D0403160

EUROPEAN TH...

DON'S ROUTE FROM SCOTLAND TO BELGIUM

SWEDEN

DENMARK

North Sea

Copenhagen

Baltic Sea

Prisoner of war camp

Barth

Pennemünde

Lübeck

Oder

Elbe

Berlin

Weser

Ems

Amsterdam

NETHERLANDS

Arnhem

Rhine

Meuse

Steldt

Antwerp

GERMANY

hièvres Airfield

Brussels

Aachen

Düren

Cologne

BELGIUM

Malmedy

St. Vith

Euskirchen

Stadtkyll

Koblenz

Dockweiler

Frankfurt

CZECH.

Bastogne

LUX.

Main

Laon Airfield

Luxembourg

Reims

Metz

Karlsruhe

Marne

Verdun

Mosel

Rhine

Danube

Inn

Seine

Yonne

AUSTRIA

MISSING

*A World War II Story of Love,
Friendships, Courage, and Survival*

Kenneth D. Evans

This is a work of nonfiction. No names have been changed, there are no fictitious characters, all events in the book actually took place. The author has taken every effort to verify the accuracy of the information contained herein, but assumes no responsibility for any errors or omissions.

Copyright © 2018 by Kenneth D. Evans

All rights reserved. No part of this book may be reproduced or used in any manner without the prior written permission of the copyright owner, except by a reviewer who wishes to quote brief passages in connection with a book review.

Library of Congress Cataloging-in-Publication data on file

Includes notes, references, and index

ISBN 978-1-7323702-0-3

Published by Starhaven Publishing, LLC

Cover and interior design by Daniel Ruesch

Maps by Gene Thorp

First Edition

Printed in the United States of America

Books are available in quantity for promotional or premium use. For information on discounts and terms, please visit our website: MissingWWIIStory.com

Dedicated to my father,
Donald N Evans,

and to the other members of The Five:
Robert (Bob) Sharp,
Gerald (Jerry) Kelly,
Kenneth (Kenny) Kalen,
and Charles (Pat) Patrick.

And to my mother,
Laura Jeanne.

and the other courageous women
who not only supported their husbands,
sons, brothers, and fathers
they sent off to war,
but who also went to work filling
the jobs they left behind at home.

CONTENTS

PART THREE

PART FOUR

INTRODUCTION

Found among my father's memorabilia following his death were a 1941 Bancroft tennis racket (strung with badly frayed catgut), a high-school state singles championship tennis trophy, a diecast metal replica of a P-47 Thunderbolt fighter-bomber, two scrapbooks crammed with photos and narratives, and two shadow boxes—one filled with athletic awards, the other with World War II medals and pins.

While looking through the scrapbooks as a teenager, I occasionally cajoled Dad into sharing memories of his formative years in a small Utah farm town during the Great Depression, along with the story about how he met my mother, Laura Jeanne, the love of his life. Using his trademark wit and sarcasm, he always made the stories interesting, never telling them exactly the same way. But I noticed that whenever I asked him questions about his World War II experiences, he quickly grew silent. My mother thought that this reticence grew from a fear that talking about such matters might bring back unwanted, difficult memories.

Near the end of his life, struggling with heart failure, Dad finally faced the demons of his past and began to compile his war memoirs. That Christmas Eve, in an emotional family fireside, he shared the unforgettable story of *his* "Night Before Christmas" in 1944, spent huddled under a pine tree in the Ardennes Forest after his fighter plane had been shot down during the Battle of the Bulge. My father remained guarded about what he shared in his memoirs, writing little of the atrocities he'd witnessed or the traumatic events he'd experienced as a fighter pilot and prisoner of war, choosing instead to take them with him to his grave. And they would have stayed there if my mother hadn't saved every letter he wrote to her during the war, along with two YMCA prisoner of war notebooks and other war memorabilia detailing experiences he was never able to talk or write about otherwise.

After my mother passed away, my sister and I discovered a box containing more than 300 love letters Dad had written to her, beginning when he went away to college up until the time he returned from the war. Also tucked in the box were letters he'd written to his parents and a few of the letters Mom had written to him while he was a prisoner of war. Following his death, she reread the boxed-up letters one last time while writing her personal history. Then, believing the love letters were too personal and intimate for anyone else to read, she claimed to have burned them. Nearly all of the letters my mother had written were indeed missing, but apparently, she didn't have the heart to destroy the others. The preserved letters and other source materials enabled me to fill in the missing pieces of my father's war experiences and tell the rest of his story, much of it in his own words.

My research, interviews, and writing have taken me on a long, meandering journey, filled with serendipitous encounters and events, providing answers every time I hit a dead-end. Studying air cadet flight training and delving deep into the war in Western Europe consumed me. I once joked that I wandered into the Ardennes Forest to research the Battle of the Bulge and didn't find my way back out for nearly six months.

Early in my writing, it became apparent that my father's life and some of the pilots with whom he served in the 368th Fighter Group of the U.S. Ninth Air Force were so intertwined that their stories needed to be included as well. The pilots nicknamed him and his two best friends The Three Musketeers. His expanded group of buddies were so close they called themselves The Five. Their stories are told using excerpts from their own letters, notebooks, scrapbooks, journals, personal histories, and mission reports, giving me the unique opportunity to glimpse the events I've written about through the eyes of those who actually lived them, forever changing my life.

My father, Donald N Evans, has been and always will be my hero. His will to overcome nearly insurmountable odds, driven by his desire to reunite with my mother, is inspiring. That he actually did so is a miracle. While his story is one of friendships, courage, and survival, above all else it's a love story, with the Great Depression and World War II as a backdrop.

2nd Lt. Donald N Evans

PROLOGUE

December 24, 1944—Eastern Belgium

Twenty-one-year-old Air Force 2nd Lt. Donald N Evans carefully placed his knife, compass, C ration tin, and two chocolate candy bars into the deep front pockets of his gabardine flight suit, then strapped on his Colt .45 M1911 semi-automatic pistol. Before pulling on his leather flight jacket, he threw some more coke into the pot-bellied stove to warm up the tent. His half-awake buddies, not scheduled to fly until later that day, thanked him for stoking the fire and wished him luck as he closed the tent flap and walked out into the early morning darkness.

Don entered the makeshift briefing room and took a seat on one of the hard wooden benches, waiting with fifteen other fighter pilots in his squadron to receive final mission instructions before taking off on the day's first sortie. He studied the large 10x6-foot map hanging on the wall, focusing on the thumbtacked red ribbon that marked Command's best guess where the fluid front lines were located. It was Day 9 of the Battle of the Bulge, and the new German counteroffensive had the Allies set back on their heels.

While waiting, Don let his mind drift back home, picturing family and friends preparing for the Christmas holiday. He longed to see his wife, Laura Jeanne, again. Separated by war, facing an uncertain future, was a lot for the young newlyweds to handle. His thoughts were abruptly cut short when his commanding officer (CO) entered the room.

Overcast skies had grounded the Ninth Air Force 368th Fighter Group for most of the battle so far, and the pilots were anxious to get back into the air. Armed with bombs, rockets, and .50 caliber machine guns, their assignment that morning was to provide close air support for American ground troops struggling to hold back the

German panzer* division advancing in the Ardennes Forest between the villages of La Roche and Stavelot near the German border. As the mission briefing session ended, their CO wished them good luck, dismissing them as dawn struggled to break through the cloud cover blanketing the bitter-cold skies over eastern Belgium.

The pilots threw their parachutes into the back of the jeep-pulled-pilot trailer, hopped in, and headed down to the flight line. After his crew chief made a final check of his P-47 fighter-bomber, Don hesitated for a moment, staring at the plane's unmarked cowling, disappointed that he hadn't had time to paint his wife's nickname, Torchy, on the front of his new plane, then climbed into the cockpit and waited for clearance to take off on his twenty-third mission.

Dense cloud cover between 1,000 and 3,000 feet forced Don's squadron to fly low to the ground, drawing fire from anti-aircraft artillery, mortar weapons, and even infantry rifles as they approached their target area. When they arrived, they found American ground troops pinned down in trenches, under bombardment from the German panzers.

During the air passes that followed, the fighter pilots dropped their 500-pound bombs and fired their HVAR** rockets, taking out several enemy tanks and armored vehicles. It was a good mission, although a number of their planes sustained flak damage. After the pilots had spent all their bombs and rockets and regrouped to return home, ground forces control radioed the 368th flight leader, Major Leary, begging him to make one more pass and take out a big German Tiger tank that was giving the infantry trouble. Leading a four-plane formation that still had some machine gun ammunition remaining, the major said, "Let's give it to 'em, then get out of here and head home—we're almost out of gas."

Don was flying "Tail-end Charlie," the trailer in their four-plane attack flight. The German anti-aircraft gunners were able to practice on the first three planes in his formation, giving them a better chance to adjust their flak guns on him. He fired his eight .50 caliber machine guns directly underneath the tank's belly, hoping the bullets would

---

*   Abbreviation for Panzerkampfwagen, a military division composed of armored vehicles, tanks, artillery, and infantry.
** High Velocity Aircraft Rockets mounted under the wings of a fighter plane.

ricochet off the ground into its vulnerable undercarriage. As he pulled up from his strafing run, he looked back over his shoulder and smiled when he saw the Tiger bellowing black smoke. BAM!!! He was rocked by an 88mm anti-aircraft cannon shell. "Evans, you're on fire!" Don's wingman screamed into the radio. "Bail out!" The engine exploded and his plane burst into flames.

Don had never bailed out of a plane—it was never part of his training. That was bad enough, but flying less than 200 feet off the ground at 400 mph, he was too low to bail out. He was in a situation from which pilots aren't expected to recover. As he offered a quick prayer for help, the bailout procedures in his P-47 tech manual flashed through his mind. He didn't have enough time or altitude to execute the recommended procedure. Instead, he decided on the other option the manual had offered—a quicker but more dangerous maneuver—and rolled his plane over. "Depending on when you leave the cockpit, you might hit the tail," he remembered reading in the manual. But he didn't have time to think about that. His plane was engulfed in fire and the cockpit was filling with smoke, leaving him only seconds to escape. In his war memoirs, Don wrote:

I think I had a guardian angel flying with me that day. I didn't panic, but for a moment, I was uncertain what to do. Then my prayer was answered. It became perfectly clear what I should do, and in what order I should do it. Flying upside down, I pushed the stick forward and hoped that my burning plane would hold together for a few more seconds and gain enough altitude to safely bail out. With one hand on the stick, I used the other hand to pull the canopy ejection lever, tear off my headgear, and hit the quick-release seat belt. Then I tried to stand up in my cockpit seat. Fighting the G force made it difficult to get up. But once I did, the slipstream sucked me out of my plane with tremendous force. As my hand came off the stick, the tail flipped up enough for me to pass by it without being hit. Then I started falling.

I was prompted not to count to three, but instead to pull my chute latch as fast as I could. I didn't even know where it was. I just threw my hand hard against my chest, hoping I'd somehow grab the release. Amazingly, my chute popped open. Having safely escaped my plane, I promised the Lord, "If you get me out of this, I'll forever be in your debt." I was close to the ground when I bailed out, and the forest below was rapidly closing in on me. After just one swing of my parachute, I hit the ground. Luckily, I landed in an opening of brush on a snow-covered side hill, just missing nearby trees. I was falling fast and hit the ground hard, sliding and rolling down through the snow and bushes. Hitting the hillside on the down slope broke my fall and miraculously nothing else.

After burying my parachute to hide it from the Germans, the whole hillside around me burst into gunfire. It sounded like the whole German Army was shooting at me. I crept over to the edge of the woods, where I saw my plane burning on the hill below me. The flames were causing the remaining .50 caliber shells in my plane to explode and fire in all directions. It wasn't safe where I was, so I started back up the hill. At least I didn't have to worry about destroying my plane before the Germans discovered it.

Don struggled through the brush and snow, not stopping until he made it to the top of the hill and the cover of the forest canopy, then collapsed on the ground. Leaning against a pine tree, he closed his eyes for a few minutes, trying to assess the situation and slow down the rush of adrenaline he was still feeling. He had several cuts and bruises on his face, arms, and legs. Applying a combination of snow and pressure stopped the bleeding and dulled some of the pain. He also had a hitch in his back, which he tried to stretch out, to no avail. But what concerned him most were his feet. He'd bruised them badly when he slammed into the side hill, and it hurt to walk. He had a general idea where he was, but the overcast blocked even a hint of where the sun was in the sky. Without the maps that had gone down with his plane, he knew he'd have to rely on his compass and his instincts to help him find his way to the Allied frontlines. Don continued:

I reached for my flight suit front pocket to pull out my compass, but to my surprise, the big deep pockets running down the front of both legs had disappeared. There were no tears or holes. The pockets were just gone.

My compass, my knife, even my C rations and chocolate candy bars were gone. Apparently, the pressure on me when I was sucked into the slipstream had been so great that it stripped the seams of the pockets right off my flight suit—just as if someone had used a thread picker—clean as a whistle. At least my .45 was still strapped to my belt. Reports had been coming in that the Germans were starting to line up prisoners when they were captured, take their dog tags, shoot them down, and then bury them in unmarked trenches. So if worse came to worst, I could at least try to defend myself.

Under the terms of the Geneva Convention, a prisoner was only required to give his name, rank, and serial number. But the Nazis weren't abiding by the rules anymore. I was sure the Germans had seen my plane go down and would be searching for me. Even though it hurt to walk, I needed to get moving to get away from my plane and to warm myself up—it was freezing, and I was getting cold.

With the overcast sky and without my compass, I could only guess which way to go. I wandered around in the forest through the deep snow, limping and crawling on my hands and knees for what seemed like miles, trying to find a way back to our frontlines. Every hundred yards or so, I ran into German tanks or soldiers. Each time, I carefully backed away into the cover of the woods and headed in another direction. At one point, just after dark, I came upon a little guard shanty. I slowly crawled toward it until I was about twenty feet away. And sure enough, a Jerry* was in it. I again quietly backed away and headed in another direction. I kept searching for a way through enemy lines until long after dark. I was in no-man's land, between the American and German main forces, where elements of both sides were fighting for position. Everywhere I turned, I ran into German soldiers.

Freezing and exhausted from hours of wandering, I finally gave up. I picked out a great big pine tree—one over fifty feet high—and scraped away the snow from its base. Then I

---

* Nickname the Allies gave to German soldiers in World War II.

curled myself around it to try and stay warm, and said to the tree, "You're my home."

About midnight, the sky lit up as phosphorus bombs began exploding in the skies directly above me. Both the Allies and the Germans used these bombs to light up the nighttime terrain, allowing patrols and outposts to monitor each other's troop movements during the night. It was a great fireworks display. All sorts of red-hot shrapnel rained down through the trees—unlike anything I've ever seen, before or since. The words of Francis Scott Key's national anthem came to me: "And the rockets' red glare, the bombs bursting in air, gave proof through the night that our flag was still there." I hoped I'd be able to see it fly again.

I was lost, cold and hungry—and I'd never felt more alone. I couldn't sleep. I got up and moved around from time to time, so I wouldn't freeze to death. I thought about the mess I was in, and wondered how I'd ever get out of it. Mostly, though, I thought about Laura Jeanne and Christmas Eve back home—wondering if we'd ever see another Christmas together.

That same night, far away from the Ardennes battleground, Laura Jeanne had a disturbing experience:

I was home alone for several hours that evening. I can't recall where the rest of the family was, but I distinctly remember that I lay on the floor by the Christmas tree, wondering how Don was spending his time that night.

During the day, there had been discouraging reports on the radio about the terrible fighting in the Battle of the Bulge. My daydreaming stopped abruptly, when all of a sudden, I had a premonition that he was in trouble. I knew something had happened to him, and I couldn't get it out of my mind.

PART ONE

Don's high school graduation photo

ONE
....

"Tough"

Fall of 1940—Lehi, Utah

Perched on her front porch swing, Laura Jeanne cast her gaze toward the two new tennis courts located just across the street. Sunlight glinted off the shiny chain-link backstops surrounding the courts, accentuating their black, freshly painted service boxes and baselines. But she wasn't focusing on the town's newest recreation hotspot. Instead, her eyes were fixed on the handsome tennis player walking onto the court.

Reaching center court, he got down on one knee, checking the center-net-strap height. Using his Bancroft tennis racket as a makeshift tape measure, he put his finger on the net where the top of his racket reached, then turning the racket head sideways, placed it above his finger, marking a spot on the net. After adjusting the net strap to the three-foot regulation height, he walked to the baseline and started practicing his twisting topspin service. Years later, with that front-porch image still clearly in her mind, Laura Jeanne reminisced:

I was enthusiastic in cheering our Lehi Pioneer teams on to victory, but I was secretly cheering for the young man who had stolen my heart without even knowing it. So many girls had a crush on him that I didn't think he'd ever take notice of me.

The star tennis player she'd fallen for had glanced her direction more often than she thought. He later wrote:

It was hard not to notice her. She was so cute. Seeing her sitting on her porch watching me play tennis made it much more difficult to keep my eye on the ball. She was only just a sophomore, but she was quite popular and always seemed to have a lot of guys paying attention to her.

When Don learned that Laura Jeanne had the leading role in the high school musical production *June in January*, he talked one of his best friends, Grant Ash, into trying out for a part, hoping it might give him a chance to meet the cute, blonde cheerleader who had caught his eye. Grant was a natural, quickly landing the role of the Bashful Swede. Don, on the other hand, had no experience acting and could barely carry a tune. But in small schools, trying out was half the battle, and he ended up cast as the Hero of It All, a speaking only role. Heralded "as the year's most humorous and cleverly written play,"[1] it brought the hero and leading lady together in real life, as well as on the stage, setting in motion an unforeseeable chain of events.

Although located in a small, rural Utah town, Lehi High School wasn't that different from other high schools across America. Still caught in the grips of the Great Depression, nearly half of the nation's students quit school by the eighth grade, forced to work on farms or in city factories to help support their families. Thousands of others, unable to find work, were "riding the rails," looking for odd jobs, roaming across America on freight cars. Most of those who graduated went straight into the job market, hoping to find work, but rampant unemployment nationwide left many disappointed. Some enrolled in vocational schools, further enhancing their employment opportunities. Fewer than five percent went on to college.[2] None of them could possibly have predicted they'd later be referred to as the "Greatest Generation."

As part of the first "nearly adult" age group called *teenagers,*[*] high school students had developed their own identity.[3] Their upbringing during the Great Depression had taught them how to "use it up, wear it out, make it do, or do without." But now, after years of wearing hand-me-downs, teens were becoming fashion conscious again. Girls were wearing muffler scarves, wool sweaters, and bright plaid skirts, and using garters to hold up their wool socks. Poplin jackets with collared shirts and sneakers were popular with boys.

---

[*] The term "teenager" first showed up in print form in a magazine article written by Edith M. Stern and published in the April 1941 issue of *Popular Science Monthly.*

And T-shirts were now showing up in classrooms and on athletic fields. In addition to core curriculum courses, high schools still emphasized physical education and sports for boys and homemaking skills for girls. However, more and more girls were making their mark in sports as well, especially in track and field, basketball, and on the tennis courts.

America's Class of 1940–41 lived in the middle of the Big Band era, dancing the Jitterbug and Swing, and jiving to their loud, rhythmic instrumental music. But they also learned to move gracefully around the ballroom dance floor. They grew up listening to the radio—not just to music and news reports, but also to dozens of weekly programs, from the Lone Ranger to Jack Benny. Their comic book heroes were Batman and Captain America. Across the country teens had fallen in love with the movies, attending showhouses on weekends, as often as they could come up with the 25-cent ticket price. This year's high school seniors were slowly rekindling the hope that had been driven from their parents' generation by the Depression, now seeing the world as an exciting and rapidly changing place. American high schools had become a microcosm of the outside world, with politics, sports, music, drama, and social activities—and Lehi High School was no exception.

Don came from a long line of farmers, tracing their way back to the early Mormon pioneers who originally settled Lehi. Back then, the locals called the town *Evansville,* naming it after Don's great-great-grandfather. Although Don joked that his middle initial N (without a period) stood for *nothing,* he was proud that it was given in honor of his father, Noble. Reflecting on his early childhood memories, he wrote:

My dad paid my grandpa $250 for the house I grew up in. It came with a barn, corral—and a pig trough back behind the house. It had ugly-gray plastered walls and no front porch. No one ever entered through our front door. It was nailed closed because the room inside had been converted to a bedroom. The place didn't look like much, but my mother turned it into a home.

My favorite memory growing up was sitting around our "Heatrola" coal-burning stove at night, eating chunks of block chocolate and pine nuts, and listening to "Amos & Andy" and "Jack Benny & Gracie Allen" on the radio.

We had a large garden behind our house filled with cucumbers, which I had to weed, harvest, and haul to market, in my little red wagon. I gave all the money I earned to my parents to help with family expenses.

My mother used to take us to visit my Grandma Varney, who lived about a mile to the east at the Lehi "Forks of the Road." She pushed my little sister LaRae in a baby buggy, and my big brother Duane and I tagged along behind. It was a long walk, but the rewards were great. Grandma always had hot bread with our choice of honey or thick, rich cream topped with sugar. And she always sent us home with delicious raisin-filled cookies. I used to love hearing her tell stories about Indians and Pony Express riders from her childhood growing up on the old Pony Express station located out by our farm.

My Grandpa Evans had a farm and ran cattle about four miles west of town, near the Jordan River. He died eleven years before I was born, leaving his family deeply in debt. My dad and his two brothers worked for years to pay them off, a hardship that became even more difficult after the "crash" of 1929. Dad worked seven days a week, but only asked us boys to work Sundays when he had irrigation turns. He wasn't a churchgoer, but mother was, and he encouraged us to go with her.

Since Dad always seemed to be working, my two brothers and I really looked forward to hunting seasons each fall. Although Dad loved to hunt, he was always serious when we went. The pheasants, ducks, and deer we harvested were needed additions to our dinner table. Huge flocks of waterfowl used to come into our farm wheat fields just before dark. One of Dad's greatest feats was bagging 16 ducks with two shots!

Farm work was hard. I hated getting up at 3 a.m. to irrigate. Stumbling around in the dark with a hoe or pick-ax trying to get water down the furrows was a mess, and irrigation turns *lasted for a long time. One hot summer afternoon, while I was taking my turn irrigating one of our grain fields, some of my buddies came by and talked me into going to the "Mill Pond" just outside town to go swimming. I had several rows set and irrigating, and figured I could sneak away for a few hours. We had a great time, and nobody even knew I was gone. But I wasn't there to get the irrigation water to the grain where the land was uneven.*

Description on photo: Place of my birth — s.w. Lehi 1923. Home as it looks in 1989 after remodeling. Ditch in foreground is where I was knocked into by a frisky old "billy goat" (age 2) Mom came to my rescue!

Later that summer, a long narrow dead spot appeared in the grain field. Feeling guilty about what I'd done—or rather not done—I confessed that it was my fault. At harvest time, Dad reminded me that we probably lost about $20 worth of wheat on that section. I never forgot that experience—and learned a great lesson.

Times were hard and my parents often went without, in order for us children to have things. In every picture I have of my

*mom, she was wearing the same dress. Dad only took her on
one vacation during their entire married lives.*

Children from left to right: Don, LaRae, Duane

*Almost all my clothes were farm work clothes. I only had
one white, long-sleeve shirt, and one tie, which I wore when
I played tennis, at student assemblies and at church. I was
grateful when Mom bought me a new white t-shirt to play in
the state tennis tournament my senior year.*

*I wasn't ever paid for my farm work. But Dad always saw
that I had a good tennis racket, balls, and whatever money he
could spare for a few dates. He taught me how to work and
be responsible—and was always encouraging me to prepare
for college. He didn't want me to be a farmer.*

During the spring of 1940, Don and a few of his friends threw
their hats in the ring, running for high school student offices. Don
was voted student body president, Iva Sunderland and Grant Ash
were elected to the student council, and Ralph Allred became senior
class president, marking the beginning of a great year for Don and

his Lehi Pioneer senior friends. Easily recognized by his curly blond hair, charming smile, and fun-loving personality, Don seemed to be everyone's friend. Recalling his student government experiences that year, he wrote:

> I enjoyed planning and being in charge of student assemblies and special activities—and especially getting out of so many classes. I never studied so little and got such good grades. One of my greatest contributions that year was organizing what I called "The Bouncer's Unit." A group of bullies were giving teachers and students a lot of trouble and disrupting school activities. I met with the school principal and asked permission to organize a special unit to deal with the problem.

> I called the two biggest, rowdiest, meanest seniors in the school to head up the unit and assigned them to patrol the hallways and control student behavior at all our activities. I let them get a secretary and call some assistants, and even got them "excused" from class once in a while to report on their assignments. That was all the reward they needed. They took to it like "ducks to water." Keeping everyone in line really made their day. The principal, teachers, and even the janitor were amazed and grateful.

> We got along great, and the bouncers started calling me "Tough"—a nickname that stuck with me even after high school.

Lehi named its senior class yearbook *Lehision 1941*. It was Volume 25—the Silver Edition—and the editors were determined to make it their best ever. It included several pieces of trivia. According to the yearbook, top student offenses that year were talking out of turn, chewing gum during class, and shooting spit wads. Don conducted all student assemblies and served as chair of the school social club. Grant headed the activities committee, coordinating everything going on behind the scenes. Ralph was in charge of the senior class project. And Iva, the school valedictorian, served as secretary. Although she tried her best to keep the student government officers in line, apparently she wasn't always successful. The yearbook editor reported the following inside scoop: "Sluffing gets some of the 'mighties' in trouble." All of them, except Iva, were caught skipping classes and given detention. Her influence eventually rubbed off on them, however, and the entire student council made the senior honor roll.[4]

Near the end of the school year, the *Lehi Free Press* wrote:

> Athletes at Lehi High School received recognition Friday at a special award-day assembly. Football and basketball honors were accepted by Don Evans and Jack Mitchell, co-captains of both teams. Recognition in tennis for girls was accepted by Captain Iva Sunderland and for boys by Captain Don Evans. To Grant Ash went the Coach Prior football medal, and to Don Evans went the Coach Nielson all-around athletic award.

Utah sportswriters and coaches selected Don as that year's all-state quarterback in football, also naming him to the all-state basketball team, both unexpected honors for an athlete from a small rural school. He finished the year by winning the state tennis championship singles title, an achievement that landed his picture on the front sports page of the *Deseret News*, along with a full-length article about his victory. Popular sports writer Les Goates reported:

> Now comes Don Evans, curley-thatched, blond and bashful, to win the state association trophy and give the Pioneers their first championship. Don is a champion because of his great love for tennis and his amazing determination. He has a natural steadiness and a splendid competitive temperament.

Years later, after seeing the faded newspaper article in a scrapbook, Don's children teased him about the words used in the article to describe him and his tennis skills. Cracking a smile and showing his keen sense of humor, he shot back:

> *My hair really was curly and blond. And twenty-five years ago, the words "awesome," "spectacular," and "unbelievable" would no doubt have been used in the article—if they'd been in the dictionary back then!*

Remembering his days on the gridiron and basketball court, Don recalled:

> *I was knocked out three times in our football game against Lincoln High School. Our leather helmets didn't offer much*

protection—good I had a hard head. Back then, the big schools still played the small schools. There was no 2A, 3A, 4A, or 5A—just the small-school farm kids against the big-school city slickers.

Lehi was such a small school that we had to "draft" guys to field a team. Even then, most of us still had to play both ways—offense and defense. Lincoln outweighed us about 35 pounds per man, and their school was about five times as big as ours. We beat them 3–0 on my 35-yard "drop-kick" field goal—just as the clock ran out.

Coach Prior let me call the plays my junior and senior years, which I often drew up on the ground in our huddle. Other times, I just winged it. The defenses didn't know what I was going to do with the ball—because I didn't even know myself. I guess that was the secret to our attack. Even Coach stood in amazement on the sidelines at all the options we came up with. Our team took first place in the District League my senior year.

Most of our basketball games weren't high-scoring affairs and were won in the 30 to 40-point range, seldom reaching 50 points in a game. Big guys were 6'2" to 6'4" tall. That year I was a 5'9" power forward, weighing in at 141 lbs.

Although basketball wasn't my best sport, I did have a few "moments" on the court. My best game was 23 points. I used a two-handed set shot from the perimeter, a moving one-handed shot from the corner, and a deadly two-handed between-the-knees foul shot.

As a short power forward, my opponent's elbows were usually about at my eye level. It seemed like I always had a black eye from one game to the next. We didn't do well at State that year, but we had a lot of fun.

Tucked away near the back of *The Salt Lake Tribune*, the commencement announcement read, "Lehi High School Prepares to Graduate Class of 1941." Lehi's fifty-eight seniors would soon be donning caps and gowns and marching across the auditorium stage to receive their diplomas. Afterward, they would join 1.3 million other graduating high schoolers around the country in the same time-honored tradition, switching the tassel on their mortarboard caps from one side to the other, signifying their achievement.

Shortly before graduation, the *Lehi Free Press* reported:

> Donald N Evans of Lehi High School has been selected to receive a $25 scholarship to Brigham Young University. The choice was made on the basis of leadership, service in activities, and character.

The scholarship was a big deal back then. Twenty-five dollars covered full tuition at BYU for an entire quarter—and the scholarship was renewable as long as the recipient maintained at least a B average. Don was about to take his first step toward getting off the farm.

Laura Jeanne Brown high school graduation photo

TWO

......

"Torchy"

The Orem Interurban Electric Railroad ran south from Salt Lake City to Provo. Originally pulled by steam locomotives, the railway was converted to use electricity in May 1910.[5] The train tracks ran right next to the Evans home, and the station house was less than two blocks to the west. Don wrote:

> *I used to hate living so close to the train station. The tinkling "toot-toot" as the train passed by our house kept waking me up at night when I was young. But I thought more kindly about the "swinging and swaying" Orem Electric when it became my only mode of transportation to and from BYU. Since I didn't have access to a car, the train was the only way I could come home on weekends. It was even my source of wheels to go on dates. Unfortunately, it wasn't too impressive to most of the girls I dated.*

The cute Lehi cheerleader he still had his eye on didn't seem to mind. Laura Jeanne Brown loved trains, which wasn't surprising, since her father operated the Denver Rio Grande Railroad Station in Lehi.

Don loved college life, but found his classes challenging, making him regret not taking his high school studies more seriously. He made up for it by working hard and studying late, determined to keep his scholarship. That fall, after reading in the *Y News* that BYU tennis tryouts were open to walk-ons, he decided to try out for the team. He not only made the varsity squad, but also quickly climbed the ladder to the number two singles spot. At the end of the season, his coach presented him with a custom-fitted letterman's sweater and a gold tennis pin.

Cheerleaders—Laura Jeanne on the left

Don took the Orem Electric back home to Lehi nearly every weekend to help on the farm—and lately, to spend time with Laura Jeanne, attending Lehi's football and basketball games as much to watch her tumble, dance, and jump as he did to see his old teams play. Besides being a popular cheerleader, she was also part of the reigning Miss Lehi royalty her junior year, making it difficult to get penciled into her dance card at the Friday night hops following the games. Laura Jeanne had a beautiful voice as well and regularly earned the lead role in her high school musicals, plays, and operas. Her high school friends called her *Torchy*, a nickname inspired by the cute, blonde, fast-talking movie character known as Torchy Blane.[6]

Don and two high school friends and former teammates, Ralph Allred and Don Johnson, batched together at BYU in a dark, cramped basement apartment with a small kitchen and two bedrooms. They called it The Hole. The guys got along great most of the time. But in cramped quarters, it was inevitable that one of them would encroach on the others' space. And they had differing views about what *cleaned up* meant. But the biggest source of contention was with food and cooking. They agreed to share kitchen duties, which included shopping for groceries and cooking meals. Some nights, however, the cook didn't show—and too often, the refrigerator and cupboards were bare. They all looked forward to returning to Lehi on weekends to enjoy their moms' home cooking, which was better than their own fare and cheaper. Don wrote:

> It was hard to make ends meet, even when your main food staple was Kraft Macaroni and Cheese. I didn't have enough money my second quarter at BYU to pay for all my books and fees. So I applied for a $20 loan from the university to help me get by. When the note came due, I didn't have enough money to pay it back.

Laura Jeanne encouraged Don to ask his father for help, but knowing that his dad had financial problems of his own on the farm, he couldn't bring himself to do it. Desperate after the university denied his request to extend the loan, Don turned to his tennis coach for help. Fred "Buck" Dixon listened sympathetically as he unloaded his financial problems. Within a few days, his coach had worked out an extension on the past-due loan and secured him a part-time job at the university farm so he could pay it back. The work was hard, putting him on the hand-blistering end of a pick and shovel—and the pay wasn't that great, but it was enough for him to make ends meet.

On the afternoon of Monday, December 8, 1941, Don and his roommates were quietly studying in their apartment, still in a somber mood after listening to the radio news broadcast that the Japanese had bombed Pearl Harbor the previous day. Along with the rest of the nation, they waited by the radio, anxious to hear from the president of the United States. In a solemn voice, Franklin D. Roosevelt began speaking:

> *Yesterday, December 7, 1941—a date that will live in infamy—the United States of America was suddenly and deliberately attacked by naval and air forces of the Empire of Japan. No matter how long it may take us to overcome this premeditated invasion, the American people in their righteous might will win through to absolute victory.*

Congress immediately approved the president's request to declare war. Wearing a black armband—symbolic of the more than 2,500 Americans lost at Pearl Harbor—Roosevelt signed the declaration that same afternoon. America was now at war.

Don and his roommates had followed the war in Europe, reading newspaper articles and listening to news reports about Hitler's invasion of Poland. But even after Great Britain and France responded to his aggression by declaring war on Nazi Germany, they, like most Americans, viewed the war as a European problem not directly affecting the United States. The nation's naive, isolationist sentiment continued even after the Germans invaded the Soviet Union and the news media started calling the conflict World War II. Most Americans wanted no part of the war until the devastating attack on Pearl Harbor—then everything changed. As Japan's European ally, Hitler was now a direct threat to America, as well as Europe, forcing Roosevelt to declare war on Nazi Germany the following day.

A patriotic feeling swept over the nation, and thousands of young men raced to recruiting offices to sign up in the armed services. Don and his roommates shared the same feelings and talked a lot about what to do. At eighteen, they were old enough to enlist, but were still under the military draft age of twenty-one. Don's father pleaded with him not to volunteer. After wavering back and forth, all three decided to remain in school, at least for the time being.

Don successfully completed his freshman year at BYU the spring of 1942. The tennis team wrapped up a successful season on the courts, and his grades were again good enough to renew his scholarship. Don was ready for a break. He felt obligated to help his dad on the farm, but also wanted to find a paying job that summer— one where he could earn enough money to pay for his sophomore year of school. It was too hard trying to hold down a job, play on the tennis team, and go to school full-time. Something had to give, and he didn't want it to be tennis.

After each harvest season ended, Don's father worked for the Utah Clay Company to supplement his farm income. Most fall mornings, the locals admired his handsome team of matched draft horses as he drove them to the clay beds west of Lehi. After a work party of men dug out the clay with picks and shovels, he hitched his team up to a skid scraper, dragging the clay into piles, which were then loaded into dump carts and hauled off.[7] When Don had trouble finding work, his father used his connections with the clay company to land him a summer job. Unfortunately, it wasn't behind a team of matched draft horses. Instead, he was again on the working end of a pick and shovel. It was hard work, but the pay was good—$5.75 a day—and he got most of his weekends off.

Don enjoyed being back home, sleeping in his own bed, and eating three square meals a day. His mom spoiled him, waking him up for work, fixing him breakfast, even packing his lunch. At night, she cooked his favorite foods for dinner and washed his filthy work clothes. Lela Evans doted on her children, seldom complaining about anything. However, like most mothers with sons old enough to enlist in the military, she worried that hers might do just that. Duane, her oldest, was already talking about joining the Navy against his father's strong objections.

Laura Jeanne moved to Salt Lake City that summer, living with a friend in a rented apartment downtown. It was quite a change of scenery for a small-town girl. She grew up in tiny Utah railroad towns with peculiar names, like Soldier Summit, Galoolee, and Thistle, where her father worked as a telegrapher for the railroad. She wrote the following about her summer in the big city:

> After my junior year, I worked as a waitress at the Lion House Cafeteria in the morning and attended LDS Business College in the afternoon. The work was difficult and demanding, but the pay was pretty good.

> Eventually, I got the coveted job of cashier, which was a lot better than cleaning up dirty dishes and washing pots and pans. The cafeteria was a popular place, and it was exciting to see city dignitaries and LDS [Mormon] Church General Authorities come there to eat. Once in a while, I even got a tip—but not often.

> I was just there for the summer months until high school started back up. I spent weeknights studying English, shorthand, and typing for my classes at the business college. But my weekends were reserved for Don.

> Our favorite thing to do was going to Saturday night dances at the beautiful Rainbow Gardens dance hall in Salt Lake City. We danced to the music of the famous Big Bands that played there, never leaving until they stopped playing at midnight.

> We also rode up the canyon for picnics and enjoyed swimming at Saratoga. Other times we just walked in the park, went to a movie, or headed across town to Watties Ice Cream Parlor. We couldn't wait to see each other every weekend.

Sensing that her carefree life might not always be so, Laura Jeanne wrote the following in her journal:

> There's a dark, threatening cloud hanging over our country. We don't want to face it, but our country is in the middle of a terrible war. Our lives have changed dramatically since the Japanese Air Force unexpectedly attacked Pearl Harbor last December. More and more of our young men are now going off to war, and it's heartbreaking when we get the news that some of them aren't coming back.

Don experienced mixed emotions as he boarded the Orem Electric that fall. He was excited to start school again and begin a new tennis season, but he started missing Laura Jeanne even before the train reached the campus stop. After arriving, he sent her the following short note:

> I got so used to being with you last summer—that it's really terrible being away now. You've cast a magic spell over me.

Don's friend, Grant Ash, the fullback he handed off to in high school, transferred from Utah State to BYU that fall and moved into The Hole with his three former teammates. Year two at school was off to a great start, especially since Don didn't have to work anymore. He didn't miss the university farm, and just thinking about the backbreaking work at the clay beds motivated him to study hard.

He signed up for some challenging courses his first quarter as a sophomore. Trigonometry and physics came easily to him, but intermediate accounting was a different story. After nights of studying late and struggling with accounting theory and complex homework problems, he wondered if he'd chosen the right major. Eventually, dogged determination paid off, and things started to click. Equally dedicated to tennis, his skills on the court improved as well, especially his topspin service.

Laura Jeanne was now a senior in high school, and Don tried to attend as many of her dances, ballgames, and performances as he could. He was now completely smitten with her and ready to take their relationship to the next step. Then the unexpected happened.

President Franklin D. Roosevelt

THREE
....

Decisions

On November 11, 1942, President Roosevelt signed a new selective service act that lowered the military draft age from twenty-one to eighteen, requiring all men that age to register for the draft. Don was eighteen years old and World War II was now staring him in the face.

The Draft Board offered college students an option to finish two years of school before calling them up, if they joined one of the military reserve units. Don and his roommates spent several late nights debating what to do:

> *I wasn't overanxious to go to war. But I was young and adventurous, and like most Americans, I felt patriotic. I was ready to enlist, but I had trouble figuring out which branch of the military to join. My brother Duane was already in the Navy and was soon leaving for the South Pacific. That didn't interest me. I knew I didn't want to join a tank battalion. And I didn't want to be in the infantry either, because I had flat feet.*

> *My roommates were all excited about becoming pilots. So I finally decided to enlist in the Army Reserve Corps with them, and we traveled to Salt Lake City to take the Aviation Cadet examinations. I'd never even been in an airplane. But I'd learned to drive a tractor on the farm, so I figured I could probably learn how to fly a plane.*

> *You had to have two years of college education to get into the air cadet-training program. So when we signed up, the recruiting sergeant promised us we'd be able to finish our sophomore year at BYU before the Army called us up.*

Two months later, the Army threw out the two-year minimum college education requirement and announced they were calling all Air Force Reserve units to active duty—effective immediately— suspending Don's college days indefinitely. He faced a catch-22 situation while he waited for his induction orders to arrive. He desperately wanted to ask Laura Jeanne to marry him, but the timing couldn't have been worse. In a few months, he'd be entering the Air Force cadet-training program, then, a year or so later, shipped overseas to fight in the war.

Don struggled for days, debating with himself about what to do. Was it fair to Laura Jeanne to get married, then leave her a few months later? And what if they got married and he didn't return from the war? Complicating matters worse, they were both underage, requiring their parents' permission to marry. Laura Jeanne was still in high school, and her parents were sure to object. A marriage proposal right then made no sense at all. In the end, however, love won out over logic—and Don started looking for an engagement ring.

Not long afterward, Don and Laura Jeanne rode the Orem Electric to Salt Lake City to visit two of their best friends. Before dinner, they stepped outside their apartment onto a small balcony. Since Don had been uncharacteristically nervous all evening, Laura Jeanne suspected what was about to happen:

It should have been a romantic moment for us. Don got down on one knee, pulled out the ring and just when he started asking me to marry him, a cat tipped over a garbage can right under the balcony and about scared us both to death. After we finally stopped laughing, I said, "Yes," and then we kissed.

When Don's induction orders arrived, he withdrew from school and returned home to live with his parents. He spent his days helping his father on the farm, but reserved his evenings for his new fiancée. Laura Jeanne was dying to talk to her girlfriends and show off her engagement ring, even though it was only a band and not a diamond, but she and Don agreed it would be better to keep their betrothal secret. Laura Jeanne only confided in her sister Kathryn, swearing her to secrecy. As his induction date drew near, the couple finally revealed their plans. Their parents' objections were predictable and made sense, but failed to dissuade the love-struck couple. It was an emotional time for Laura Jeanne—her heart told her that marrying Don was the right thing to do, but her head wasn't quite as sure:

I was just seventeen years old and still in high school. Don was soon going to leave for air cadet training. It seemed like I was just going through the motions of living and trying to stay focused. It was difficult to be enthusiastic about school and still try hard to maintain good grades, but somehow I did. I was now engaged, so my social life was soon going to come to an abrupt halt.

Don and Laura Jeanne talked and prayed, struggling with what they should do. In their search for guidance, they met with their church patriarch and each received a blessing.* Laura Jeanne wrote the following about the experience:

Our blessings promised us that if we were faithful in living the gospel of Jesus Christ, we'd be "preserved from the tragedies of war." Don was further promised, "The power of the Lord will go with you and bless you in times of danger and guide your footsteps..., and you will return home safely when the war is over." Those were the comforting words that I needed to hear, as I was about to say good-bye to my best friend, my sweetheart, and my future husband.

Air Cadets were required to pledge that they wouldn't interrupt their flight training for marriage, meaning the newly engaged couple had to marry right then or wait until Don graduated from cadet training ten months later. Laura Jeanne wanted to get married immediately. But Don made the final decision, insisting she graduate from high school first. That appeased their parents, who were still hoping the ill-timed engagement would extend until after the war. But the couple, having vowed to wed before Don went overseas, immediately started working on their mothers to give them their blessing—and their written permission. Since the Air Corps usually gave newly commissioned officers a few days leave after earning their

---

* Patriarchal blessings in The Church of Jesus Christ of Latter-Day Saints (Mormon Church) include guidance, direction, and promises, with fulfillment conditioned on the recipient's faithfulness in living gospel principles.

wings, the couple secretly planned to get married as soon as Don completed his flight training.

Their last date was a romantic picnic in a nearby canyon. Laura Jeanne wrote:

> *We went with Don's friend Dee Schow and his soon-to-be fiancée Marcelle to a beautiful picnic spot up American Fork Canyon. We had fried chicken and all the trimmings. We ate while sitting on the rocks on the edge of the riverbank.*
>
> *It was both a sad and a happy time. Dee had joined the Navy and would soon be leaving for the South Pacific. And Don was leaving early the next morning to enlist at Fort Douglas. There on the edge of the river we had our farewell kiss. Uncle Sam and the war were now in control of our future.*

Last date before Don enlisted at Fort Douglas

The Army established Fort Douglas in 1862 as a small military outpost east of Salt Lake City and stationed Union troops there throughout the Civil War, in part to keep an eye on the Mormons. During World War I, the Army used the fort as an internment camp to house German prisoners. After the war, it became home to the U.S. 38th Infantry. Later, the Army added an airfield, and the 7th Bombardment Group flew B-17s from the base. Now, at the beginning of World War II, the old fort was serving as an Army mobilization and training center.[8]

Although attempting to put on brave faces, Don and his BYU roommates were apprehensive as they entered the gates of Fort Douglas on April 12, 1943. The base "welcoming committee" herded them through an unorganized processing operation, treating them more like numbers than people. At the end of a long day, Don wrote:

We've been pretty busy getting instructions, marching around, taking exams, and going to mess. We stood in line after line getting every shot known to man. Afterward, we were issued a beautiful new khaki wardrobe.

The Army insists that we make our bed "their" way and fold our blankets in such a manner that they hold you tightly in bed once you get there. My hair is now shorter by some inches, but there's still a curl in the front.

On their second morning at Fort Douglas, the inductees experienced their first Army "SNAFU" (Situation Normal All Fouled Up):

After breakfast, we lined up, and they started calling out names and making assignments—mostly to Tank Corps and Infantry Units. We got nervous when they started calling men from Air Force Reserve Units like ours and assigning them there instead of to air cadet training.

You guessed it—they called out our names too and assigned us to the Army Tank Corps. We didn't waste any time searching for the sergeant in charge to plead our case. We hounded him to verify our promised air cadet assignments. He finally checked it out and got us out of the Tank Corps, but made no promises as to where we'd end up. Now we're back to waiting.

Sunday afternoon, the Army granted the remaining inductees a short leave, allowing Don to spend a few hours with Laura Jeanne and a few close friends. After returning to the base that night, he wrote:

The wind is howling outside, it's raining hard, and I'm missing you terribly. It was so hard saying goodbye to you again.

Monday morning, the Lehi contingent's orders finally came through. The military dashed their hopes of being assigned together, transferring Don Johnson to the Marine Air Force and sending Grant, Ralph, and Don to the San Antonio Air Cadet Center (SAACC). It was the last time the four of them would ever be together.

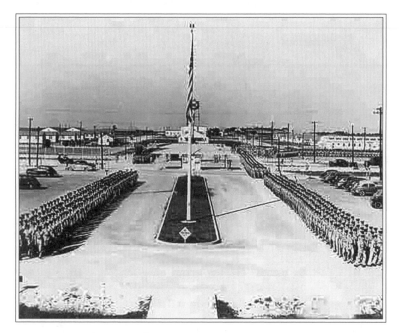

San Antonio Aviation Cadet Center (SAACC)

FOUR

Classification Battery

Don had never been outside Utah. And unlike Laura Jeanne, who grew up riding the rails, this was his first trip on a passenger train. The railroads had placed every possible sleeper car across the nation into service to help transport American troops. Since the Pullman Company built far more of these specialty cars than anyone else, passengers generally referred to them as just "Pullmans." Each coach had a double bed in its lower berth, which transformed into a seat, and a single bed in the upper. The Pullman Company converted baggage cars into rolling kitchens, and even supplied them with a porter and conductor. Steam locomotives pulled the trains at speeds approaching seventy miles per hour on level stretches and even faster downhill, but they slowed down to a crawl on long uphill climbs.

The air cadets traveled a route that angled southeast to Grand Junction, then wound its way through the Rocky Mountains. The scenery on the first leg of their journey, with its mountain ranges and valley farmlands, reminded Don of home. As they traveled farther east, the elevation gradually dropped and the pines and quaking aspen gave way to juniper and mesquite trees, sagebrush, and prickly pear cactus. Once they reached the New Mexico-Oklahoma-Texas tri-state border area, they veered south through the southern end of the Great Plains, where the landscape transitioned from plateaus to flat lands dotted with mesas and unusual rock outcroppings. Buffalo grass, brushy canyons, yucca, blooming desert cactus, and wildflowers covered the sweeping plains and rolling hills between Amarillo and Fort Worth. Grazing cattle, scattered all along the route, blended in with the countryside. The only things out of place were the hundreds and hundreds of oil wells speckling the horizon in all directions. Don was fascinated by the constantly changing scenery flying past his window—which he now kept open, since it was getting warmer and stickier as they approached San Antonio.

Don, Ralph, Grant, and fourteen other cadets from Fort Douglas reached SAACC on April 24, 1943. The cadets arrived sweaty and uncomfortable, still wearing the heavy wool uniforms the Army had issued them at Fort Douglas, which were fine for the cool Utah weather, but the temperatures in the subtropical San Antonio climate were already 90 degrees and climbing higher each day. The Utah cadets weren't happy when they found out the Army had shipped most of their luggage, including their lightweight cotton uniforms, on a different train not scheduled to arrive for two more days, forcing them to wear their hot wool clothing.

The new air cadets were transferred from the railway station to the SAACC Classification Center, given a few instructions, then placed in quarantine. Over the next two weeks, they were processed, given extensive physical and mental examinations, inoculated for everything from tetanus to smallpox, and began taking tests known as the Classification Battery.

In his first letter to Laura Jeanne, Don demonstrated that he hadn't lost his sense of humor:

> *How is y'all today? Ah feels fine, my deah. Ah hopes y'all kin rid this here lettah. The guys heah 'bouts don't know whethah I'm frum the South or the North. I kin mimic and keep up with the best of these southern boys.*
>
> *I just received my first real G.I. haircut. Here at SAACC they call it the "Cadet Clip." The barber left a little over an inch on top so the top of my head won't burn in the Texas sun. The fellows, including myself, are a sorry looking sight. Oh well, at least I won't have to worry about combing my hair anymore.*
>
> *Gee whizz—it's surely hot down here. My face and neck are burned. Even the drinking water is warm. They don't use stoves down here, they just lay the stuff out on the pavement. These Texas boys say that the summer heat usually ranges from 110 to 120 degrees and sometimes points higher. Ah reckon ah kin stand it if these here boys kin!!*

The Classification Battery helped the Army assign cadets where they'd have the best chance of success—as a pilot, navigator, or bombardier. The Air Corps designed the first series of tests to measure general knowledge and aptitude, leadership abilities, and intellect. Next, they put cadets through extensive psychomotor tests to assess their eye-hand-foot coordination, visual acuity, and their ability to perform under pressure. At the end of classification testing, an Army psychologist thoroughly grilled each candidate.[9]

An astounding ninety-seven percent of the air cadets entering training wanted to be fighter pilots. In addition to scoring high on the classification tests, fighter pilot candidates couldn't be more than five feet ten inches tall and weigh more than 160 pounds. The selection odds weren't in their favor, guaranteeing there would be many disappointed air cadets when the Air Corps announced classification results.[10] After the tests, the waiting game began. They woke the cadets at 5:30 a.m. and turned the lights out at 10:00 p.m., but gave them little to do in between—apparently intent on teaching them the long-standing Army tradition "Hurry up and wait."

Don hadn't heard his name at mail call since he arrived at SAACC, waiting nearly two weeks before he received his first letter from home. Then, just as he started to open the envelope, the drill sergeant called the cadets to formation:

Honey, I almost died before I got back. I'm terribly glad that you've missed me so much—because I've been as moody as all get out. I hope you never get used to not having me around. And congratulations on passing your Civil Service Exam! I hope you can get a good job close to home.

I haven't called you on the telephone because I've been in quarantine. And about the telegram... Some of us sneaked (without permission) into the station at San Antonio to try to send a few. I got one off to my parents, then just as I was addressing one to you, some guards showed up and paged us—at the point of a gun—and wouldn't let us finish. Please don't be upset with me and think that my folks come first, and then if I have time, you come next. I know it looks that way but—never mind—I guess the damage has been done, and it's just one more black mark on my record.

The food here is good, but it's too darn hot to eat much. All I do is sit at the table and sweat and pass the iced tea and then sweat some more. The iced tea looks really tempting, but I haven't broken the Word of Wisdom* and don't intend to—even if I have to drink warm water all the time. I'd give a dollar right now for a cool pitcher of good old Utah water.

All the guys, me included, are bored and anxious to know what's going to happen to us.

Three days later, Training Command announced air cadet classifications. During a break that afternoon, Don shared his good news with Laura Jeanne, writing:

I made it! I'm one of ten cadets in our group classified as a pilot. About forty cadets were classified as bombardiers and six as navigators. Gee, honey, I'm so happy! I can't wait to get in the air. Grant and Ralph were classified as bombardiers. Grant feels kind of upset and is going to try and get changed to a pilot. All three positions are really good ones, but most fellows want to be at the controls.

Grant just came back from talking to HQ. He's decided being a bombardier is ok—so he signed up.

Now we just have to wait for our Preflight Training assignments. I could go to Nashville or Santa Anna, but most likely I'll go across the road to the training school at SAACC.

While the air cadets waited for their preflight training assignments, SAACC assigned them guard duty, KP (kitchen patrol), and PT (physical fitness training), which the cadets renamed *physical torture,* but most of the time they were bored with little to do, wondering if the Army really knew what it was doing or just making things up as they went along. Ironically, their query wasn't far off the mark.

Air Force Training Command had been scrambling for more than a year to ramp up its pilot training programs to accommodate the huge increase in pilot candidates. Before Pearl Harbor, there were fewer than 17,000 cadets in flight training programs in the

---

*   The LDS (Mormon) health code discourages the use of tobacco, alcohol, coffee, and tea.

United States. One year after the attack that number exploded to nearly 90,000, many kept waiting in classification centers like Don's group—stuck in limbo for up to six months.[11] Pilot training programs had undergone dramatic changes since the U.S. entered the war, and the programs were still evolving in May 1943, as the new air cadets at SAACC waited to begin preflight.

———————

Don got along well with the guys on his post, but when they took off to go places and have fun, he generally stayed behind. One lonely evening, he bemoaned his situation to Laura Jeanne, writing:

All the guys have gone to the show again tonight. I haven't been to one as yet. I don't seem to have time to keep up on my correspondence and still take in the activities they do. I've been trying to keep in touch with all my friends at home and in the military, as well as all the family. I don't mind writing. It helps me feel closer to home.

While I was reading your last letter, I got all choked up inside. I feel so lonely and blue. I never thought life could be so miserable. Every time I look at the last picture we had taken together in the canyon, I just want to leave the Air Corps and come straight home to you.

I don't know how much longer I'll be able to stand being away. Things look so dark to me right now. We're so far away from each other, and it will be a long time before I can get a furlough. I don't know when I'll get an open post—but when I do, I'm going to call you. I'm desperate to hear your voice again.

Don read and reread Laura Jeanne's letters at night, reminiscing every date, dance, movie, and fun time he could summon to his memory. He exhausted his vocabulary describing his love and lonesomeness in his letters, and even resorted to writing poetry. The thought of missing her high school graduation exercises, not hearing her sing her solo, and knowing she would spend the night alone at home instead of at the graduation dance and party left him deeply depressed. One of Don's buddies finally got him out of his funk, dragging him into town to buy her graduation presents. He even sweet-talked their cute sales clerk into modeling a satin robe.

Life wasn't easy for Laura Jeanne back home either:

After Don left, I spent my time studying and preparing for graduation. On May 15, 1943, the big day finally arrived. I made the honor roll and sang a vocal solo at our graduation exercises. Instead of going to my graduation dance and party, I went home and waited for the telephone call I hoped would come from my cadet sweetheart.

Earlier that day he'd sent me a beautiful corsage, a card, and a lovely satin robe. The evening was complete when the phone rang and I was able to hear his voice again—and listen to the words "I love you and miss you terribly."

Laura Jeanne was in a quandary about what to do after graduation. Should she start college, as she'd always planned, or look for a job and try to save up some money before getting married? She listened to advice from her friends and family, wavering back and forth. In the end, the pragmatic choice won out. After passing the Civil Service Exam, she began interviewing to find a full-time job. Competition for good jobs was increasing as more and more women were now entering the work force. The first position she applied for went to someone with more experience, but she impressed an Army officer during her second interview, and he hired her on the spot. Her new employment, however, wasn't without its challenges:

I had to leave home at 5:30 in the morning and travel through mountainous terrain west of Fairfield, Utah, to get to the Tooele Army depot by 8:00 a.m. There were six passengers in the car and the roads were dusty with lots of dangerous curves.

I was secretary to Capt. Rosenbach. He was the most demanding, arrogant, ornery Army brass boss ever! The only good thing about my job was my salary. I worked hard and was quickly promoted, allowing me to save a few dollars for whatever events might happen in the months to come.

––––––––––

On May 26, 1943, more than a month after arriving in San Antonio, Don finally received his preflight training orders. As he hoped, the Army was sending him across the road to train at SAACC.

Signal Corps Balloon and Wright Brothers' Military Plane

FIVE

Hazing and "Gigs"

The Army created the Signal Corps Air Service at the beginning of the Civil War. While the North and the South didn't engage each other in the air, pilots from each side flew military balloons, observing battles and troop movements. Thirty-five years later, the Signal Corps deployed a balloon again, this time in the Spanish-American War. After flying the Army's only hand-sewn balloon all the way to Cuba, a courageous pilot provided logistics from his aerial perch to Teddy Roosevelt and his Rough Riders as they charged their way up San Juan Hill. In 1908, the Signal Corps purchased an aircraft from the Wright Brothers and began training a few brave soldiers to fly.[12,13]

In 1916, the newly created Army 1st Aero Squadron, led by General John "Black Jack" Pershing, helped chase Pancho Villa back to Mexico after he invaded the U.S. during the Mexican Revolution, proving that planes could do some things better than men on horseback. Few leaders envisioned their military potential at the time, but that was about to change.

When America entered World War I in 1917, the Army Air Service consisted of a few obsolete airplanes, a handful of experienced pilots, three pilot-training schools, and very few qualified instructors— paling in comparison to the strength of the Germans and their European Allies.[14] The War Department immediately began setting up aviation schools throughout the country to try to catch up. Nearly 40,000 young men applied to enter the new pilot training programs. Entry into the Air Service wasn't easy. Candidates had to be under age twenty-five, have two years of college education, and be "athletic, honest, and reliable." Now called "flying cadets," they spent eight weeks in ground-school classes, then six to eight weeks at a primary flying school.[15] Their combat training took place in Britain, France, and Italy, since America had no advanced training planes and no qualified combat instructors.[16]

President Woodrow Wilson, responding to criticism for America's poor aircraft showing early in the war, removed the Army Air Service from the Signal Corps and placed it directly under the War Department. By Armistice Day in November 1918, the Air Service had trained nearly 9,000 pilots, and America had become serious about building military aircraft.[17]

Following World War I, the United States dramatically decreased military funding. American citizens, politicians, and most military leaders bought into the myth that World War I *was* "the war to end all wars." Feelings of apathy and isolationism spread across America. The Army Air Service faced fewer reductions than other military branches and was able to continue modernization efforts after the war. Flight training programs were consolidated and improved, and America began building low-wing, all-metal monoplanes.[18]

In 1920, Congress passed legislation making the Air Service a combat arm of the Army. Six years later, they changed the name again—this time to the Army Air Corps. With entry into World War II looming, the War Department foresaw the need for an expanded aviation arm and created the Army Air Force (AAF). The Air Corps still oversaw all flight-training programs, technically operating as a branch of the AAF, but for all practical purposes, the Army had replaced it. Several prominent leaders argued for the AAF to become a separate and equal military branch of the armed services. In a compromise, the War Department made the AAF co-equal to the Army Ground Forces.[19]

In 1941, the AAF changed the name of its flying candidates to "air cadets." Although they were now addressed as "Mister," cadet pay remained unchanged at $75 a month, the same as it was in World War I. Ground schools evolved into "preflight schools," but there was serious disagreement among Air Corps Training Command leaders about course content, length, and how much military discipline and physical conditioning to emphasize. Gradually, the focus shifted to technical knowledge and academic subjects to keep up with the advances in aviation technology. However, the Air Corps didn't introduce a standardized curriculum for its preflight schools until April of 1943, just as Don entered pilot training.[20]

The Air Corps adopted the West Point Code of Cadet Discipline and Honor as the model for its preflight schools. The cadets soon fell into the typical military class system, where hazing and harassment were common practice. That May, following the disclosure of several embarrassing abuses, the Air Corps officially abolished the practice.[21] However, hazing of underclassmen was a time-honored tradition, and military traditions die hard. Even though the practice interfered with the primary mission of the schools, Training Command turned a blind eye and did little to eliminate it.[22]

Hazing at SAACC started the moment Don crossed the road on his first day at preflight:

When we underclassmen were lining up this morning, the "uppers" (upperclassmen) were hanging on the fence, waiting for us like a pack of hungry wolves—the kind that likes raw meat.

Every time we want to leave the barracks, we have to take a co-pilot (another underclassman) with us. And when we get outside, we have to do double-time everywhere we go. We pop to attention whenever the "uppers" enter our barracks, then salute and address them as "Sir." In fact, we even have to salute the water fountain before we drink and say, "Sir, aviation cadet Evans reporting to ask a question. May I have a drink, Sir?" And when we're eating and want something, we must say, "Sirs, is anyone using the pineapple preserves? If not, will someone please pass them?"

The temperature in South Texas was now reaching a scorching 105 to 115 degrees by mid-afternoon. Preflight classes weren't scheduled to start for another week, giving the new cadets' drill instructor a head start to whip them into shape. They marched and did calisthenics during the heat of the day and struggled through lectures at night in stifling classrooms—on top of their regular KP and guard duties.

Air cadets received demerits, known as "Gigs," for breaking rules and exhibiting bad behavior. As a carryover from the military class system, the Air Corps still authorized upperclassmen to give demerits to underclassmen, arbitrarily at times, as punishment for even the smallest infractions:

Some of the things the "uppers" make us do are pretty funny. We have a six-foot, four-inch guy in our barracks, and every time an "upper" cries out, "Where's my boy?", he has to yell (and I mean yell) in a real loud voice, "You-u-u who-o-o, here I am, Sir." It's really comical and gets us all laughing, and then they give us a "gig" for laughing.

Every time one of the "uppers" finds anything wrong with our personal belongings, our bed or floors, if we're late for formation or class, or even if we just look "slouchy," they give us a gig. A gig counts so many demerits and when you get more than seven in a week (which is quite easy), you have to walk with a gun on your shoulder for an hour for each one over seven. I haven't had to walk—yet!

Just plain drill

Despite the sweltering South Texas heat and occasional bouts of homesickness, Don excelled in preflight, performing near the top of his class. Although his long days seemed routine and tedious to him, Laura Jeanne loved reading about his training experiences and was constantly asking him questions:

You asked how I'm doing and I almost wrote, "Fine, Sir!" Actually, it's more like "relatively fine under the circumstances." I'm lonesome, broke, tired and sleepy, have two sore arms (from shots), two sore feet (from marching), no free time, and I'm hot.

We went into the pressure chamber this morning. They tested us to see if we can take it up where the oxygen is scarce. At 28,000 feet, they had us take off our masks for six minutes. It makes you feel sleepy and then kind of like you're just about to pass out.

We have courses in code, math, and identification of naval vessels and enemy aircraft. Every day (including Sundays), we're up at 5:00 a.m., shave, mop floors, make bed, and then chow. Next, formation is at 8:00 a.m., followed by lectures, drill, PT, lunch, more classes, then dinner at 5:00 p.m. We use our free time to shine shoes & brass, and do our washing, etc., then we study until 9:30 p.m., shower, and prepare for the following day. At most, I might have one hour of my own. Our cadet motto is "War is hell, but Preflight is worse!"

In a humorous attempt to apologize to Laura Jeanne for not writing more often due to his hectic schedule, Don penned the following anecdote:

I don't think I ever told you about the big, beautiful cockroaches we have down here. There are so many in our barracks that each cadet is in charge of 500. The little beggars get into our lockers and change things around so that I can't find a thing. Consequently, I have to spend a couple of hours each day training them and giving them military discipline!

Every Saturday we get our cockroaches organized and have a parade. Mine have won twice, and I'm mighty proud of them. However, I got kind of sore the other night when they came in from an open post drunk—and kept shaking my bed. Gee whizz, I didn't get any sleep.

Anyway, I was attempting to tell you that my writing has been interrupted by a scheduled drill formation for my cockroaches. Honey, I don't mean that my little pets come before my writing to you, but if I don't meet them when a formation is scheduled, they just take over and all pile into bed with me. You can see what I'm up against, can't you?

———————

In addition to coping with upperclassmen antics, Don also had to placate an anxious fiancée, who had started pressing him to move up their wedding date:

In answer to your letter about getting married earlier than planned, the soonest I could possibly get a furlough would be in September. If not then, it would have to be next spring when I graduate. We can try for September, honey, or we can wait until next spring or next summer, whatever you think best.

I've written to both our folks about our desire to get married before next March when I get my wings—if I don't wash out. They feel strongly that we should wait. I'm perplexed as to whether we should do as our hearts tell us, or if we should use our heads as well, and consider our parents' wishes.

Unaware he was about to open Pandora's Box, Don suggested in his next letter that they consider delaying their wedding plans:

Honey, I don't know where I'll be in September. And I don't like to talk about it, but some of the best guys from our old upper class just washed in Primary. Usually not more than 20 to 30 percent of those who start out in training to be fighter pilots complete the entire course. And only the top 10 percent of the remainder get commissioned second lieutenant. The rest become flight officers. They say that either you have the ability to fly or you don't, so I'll just have to wait and see what happens.

Anyway, if I wash out, I don't know where they'll send me. I don't know how to plan for something like that, so it's probably better for us to wait until I find out for sure or until I get my wings. I want you to know that my heart's desire is to get you here as soon as possible.

Laura Jeanne's reaction to postponing their wedding caught Don completely off-guard. The uncertainties surrounding their future were a lot for a seventeen-year-old teenage girl to handle, providing fertile ground for doubts and impatience to take hold. In his next letter, Don tried to assuage her feelings:

I'm sorry that my letter made you feel so upset. When I said I thought we should wait it was because I thought it would be better for you, darling. But if you want to get married next month, then I'm willing to raise hell and high water to make it happen.

Our folks are doing what they think is best by telling us to wait. But we still need their permission to get married. So if that's what you want for sure—then we need to convince them to change their minds.

If there isn't a branch of the Church where I'm assigned, we can have a military wedding, or get married by a justice of the peace. Military weddings are quite formal. The groomsmen wear sabers and there's saluting and stuff. I think you'd enjoy it. I need a lot of help with this—I've never been involved with wedding plans for anyone before. So give me all your suggestions as to how or what you'd like. And speak freely, my dear, for you won't be free for long!!

With only two weeks of preflight left, the pressure was off the surviving cadets. They knew they would graduate and were content with killing time, waiting for their new assignment to come through. They celebrated by shooting sub-machine guns at the firing range, watching movies, and placing bets on where the Air Corps would send them for primary flying training.

On July 27, Don graduated from preflight and received orders to report to Curtis Field. That night he wrote:

The Army Air Corps has finally announced the place of our wedding bells!! It's Brady, Texas, a small town of around 5,000 people, located 140 miles north of San Antonio. We're leaving here at 5:30 a.m. on July 30, and we'll get there by August 1. Some of the guys aren't too happy because they don't even sell liquor there. Oh, what will I do? It'll probably be about a week before we start flying. I can hardly wait!

And don't worry about the CO—I'll take care of him. It isn't necessary to ask his permission, but I intend to talk to him anyway, as well as with the chaplain. As soon as I get there, I'll start on our plans. Trust me—I'll take care of everything.

Unfortunately, Don was naive when it came to military protocol. An air cadet's commanding officer had absolute authority over him, rarely granting exceptions to a cadet's pledge not to marry before earning his wings. The Air Corps had justifiable reasons for requiring the pledge—a wedding could easily become a major distraction, negatively affecting a cadet's flying training. The Army was making a significant investment in time, money, and resources to train its fighter pilots. And with America at war, when push came to shove, the Army always won out.

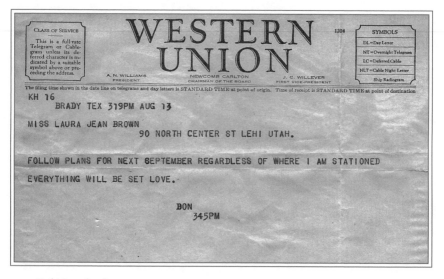

CLASS OF SERVICE

This is a full-rate Telegram or Cablegram unless its deferred character is indicated by a suitable symbol above or preceding the address.

WESTERN UNION

1204

A. N. WILLIAMS
PRESIDENT

NEWCOMB CARLTON
CHAIRMAN OF THE BOARD

J. C. WILLEVER
FIRST VICE-PRESIDENT

SYMBOLS

DL = Day Letter

NT = Overnight Telegram

LC = Deferred Cable

NLT = Cable Night Letter

Ship Radiogram

The filing time shown in the date line on telegrams and day letters is STANDARD TIME at point of origin. Time of receipt is STANDARD TIME at point of destination

KH 16

BRADY TEX 319PM AUG 13

MISS LAURA JEAN BROWN

90 NORTH CENTER ST LEHI UTAH.

FOLLOW PLANS FOR NEXT SEPTEMBER REGARDLESS OF WHERE I AM STATIONED

EVERYTHING WILL BE SET LOVE.

DON
345PM

Calming the dust storm

SIX

"You'll Be Sorry!"

Before World War II, military instructors at U.S. Air Corps bases conducted all phases of pilot training. After Pearl Harbor, however, the Army couldn't handle the huge influx of new air cadets. To meet the need for additional instructors and airfields, they entered into a joint venture with fifty-six of the best civilian flying schools across the nation.[23]

The Air Corps divided primary flight training into four phases. In pre-solo, cadets flew general light aircraft, learning forced landing techniques and recovery from stalls and spins. Next, in intermediate, they learned to fly standard patterns known as elementary 8's, lazy 8's, pylon 8's and chandelles (a steep climbing turn executed to gain altitude while changing direction). During the accuracy phase, they practiced various types of approaches and landings. And in the final acrobatic phase, the cadets were required to execute loops, Immelmann maneuvers (evasive turns), slow rolls, half-rolls, and snap rolls (a spin on a horizontal axis). To graduate from primary training, the cadets were required to have sixty-five hours of flying time, pass their ground school tests, and make at least 175 landings.[24]

On July 30, 1943, Don and 263 other air cadets from across the nation (officially recognized as AAF Class 44-B) arrived at the Brady School of Aviation. As the nervous cadets stepped off the bus, the upperclassmen on base greeted them with the familiar cadet welcome, "You'll be sorry!"[25]

The training aircraft used at Brady was the Fairchild PT-19A, a two-seater—twenty-eight feet long with a thirty-six-foot wingspan, and a 200 HP engine. The low-wing monoplane could fly up to 132 mph and climb to an altitude of 15,300 feet.[26]

Don was eager to escape the restrictive confines of ground school classrooms and get into the sky—something he'd been dreaming about ever since he left Fort Douglas:

> *Curtis Field is rather small, but the food is good, barracks clean, and it's only two miles from Brady. I'm now a "red-tagger." We have to wear nametags on our shirts; a "lower" is red and an "upper" is blue. About 150 upperclassmen have already soloed. They started with about as many cadets as our class, but a lot of their guys have already washed out.*
>
> *They have about 135 PT-19s on the field. We'll probably take our first ride in one next Thursday. I can't wait! It's been a long, hard day, so I'm hitting the sack. I'll start working on our wedding plans tomorrow.*

Don found Brady to be as billed, a typical one-horse, cowboy town that locals proudly called the "heart" of Texas. The usually quiet, rural community was bustling with activity when he arrived. The government was building an internment camp nearby to house German POWs, filling up the small town's limited housing with out-of-town workers, including the uninviting rooms at the Brady Hotel. Although disappointed with his findings, Don tried to sound optimistic the night of August 4, when he placed a telephone call to Laura Jeanne on her eighteenth birthday, reassuring her everything was going to work out for a September wedding.

The next day, the Class 44-B air cadets at Curtis Field climbed into the cockpit of their first training aircraft. Flying an airplane was everything Don dreamed it would be and nothing like driving a tractor:

> *What a thrilling day! My first trip up was sensational. Flying is an even greater sport than I thought. Of course, we didn't do many maneuvers today, but I know enough to know I love it. Our trip today was merely to acquaint us with the plane and the area where we're going to fly.*

The PT-19 doesn't fly very fast, but it's stable. I didn't feel a bit uneasy during any of my flight, but when we start spins, dives, etc., I think I'll get quite a sensation.

Unfortunately, Don's wedding planning wasn't going as well as his first trip into the wild blue yonder. He hadn't been able to find a place for Laura Jeanne to stay, and there wasn't a Mormon chapel within the limits of his 50-mile travel restriction. On top of that, he wasn't sure he'd even be there in September. A number of cadets in his class had washed out after just one week. He cautiously shared the discouraging news with her in his next letter, suggesting that they consider postponing their wedding until things were a little more certain.

Nothing like driving a tractor

Unaware of the difficulties her fiancé was encountering, Laura Jeanne picked out a diamond wedding ring, and for the next few days, she was on top of the world. Then Don's letter arrived. She fired back her response that same evening:

> *Maybe it just isn't meant to be. Nothing is working out the way I hoped and planned. I do not intend to wait until your graduation and commission to get married. Please arrange for our marriage as soon as possible, or I'm returning your ring and calling the whole thing off!*

It took a week for her letter to reach Don in Brady. Stunned by her response, he immediately wrote back:

> *I never should have mailed that letter suggesting another delay. I just knew another change in our plans would upset you. I've been cooking in my own stew ever since I put the letter in the mail. I'm so messed up by all this that I'm doing practically nothing in a constructive way with my flying.*
>
> *Honey, please don't ever write another "word" inferring such things as "might be better if," etc. You hit the nail on the head when you said that we're taking a big chance on getting married at any place or time with our prospective future so uncertain. I too want to live "now," and that can only happen by having you with me.*
>
> *They say by mid-September many of the construction workers may be gone from Brady, and things might open up for a place you could rent. I'll have everything ready on this end as soon as you can come, regardless of whether I'm in Brady or wherever.*

Don slept fitfully that night, unable to get Laura Jeanne's stinging words out of his mind. Worried that his letter wouldn't reach her soon enough to calm down the dust storm he'd created, he rose early the next morning and sent a telegram that read: "Follow plans for next September regardless of where I'm stationed. Everything will be set. Love, Don."

Unfortunately, Don's plans quickly unraveled. His CO refused his request to get married, reminding him of the pledge he'd made when he enlisted. Conflicted and powerless, he could only hope his next CO would be more understanding and that Laura Jeanne would accept the delay. The distractions caused him to lose his edge in training and he struggled both in the air and in ground school. After failing to make a successful three-point landing on successive flights with his instructor, he only had one more chance to land on his own or he'd wash out of pilot training.

Don's next attempt at a three-point landing was picture perfect, and three days later, he took to the air on his first solo flight. His instructor awarded him a certificate that read:

> Let the world know by this certification of a deed achieved, that on this 23rd day of August 1943, Donald N Evans alone took the controls of one PT-19A aircraft and, without the assistance of naught but his new-born ability and Irish luck, did take off and bring to the solid earth again his ship, while I, his instructor, watched from a distance, my fingers firmly crossed.

Then Don's air cadet band of brothers hauled him off, tossing him into the showers in accordance with an old Air Corps tradition.[27] He couldn't wait to share his good news with Laura Jeanne:

> *Honey, I soloed Monday! I made three takeoffs and three landings with no instructor—and I didn't even have to bail out! I also soloed around the field today the same way. This is really great sport! It's great to be able to fly without an instructor screaming in my ears. I was so happy that I had to holler out loud at myself!*

> *Tomorrow I get to check out a ship of my own and go a few more miles from the field to practice stalls, spins, eights, etc. About 25 of our guys have washed out already. I think I'll last for at least another week. And who knows—maybe even longer!*

Don was on an emotional rollercoaster, high one day after performing well in the air, and in the dumps the next after failing to do anything right. But at least things had finally settled down at home, thanks to a wise and loving mother who not only helped Laura Jeanne develop patience, but also gave her permission to marry, as soon as she and Don could make arrangements.

A few days later, Don again felt like he was on the bubble, unsure whether his performance in the air was good enough to keep him in the program:

I don't believe I did a half dozen things right this afternoon. My instructor told me I'd have to get on the ball because our 20-hour check rides start Monday. They say there'll be about 30–40 guys wash out next week. And if I don't "come to" soon, I'll be one of them.

I never dreamed life could be so mixed up and unsettled. Pilot training is the most unpredictable, nerve-racking thing I've ever encountered. I don't know from one day to the next if I'll wash out.

You asked me enough questions in your last letter to stump the "Quiz Kids." * First of all, the last I heard of Grant, he was in South Texas completing a gunnery course and was about ready to go to advanced bombardier school. Dee finally got married. He's still in Idaho, but the Navy is shipping him this way too. I hope our paths cross again while we're all here in South Texas.*

The following week, Don not only passed his critical 20-hour check ride, but was also promoted to Cadet Commander of Squadron B, which consisted of 125 men. With his confidence restored, his old swagger returned, and he started having fun again.

Back home, Laura Jeanne and her mother were in the middle of planning a wedding shower and arranging for their trip to Texas. Don attempted to reassure his fiancée after sensing from her most recent letter that she was overwhelmed by an uncertain future, still unsure when and where—even if—their wedding would take place:

I know you're worried about all our plans coming together. Mom wrote me an encouraging note, saying, "Don't worry— things usually have a way of working out OK. And I plan on making a trip to Texas to give my son away whenever they do." I hope your mother is able to get a substitute teacher for her classes and come down too.

---

* A radio series popular in the 1940s.

Don purposely didn't mention the aircraft accident that took place earlier that day during flight training, not wanting to give Laura Jeanne anything else to worry about. It was the first of many tragic accidents that occurred during his flight training. In his war memoirs, he wrote:

We had a few "hot dogs" in our group that had done some flying while they were in college. Once we started to solo in Primary, they started showing off—buzzing the tower and doing crazy stunts. One of them was killed when he tried to fly his plane under some telephone wires. After that, the group settled in better and concentrated on following established flying procedures.

As their wedding date approached, Laura Jeanne quit her job, giving her more time to hang out with her friends. Several of them tried to convince her that getting married now was a mistake. Looking to Don for reassurance, she wrote another letter, asking him if he really loved her and was completely sure that getting married was the right thing to do. Don responded:

From what you wrote in the letter I read today, honey, I'd say you have a slight case of bride's jitters. I'm sorry things haven't worked out the way you planned. And darling, the answer to your question is YES. I'm sure about us, and I love you with all my heart and soul.

I'm fully in favor of our current wedding plans, but I won't hold you to them if you think you aren't ready to come. I know how you must feel with your friends and everyone telling you that you're foolish to get married so young and leave home to come out here to live in the middle of nowhere.

I'll call you as soon as I can, and we'll get everything all figured out. Know that I love you and miss you more than you can imagine.

Want to hear about me for a minute? Well, we've passed the halfway mark, and I'm still in the running. I have about 30 hours now, and by the end of next week, I'll be due for a 40-hour check ride. I went into clouds yesterday for the first time, and oh, what fun! I think I'm really learning how to fly!

Don anxiously waited for the telephone operator to connect his call. Working out relationship issues through the mail was painfully slow and difficult, nearly impossible. He hoped to have better luck over the phone. Although eager to have Laura Jeanne join him, he was patient and willing to wait until she was ready. She didn't seem sure what she wanted—wavering between getting married immediately and calling the whole thing off. Hearing Don's voice on the telephone, however, rekindled the spark in their long-distance relationship, and before saying goodbye, marriage plans for the middle of October were back on track, pending his next CO's approval.

In her next letter, Laura Jeanne asked Don about "check rides." He explained:

> Check pilots ride with each guy about four or five times while we're here in Primary to see if we're progressing fast enough. If not, then they give you another ride the following day. If you're still doing badly, then they wash you out. I'm still in the top 10 of our flight in my ground school courses and made out fairly well in today's check ride. I might make it through this doggone Primary school after all. Keep your fingers crossed, darling, for good luck—and so that ring doesn't fall off, OK?

> Our classes will be finished up in about a week and a half. I now have 47 hours in the air. This coming week is really important, since I'll probably get a couple of check rides. We also plot and fly a cross-country course next week that will cover about 150 miles.

Don passed his final check ride, qualifying him to move on to basic flying training. While he made it sound routine in his next letter, it was a big deal—and all the graduating air cadets were celebrating.

At the beginning of primary flight training, the Air Corps issued each cadet a small 5x7-inch black *Pilot's Log Book* where flight dispatchers recorded and certified the cadets' flight data. Don's log recorded that he graduated from primary with a total of sixty-five hours in the air—twenty-eight flying with an instructor and thirty-seven flying solo.

On the morning of October 1, 1943, the Brady Class 44-B graduates shoved off for Goodfellow Field in San Angelo, eighty miles west.

Wedding day with both moms

SEVEN
....

Mr. and Mrs.

The Army Air Corps was only willing to farm out pilot training to civilian contractors up to the primary flying school stage. After that, they took complete control, requiring the War Department to build dozens of basic and advanced flight schools all over the nation. When San Angelo civic leaders learned that the military planned to build a basic flight school in West Texas, they traveled to San Antonio to convince the War Department that their city was the best location for the proposed school. The town fathers sealed the deal when they offered the War Department 640 acres to build on at the lease rate of $1 per year.[28] Named Goodfellow Field, in honor of a former San Angelo resident killed in France during World War I, the new school was operational the following year.[29]

The mission of basic flying schools was to make military pilots out of the recent primary graduates. In basic, the air cadets learned to operate a bigger, more powerful, and more complex plane—flying by instruments, in formation, and cross-country. The Air Corps divided basic into two main phases. The first, or transition phase, involved becoming familiar with their new plane and its operation. In the second or diversified phase, the cadets learned accuracy and acrobatic maneuvers, studied air navigation techniques, and learned to fly by instruments both day and night. At the conclusion of basic, the officers at the base divided the cadets into two groups: those qualifying to train in single-engine fighter planes, which nearly all the cadets wanted to do, and those selected for multi-engine bomber aircraft training.[30]

Basic instructors at Goodfellow Field trained the cadets in the Vultee BT-13A Valiant. Like their first trainer in primary, it was a two-seater, but more than twice as powerful with a 450 HP engine, enabling it to fly up to 183 mph and climb to an altitude of 16,500 feet. The Vultee also had fixed landing gear, a two-pitch propeller, two-way radio communications, and upgraded flight instruments. The rear cockpit had an additional feature—a curtain that instructors could draw closed to block the cadet's vision, forcing him to fly using the plane's instruments. Cadets nicknamed their trainer the *Vultee Vibrator*.[31] Besides being noisy, "it rattled and shook so badly it felt like all the screws and rivets were coming loose and the panels were about to drop off, especially as it approached stall speed and in aerial maneuvers."[32]

AAF Class 44-B graduates from primary schools in Brady and Ballinger, Texas, arrived at Goodfellow Field on October 2, 1943. This time they weren't fazed by the catcalls as they passed through the front gates. After reporting to their barracks and unpacking their footlockers, Colonel Glenn L. Davasher, their new CO, called the trainees to the Quadrangle. Following a short welcome speech, he gave them a few instructions, then marched them off to chow.

Flight Time, the newspaper published on the base, reported:

> Class 44-B is the first class entering Basic at Goodfellow that was part of the College Training Detachment. As such, these cadets are much better prepared for the academic work at Preflight and Primary schools, and will find their college training a great help in Basic as well.

> Class 44-A moved to the west side of the mess hall today as Class 44-B takes over the east side. Unlike most College Training Detachments who receive a five-month course while at college, these cadets were shipped directly to the San Antonio Classification Center and from there straight to Preflight.

At the end of his second day at Goodfellow Field, Don mustered up the courage to meet with his new CO to plead his case, praying that he'd receive permission to get married. He was under the gun and feared what might happen if he failed again:

My CO immediately reminded me of the rules and said, "You can only get married when you graduate and get your wings. You made that pledge when you enlisted in the Air Corps. You'll just have to wait until you get commissioned."

Well, then, I said, I'm in real trouble. I showed him the letter that I received from Laura Jeanne the month before. He softened up some and said, "Hey, pal, you are in deep trouble. You've got a good record, so I'll tell you what. If you'll commit to hang in there and not let getting married distract you, I'll work it out so you can get a little time off to get married. Go send her a telegram and let her know."

Pratt-Whitney -- 450 H.P.
"Vultee"
BT-13A

9 weeks Training — 5 ¾ hrs before "Solo Flight" 23 ¾ hrs Total

Later that night, Laura Jeanne made the following entry in her journal:

I received a wonderful telegram from Don today telling me to make the necessary arrangements for our wedding, which is scheduled to take place on October 13, 1943. It looks like I'm really going to get married after all.

War casualties were mounting all over the nation. The losses seemed to hit hardest in small rural towns like Lehi, where nearly everyone knew each other. Every day the war was drawing closer and closer to Laura Jeanne, prompting her to write:

All around me now, there's evidence of the war's influence. My friends are being either drafted or enlisting in the different branches of the armed services. My brother Howard and Don's brother Duane are both in the Navy. Our wonderful little town of Lehi is beginning to experience the anguish of losing loved ones.

The Lehi Free Press reports a list of casualties on a weekly basis now. The heartache I feel being separated from my sweetheart is relatively minor compared to the devastation these families must feel at the loss of a family member.

As the date for our wedding grows closer, my parents continue to be apprehensive about sending me off to unfamiliar parts of the country where I'll be alone, far away from the support system of family, friends, and church.

With their wedding plans now on track, Don was able to concentrate on flight training without distractions. And his renewed focus didn't come any too soon—basic flying training was much more demanding than primary and becoming increasingly more competitive each day:

Our training at Goodfellow was packed solid from daybreak to bedtime. They gave us a bunch of manuals and handbooks to study, but not nearly enough time to study them. When we weren't flying or in ground school classes, we marched and did PT for hours at a time, and often ended the day running a two-mile obstacle course.

I liked flying the Vultee. It was more like a combat airplane than the PT-19. Besides learning to fly a new plane, we also had to

*learn how to be our own navigator and bombardier. Everything
at Basic flying school was very intense—nothing was easy.*

On October 9, *Flight Time* mourned the loss of two training
pilots killed at Goodfellow Field in a mid-air collision. A few days
later in an editorial cartoon, the base newspaper reminded the air
cadets of the alarming accident statistics in flying training programs
across the nation.

The *"Grim Reaper of Carlessness"*

Marriage announcements printed in the *Lehi Free Press* and *Deseret News* read:

> Mr. and Mrs. L. B. Brown announce the engagement and forthcoming marriage of their daughter, Miss Laura Jeanne Brown, to Aviation Cadet Donald N Evans, son of Mr. and Mrs. Noble Evans.

> The bridegroom-to-be has completed his primary flight training at Curtis Field, Brady, Texas and transferred to Goodfellow Field in San Angelo for basic training. Cadet Evans attended Brigham Young University at Provo.

> Miss Brown, accompanied by her mother and Mrs. Evans, will leave next week for San Angelo, Texas, where the marriage will take place. Both young people are graduates of Lehi High School and very popular among the younger set of the city.

In her personal history, Laura Jeanne recounted her emotional trip to Texas:

> *My dad arranged for railroad tickets to San Angelo for my mom, Don's mother, and me. It was necessary for each of us to have a parent present at the wedding, because we were both under age and needed their permission.*

> *As we boarded the train and started on the long anticipated journey, a pang of fear entered my heart. I began asking myself questions like: "What am I doing going to Texas to marry someone that I haven't even seen for over six months?", and "Am I really old enough to get married? I just turned 18 two months ago!" Panic set in and I was losing control of my emotions. It took me several hours before I could finally get hold of myself. After all, I kept thinking, "Aren't my dreams finally coming true? What was there to be afraid of?" But I was afraid.*

> *Traveling on the train was like re-living memories of my childhood. I grew up with my own D&RG Western Railroad pass, and I'd traveled to Denver, Colorado Springs, Los Angeles, even to San Francisco. So it wasn't a novelty for my mother or me—but for Don's mother, it was an exciting new*

adventure. This was her first time away from her husband in all the years they'd been married, and her first experience on a big, luxury railroad train.

Our trip was uneventful, except for the times we were delayed because of government troop trains, since they always had priority. We enjoyed waving to the soldiers as they passed. There were tanks, trucks, and men in uniform all along the way. Evidence of supplies and manpower was visible everywhere we went and brought the reality of our country's war involvement close to home.

Don had a four-hour pass to meet us at the railroad station, and our train arrived about three and a half hours late. Foolishly, I wasted nearly fifteen minutes by refusing to get off the train. I thought I had my emotions under control and was getting excited to see my future husband, until the crucial moment finally arrived. Then I had a change of heart, deciding that I was making a big mistake. I was so frightened I nearly got sick to my stomach.

Both mothers were frantically trying to persuade me to at least get off the train and tell Don that I'd changed my mind. I think they both knew that as soon as I laid eyes on him everything would be all right. I tried to take that first step off the platform, but I couldn't do it. My mother had to give me a push and a shove to get me to move my feet.

They were right! My heart nearly melted when I saw Don standing there in his uniform. He ran toward me, took me into his arms, hugged and kissed me, and told me that he loved me more than anything in the world. Tears of joy filled my eyes.

Our reunion only lasted a few minutes. Don introduced us to two Mormon missionaries that accompanied him to the train station, Elder Peterson and Elder Heaton, and assured us that plans had been made for everything. As he got on the bus to return to the base, his last words were, "See you tomorrow night, and remember, 'Torchy,' I love you!" "Tough" and "Torchy"...it's hard to believe that we went through high school with such nicknames—but it was just what I needed to hear.

The missionaries took us to the home of one of the Church members. They prepared a lovely dinner, then furnished us with the best bedroom accommodations in their home.

After getting permission from his CO, Don worried about the difficulty of making wedding arrangements while being restricted to the base. Desperate for help, he contacted the leader of the small LDS Church congregation in San Angelo. The next day, two young Mormon missionaries came to see him at the base, eager to help. With the assistance of local Church members, they arranged for the chapel, the flowers, the program, and the refreshments and even rented a place for Laura Jeanne to live near the base. Laura Jeanne continued:

The missionaries stopped by on the morning of October 13 (our wedding day) in an old truck and took me to see the small apartment they'd rented for me to live in. It wasn't exactly my idea of a honeymoon suite, but it would meet my needs. Mom, Don's mother, and I spent the afternoon getting ready for the big event. I didn't have a wedding dress, but mother had purchased me a wool suit that nearly matched the color of Don's uniform.

When we entered the small, modest building the San Angelo Church members used as a chapel, I was surprised to find it filled with beautiful flowers and beautiful people. All twenty members in that little branch were present for our wedding, and they didn't even know us. I couldn't believe my eyes.

Don's pass to get married started at 8:00 that evening and ended at 6:00 the next morning. As soon as he was released from the base, he rushed to the church, stopped outside the door for a moment to gain his composure, then made an entrance:

As the missionaries were introducing us to the members, suddenly the room became quiet. My handsome Air Force pilot walked in, took me by the arm, and escorted me to the front of the room. He presented me with a beautiful gardenia corsage and gave a nod to the missionaries to begin the service.

Elder Heaton had never performed a marriage ceremony, and he was more than a little nervous. We both said, "I do" at the proper time, and officially became Mr. and Mrs. Donald N Evans.

Following the ceremony, everyone left the chapel and went to the home of one of the members who lived close by where an open house was given in our honor. No presents, of course, but delicious food had been prepared and brought in for the special event. Texans are known for their wonderful hospitality, and we were certainly appreciative recipients.

Our mothers were taken back to the member's home we stayed at the previous evening, and Don and I were escorted to our first home. It all seemed like a storybook kind of fantasy!

The alarm clock went off at 5:00 the next morning, bringing Laura Jeanne's "fantasy" to an abrupt end. A few minutes later, the bus going to the base stopped on the corner near their newly rented apartment. A kiss good-bye, and Don was off to Goodfellow Field. Later that morning, the missionaries picked up Laura Jeanne and the two mothers in their old truck and drove them to the railroad station. Finishing her story, she wrote:

Saying goodbye this time was really hard for me to do. I felt homesick even before the train left the station. The missionaries assured me that they'd show me around the town and help me get settled in. It was a routine that all Army wives had to become accustomed to. I was now on my own.

I was allowed two short visits a week, in the evening, to see my husband at the base. The routine was easy enough to learn. No telephone calls, no privacy, and no time together alone, no show of affection, etc., etc., etc. Don was allowed to have an overnight pass every other weekend, and that's what we looked forward to.

Shortly after their wedding, the new couple had a surprise visitor, Grant Ash, who was on leave between gunnery and bombardier schools in South Texas. Don and Grant enjoyed reminiscing and catching up since their separation at SAACC five months earlier. Laura Jeanne invited their two missionary friends to join them for dinner that evening. A picture taken of the three Lehi High School alumni and the two young missionaries became a cherished possession.

Link trainer

Don's Pilot Flight Log recorded that he flew nearly every day he was in basic. In addition, he recorded seven flight sessions in a *Link Trainer*, a blind-flying simulator that looked like a short, stubby aircraft. His 44-B Class Book described what it was like learning to fly by instruments with your feet on the ground, using a bunch of gadgets and dials:

> The Link Trainer provided a pilot with a realistic replication of actual flying. It had a control column, control wheel, two foot pedals, and various flight and navigation instruments. An instructor sat at the desk and transmitted radio messages which the cadet in the Link heard through his earphones. Inside the cockpit, the cadet relied on instruments to "fly" the Link through various maneuvers while his navigational course was being tracked.

An anecdote circulating around the base depicted how realistic flying a Link seemed to the trainees, claiming that when an instructor told one of the cadets he'd run out of fuel, he broke his ankle when he leaped from the Link trying to parachute to safety.

On October 27, the air cadets flew their first solo cross-country flight. At times, it was a comedy of errors, an aerial version of Keystone Kops. *Flight Time* reported:

> The cadets of Class 44-B are really seeing Texas in the "rough" now that they've started their cross-country trips. Many curious instances have been taking place. On one triangle trip from the base to Hamilton and Cisco, one of our boys ended up in Waco (216 miles east of Goodfellow)!

> The most curious reoccurrence is the number of pilots getting lost somewhere around Sweetwater, Texas—home of the *Women's Auxiliary Flying School*. There are reportedly a lot of cuties learning to fly there. What the instructors can't figure out is how, when lost and unable to locate the base, 50% of the cadets are able to find Sweetwater!

Following several weeks of instrument and navigation training, the cadets went on their first solo cross-country night flight. They wondered how Army brass always seemed to schedule that dreaded flight to coincide with overcast skies and a waning moon. Don vividly remembered:

> *I studied the course I'd plotted on my map, marking the miles and compass headings on each leg of my night flight over the sparse Texas desert. I mapped a triangle pattern to two cities, then back to home base. I calculated my flight time at about an hour and a half, and I had about two hours of gas. My goal was to make it back to my base in one piece—with some gas still left in the tank.*

> *It was a dark, overcast night, so I had to rely on my compass, airspeed indicator, and needle and ball* for everything. I also had a low frequency radio, but that didn't help me until I was on the last leg of my flight. I was able to spot each city I'd plotted on my map, and after passing over the second one, I angled back for the base. Then I tuned the radio into the base frequency and started listening through my headphones for sounds emitting from the base radio tower. We called this "getting on the beam."*

Getting on the Beam

> *Since the beam was sent out in a straight line, it was necessary to fly back and forth in order to bracket the sound as you ran across it, then change your course as you went. Pretty soon*

---

*   Gyro instrument pilots used to indicate the rate of turn and the bank angle.

you'd hear a constant signal, and know you were "on the beam." If the signal started to fade out, but was still constant, you knew you were going in the wrong direction. I remember how relieved I was when I finally saw home base and knew I wasn't lost. Not all the guys fared as well as I did that night.

Pilot training was problematic, as evidenced by the high number of air cadets washing out at each stage of their training. Good study habits and Don's high aptitude for grasping aviation principles contributed to his success in ground school courses and in the air. Don loved to fly, and his enthusiasm for soaring in the sky was contagious. Now that Laura Jeanne was by his side, he was convinced that nothing could hold him back from realizing his dream to become a fighter pilot.

Don's Flight Log recorded that he passed his final check ride on December 2, finishing basic with 156 landings, eighty-three flight hours, and eleven hours in a Link Trainer. All that remained for the graduating air cadets in Class 44-B was to receive their final evaluation—the one that determined if they'd been selected for advanced flying training in a single-engine fighter plane or a multi-engine bomber.

As soon as the bus reached his stop, Don jumped off and raced around the corner to his apartment, excited to tell Laura Jeanne that he'd been selected for advanced training as a fighter pilot. Two days later, he boarded a troop train headed south to the Mexican border, leaving her with the daunting challenge of following him.

Pinks and Greens

EIGHT

....

Pinks-and-Greens

In stark contrast to the desert hill country of Brady and San Angelo, palm trees and orange groves surrounded Moore Field. Named after a young pilot killed in France during World War I, it was the Army's newest, and arguably best, advanced flying school for single-engine planes.[33]

The Air Corps divided advanced flight training into five phases. The first, instrument training, was a continuation of the methods learned in basic, including additional time in a Link Trainer. The next phases—transition, navigation, and formation—all required night flights. The final phase, acrobatics, included training in air combat maneuvers and fixed gunnery. At the end of advanced training, officers at the base selected the cadets who showed the highest aptitude to be combat fighter pilots, assigning them to additional gunnery and fighter transition courses.[34]

The training aircraft used at Moore Field was the North American AT-6 "Texan." Similar in size to the BT-13A flown in basic, the new trainer had a more powerful 650 HP engine, could fly over 200 mph, and was fitted with a single fixed .30 caliber machine gun. Reportedly hard to handle on the ground and challenging to fly, the Texan was unpopular with some air cadets. Despite that—or maybe because of it—many considered the AT-6 the best aircraft for training fighter pilots.[35]

On December 5, 1943, 275 AAF Class 44-B air cadets arrived at Moore Field, eager to climb into the cockpit of their first fighter aircraft. Base commanders divided the trainees into four squadrons of eight to twelve flight groups, each consisting of six to eight air cadets. Don was assigned to the Third Fighter Squadron, E Flight.

Laura Jeanne recorded the following in her personal history:

I was excited for Don, but otherwise in shock. I knew this day was coming, but I wasn't prepared for it. And Don and the other graduating cadets were leaving the very next day. Fortunately, a few of the cadet wives took me under their wings and helped teach me the ropes.

Mission, Texas, was the closest city to Moore Field. It was a small town of around 10,000 residents and was reported to have available housing and regular bus transportation to the base. The wives decided that would be the best place to stay for the next nine weeks, so we booked our tickets and followed our husbands.

Being married to an air cadet was a challenge. Wives spent a lot of time alone in remote locations, tagging along behind their husbands, and received no support from the Army. Laura Jeanne understood what she'd signed up for, though, and made the best of a difficult situation in the face of an uncertain future, intent on spending every possible moment with Don before he went overseas to war:

After arriving in town, I made a bus trip out to the new base to see Don and get some badly needed moral support. When I returned to Mission, I bought a local newspaper and started searching out the "for rent" ads in hopes of finding a place to live. After lots of walking and knocking on doors, I found an apartment with kitchen privileges like we'd had in San Angelo. And a few days later, I took a secretarial job at a grapefruit farm near town, since we needed the extra money.

Don got passes to come home every weekend, and I took the bus out to visit him on the base two to three times a week. We lived right on the border, and the Mexican food was really good. I also enjoyed the flowers and palm trees, and the warm weather in South Texas—but it still wasn't home.

Don quickly immersed himself in the flight-training program at Moore Field:

Advanced was a lot more fun than my previous flying training. I loved flying the AT-6 Texan. It went faster and flew higher than the previous planes we trained in. We used oxygen masks when we flew at higher altitudes, but we also learned to fly at near ground level. I couldn't wait to climb up into the blue every day and practice our air maneuvers and engage in mock aerial battles.

The aspiring fighter pilots also studied navigation methods, honed their instrument proficiency in Link Trainers, and learned how to dive-bomb, dropping bags of calcimine* on targets. But before they could fire the AT-6's machine guns, they had to learn how to lead and hit a moving target. First, they practiced breaking clay pigeons with a 12-gauge shotgun. Then they advanced to firing BB guns at a moving target as it sped around a circular track that one of their instructors had ingeniously fitted to their Link Trainers. After shotguns and BB guns, gunnery training turned serious, transitioning to the .30 caliber machine guns mounted on their planes.

As the Christmas season approached, Laura Jeanne's thoughts turned to family and friends back home. Although missing them terribly, she was happy to be with Don, loving him more than she ever thought possible:

Don's mother sent us a delicious fruitcake for Christmas, and we ate to our heart's content when it arrived. Texas was known for its big cockroaches and tiny ants. Since they got into everything, Don devised a clever plan to keep them out of our fruitcake. After wrapping it carefully and tying some twine around it, he hung it from the pull chain of the light fixture in the center of the room. We nearly cried the next day when we pulled down the cake and observed that the ants were having a feast inside the wrapping.

The CO allowed the wives to spend Christmas afternoon with their husbands at the base and take a tour of the facilities.

---

* A low-cost whitewash material used to mark where the mock bomb hit the ground.

Don had arranged for me to take a trial run in one of the Link Trainers. Thank goodness, it was only a flight simulator and not a real plane, or I'd be on the deceased list. I wasn't able to make the necessary corrections to get me out of spins and rollovers and terrible dives. I doubt Don had laughed that hard since the cat tipped over the garbage can the night he proposed to me.

We ended our visit in the lounge area of the base singing a few Christmas carols before our farewell ritual at the bus stop.

Each pilot-training stage brought an increased element of risk, even when the cadets flew with their instructors. Moore Field trainees had another sad reminder of the dangers when a nineteen-year-old air cadet and his flight instructor, a seasoned lieutenant, crashed and died on a routine training mission at the base.

Competition and failure to master advanced air combat skills continued taking their toll on cadet numbers, causing more and more pilots to wash out in advanced training. Those who survived eagerly looked forward to their next step—leaving the AT-6 Texan parked on the runway and climbing into the cockpit of a P-40 Warhawk fighter plane:

I've flown several hours in a P-40 fighter, a single seater being used in the Pacific Theater of War. It's quite a machine with a great deal of power, over twice the HP of the AT-6, It can fly over 350 mph, and lands at about 100 to 105 mph. In a turn, you can "black out" with no trouble at all. It's really a hot number—kind of like my Torchy.

On my first flight in a P-40, I was part of a formation of eight planes, four in each flight. We took off with our instructor, and everything went fine until we came in to land. One cadet wasn't able to land his plane. He came in several times, but his depth perception kept throwing him off, and he couldn't get lower than about 40 feet. Finally, one of the instructors flew wingtip to wingtip with him, telling him when to cut his power, and guided him to the ground. Fortunately, I was able to get my plane up and down successfully the first time.

A few days before graduation, the Air Corps gave the cadets money to buy officer dress uniforms called "Pinks-and-Greens,"* (smartly fitted wool pants and a jacket), expecting their soon-to-be officers to look sharp at their upcoming graduation ceremony. The printed graduation announcement read:

> The Army Air Forces Advanced Flying School of Moore Field announces the graduation of Class 44-B Tuesday morning, February eighth, nineteen hundred and forty-four at eleven o'clock at Moore Field, Texas.

Laura Jeanne beamed with pride as her husband walked up the stairs to the podium and received his pilot wings. And since he graduated among the top ten percent of his class, he received his commission as a second lieutenant in the AAF as well. The Air Corps assigned Don to complete his fighter pilot transition training at Moore Field and his gunnery training at nearby Matagorda Island. But the best news of all, at least for Laura Jeanne, was the announcement of a two-week furlough, effective immediately.

Although she'd done her best to conceal it, Laura Jeanne was suffering from a severe case of homesickness. With the cure only a few days away, she eagerly packed up her belongings. The following day, they boarded a passenger train headed for Utah:

> *The two-day train ride back home was long and tiring. There were more soldiers than regular passengers on the train and not enough seats to go around. Don was so exhausted from his training he could have slept anywhere, anyplace, anytime—and did so most of the way. But trying to sleep while sitting up wasn't one of my talents.*

> *The first glimpse of the beautiful Rocky Mountains helped me forget all the discomforts of the trip. I was so excited to return home and be with friends and family again.*

> *The timing of our return home coincided with my brother's furlough from the Navy. It was wonderful to see him and his*

---

* *The "Pinks" were dress pants, which were actually a light grey color with pink color tones, while the "Greens" were dress jackets, referred to as blouses. In November 1944, the newly designed short-waisted "Eisenhower Jackets" became standard issue for fighter pilots, replacing their dated old-style blouses.*

*new wife again. We stayed at my parents' home during Don's
leave, visiting friends, and going on dates, just like we did
before he entered the military.*

*Soon after arriving home, we arranged to go to the Salt Lake
Temple to be sealed* forever as husband and wife. It was the
highlight of our trip home. Two wonderful people were able
to join us, Elder Peterson, just returned from his mission in
South Texas, and Don's grandmother, Rose Varney. It was
such a beautiful day.*

Salt Lake Temple — Feb. 17, 1944

---

*   The Church of Jesus Christ of Latter-day Saints (Mormon Church) believes that family
      relationships can continue past death, replacing the words "until death do us part" with
      "for time and all eternity" in temple wedding and sealing ceremonies.

Toward the end of Don's leave, Laura Jeanne caught the flu and remained at home, promising to rejoin him as soon as she felt well enough to travel. His return trip to Moore Field was cold, tiresome, and lonely—there were no Pullmans, the riding cars were unheated, and the hard, straight-backed seats were too uncomfortable for even him to sleep on.

Laura Jeanne soon recovered from the flu, but now suffered from a new malady, dreading the thought of leaving home again so soon. Her brother and his wife were still in town on leave, her favorite aunt was visiting from Denver, and her friends were begging her to stay. She grappled with conflicting feelings, torn between her desire to stay home and her longing to be with Don. In a quandary, she stretched the truth a bit, telling him that she was slowly starting to feel better, suggesting that it might be best if she waited to join him at his next post.

Matagorda is a barrier island located in the Gulf of Mexico northeast of Corpus Christi. Meaning *thick brush* in Spanish, it got its name from the dense thickets that once grew along its coastal waters. The narrow island, stretching thirty-eight miles in length, has a long and colorful history.[36]

The now extinct Karankawa Indians were Matagorda's first known inhabitants, attracted there by the island's abundant fish and game. During the Civil War, the Confederates set up a strategic Army post that housed more than 500 troops. By the early 1900s, the island had become home to several cattle ranches and gained a reputation for its excellent hunting and fishing. In the 1930s, the Army Air Corps refurbished an old Coast Guard station, using it as a retreat. Nicknamed the *Matagorda Hunting and Fishing Club*, the popular destination spot was soon restricted to senior officers and their upper-crust guests.[37,38]

Since the island was relatively flat, remote, and near the mainland coast, the Air Corps determined it would make an excellent location for a fighter pilot training base. In November 1940, the War Department, using eminent domain, acquired nearly 19,000 acres on the northeast end of the island to build an airfield and gunnery range. Three years after confiscating their property, the government paid the landowners a paltry seven dollars an acre in a controversial settlement.[39]

The new military base included several long airstrips, secondary runways, hangars, barracks, and a small flight school. Army engineers dredged the bay, using the excavated material as a base for the concrete runways. The resulting underwater excavation pit created a popular fishing spot for redfish and speckled trout, which anglers soon began calling the *Army Hole*.[40,41]

Don's unit was bused to Corpus Christie, then transported by ferry to the training base at Matagorda, arriving late afternoon on the last day of February. In his first letter from the island, he wrote:

> *How are you feeling, honey? I can't wait until you're well enough to come back down and join me. I miss you so much. I haven't heard from you since I returned to Texas, and I'm about going nuts!*
>
> *We fly all day, off and on, then clean our aircraft machine guns in the evening. It's really a lot of fun shooting at targets from an airplane wing gun. The targets are 6 feet x 6 feet and slanted on the ground. We fly around 800 feet in the air, peel off and fire at the target at a distance of 150–250 yards, then skim over it just a few feet off the ground and pull up—great sport, huh?*

Don's Class 44-B cadet book, *Avengers,* included a brief narrative describing the Air Corps version of the pilots' experience on the island gunnery-training base:

> A never to be forgotten part of training was the time spent on Matagorda Island. Far different than the early "camping out days," Matagorda today presents a much different picture, with barracks instead of tents, paved runways, theater, P.X., etc. The only thing missing is feminine beauty, but even despite this handicap, it was a wonderful experience—one, truly, never to be forgotten.

Don described his experience on Matagorda a bit differently in his next letter to Laura Jeanne:

Our training base is on a really desolate part of the island. All you can see is sand and water—and craters from all the bombs that have been dropped. There are no tables in the barracks to write a letter on, and the beds are almost as bad as at Preflight. The food isn't up to par, and the water is salty—not fit to drink.

I'm comfortably cuddled up in my sack under mosquito netting while I'm writing. You wouldn't believe the size of the mosquitoes over here. The gas crew pumped 40 gallons into one the other day before they realized it wasn't a plane. The movies at the theater are all old. And there isn't a woman on the island—not one. You should hear the guys howl when they see a gal in a picture show.

After inexplicably holding the pilots' mail for more than a week, Moore Field finally forwarded it to Matagorda on the local ferry. Don's initial excitement quickly waned when he read that Laura Jeanne was considering waiting until his next assignment to rejoin him:

How's my sweetheart today? Lonesome and anxious to get to Texas and be with her Mr. Lt., I hope. I'm sure ready for you to be back and don't like the idea of you waiting to join me at my next post. I wish I knew what you were planning. Hope you're there to surprise me when I get back.

So far, I'm doing ok in ground gunnery. I even earned a medal. Hope I do as well in aerial gunnery. This moving sleeve target they tow behind an airplane is no cinch to hit, but I'm going to do my best. It's a lot of fun competing against everyone here.

No flying today due to low stratus clouds and bad weather. Most of the boys stayed in the barracks and relaxed, but a few of us "eager beavers" got some fishing poles and a rowboat and headed out into the Gulf of Mexico. We've been hearing about the wonderful fishing off the coast of Matagorda in what's called the "Army Hole." They say the fish are pretty big and really put up a scrap when you get one on your line.

Of course, I had to go and "brag up" my trout fishing skills to the boys before we left. I'm embarrassed to write that we

*didn't even get a nibble. Anyway, we had a lot of fun rowing
around in the boat.*

Severe weather prematurely ended gunnery training on what the
pilots sarcastically referred to as "Paradise Island." In his final letter
from Matagorda, Don wrote:

*"Mother Nature" has stationed all her nasty weather here,
marooning us on this godforsaken desert island. The wind is
howling and the windows are rattling. We haven't been able
to fly for the past three days, and I've about gone nuts. Being
trapped here is starting to get to all of us.*

*Everything is packed and locked up tight down at the flight
line just waiting for the weather to clear so we can take the
ferry shuttle back to Moore Field.*

Don was deeply disappointed when he returned to Moore Field
and Laura Jeanne wasn't there:

*Well, we finally got back to Moore Field. I wish you were
down here with me, honey. But I know how homesick you
are and how badly you wanted to stay there, especially while
your family is all in town. Everything seemed to be against
your coming back to Mission.*

*It doesn't make much sense for you to come now—but I
order you back to active duty with your husband, as soon
as I get reassigned. Of course, you'll get 10% more pay and
oodles of hugs, kisses, and side benefits!*

Don completed his transition and gunnery training with ninety-
three flying hours in the AT-6 Texan and twelve hours in the P-40N
Warhawk. The Air Corps assigned most of the Class 44-B pilots from
his squadron to P-38 transition training in Arizona, but sent him
a different direction, separating him from his flying buddies. Right
after receiving his new orders, he headed for the base phone booth:

*Here I sit at the Officers Club, sweating out a phone call to
my honey. So I thought I'd drop you a short note while I'm
waiting. "Only a one to two hour delay," the operator said.
Hope the phone rings soon—I'm going nuts waiting.*

Anyway, hopefully I'll soon be telling you that my next assignment is to Harding Field in Baton Rouge, Louisiana. I'm so anxious to talk to you and get things straightened out. I don't know whether I'm coming or going—but I hope to soon be holding you in my arms again and squeezing you tight.

After a two-hour wait, Don's phone call finally went through. Hearing his voice brought tears to Laura Jeanne's eyes, causing her to realize how desperately she missed him. Taking courage, she decided it was time to say goodbye to family and friends and promised to rejoin him in Baton Rouge as soon as she could get there. They were just the words Don needed to hear.

———————

Laura Jeanne stepped aboard the passenger train, handed the conductor her one-way ticket, then sat down on the hard bench seat of her riding car. Leaning her head back, she took slow, deep breaths, trying to calm her jittery nerves as she waited for the train to leave the station:

I dreaded leaving my family and friends again. Saying goodbye wasn't easy, but I mustered the courage and did it— with more faith and determination than I thought possible. Traveling alone made me feel somewhat anxious, but I was really looking forward to being with Don again, and that helped calm my nerves.

The train ride was long and uncomfortable, and with the usual stops and delays along the way, was running behind schedule. It had "Pullman" sleeping cars, but I had nearly as much trouble sleeping in my sleeper berth as I did on the hard straight-back seats of the riding cars.

Don's new CO had issued him a two-hour pass to meet Laura Jeanne at the rail station, located a short distance from the base. While waiting, he grew anxious, experiencing mixed emotions— excited to see her again, yet still musing over her decision to remain in Utah, rather than join him at Moore Field the previous month. He finally decided to put it behind him and not bring it up again. After his pass expired, he returned to his post disappointed, hoping to hear from her later that day.

The delayed passenger train rolled into the Baton Rouge station several hours behind schedule. Laura Jeanne was exhausted as she walked down the platform steps and took her luggage from the porter. Disappointed and a little apprehensive when she discovered Don wasn't there to meet her, she bravely took it all in stride:

I'd been in this situation before, and I knew what to do. I'd become an old pro by now, so it wasn't frightening anymore. After checking into a hotel, I got word to Don through the base dispatcher that I'd arrived, then fell on the bed, exhausted from my long journey.

Don rushed to meet her that evening as soon as he could get away from the base. When she tried to apologize for not rejoining him in Texas, he silenced her with a kiss, and the warm smile on his face told her he'd already forgiven her. With tears in her eyes, Laura Jeanne silently vowed to be there for him every moment from then on until he went overseas. Don couldn't have been happier—his upside down world had finally been turned right side up again.

P-47 "Thunderbolt"

NINE
....

"Live Five with the Jive Drive"

The Army Air Corps managed pilot transition training at Harding Airfield for several different types of fighter aircraft used in Europe and the Pacific. Instructors conducted bombing mission drills at nearby Hammond Bombing and Gunnery Range, while aerial combat drills took place over Lake Pontchartrain, one of the largest wetland estuaries in the world. The Air Corps had recently introduced a new combat training program at Harding designed specifically for P-47 *Thunderbolt* pilots. Don became part of the second pilot group to enter the new program.

From first sight, Don was in awe of the Republic P-47, the largest, heaviest, most expensive single-engine fighter plane in history. Early models were plagued with a myriad of performance issues and setbacks both in testing and in initial combat situations overseas, but Republic finally got it right in late 1943 when they rolled out their "D" model. It was all they hoped it would be, and the AAF was soon shipping them overseas by the droves, building more P-47s than any other U.S. fighter plane in history.[42]

Even with a name as commanding as Thunderbolt, the P-47 was given another handle—the "Jug," which many assumed was short for *Juggernaut*. However, the pilots who flew the fighter-bomber alleged the tag came from the P-47's close resemblance to an old-fashioned *milk jug*.[43] Regardless of its origin, the nickname stuck.

In fact, the P-47 really was a "Juggernaut" of an aircraft. With a wingspan of forty-one feet, over fourteen feet high, thirty-six feet long, and weighing in fully loaded at nearly eight tons, it was one big fighter plane. Its 2,000 HP turbo-supercharged engine gave it a maximum flying speed of 433 mph. It had a service ceiling of 42,000 feet and a range of 1,100 miles with auxiliary fuel tanks. Armed with eight .50 caliber machine guns (four on each wing), the P-47 could also carry ten five-inch rockets or 2,500 pounds of bombs—or a combination of the two, giving it the most firepower of any AAF fighter aircraft in World War II. And when it went into a dive, the P-47 could exceed speeds of 700 mph.[44]

Jerry Kelly and Bob Sharp

Bob Sharp and Jerry Kelly were among the recent Advanced Flying School graduates receiving orders to report to Harding Field for P-47 combat training. Following a brief furlough, they boarded a troop train headed for Baton Rouge. In a letter to his mother, Jerry wrote the following about their trip:

Lt. Sharp and I came on from Salt Lake together. We had a pretty good trip. He's a good Joe. We're bunkmates now. We met a girl on the train yesterday—very, very nice. She's a sophomore at LSU and belongs to the Kappa Alpha Theta Sorority.

I just loved to sit and listen to her talk. She has the most marvelous drawl I've ever heard! It's wonderful. She invited us up to LSU and said she'd introduce us to some of the prettiest gals in the South. I think I'm going to like this southern hospitality.

Don met the two pilots from Salt Lake City in their first ground school class at Harding. Although the three immediately clicked, becoming friends from the start, they couldn't possibly have imagined how intertwined their lives would soon become.

Bob and Jerry grew up in Salt Lake City and, like Don, each had an older brother and a close relationship with his mother. Sadly, when Bob was only two years old, his father abandoned his family in the middle of the Great Depression. The three Utah flyboys shared similar values and had a number of common traits. Each was good-looking and smart, made friends easily, had a great sense of humor, and shared a zest for life. However, when it came to their relationship statuses, the similarities ended. Don was newly married to the love of his life. Bob really liked a girl back home named Louise, but wasn't sure she felt the same way about him. And Jerry's girlfriend, Lucille, wanted a more serious relationship than he did, causing him to fret over how to tell her he didn't feel the same way.

The three Utah pilots lived quite different lives growing up. Robert (Bob) D. Sharp, as early as grade school, appeared destined to become a fighter pilot. Reminiscing about his early life, he later recounted:

After my father abandoned us, my grandmother opened her home, taking in my mother, my older brother, and me. I had a great childhood with my dog and my bike, and can't imagine being any happier than I was.

I started my flag waving and "love of the USA" philosophy early in life when I joined the drum and bugle corps at Longfellow Grade School in SLC. I continued with it during my years at Bryant Jr. High School and enrolled in the ROTC for three years at West High School. I really liked it and worked hard to advance and learn the Infantry Manual. I was a lousy student in High School (C minus or even lower), except for physics and math, where I did pretty well. Somehow, I managed to get into college.

I took a military class on aircraft sheet metal repair and got a job at Hill Air Force Base while I went to the University of Utah. World War II had started by then, and the draft was imminent. Rather than wait around to be drafted and end up in the infantry, something I never fancied, I put in to join the Air Corps. I always liked to drive fast and enjoyed pushing my 1935 Ford coupe, with a hot V-8 engine, to its limits. Flying a fighter plane seemed like the ultimate in speed and a lot more fun than being on the ground marching, camping out, and getting shot at on the front lines somewhere.

I passed the initial tests in Pre-flight, then went to Primary in Tucson. On several occasions, I thought I'd wash out, but somehow I advanced thru each training phase until I made it to Harding Airfield for P-47 training.

Gerald (Jerry) B. Kelly was a year younger than Don and Bob, and clearly wasn't cut from the same mold as either of them. He grew up on the east side of Salt Lake City, where his family operated two businesses. It was an affluent area, but times were tough, and his family lived in a small basement apartment below their business building. Running the two shops was a family affair. Jerry preferred hanging out at his mom's business, Mrs. Kelly's Bakery, helping her after school and on Saturdays. He loved eating his mom's famous pastries and delicious roast beef sandwiches, especially when he could down them with a bottle of ice-cold milk. Early each morning, Jerry's father fried the day's supply of donuts before opening up Kelly's Barbershop next door to the bakery.[45]

Blessed with his mother's tender heart and his father's sense of humor, Jerry made friends easily and was popular with his classmates. While serving as senior year class president at Granite High School, his efforts on the senior class project raised $1,200 in war bonds and landed his picture in the *Salt Lake Tribune*. Jerry took his education seriously, earning straight A's in high school and graduating with honors. He attended the University of Utah until midway through his second semester, when he and his best friend from high school enlisted in the Army.[46]

At the beginning of pilot training, Jerry received a letter from his grandmother urging him to remember who he was and to live up to the values and standards he'd learned growing up. In response to her admonition, he wrote back:

> *If ever there was a place where a fellow could lose his ideals, this is it. But I'm trying hard not to. I'm not letting these fellows around here lower my standards. I know what's right and wrong and I'll stick to it no matter what.*
>
> *It seems like I'm the only guy on the whole base who hasn't started swearing. Everyone's always asking me when I'm going to start. I tell them I sincerely don't believe that I should use language here that I wouldn't use anyplace else.*

Like Don, Jerry struggled with his three-point landings during training, and was afraid at times that he was going to wash out. But he persevered, advancing through each stage of training, finally arriving at Harding Field eager to fly a P-47.

The three Utah boys soon made friends with two guys from Missouri—Kenneth (Kenny) E. Kalen and Charles (Pat) Patrick. The Missourians had been friends since the beginning of their training, meeting on a latrine detail, of all places. Unlike Don, who'd been separated from his friends at each stage of his training, these two stayed together from the start, not leaving each other's side until after the end of the war. They lived a little different lifestyle than the other three, but the war made strange bedfellows. The chocolate milkshake-drinking Mormons from Utah hit it off great with the two beer-drinking roughnecks from Missouri. Don hung out with his new friends during the day, but as soon as they completed their training, he rushed home to be with Laura Jeanne.

Jerry and Bob became fast friends and were inseparable at Harding Field. Describing their close relationship in a letter to his mother, Jerry wrote:

> *It's a funny thing, but Sharp and I are practically a carbon copy of each other. We think the same about everything and like the same things. We share the same values, and both of us plan to keep on living them while we're gone.*
>
> *Sharp doesn't smoke, drink, drink coffee, or pick up women. At times when we're just standing around in town with nothing much to do he says, "Kelly, sometimes I wish that*

we did, you know, do all that stuff—then life in the Army would be much simpler." But then as soon as a couple of our buddies offer to buy us a drink, he says, "Oh, no thanks, never touch the stuff myself." And when we see the same beautiful gal on the streets—we both just look, we haven't got any guts at all.

Got to go, Kalen and Patrick just challenged us to a basketball game—the losers to pay for milkshakes. We have to uphold the good name of Utah.

Kenny Kalen and Pat Patrick

The Utah boys struggled as the temperatures started rising, while their Missouri buddies just smiled and poked fun, seemingly unaffected by the hot, sticky, Louisiana weather. None of their initial training at Harding Field was in the air. Instead, they watched combat films and sat through lectures, struggling to stay awake in their stifling classrooms. When the Army began issuing bedding rolls, helmets, packs, parachute bags, and other equipment, and initiated another round of typhus and cholera shots, the guys started feeling the war overseas creeping up on them. In a letter to his father, Jerry wrote:

There are a lot of boys here now that have come back from combat, and they give us lectures on gunnery and stuff. This is mighty serious business, Pop. I sorta always thought I'd never get into combat. The war and fighting are now beginning to come uncomfortably close to home. I'm scared to death at the thought—but everybody else is too—we all just manage to bluff our way through.

Don and his new buddies were excited when they climbed into the cockpit of a P-47. Their new fighter plane was not only fast, but also remarkably stable on the ground and in the air. And unlike the other planes they'd flown, its cockpit was large and roomy, providing a good fit for the pilots.

Earlier that month, Jerry's beloved University of Utah basketball team became a surprise addition to the NCAA tournament field after two Arkansas players were injured in a car accident and their team dropped out. The Utes went all the way to the finals, defeating heavily favored Dartmouth 42 to 40, winning the championship game in overtime. Coming out of nowhere, Utah became the first "Cinderella team" to win the NCAA tournament. And they did it in the middle of a World War against Japan, in storybook fashion— with two Japanese-American players. Incredibly, one of them was on release from a relocation camp* in Utah.[47]

The underdog teammates called themselves *The Live Five with the Jive Drive*. After their victory, Jerry started calling his new Utah and Missouri buddies *his* Five, hoping that the matching nickname would bring them his Ute team's good luck and take them safely to the end of the war and back home again.

---

* After Pearl Harbor, Congress ordered the incarceration of over 120,000 Japanese-Americans in prison-like camps located in remote desert areas of the Western United States. More than two-thirds of those forcibly interned were citizens of the United States who had shown no sympathy toward Japan—or any disloyalty to America.

Base personnel at Harding Field rigged up an intriguing system for the pilots' air-to-air gunnery training. A brave P-47 pilot from the base staff towed a 4-foot x 20-foot screen-mesh, banner-type target for the pilots to fire at with their .50 caliber machine guns. Base aircrew attached a long cable to the plane, connecting it to the front tow bar of the target. A heavy ball hung on the bottom of the contraption, enabling the target to fly vertical. As the tow plane took off, it dragged the target into the air, then once they were over Lake Pontchartrain, the shooting started.

The pilots trained with ammo dipped in paint, a different color for each plane in the flight. Hits left a colored mark on the flying target as they went through the sleeve, allowing instructors to later tally scores. Occasionally, pilots shot the ball weight off the target, causing it to roll, making it difficult to hit. Somehow, Bob was still able to score hits while the target was flying horizontal, a skill that caught the attention of his instructors.

The pilots did most of their shooting when they were on a pass going down toward the flying target, minimizing the danger to the tow plane. The P-47s were generally going around 350 mph, pulling nearly 4Gs when they started firing. Surprisingly, there were few accidents in these Wild West shooting drills.

In air-to-ground gunnery drills at Hammond Bombing and Gunnery Range, forty-five miles east of Harding Field, T-Bolt pilots dropped 100-pound general-purpose bombs, launched 2.25-inch practice rockets, and strafed 10-foot-by-10-foot slanted panel targets with their .50 caliber machine guns.

Although more advanced than the iron sights used in World War I, sights in World War II fighter planes still required a lot of pilot judgment and instinct. When P-47 pilots fired their machine guns, it was practically like using the whole aircraft as the sighting device. The Thunderbolts eight .50 caliber machine guns were "harmonized"— meaning they were aligned to fire at a slight angle, so the bullets intersected at a preset bore-sighted distance. The pilots practiced strafing at distances of 900 to 1,200 feet while making shallow dives toward the target, flying more than 270 mph.[48] During their strafing drills, the object was to hit the targets with as many bullets as possible. Afterward, instructors counted the number of hits, compared them to the number of rounds fired, and recorded the pilot's score.

To help the trainees recognize when to fire and where to pull up from dives in their air-to-ground gunnery drills, lead-in and foul line markers were placed on the range. Tracer bullets* were generally fired from the P-47's machine guns during strafing exercises. If a pilot fired his harmonized guns too early, in front of the foul line, the bullets crossed over and spread out, missing the target on each side. When they fired very far past the foul line, the opposite happened, and the bullets didn't have time to come together on the target. Flying past the foul line had another downside as well: it put the plane dangerously close to the ground.[49]

Advanced aerial and ground gunnery training wasn't without risks. The pilots had more to worry about than just washing out because of poor shooting scores, safety violations, or flying sloppy patterns. Sometimes they experienced "target fixation," focusing so intently during a strafing run that they were drawn into the target, unable to pull up soon enough. Crossing too far over the foul line before pulling out at best raised a lot of dust—and at worst, caused the pilot to fly into the ground and die.[50]

Although their instructors cautioned them otherwise, a lot of illegal mock combat fighting and stunt flying still occurred. Pilots, including the Five, seldom passed up a chance to make a fighter pass at a plane that strayed in from another training field. And there was always the exhilaration of buzzing the tower. Air Command frowned on such stunts, especially those flown at low altitude, wanting their fighter pilots to arrive overseas in one piece—not buried somewhere in Lake Pontchartrain.

The Five closely followed the war overseas, especially in the European Theater of Operations (ETO) where the AAF would most likely send them. The emphasis placed on air-to-ground gunnery training at Harding Field was in direct response to the P-47s' changing role in air combat. The Thunderbolt entered the war flying escort missions for medium and heavy bombers. But even with auxiliary fuel tanks, P-47s didn't always have the range necessary to escort bombers

---

* Tracer bullets had a small, brightly burning charge that made it visible to shooters, enabling them to follow the bullets' path and make aiming corrections on the fly.

to their targets deep inside Germany and back home again. Whenever they found the big bombers unprotected, the *Luftwaffe** would move in and attack with disastrous results. In response, Air Command started sending P-47s on shorter-range escort missions, leaving them with unused fuel and weaponry on many of their return flights.[51]

A few enterprising Ninth Air Force P-47 squadrons started looking for targets of opportunity to attack after completing their escort missions. Once Air Command noticed how effective they were at destroying railroads, trucks, and tanks, and fighting Luftwaffe fighter planes in air-to-air-combat, Thunderbolt pilots earned themselves a new job. Their primary missions now focused on strafing and bombing enemy targets in close air support of Allied armored and infantry divisions near the frontlines. P-47 pilots were the only flyboys in World War II recognized as fighter-bomber pilots. And in their new role, they helped turn the tide of the war against Germany.

Jerry was now having second thoughts about the letter he'd written to Lucille a few weeks earlier, explaining that although he liked her a lot, he wasn't looking for a serious relationship. Kindhearted by nature, he hadn't intended to hurt her feelings and hoped they might remain friends, but he had enough experience with girls to know that wasn't likely. He wasn't sure how she reacted to his letter, but he had a good idea when she didn't write back to him—ever. Writing with the fountain pen Lucille had given to him as a token of her affection, Jerry lamented his unattached status in a letter to his mother:

My love life is now officially, literally, truly shot!! So I've transferred all affections to my trusty old P-47. Sharp said that if it weren't for the letters I get from you, Mom, I'd never get any mail at all. And it's true, except for getting the Salt Lake Tribune.

Bob gets mail from his mom and from a lot of boys in the service. But the girl he likes, Louise, doesn't write him often— maybe once a month—so I kidded him back. And then he said, "Well, what if she did fall for me? I'd go home, and

---

* The official name of the Nazi Air Force in World War II.

she'd probably just give me a fountain pen, then that'd be
the end." That stopped me—I couldn't think of a comeback.

Jerry's older brother caught him completely off guard when he walked into his barracks, unannounced, on Easter Sunday. Gene, who had just completed glider-pilot training, was waiting for the Navy to send him to the Philippines. He'd traveled all day by train to spend a few hours with his brother before they left to fight on opposite sides of the globe. Jerry wrote:

I had a swell Easter. Gene came in on some sort of day leave,
and we spent the evening from about 4:30 till 11:30 just
talking and having a good old reunion. I was sure glad to see
him, because I didn't think we'd get together again until after
the war.

He and Sharp and I had dinner, then sat around and talked
until he had to catch a train back. Sharp thinks Gene is really
the "clear stuff." He says he wishes he and his brother got
along the way Gene and I do. I'm a pretty dog-gone lucky guy
to have a family like I've got. And that stuff about "absence
makes the heart grow fonder" is just about right.

The two brothers lingered at the train station, reluctant to say goodbye until the conductor shouted out the final boarding call. After one last hug, they wished each other good luck in the war, then Gene stepped on the train. As it pulled away from the station, he turned and waved to his little brother for the last time.

―――――――

The Five performed well in their aerial and ground gunnery, all advancing to final combat training. Others didn't. It was nerve-racking for the pilots, not knowing their fate from one day to the next. At each stage of flight training, their future rested in the hands of a few instructors, who constantly tested, reviewed, scored, and graded their performances.

During their last few days at Harding, the Five watched hours of battle combat films. Then, as a graduation gift, the Air Corps medical staff gave them another round of typhus, cholera, and smallpox shots. Their CO confirmed the rumor that a few of the pilots might end up in outlying air bases to complete their final combat training, but that most of them would remain where they were.

As expected, Jerry, Bob, and the Missourians received orders to finish their stateside training at Harding Field. Don, however, wasn't so lucky. Once again, his buddies went one way, and he went the other.

Final furlough before going overseas

TEN

"Remember…I'm Loving You Always"

Before the fall of 1942, Bruning, Nebraska was a quiet village with fewer than 300 residents. That all changed when the Army decided its location and terrain made an ideal spot for a military flying school. Exercising eminent domain, the government evicted twelve farmers, giving them ten days to vacate, then immediately began construction. Pocketing a measly settlement of $49 an acre, the displaced families watched helplessly as Army engineers bulldozed their farms, destroying their livelihoods. Embroiled in the middle of a world war that was threatening the American way of life, the government justified its actions, giving military needs unfettered precedence, even when they trampled the civil liberties of her citizens.[52]

The new Bruning Flying School was huge—with 234 buildings, three 6,800-foot runways, and three large hangars. To accommodate its burgeoning 3,500 military and civilian personnel, the Army also added housing units and a recreation hall.[53]

By the time Don and Laura Jeanne arrived, Bruning had become a bustling community. Housing was scarce, forcing them to search in outlying towns for a place to live. They finally ended up in Fairbury, a small township located twenty-eight miles southeast of the base. The older brick home they rented had a covered front porch supported by attractive pillars, reminding Laura Jeanne of the entryway at her parents' home. Surrounded by farmland and with a railroad running down the middle of Main Street, Fairbury felt a lot like their hometown and provided the newlyweds with the closest thing to a normal relationship they'd experienced so far in their marriage. In a rush of nostalgia, Don later reminisced:

> *The days at Bruning Airfield were long. However, the nights made up for it a million times over. I had to travel to the base early every morning and got home well after dark each night, but it was worth it to be able to live together.*

> *I hated hearing that darn alarm clock go off early every morning, though. Laura Jeanne always looked so peaceful and content laying there on the bed asleep. I didn't have the heart to wake her up as I got ready to go to the base, but I always stole a kiss from her before I left.*

While Laura Jeanne generally stuck to her pledge "not to complain or act homesick, and make every moment together with Don special," it wasn't always easy:

> *On May 9, 1944, I was suffering from a severe case of homesickness. Don gave me a beautiful corsage for Mother's day, and it should have been a happy day. We called our mothers, wished them well, and expressed our love. But talking with my mother made things even worse for me. On top of everything else, I was feeling disappointed that my expectations of getting pregnant hadn't materialized. I wanted so much to be a mother, and Don would soon be leaving for the war. I was feeling sorry for myself and started to cry.*

> *Don tried in his own teasing, humorous way to change my mood. It usually worked, but this time it backfired. I told him he was being insensitive and that he just didn't understand. Then we each raised our voices and said things we didn't really mean. It was our first quarrel. We both quickly apologized, then Don put his arms around me, and we shed a few tears together.*

While at Bruning, Don was part of the P-47 Pilot Replacement Training Unit (RTU) of the Ninth Air Force 36th Fighter Group. His squadron flew friendly flight against P-51s and practiced escort missions with flights of B-17 and B-24 bombers from a base in Sioux

City, Iowa. It was good training for both the fighter pilots and the big bomber crews, occasionally leading to a little hot-dogging and mock air attacks:

> *Sometimes we buzzed the big bombers to give them a taste of what it was going to be like when they faced German planes over enemy territory. They seemed to enjoy our mock attacks. I always ended our little encounters by waving and wiggling my wings at them. The Jerries, of course, wouldn't be doing that.*

Don's squadron regularly flew formation drills, four planes flying together in two elements, each with two ships. Each element leader had a wingman flying at his side, slightly behind him, responsible to watch out for his leader and warn him of any danger from behind. Alone, a pilot was at great risk, but when a wingman had his back,* both pilots were safer and more dangerous to the enemy. The RTU pilots at Bruning also received advanced training in navigation and instrument flying, culminating in demanding, cross-country training missions flown above the vast Great Plains:

> *The flat land of Nebraska seemed to spread out forever, and there weren't many identifying, physical landmarks to relate to when I was in the air. On my training flights over the sprawling prairies, I developed a greater appreciation for flying with a needle-ball, compass, and airspeed indicator. There was a lot of mental, as well as written, calculation required to plot a cross-country flight course and not get lost.*

> *It was a challenge being your own navigator, especially on night flights. Quite a few P-47s came in on their bellies out in farm fields and other open spaces because they miscalculated their mileage and ran out of gas. I was grateful for the math and calculation skills I'd developed. They kept me from ever having any gas problems in my flight training.*

---

* The saying "I've got your back" owes its origin to pilots flying in World War I and soon became the reassuring expression every element leader wanted to hear from his wingman.

While reading the *Milligan Review,* the weekly newspaper covering the Bruning area, Laura Jeanne paused, took a deep breath, then reread the front-page article:

> May 17, 1944...A fatal air crash at Bruning Airfield occurred Wednesday evening, when a P-47 fighter plane and a basic trainer plane collided in mid-air. Both pilots were killed on impact.

It wasn't the first such news story she'd read—accidents in flight training were all too common. But for some reason, this one was especially disquieting. She knew pilot training was dangerous, and Don's attempts to downplay the risks inherent in flying did little to keep her from worrying about his safety. The deadly crash brought a feeling of sadness and loss to the base and the surrounding communities. Too many others felt those same sentiments, as training accidents had escalated all across the nation.

Don tried to honor a promise he'd made to Laura Jeanne at the beginning of flight training to be safe and not take unnecessary risks while he was in the air:

> *I really liked flying the P-47. Though I did have some "fun" in the air and pulled off a few stunts, I wasn't reckless like some of the "hot-rod pilots" on base that liked to buzz barns, animals, and even farmers on their tractors. I had enough close calls without doing anything that stupid.*

A short time later back at Harding Airfield, Jerry described the worst P-47 training accident ever experienced on the base:

> *Some former Basic Training [B.T.] instructors started flying today and checked out the 47s for the first time. The results of their morning flying were twelve airplanes damaged, including two that are completely washed out. The accidents included two nose-overs from pressing the brakes too hard and several taxi accidents. One guy even ground looped, which is next to impossible in a P-47—but somehow he did it!*

> *The worst was a stupid mid-air collision. Two pilots, who were flying too close together and weren't paying attention, plowed right into each other. The guy that got run into fell onto a wing and was able to safely bail out. The other pilot*

was killed when his plane exploded in midair. Everything about that bunch of B.T. drivers was inexcusable today.

But don't let this scare you, Mom, because nothing like this ever happened to our bunch.

Despite Jerry's attempt to comfort his mother, wives and mothers of training pilots across the nation were all fearful something like this could happen—and with good reason. The road to becoming a fighter pilot in World War II wasn't a safe one. During 1944, the year the Five completed their pilot training, the Air Corps reported 11,385 training accidents, too many ending in tragedy. That year, training pilots wrecked 1,945 training planes, resulting in 1,446 fatalities. P-47 casualty rates were the highest. Of the 1,303 reported accidents, T-Bolt pilots totaled 474 planes, resulting in 217 fatalities.[54] Learning to fly a fighter plane wasn't as easy—or nearly as safe—as learning to drive a tractor. And the "Grim Reaper of Carelessness" was taking a toll on America's pilots in training, preventing far too many from ever making it overseas.

———

Don and all the base personnel at Bruning cheered when the front-page of the *Stars and Stripes** declared victory in the largest seaborne invasion in history. The article read:

On June 6, 1944, more than 160,000 Allied troops landed along a 50-mile stretch of heavily-fortified French coastline to fight Nazi Germany on the beaches of Normandy, France. Gen. Dwight D. Eisenhower called the operation a crusade in which "we will accept nothing less than full victory."

More than 5,000 ships and 13,000 aircraft supported the D-Day invasion, and by day's end, the Allies gained a foothold in Continental Europe. The cost in lives on D-Day was high. More than 9,000 Allied soldiers were killed or wounded, but their sacrifice allowed more than 100,000 soldiers to begin the slow, hard slog across Europe to defeat Adolf Hitler's crack troops.[55]

---

*   Daily newspaper of the United States Armed Services printed in nearly all operating theaters of World War II.

Two weeks after D-Day, Don completed his final P-47 combat training at Bruning Airfield, beating the odds and officially becoming a fighter pilot. While Laura Jeanne was happy for him and couldn't have been prouder, she dreaded what it meant:

Don received orders to report back to Harding Field on July 1, 1944. He didn't know where he'd go next—only that he'd be sent somewhere overseas. He was granted a two-week furlough to escort me back to Utah.

The train trip home was somber indeed. We had time to reflect on the few short months we'd been married and how quickly the time had passed. Don seemed oblivious to the hustle and bustle of all the servicemen, the crowded train, and of even some rowdy behavior. He just held me close, not wanting me to leave him for even a moment. It was as though fear had entered his heart for the first time, and he was having a difficult time dealing with it. I was determined that when it came time for our final farewell, I'd muster all my strength and be strong for his sake.

When we arrived home, we found Don's father suffering from heart problems. His work on the farm was very strenuous, and he continued working even after being warned not to by his doctor. He had no other choice, since his two oldest sons were both serving in the military.

Several families in Lehi requested hardship waivers from the draft board to allow at least one son to be exempt from military service and remain home to help out. A few prominent families in the city had their request granted. However, Don's father wasn't so fortunate. The only one left home to help him on the farm was Don's fourteen-year-old little brother.

The rest of the Five back at Harding Field completed their final combat training at the same time as Don, returning home on a two-week furlough to say their goodbyes before going overseas. Bob, however, faced a decision at that point. Having excelled at aerial gunnery during training exercises, Air Command asked him to remain at Harding to serve as an instructor. It was an attractive offer. He'd be able to put in his time flying the fighter plane he'd grown to love without having to face the enemy in combat. Years later, he jokingly shared his response to the Air Corps officers who offered him the position: "I told the powers that be that I wanted to stay with my buddies—then convinced them to send me into combat instead. Was I nuts or what?"

Jerry didn't see or talk to Lucille, his old girlfriend, during his leave home. However, he did start calling on a young woman named Myrlene. Things went well between them and they agreed to write each other, releasing him from his pledge to transfer all his affections to his trusty old P-47. Bob spent most of his furlough with Louise, even taking her with him on visits to the Kelly home. She was attractive and fun loving. It was easy for Jerry to see why Bob liked her so much.

Throughout his training, Jerry endured good-natured ribbing, sometimes because he didn't drink, smoke, or even swear. But most of the time, the guys razzed him simply because he didn't look old enough to be a fighter pilot. They teased him relentlessly asking, "When are you going to start to shave?" or "How does it feel to still be tied to your mother's apron strings?" He never let it bother him, though, affably taking it all in stride, even using it as motivation. In the end, Jerry had the last laugh, not only earning his wings, but also beating the long odds against becoming a fighter pilot. He actually did shave from time to time—but not very often.

In his mother's eyes, Jerry was still a skinny teenage boy, too young and innocent to be going off to war. Worse yet, she was haunted by a premonition that if he went overseas, he'd never return. He pleaded with her to have faith and stop worrying so much about him, "Mom...I'll come back." It was hard enough when her oldest son, Gene, left for the Philippines. Now, sending her second son off to war, she feared she might never see either of them again. During an emotional conversation at Jerry's home before returning to Baton Rouge, Bob spoke up, trying to comfort her, saying, "Don't worry, Mrs. Kelly, I promise to take care of Jerry and bring him home safely."

A few miles to the south in Lehi, a similar conversation took place at the Evans home. Don's parents, also struggling with the thought of sending their second son overseas, shared Mrs. Kelly's fears that they might never see their boys again.

Laura Jeanne was constantly by Don's side during his final days before going overseas:

Our time together came and went all too quickly, We made the rounds to family and friends, then it was time to go to the railroad station in Salt Lake City for our last good-byes. It was an emotional time for Don's mom and dad. Sending another son off to war was terrible for them. I understood their feelings. I, too, was feeling a sense of loss that I'd never before experienced.

Everyone cried at the station, except Don and me. I thought he might miss his train because of that last, wonderful, lingering kiss...but he didn't. He did, however, see me smiling as he waved from his window seat, just as I'd promised myself I would.

As soon as the train pulled out of sight, though, I fell apart. I didn't know when, or if ever, I'd see him again, and I couldn't hold back the tears any longer. Don's parents tried to comfort me, but I was inconsolable.

It was a long, quiet, sad ride back home to Lehi.

As Don's troop train pulled out from the station, the melancholy feelings he experienced during his recent trip home from Nebraska returned. Tears he'd held back when saying goodbye to Laura Jeanne now filled his eyes, and a feeling of gloom fell over him. Since the war waged by the Germans and the Japanese was a threat to all Americans, Don and 16 million other U.S. soldiers willingly put their country first and their lives on the line to protect their loved ones back home. While he didn't consider himself a hero, he was confident that he could muster up enough courage to face whatever the Army or the enemy threw at him.

Don's glum mood didn't come from fear, but rather from uncertainty. He'd just told Laura Jeanne and his parents not to worry, promising them, "I'll come home safely after the war." But he really didn't know if he'd be one of the lucky ones to make it back home, or if he'd just said goodbye to them for the last time. It was a lot for a twenty-one-year-old to deal with, and he couldn't think of anything else as his troop train lumbered through the Midwest, then veered south toward Louisiana.

Even with the windows open, the travel cars were hot and uncomfortable. Uncharacteristically, Don had trouble sleeping, dozing in fits and starts during most of the trip. On the second day, his troop train missed its connection in Kansas City, forcing the passengers to spend the night in the railroad yard in their Pullman. The following day, they finally rolled into the Baton Rouge station.

Shortly after arriving back at Harding Field, Don ran into Bob and Jerry, who reported they'd seen Kenny and Pat on the base as well. The Five were excited to be reunited, even if it was only for a few days while they waited for orders to ship out.

While it still didn't seem to bother the Missourians that much, the Utah boys sweltered in the heat and humidity, finding it nearly unbearable. After cooling off in the base swimming pool most of the afternoon, the Five reported to an Indoctrination Unit, where they spent the next few days attending boring lectures and signing endless government forms. Later in the week, the Air Corps issued them the latest and greatest military gear made especially for combat fighter pilots, including new headgear, improved goggles, and comfortable, new A-10 leather gloves. They even received a new wristwatch. The final item issued was an impressive Colt Model 1911 .45 semi-automatic pistol. In a letter to his mother, Jerry quipped:

Sharp immediately zeroed in on his new .45 pistol, forgetting about all the other gear. He's as happy as a kid with a new toy. He takes his .45 out, looks at it, pulls the trigger, and then puts it back in the holster. And in a few minutes, he does the same thing over again.

Once their indoctrination concluded, the guys had nothing to do but hurry up and wait. At night, they went to movies and enjoyed chocolate milk shakes and root beer floats, while keeping an ear close to the rumor mill. Stories were flying around everywhere. Word eventually leaked out from HQ that they'd be shipping out from somewhere up north and sailing across the Atlantic Ocean on a troopship. This terrified some of the men more than the thought of enemy combat. The Five predicted they'd start out in England, since the Eighth and the Ninth Air Forces both had P-47 training bases there. But exactly when they'd leave was anyone's guess. They heard a different story each day. The most recent one was, "Don't send your laundry out for cleaning unless you never want to see it again." On July 11, after a week of waiting, the Five boarded a government troop train headed for New York City.

––––––––––

For a young man from a small rural town, Don had logged a lot of railroad miles, all courtesy of Uncle Sam. Unfortunately, sightseeing on his trip up the East Coast was limited to short glimpses out the window of their fast moving train. When the Five arrived, they found the world's largest city inundated with hundreds of thousands of soldiers waiting to be processed and shipped overseas. In his final letter posted from the States, Don wrote to Laura Jeanne about his layover in the Big Apple:

We had a pretty good trip up here—went through a few new states—got a glimpse of the Capitol and Pentagon buildings in D.C.—and saw a few other sites along the way. I haven't had much time to write, so please slip up home, and tell my folks that you heard from me, OK?

I didn't get up until 9:30 this morning—and even then, I didn't have to. We went to a show last night sponsored by the Special Service Club featuring, Ann Sheridan, Ben Blue, Ethel Merman and Spike Jones and his City Slickers Band. It was surely a good show, and your hubby was right down on the front row. In fact, I was in front of the front row on the hard asphalt floor of an open-air theater, since they were a little short on seats. Thousands and thousands of soldiers were there. I'm still hoarse from laughing so much.

I had my haircut today, and barely got out of the barbershop with my life. Some crazy Italian went after me like he was shearing a sheep. Believe me, honey; he cut pretty close to the bone. And to finish the job he used fire! Honest, he singed it with a blowtorch, and I smelled like a burnt chicken when I left.

At the end of the week, the Five received their deployment orders and were assigned to the same troopship headed "somewhere in England." Remaining with friends during a move was a new experience for Don. But all the news that day wasn't good. Their outfit's mail failed to catch up with them while they were still stateside, leaving Don deeply disappointed. He'd hoped Laura Jeanne's beautiful 8 ½ x 11-inch high school graduation photograph would arrive before they shipped out. She sent it, but an overzealous Army censor rejected it for some unknown reason, returning it to her undelivered.

Don was able to get one last telephone call through to Laura Jeanne before leaving on his overseas voyage. They each grasped for the right words to say as their call ended, not knowing when they might hear each other's voices again. Saying goodbye was too painful and suggested a feeling of finality. Instead, the last words Laura Jeanne heard were, "Remember...I'm loving you always."

True to her vow, she remained strong, somehow controlling her emotions right up until she heard the telephone click, then broke down in tears, praying it wouldn't be the last time she ever heard his voice.

PART TWO

Queen Elizabeth

ELEVEN
....

Crossing the Pond

In the fall of 1936, John Brown & Co. began building a new Atlantic liner destined to become sister ship to the famous *Queen Mary*. A year later, Queen Elizabeth christened the ship now bearing her name, smashing a bottle of champagne across her bow. Dockworkers then lowered the dull-grey-colored liner into the water and towed her up the River Clyde into Scotland to be fitted-out. Great Britain feared that if the conversion took place in England, the *Queen Elizabeth* would become an easy target for the German Luftwaffe. To sink the largest ship ever built would have been a coup for the Nazis and a bonanza for their propaganda machine. The British didn't intend to let that happen.[56]

After her engines were installed, the ship left the wharf and headed out to sea. As part of an elaborate scheme to confuse German spies, British intelligence intentionally leaked word that the ship was making a "short positioning voyage" to Southampton, on the south coast of England, to be fitted-out as a troopship. The Brits even booked hotels there in the names of John Brown & Co employees to authenticate the ruse.[57]

Once the *Queen Elizabeth* was out to sea, her captain opened the ship's safe and read his sealed orders. Later that same day, a squadron of Nazi bombers flew over the English Channel where the *Second Queen* would have been berthing had she actually sailed for Southampton. Instead, the new liner was safely racing west across the Atlantic, arriving in New York Harbor on March 7, 1940. Since her maiden voyage was such a well-kept secret, the new ship created quite a stir when she pulled into port.[58]

The *Queen Elizabeth* received her initial fitting-out in New York, then sailed to Sydney, Australia, to complete her conversion to a troopship. After returning to the United States, ship workers increased the *Queen Elizabeth's* carrying capacity from 5,000 to 10,000, enabling her to transport an entire division of American troops. She carried more than 750,000 troops and their equipment safely across the Atlantic during her time as a troopship—traveling alone and unescorted, relying solely on her speed and unpredictable zigzag-course maneuvers to protect her from German U* Boats.[59]

───────

Don had never gone to sea and the biggest vessel he'd ever boarded was the rowboat he took fishing at Matagorda Island. The size of the *Queen Elizabeth* and the vastness of the Atlantic Ocean amazed him:

> *We left New York on July 16, heading out of the harbor past the Statue of Liberty and out to sea. This has been an enjoyable trip, but the ship is very crowded with military personnel. The upper-crust officers have good accommodations, but regular officers like us and the enlisted men don't.*
>
> *We've only been eating two meals a day, but they're really first class, as you might expect on the Queen Elizabeth. Your hubby eats enough to last the whole day thru. And nope, I haven't been seasick. It's hard to believe that you could travel for so many days and not see land. I hope I can show you someday just how big the ocean really is.*
>
> *Every day before we left the States, I expected a letter from you. And every day I ended up terribly disappointed. It's been almost a month since we've received any mail, and now I don't expect any for another couple of weeks. Nothing but bad luck!*

On July 22, 1944, after six days at sea, the *Queen Elizabeth* put into port at Greenock, Scotland. The Five were eager to go ashore and set foot on dry land again. A few hours after landing, they boarded a

───────

*   *U was short for Unterseeboot, meaning "undersea boat." German submarines caused havoc by attacking ships crossing the Atlantic, especially during the early part of the war, and had the firepower to sink even the largest Allied troopships.*

train, beginning a long, winding ride across the United Kingdom to the small town of Shrewsbury, located in the center of England.

———————

The Royal Air Force (RAF) base at Atcham, aka "Station 342," was located five miles east of Shrewsbury. In 1942, the RAF turned the facility over to the United States Eighth and Ninth Air Forces to use as a training base to prepare new fighter pilots for combat.[60] Don's luck with his buddies from Harding Field continued—the Five not only ended up at the same base, but in the same flight squadron and barracks as well.

RAF Atcham Station 342

The weather at Atcham was humid and cool, and the sun was seldom visible. Thick, low-lying *scud* clouds frequently delayed the pilots' morning takeoffs, providing them with a lot of practice flying in fog and rain. They trained in the *Razorback* version of the P-47D, which earned its name from the ridge behind the pilot's canopy. The first thing their instructors taught them was to forget everything they had previously learned about flying combat formations.[61] Apparently there were still a few disconnects between training in the States and actual combat overseas.

In his first letter to Laura Jeanne posted from England, Don wrote:

It's been overcast since we arrived, and they say it isn't likely to change. They have really long days over here. It's 11:30 p.m. and it just got dark a little while ago, and it gets light about 4:00 a.m. We should be flying pretty soon. However, no combat for a while yet.

The base is really spread out and has a lot of hills. We have bicycles to run around on, and riding is a lot of fun. They also have tennis courts here at the base. I doubt I'll ever get enough time to play—but I hope so. This English money system is really a mess at first, but I'm beginning to understand it. And they drive on the left side of their narrow roads.

The new arrivals at Atcham were on cloud nine when their overseas mail finally caught up with them. Relieved to learn that his buddy Grant Ash had survived being shot down a few weeks earlier, Don used the good news to try to allay Laura Jeanne's growing fears about his own safety:

I'm writing with a sandwich in one hand and a pen in the other. They serve free sandwiches and coffee or cocoa after 9:00 p.m. every night at the Officers Club, and it surely hits the spot. I guess it's not exactly free, since we have to pay club dues. Earlier, we saw a show at the clubhouse. They have a small screen, which isn't the best, but it's entertaining.

I was glad to hear that Grant and his crew were reported as OK.* That goes to show we have a very good chance to make it over here—even if we get a bad break. So please don't worry so much about me, okay? Just have faith and keep saying your prayers—and everything is going to come out all right.

I'm headed for a shower and shave before hitting the sack, then I'll start dreaming about you. I can still feel those cold little feet of yours trying to warm up on my back. I'd give a million dollars to have them there again.

Following a week of lectures, ground school instruction, and link training, base command cleared the new arrivals to begin air combat training. The P-47s on the base were newer and faster than those they

---

*   Grant Ash's B-24 bomber, flying a combat mission for the 15th Air Force, was shot down near Vienna, Austria on May 24, 1944. He was able to bail out safely, but was soon captured by the Germans and sent to Stalag Luft III, a POW camp in Sagan, Poland.

flew in the States, and the Five were eager to climb into the cockpit and try them out. Don wrote:

> We start flying tomorrow, and I can't wait to get out of this scud and up into the blue again. By the way, I met an old "Y" tennis buddy, Mark Boyle, of Provo, who's serving as a flight instructor on our base. He's a captain in the Eighth Air Force and is leaving for home in the not too distant future, since he's done his share over here.

Laura Jeanne hung on every word Don wrote in his letters to her, pleading with him to answer her questions and write in more detail about his life and experiences overseas:

> I had to laugh when I read what you wrote about my bad points as a writer, but I'm inclined to agree with you. I've been spending most of my time wondering what I could write that wouldn't be censored, so I haven't written much about anything. But there are plenty of things that I "can" tell you. Resolution: I shall endeavor in the future to tell you more about what's going on in the life of your Mr. Lt. Maybe I'll become a fair war correspondent one of these days yet.
>
> The guys from Harding and I live in the same shack and are still in the same squadron. We haven't been off the post as yet. However, I think we'll go take a look at the English town near the base one of these days.
>
> Honey, I didn't realize that your birthday was coming up so fast, and thinking about it a week in advance is thinking about it several weeks too slow when we're so far apart. I'm ashamed of myself for being so darned absentminded—what a knucklehead. This letter will get there too late now, so all I can say is I hope you "had" a very happy birthday and pray we can spend your next birthday together.

A few days later on a return trip from nearby Shrewsbury, the Army truck transporting Don's squadron was involved in a traffic accident:

*We went to town today for one of our classes and on the way
back our truck hit a blinking "Limey* Taxi." The English
cars are only about the size of our Willys jeeps. Net result—
one banged up limey car, but no serious injuries. We call
an Englishman a "Limey," and they call us "G.I. Joe."**
Everyone gets along remarkably well—although it's really
hard to understand them at times.*

Don, Bob, and Jerry were now inseparable. They were seen
together so often that the other pilots started calling them the Three
Musketeers, a tag that stuck with them the remainder of the war.
Since their footlockers containing most of their extra clothes and
gear hadn't yet made their way to the base, the guys were forced to
hand wash their dirty clothes:

*Here's one for the books. Your hubby, along with Sharp and
Kelly, did a splendid job of cleaning our clothes last night
down on the line with 100-octane gas. We dunked them in all
over, after rubbing out the dirty spots with a cloth. And did
they ever smell—phew! However, after a day in the breeze,
they're in good shape again. Now all we have to do is press
them.*

The pilots' waylaid footlockers finally arrived at the base the
following day. After opening their trunks, the men fumed in disbelief:

*Some "blankety-blank" rifled through my bags, and two pairs
of shoes and several other things were missing. It made me
so damn mad I yelled! Bob and Jerry and a lot of other guys
had stuff missing too. It wasn't the Limeys, but our own guys
in the American Army that stole our stuff! I'll have to send
away for more shoes. The other things will probably cost 5£
(about $20) to replace—that's if I can find them in town.*

---

*   *The nickname Limey originated in the 19th century when British sailors on long sea voy-
ages chose limes instead of the more commonly used lemons to prevent scurvy.*

** *The letters G.I. were initials for Government Issue, in common use since World War I. The
Army stamped G.I. on all kinds of equipment, from helmets and rifles to tanks and aircraft.
The initials were also used as an adjective to describe almost anything to do with the Army
or the Air Force—and eventually were even associated with the men themselves.*

Sorry for the rash words that slipped out of my pen, honey. I guess I'm still a little angry.

None of the Five particularly liked England, its continual bad weather, or the English ways of doing things. According to Bob, even the training missions they flew over the English countryside were trying:

Cross-country flying in England was a bear. Everything looks the same and there are so many roads and creeks that it's impossible to tell where you are. We often got disoriented while flying and were lucky to just get back to the base most of the time. And the weather was usually so bad that it added to the navigation problems.

The Brits at Atcham had organized a tennis match, pitting their best players against the best Yank racqueteers on the base. Mark Boyle pulled a few strings, convincing the club operators that Don would be a good addition to the upcoming match. Having never played on a grass court before, he was doubly excited—and couldn't wait to get his hands on a tennis racket again:

Looks like they're going to have a little tennis match here tomorrow night. I've been invited to play, but our flight instructor may not let me. He's a bit peeved at us for not reporting to the flight line tonight after chow. We didn't know about it—but he insists that we "should" have known. So from now on we'll report and stay on the line after supper, whether we fly or not! Rather rough, eh? What an old bean.

Later that night, Mark pressured Don's flight instructor to convince him that he needed Don as his doubles partner to help the Americans defeat the Brits, who had home-court advantage:

I played in that tennis match after all. They had Mark and I scheduled to play No. 5 doubles, but after our coach saw us warming up, he put us up against the Brits top team instead. We trounced them 6–0 and 6–2 for an amazing victory. They didn't have any singles matches, but it was still a lot of fun. I played again today and was hitting the ball pretty well for the shape I'm in.

The air raid sirens had been silent at Atcham since the Five arrived. In fact, the new arrivals at the air base hadn't experienced any *real* effects of the war, making the pilots' mock air battles almost surreal, like war games. The Yanks on the base took every opportunity to go fast and have fun in the air and on the ground. In addition to flying unauthorized maneuvers and buzzing the tower, they also engaged in ground dogfights on their bicycles. Don wrote:

> *I flew this morning and again tonight in a two-ship formation. And did we ever have fun! We fought everyone we could find for a couple of hours. Of course, it wasn't the real McCoy, but we pretended that we shot several of them down. Afterward, we came barreling down from 7000 feet screaming over the field and control tower, then pulled up doing about 400 mph.*

> *I'm having quite a time with my bicycle. The back wheel is all bent out of shape due to a little individual combat I had with some of the boys the other day. I have to go everywhere on foot now until I can find time to fix it. I'm getting in shape, tho—I must walk about six miles every day to get around the post.*

Bob liked going fast as much as the next guy and did his share of buzzing the tower. But he didn't like the thought of hiking all over the base, so he avoided ground dogfights like the one Don was in. However, the bicycle combat stunts prevalent at Atcham clearly amused him. He later wrote:

> *Pilots on the base were forever pulling firing passes on one another as they sped up and down the hills running through the airfield on their bicycles—and the crashes were awesome! We had many of our finest in the hospital recovering from injuries and abrasions acquired during these bicycle pursuit-curve attacks.*

Keeping his resolution to Laura Jeanne, Don did his best to answer her questions and tell her about his experiences more colorfully and in greater detail:

> *I'm sorry I can't answer more of your questions, honey. There are some things I can't tell you about—they'll have to wait*

until after the war. About the countryside, however, the most beautiful scenery I've seen so far was in Scotland.

I finally got to take a ride in a B-17. I sat right up in the nose with the pilots and could see everything. Most of England, Wales, and Scotland looks like a big jigsaw puzzle from the air because they separate their little pieces of farmland by rock walls instead of fences. Everything looks green and pretty from the air.

And about the girls over here, they aren't nearly as attractive as those in the States. They don't wear stockings, and since they have very little sun over here, their legs are pasty white and unattractive. Too bad these gals don't have legs like my wife's—woo-woo!!

The only letter I got this week was from the government, informing me that you haven't been receiving my pay allotment because the main office in Baton Rouge messed the paperwork up. Believe me—I'd like to have a few words with them, since it took them four months to notify me! Tomorrow I'll get the major in the finance office to get this SNAFU straightened out. Try to be patient and please don't starve in the meantime. And don't sue me—I'll come thru—I hope.

Mail was every soldier's lifeline to their friends and loved ones back home. When it was cut off, especially for extended periods, their morale and performance suffered, regardless of where they were or what they were doing. Inexplicably, Don's letters seemed to come in bunches, often weeks apart, even though the Army delivery service regularly picked up and sent out the mail:

Well, darling, I'm sweatin' out my mail again. I know you're writing, but I'm just not receiving. I don't understand it. It's hard to write tonight, 'cause there's a lot of gabbing going on. And we have one character in our shack that snores and talks in his sleep. He's already started up tonight, even before the lights are out!

If I ever snore like that, honey, just roll me over and stuff something in my mouth. Or you could just put your lips next to mine and stop me that way. Yeh, that's definitely the best way to deal with the problem.

I'm still trying to get my shoes replaced. The first pair I ordered was too small, so I had to send them back. I hope the guy who stole mine is getting all kinds of blisters on his feet.

The Five finished their final combat training at Atcham the evening of August 16, and celebrated by buzzing the field a few times in various formations, to the chagrin of the tower air controllers. The next day, HQ posted Confidential Special Order number 229 on the bulletin board, assigning the newly trained combat pilots to thirteen different fighter groups. Following a last-minute change in Don's assignment from the Eighth to the Ninth Air Force, the Five remained together as part of the eleven P-47 pilots assigned to Site "A-3" in Cardonville, France, becoming part of the 368th Fighter Group. Don was surprised when he learned his CO had appointed him Officer in Charge of his group.

```
                    368TH FI GP   SITE A-3
                   2D LT DONALD N  EVANS  0711973  (OIC)
2D LT KENNETH E  KAIEN   0770302      2D LT ROBERT M  PACE   0770112
2D LT GERALD B   KELLEY  0770305      2D LT KENNETH D  PAELER  0770380
2D LT GRADON E   MONGAR  0770363      2D LT CHARLES B  PATRICK  077038
2D LT GEORGE A   MYERS   0770108      2D LT NEALY C   RIEMANN   _10___
2D LT TALBERT S  NEWHART 0770373      2D LT ROBERT D  SHARP   0770430

          - 2 -   C-O-N-F-I-D-E-N-T-I-A-L   - 2 -
```

ETO orders to the continent

The Five looked forward to leaving England, eager to see the sun again and excited to join the fight to defeat the Nazis. In his last letter posted from Atcham, Don wrote:

Well, honey, I'm going to France soon, so I'll be sending my footlocker home with some clothes and other articles that I don't need or can't take with me. Sorry about the dirty clothes, but you know how much I hate to do laundry.

Is that pin-up picture for my wall on its way here yet? I'm still "not" so patiently waiting for it. I should have sent you a picture of myself earlier today. The water system has been out for five or six days now, and I haven't showered or shaved in all that time. Tonight we had enough water to do both jobs. I think I look and smell a little better now!

It's blackout time, so I must say "Bonne nuit," my darling. I've started practicing my French.

The Five were finally heading to the Continent—and going to war.

Laura Jeanne was uncertain what to do with her life after Don went off to war. She considered joining her friends in college, then wondered if it made more sense to get a job, save some money, and start school with Don when he returned from the war. She forced herself to think in terms of *when*, not allowing *if* to enter her mind, unwilling to think about what her life might be like without him. It was a difficult decision, and her friends and family didn't make it any easier, giving her conflicting advice. In the end, she decided to find a job, postponing college for the time being:

I was grateful that my parents welcomed me back to live with them while Don was overseas. I found employment with the Office of Price Administration, just across the street from their home, where the OPA administered the affairs of supplying ration books to the citizens of Lehi.

Many items of necessity were now being rationed. I learned that there was a big difference between wants and needs. Some were willing to sacrifice and try to get along on the bare necessities, while others wanted more than their fair share.

We issued stamps for shoes, soap, sugar, coffee, flour, cigarettes, gasoline, and tires for machinery and cars. Ration coupons became as important and valuable as money in obtaining necessary commodities. I was in a good position to trade my coffee and cigarette stamps to people who wanted

*them badly in exchange for their shoe and sugar stamps. All
kinds of items became quite scarce.*

*When we saw a line of people outside the grocery store,
we automatically joined them, just in case there might be
something there to buy we desperately needed. I especially
missed not being able to obtain nylons, so I did the next best
thing. I used liquid stocking makeup, as did all the other
young women. It was a really messy job painting your legs!
Everyone had to learn to get by on less and be frugal with
what they had.*

War Ration Book

In an attempt to control costs and fairly distribute items in short
supply during World War II, the OPA froze prices and instituted
rationing. More than 8,000 local offices administered programs
across the nation, issuing ration books with removable stamps to
each member of a family. Once stamps were used to buy a particular
rationed item, no more of it could be purchased until the OPA issued
the next month's ration books.[62]

Special stickers rationed gasoline. Most were "A" stickers, which allowed the purchase of three or four gallons of fuel each week. Those considered essential to the war effort, like doctors and workers in the military industry, were given "B" and "C" stickers, making them eligible to receive up to eight gallons a week. Truckers received a "T" sticker, getting them unlimited fuel when they were hauling supplies critical to the war effort. And the OPA issued an "X" sticker, which had no fuel limitations, to police officers, firefighters, clergy, and civil defense workers. In a further attempt to conserve tires and gasoline, a national speed limit was set at 35 mph.[63]

Not surprisingly, the desire for the most sought after ration stamps and gasoline stickers drove selfish behavior and corruption, not only on the black market, but also at the highest levels of government. A scandal erupted when the press corps reported that 200 Congressmen had received the coveted gasoline "X" sticker. Even after the media exposed the under-the-table dealings, the politicians refused to relinquish their stickers.[64]

Shortages arose at home, in part because of massive shipments of materials and supplies to the military overseas. Some goods were in short supply because they were previously imported from countries the U.S. was now fighting in the war, others because they could no longer be safely shipped from Europe or South America. Coffee and sugar were in the latter category, becoming so scarce that the production of Coca-Cola stopped for a time.[65]

Salvage campaigns sprang up across America to collect scrap metal, rubber, cooking fat, and even rags, all of which were recycled into weapons, ammunition, gas masks, and explosives. Japanese silk imports dried up after the war began, causing the War Production Board to launch silk and nylon stocking drives for use in making parachutes and cords. While the scrap drives had limited impact on war production output, they promoted a strong feeling of patriotism throughout the nation.[66] Americans, still recovering from the Great Depression, coped remarkably well, continuing to "use it up, wear it out, make it do, or do without"—just as they'd been doing for more than a decade.

368th Fighter Group Insignia

TWELVE
....

Normandy Beach

The U.S. Ninth Air Force emerged in August 1943, following an AAF restructuring of the VIII Air Support Command. Two months later, SHAEF (Supreme Headquarters Allied Expeditionary Forces) moved the Ninth to England under orders to build a Tactical Air Armada for the upcoming invasion of Europe. By June 6, 1944—D-Day—it had become the largest air force in history, with 250,000 men and 3,500 airplanes. Its aircraft consisted of fighters, bombers, and troop carriers; its militaries included air defense, engineering, and service commands.[67] During the Normandy Beach Invasion, Ninth Air Force fighter planes provided air protection for paratroopers as they jumped out of transport planes onto the French coastline, then followed up with massive air strikes as the Allies stormed the beachheads.[68]

The Ninth Air Force 368th Fighter Group was the first air unit stationed on Normandy Beach following the invasion. Each of its three squadrons, the 395th *Panzer Dusters*, the 396th *Thunder Bums*, and the 397th *Jabo Angels*, consisted of twenty-six aircraft and thirty-six pilots, divided into four flights. The squadrons had their own call signs, aircraft identifications, markings, and logos, along with their own colors painted on the forward section of their aircraft's nose cowl.[69]

Air Command assigned the Five to the 397th Jabo Angels. Their P-47s had blue cowls and went by the radio call sign *Tropic*. Their logo was a crazy-looking cowboy caricature with a 10-gallon white hat, red bandana, and handlebar moustache. Mounted on a winged chestnut steed, the wild-eyed bronc rider had both hands held high, pointing his six shooters into the sky. The word *Jabo* came from a combination of two German words. The first two letters *"Ja"* were

from the word *Jaeger*, meaning "fighter." Adding them to the first
two letters of *Bombenleger* (*"Bo"*), German for "bomber," formed
the word *Jabo*. "Angels" was an amusing add-on with an ironic
twist; the 397th pilots never considered themselves messengers sent
from heaven.

Airstrip "A-3" was located four miles from Normandy Beach
near the small town of Cardonville, France. Soon after the Allied
landing, the Ninth Engineering Command constructed a makeshift
5,000-foot steel, square-mesh runway on the beach. After D-Day,
the 368th flew close air support missions from Normandy Beach,
paving the way for the Allied armies to advance across Nazi-occupied
Western Europe.[70]

Bob recounted the following humorous experience that took
place on their trip from RAF Atcham to Cardonville:

> *We flew to the Continent in a B-17. On the trip across the
> English Channel, Jerry unfortunately lost his fabulous crush
> hat. Our standard dress cap was nicknamed a "crush cap."
> It had a short leather bill and wire stiffeners in the top rim of
> the cap, which kept it in proper regulation shape. Since we
> wore headgear over our caps when we flew, nearly everyone
> took out the wire to make it more comfortable. This allowed
> the sides of the cap to go floppy, giving it a "crushed look."*
>
> *Jerry had been shaping his hat for months, and was pretty
> proud of the way it looked and fit his head. He was standing
> in the middle of the airplane and the hatch was open.
> Suddenly, his hat was swooped off his head and flew out into
> the English Channel. Jerry was speechless.*

Don missed seeing Jerry's crush cap incident. Even though he
was Officer in Charge of the eleven pilots ordered to Strip "A-3," he
missed the entire trip. In his next letter to Laura Jeanne, he explained:

> *Some of us got left behind in England. It seems that the word
> didn't get around fast enough about our departure flight. So
> there I stood, still at Atcham, while my buddies were on their
> way to France to fight in the war! Those of us left behind*

were kind of worried for a while, but we soon got back on the ball, hopped another flight, crossed the Channel, and made it to the Continent.

It was a warm, sunny afternoon when the new fighter pilots landed on the coast of France. When they arrived at the makeshift airfield at Cardonville, everything was in commotion—men were packing crates, loading trucks, and rushing around everywhere, while crowds of French citizens watched all the goings-on. The Ninth Air Force 368th Fighter Group was preparing to move out.

Charged with orders to provide close air support and protection for the exposed flank of General George S. Patton's Third Army, the fighter group was now too far away to do that effectively, forcing them to pull up stakes and move closer to the frontlines. After a quick welcome, the 397th Squadron leader tasked the "new boys" with setting up their tent, instructing them to dig a trench next to each of their cots. Hopeful that Don would eventually find his way to the airstrip, they set up an extra cot and even dug him a trench. Don continued:

After arriving at Normandy Beach, I stuck out my thumb and hitched a ride to the airfield. When sack time came around that night, I surprised my four mates with a cheery "hello," then readied myself for the ribbing that I knew would be coming.

I'm still with my buddies. They're all crazy as the dickens (present company included). There's a little Renault tank and a German motorcycle here in camp that we beat up a muddy road with today—even our CO likes to have fun with us. I'm definitely happier now that I'm with my own outfit.

It rained intermittently throughout the Five's first night at Cardonville. Off in the distance they heard the eerie sounds of bombs, keeping them awake most of the night—everyone that is, except for Jerry. Describing their temporary new base to his mother, he wrote:

Here we are. Signs of the war are all around. France isn't so bad, although there's definitely been a war going on around here. There are bomb craters everywhere and every little town is about half demolished. It still seems unreal to me

*that people could be fighting and killing each other on such
a nice day.*

*We're living in tents and the food here is pretty good. Sharp,
Kalen, Patrick, Evans, and I were mighty lucky. Not only
did we get assigned to the same fighter group, but also to the
same squadron! The other guys in the squadron are really a
bunch of good guys.*

*The guys said there was quite a bit of flak and bombing
toward the east last night, however I didn't hear or see any of
it. I was asleep in my sack.*

The next few nights at Strip "A-3" remained nerve-racking.
Don adapted quickly to the nighttime war noises, soon sleeping
as soundly as Jerry. However, Bob and the Missourians still slept
uneasily, waking up off and on throughout the night. Bob recalled:

*The nights at the airstrip were seldom peaceful. Flak was
always bursting overhead. We had to dig a trench beside our
bed to sleep in—or sleep next to and fall into—whenever
there was a bombing or strafing of our steel-mat airfield.
Sometimes "buzz bombs" would come flying over us, and
now and then, a fighter would be on the tail of one of them.
Eventually, we all got used to the noise and were able to
sleep well.*

———————

One week after the Normandy invasion, Hitler started launching
a new weapon on the British. Air raid sirens screamed loudly nearly
every night in London, as odd-looking, jet-propelled, unmanned
aircraft called "V-1s" (short for Vengeance weapons) approached
the city. Shortly after the siren alarms sounded, these flying bombs
became visible, making an ominous buzzing sound as they fell from
the sky. The British gave them colorful nicknames like "doodlebug"
and "farting fury," but the name that stuck with most British and
Americans was "buzz bomb."[71]

Powered by a simple pulsejet engine, V-1 rockets were twenty-
seven-feet long with a wingspan of nearly eighteen feet. Officially the
world's first cruise missile, they were able to carry a high-explosive

warhead weighing 2,100 pounds up to 150 miles at a speed of 375–400 mph. Although unable to strike small strategic targets, the cheap and easy-to-build weapons were able to hit a target the size of London.[72]

V-1 "Buzz Bomb"

During the first week of missile launchings, the skies over London rained more than a hundred buzz bombs each day.[73] Blasts from the rockets wrought death and destruction on everything near their detonation point, cracking windows up to a mile away. Determined to further break the spirit of the British people and bring them to their knees, Hitler ordered his scientists to start working on an even more sophisticated missile with greater accuracy, range, and destructive power.

Although the air raid sirens succeeded in eliciting fear in Londoners and the V-1 attacks killed and maimed tens of thousands, they were ineffective from a military standpoint, and they failed to create the degree of terror Hitler assumed they would. The Brits remained resolute, unwilling to surrender. The Nazi leader greatly underestimated the heart and grit of the English people and their ability to endure the worst Germany could throw at them. Even after realizing that his homicidal objective in England was failing, Hitler ordered V-1 bombings to continue, simply as revenge against England for participating in the D-Day invasion.

The British fought back against the Vengeance weapon attacks with limited success. Anti-aircraft defenses were set up southeast of

London, but they had difficulty taking out the fast-flying bombs. The British sent up more than 2,000 tear-drop-shaped barrage balloons, which were tethered to the ground with steel cables. The low flying missiles collided with the cables, causing them to crash or veer off course. Although this defense was successful at first, the Germans soon countered, ingeniously attaching cable cutters to the wings of the buzz bombs.[74]

In the end, the best defense against the rocket bombs was a good offense. British fighter planes underwent special modifications, enabling them to go faster than the flying bombs. RAF pilots, flying customized Spitfires and Tempest fighter planes, attempted to take them out in several ways—all of them dangerous. The most common method was to approach from the side and fire at the bombs as they crossed the pilot's path. The fighters also tried chasing them down from behind, as Bob wrote about, but this was a tricky maneuver. If the fighter plane was closer than 200 yards when the V-1 exploded, the aircraft would also go down. After running out of ammunition, a few enterprising British pilots started placing their plane's wing tip under a wing tip of the flying bomb, knocking it off course when they banked away. Others bravely flew out in front of the buzz bombs, letting their slipstream spin the rockets out of control, a tactic even more dangerous than wing tipping.[75]

The Nazi scientists' second-generation vengeance weapon, the "V-2," was a different story altogether. Much more accurate than its predecessor, it traveled at an amazing 3,400 mph, becoming the world's first long-range ballistic missile to enter space. Against these new Nazi super weapons, the Allies had no defense.[76]

Over 15,000 German V-bombs struck England and Belgium during the war, killing an estimated 15,000 and wounding an additional 47,000. Although most casualties were Londoners, the Belgian cities of Antwerp, Brussels, and Liège also suffered significantly. Flak, barrage balloons, and fighter planes were able to destroy nearly 6,000 incoming V-1 rockets before they reached their targets, or casualty losses would have been greater.[77] Not surprisingly, Hitler forced more than 60,000 prisoners, working in dangerous, brutal, work-camp conditions, to build the Nazi V-weapons. An estimated 20,000 of them died while producing the destructive rockets.[78]

V-2 Rocket

Early on the morning of August 23, the first part of the 368th Fighter Group broke camp in a downpour and began heading to the east. Moving a convoy of men, equipment, supplies, and planes from one air base to another was a daunting task under the best of circumstances. Heavy rains and sticky mud made it much worse, turning the fighter group's move into a tough slog. Father Don Cleary, chaplain for the 368th, wrote the following about their first relocation journey in a newsletter he published for friends and colleagues at Cornell University:

Our trip of some miles brought us contact at close range with the results of war on civilian communities. Whole villages lay flat—others completely untouched—Churches with only jagged walls standing—houses toppling over one another, and through it all, people were trying to be cheerful while clambering over the ruins of their homes, their stores, and their towns. Here and there were women in black veils, mute testimony to a recent death in the family.

Father Don Cleary, 368th FG Chaplain

What a price the common people have to pay to be delivered from a foreign tyranny! They received us at first with reserve, not knowing what we were going to do—what our presence would mean. Since then they've warmed to us, and now, nothing is too good for the Americans!

I visited Caen and St.-Lô. The former may be restored someday—the latter, never. All that remains is the crumpled shattered remains of what once had been a lovely city.[79]

Jerry added some poignant comments of his own in a letter to his mother:

France, in most places, doesn't even look like it's been in a war. The countryside looks peaceful, green, and pretty, except for an occasional burned German Tiger Tank. But the towns are in a terrible fix. In some there's not one intact building still standing, I've seen pictures in the newsreels of the damage that war causes, but it really sinks in when you stand and look at it.

Mom, whoever invented war? We're winning—but even the winner loses.

The French people are awfully glad to see us Americans arriving. They actually line the road and wave at every vehicle that passes—they do it hours at a time, too. And I was really surprised when they actually and truly threw flowers at us.

I never knew that the US Army had so much equipment. There are endless streams of trucks and guns and everything. The Germans don't have any chance at all—not a one.

Chartres, Cathédrale Notre Dame

THIRTEEN
....

Chartres, France

Chartres, an ancient Gallic city in northern France, is famous for its beautiful Gothic cathedrals and stained glass windows. First conquered by the Romans, then sacked by the Vikings, and later controlled by England, the French city has a long history of foreign sieges and occupations.[80]

At the beginning of World War I, the French built a military flying school in Chartres on the site of an old cavalry field. During the Battle of France in World War II, the Germans captured the airfield and used it as a launching pad for the Luftwaffe's destructive "blitzkrieg" air raids over London. Following the D-Day invasion, Chartres became a popular target for Eighth Air Force heavy bombers. Later, Ninth medium bombers and P-47 fighter-bombers took their turn at the airfield, finally forcing the Germans to abandon it on August 21, 1944.

Five days later, the 368th was flying combat missions from Chartres—thanks to the incredible rebuilding efforts of the Ninth Engineer Command.[81] They played a critical role in the Allied surge toward Germany, constantly rehabilitating captured German airstrips near the frontlines. Damage from Allied bombing made their job difficult, and the retreating Germans made it worse, mining the airfields with explosives and attempting to destroy everything of strategic value before they withdrew.

Readying seriously damaged airfields was a formidable task—de-mining unexploded munitions, clearing away wrecked aircraft and bombing debris littering the airfields, filling up bomb craters, patching up holes in runways, and restoring what they could of abandoned buildings and barracks. The engineers moved in immediately after the Luftwaffe withdrew, which made their task dangerous, as well as challenging.

After making the reclaimed air bases operational, the Ninth engineers had their hands full keeping them that way. Enemy attacks damaged buildings and put additional holes in the runways. And sometimes the pilots themselves made new craters, jarring bombs loose during takeoffs and landings on the bumpy, war-torn runways. The holes were repairable, and the AAF could swap out the wrecked P-47s for new ones—and sadly, even the pilots, who seldom survived such mishaps, were replaceable.

Moving in to Chartres Airfield "A-40"

The new 368th base, Airfield "A-40," was located 215 miles inland from Normandy Beach, right behind enemy lines. On August 28, all three squadrons took to the skies and christened the new airstrip by destroying nearly 300 enemy motorized transports, tanks, halftracks, and trucks, setting a modern military record. However, they paid a price for their success—a 396th Panzer Duster pilot died on a strafing run when he hit a tree and crashed.[82]

P-47 fighter-bombers had become the Allies' most effective weapon in their push across Western Europe toward Nazi Germany. In addition to providing close air support for the ground troops, Thunderbolt pilots matched the German Luftwaffe in air-to-air combat. And with their bombs, rockets, and machine guns, they'd proven adept at destroying enemy aircraft installations, roads, rail lines, bridges, trains, armored vehicles, and tanks.[83]

The effective teamwork of the Ninth Air Force and General Patton's Third Army proved to be instrumental in the success of the P-47's air-to-ground combat operations. Radio communications between the two allowed them to make combat decisions in real time. Experienced combat pilots rode along with Army tank columns, directing aircraft ground attacks from the frontlines right as the missions took place.[84]

Château de Mon Grande

After arriving at their new base, the men set up tents in the mud while the Ninth engineers began efforts to clean up a once-grand château where the chaplain and most of the officers planned to stay. Men shoveled and swept out as much dirt, garbage and debris as they could—and even won a battle with a swarm of bees that had taken up residence there.[85] Father Cleary wrote:

Our base is one the Germans had used, and naturally, as a result of our bombings, is well beat up. We're living in a nearby château, formerly a German headquarters and originally the home of Mon Grande [a French Baron] now living in Paris. It hasn't any roof, but the other three floors are intact. And, after sweeping out the filth left by our "super race" predecessors, it is very livable. It leaks in spots, but no one complains very much.[86]

In his first letter to Laura Jeanne from Chartres, Don quipped:

I feel like I'm working for a Boy Scout rank advancement, digging trenches and putting up tents in the mud after our last move. The five of us are temporarily crammed into a small tent with all our gear. I've spent a couple of cold, uncomfortable nights, and seen the results of a pretty rough war. I'd give a hundred dollars for a hot bath and a good hot meal.

Maybe I'm not enjoying life over here like the boys stationed in England, where I could have stayed, but the experiences, etc., I've had and what we can do over here, is far more valuable than the comforts I could have had by staying in England.

I was originally assigned to the Eighth Air Force and my buddies were all assigned to the Ninth. I didn't mind, since I'd have been with some of the boys I trained with in the States. But Kelly and Sharp both pleaded with me to try and get my assignment changed so we could stay together. So I did—and here I am! Anyway, I think I can do more good here with the Ninth flying close support for our troops on the front line.

I miss hearing from you so much. Life with no mail is hell, to say the least. I can go without a lot of things—but I love my mail!

A few days later, the Five got out of the rain and mud and moved from their overcrowded tent into the nearby château:

Boy oh boy, have the five of us ever been booted around this old château. Since we're new in the outfit, we have no seniority. After getting kicked out of a room up front, we moved our baggage and equipment into a dark, undesirable room behind the kitchen, only to be booted out again. So we carried everything to a room on the top floor of the three-story house. By this time, we were plenty sick of getting pushed around, and decided we weren't going to move again—no matter what!

We're packed in our little room like a can of sardines. We have a kerosene lamp, a little stove, and one little hole in the wall that we call a window! In spite of all this, we take everything in stride—laugh at hardships, have a great time, and act pretty crazy most of the time.

I have the hardest darn mattress on my cot. Every morning I wake up half paralyzed, feeling like I've spent 10 days on the rock pile. I need to find one that's more comfortable—and soon. I'd gladly settle for that lumpy old sack we had in Fairbury—especially if you came with it! The lights went out a while ago. I've been writing with Jerry's flashlight, and he needs it back to finish a letter to his mom, so goodnight.

Packed like a can of sardines

With his flashlight in one hand and fountain pen in the other, Jerry wrote:

Special Service has put up a small tent and they're showing 16 mm films. The sound system was pretty good and we enjoyed the show a lot, although it was kind of silly in places. There was nothing about war in it. Maybe that's why I enjoyed it so much.

Between Sharp, Evans, and I, we do an awful lot of dreaming about home. Sharp wants a chocolate milkshake, I want a roast beef sandwich with a glass of milk, and Evans just wants to go home to his wife. I haven't got any news from home for so long, I don't know what's going on. This no mail situation is no good!

Did I ever tell you about Evans? He's from Lehi, 21 years old, and a really nice guy. He's quite good looking, and I'll bet Ruth [Jerry's younger sister] would think so too, but he's already married. He's a Mormon boy, and he and Sharp and I fit together perfectly.

Kalen is from Parkville, Missouri, 21 years old, and he's a good guy too. He smokes, which I don't particularly care for, but there are far more boys over here that smoke, than those that don't. I believe if I do what I want to, and they do what they want to, then there'll be no friction of any kind.

Patrick is from Joplin, Missouri, 22 years old, and is the other member of the Five. He's a good guy too, and he laughs a lot.

On September 1, the Ninth Air Force announced that trips to Paris would begin for limited groups of officers. One week earlier, metro workers, police officers, and postal workers all went on strike, effectively shutting down Paris. The next day, about 20,000 French Resistance fighters set up barricades, beginning a citywide insurrection, just as they'd done in the French Revolution 150 years earlier. As they fearlessly attacked the well-armed German garrison overseeing their occupation, it looked like a slaughter was in the making. Then, thousands of Parisians joined the outnumbered Resistance, evening up the odds.[87]

Fighting violent battles throughout the capital, the rebels took control of large parts of Paris, determined to hold on until the advancing Allied forces arrived. However, Allied Supreme Commander General Dwight D. Eisenhower feared that Hitler's order "Paris must not fall into enemy hands except as a field of ruins" might be carried out if the ancient city were attacked. Considering Paris far too valuable historically and culturally to risk its widespread destruction, he decided to bypass it altogether on his push toward Berlin.[88]

The Allies' inability to coordinate efforts with the rebels inside the city further complicated the situation. Communists, Fascists, and other French radical groups were all fighting among themselves for power. Eisenhower didn't want any part of French politics and was already suspicious that Free French Army leader General Charles de Gaulle would use the liberation of Paris for political advantage, declaring himself head of a new French government.[89]

In the end, none of it mattered. De Gaulle and the French Army defied orders and headed there anyway. With his hand now forced, Eisenhower had no choice but to go along and sent Patton's Third Army to join the French in the Battle for Paris. To their surprise, the Resistance leaders in the capital struck a temporary ceasefire agreement with General Dietrich von Choltitz, commander of the German garrison, halting most of the fighting before the Allies even arrived.[90] While more than 500 civilians and nearly 1,000 French Resistance fighters died in the uprising, von Choltitz's unexpected surrender, disobeying his Führer's command to leave Paris in ruins, cut short the mass destruction Eisenhower feared from an attack, leaving the city mostly intact.[91]

Controversy still surrounds the German commander's motives for sparing Paris. He claimed to have done so out of his love for the city, believing Hitler was insane to have issued such an atrocious order in the first place. However, von Choltitz's brutal treatment of the people of Paris throughout their four years of Nazi occupation suggests otherwise. His surrender was more likely the result of seeing the handwriting on the wall. Hugely outnumbered by the Allied forces marching toward the city, his troops would have been devastated had he chosen to oppose them. And if the commander had followed through with Hitler's orders, he'd have undoubtedly experienced a much different fate from the Allies. Instead of becoming a POW, eligible for release at the end of the war, the War Crimes Tribunal likely would have subjected him to prison time—or worse.[92]

Hollywood later portrayed von Choltitz as a humanist, hero, and the savior of Paris. French Resistance fighters and many other Parisians found this characterization offensive, claiming he killed and brutalized the people of Paris throughout the German occupation, then later tried to alter history so it would shine more favorably on him.[93] Regardless, the general's actions spared Paris. His decision not only saved thousands of lives, but also preserved the historical and cultural treasures of the famous City of Light. The people of Paris were so excited to be liberated from their long German occupation that they began a parade for de Gaulle and the Allied Troops even before shooting in the streets had ceased.[94]

The Five still hadn't flown since arriving on the Continent. Boredom was setting in, and they were growing restless, eager to get into the combat flying rotation and take a crack at the Germans. Bad flying weather and too many pilots with seniority kept them out of the sky. Adding insult to injury, their mail was waylaid somewhere as well.

Sitting around with little to do made time creep by slowly. Don spent endless hours stooped over a makeshift wooden crate writing letters to Laura Jeanne. Always using his fountain pen, rather than a pencil with an eraser, required him to organize his thoughts carefully before putting pen to paper. Remarkably, he made few mistakes, seldom crossing out a line or a word.

Over the next few days, their CO had the "new boys" spend time with each of the various squadron departments at the base:

I'm sitting in front of the tech supply tent getting acquainted with the guys and enjoying the sun. There still isn't much for us to do. Today I carved my name and serial number on the back of the bracelet you gave me. I also inscribed "Laura Jeanne" on it—for sentimental reasons.

On September 4, Don's number finally came up. Even though it was only a training mission and didn't count as combat time, he couldn't wait to climb into the cockpit of a P-47 again and take to the skies over France.

While assigned to the communications department the next day, Don spent his time listening to the radio, getting all the latest war news and hearing good old American swing music. That night, he used up the last of the stationery he'd brought from England in a letter he wrote to Laura Jeanne:

> *I quite enjoyed myself today, but that darn music made me terribly lonesome for my favorite dancing partner. That's the first time I've listened to a radio for a long time.*
>
> *We still exist on K-rations. They consist of several "hard" heavy crackers, orange-lemon powder or coffee powder & sugar, and an indigestible fruit bar or some type of candy. Occasionally, we get chocolate, a stick of gum, a can of cheese, or some kind of meat. It's quite repulsive to say the least. The congressman who said K-rations were pretty good should be made to live on them for a few days.*
>
> *We do have a good breakfast, though. We have our own cook at the château, and he makes the best darn hot cakes, fresh eggs, and sausage every morning.*
>
> *I have hopes of visiting Paris. They're starting to give out passes to officers to visit there now. They say it's really a beautiful city. So if I get the chance—it's off to Paris I go.*

Several days later, bored, with little to do, and completely out of writing paper, Don talked Jerry and two other Jabo Angels into quietly slipping away for a visit to the nearby city of Chartres:

> *What do you think of my new blue stationery? I was a bad boy today! They wouldn't let me fly, and I was kind of tired of things in general, so I went out the gate and thumbed my way to a nearby city—of course the city was "off limits" to military personnel, but that didn't bother us. A couple of other guys went along too and fortunately one of them could speak fluent French.*

We looked the place over and did a little shopping—that's where this stationery came from. Fifty single sheets like this for 100 francs ($2.00). Expensive? Yes, but I was plenty lucky to get any at all and then I would be writing on that tissue paper I mentioned once before!!

Anyway, I got some nice pictures for our scrapbook. I also visited a very beautiful cathedral while there. And that's all there was to our little escapade! So, other than the fact that I left the field without getting permission and visited an off-limits city, I wasn't a bad boy after all.

I've got to go for now. Bob just challenged the Missourians to a game of pinochle.*

Jerry only bought half as much stationery as Don during their AWOL trip to Chartres. It was more than enough, though, since he wrote fewer letters. While Don composed long love letters to Laura Jeanne nearly every night, Jerry usually waited until something "letter worthy" happened before getting out his fountain pen. His letters took him much less time to write since he didn't have to wordsmith a thousand different ways to say, "I love you, miss you, think about you always, and don't know how I can live without you," as Don did.

In his next letter to his mother, written on the "ritzy" stationery he bought in town, Jerry expressed his disdain for the British role in the ETO. While seemingly harsh in his criticism, his feelings represented those of most American soldiers fighting in Europe:

The news about the war we're getting is certainly good, but we probably hear less than you folks back home. The only news we get is that picked up on the radio from BBC,** and some of it really burns me up! The English talk like they're winning the war all by themselves. They report that the

---

*   A card game popular with U.S. soldiers serving in the ETO during World War II. Ironically, German immigrants originally brought the game to America. Played with a unique deck of forty-eight cards, up to four players attempt to accumulate points by wining tricks or by melding a combination of cards. A meld of the Jack of Diamonds and the Queen of Spades is known as "Pinochle."

** British Broadcasting Corporation, the public-service radio broadcasting station for the United Kingdom

Americans just sort of follow behind the English drives. Of course, they're all diplomatic about it.

The real truth is the English were dug in their own foxholes at Caen so deep that they couldn't see out. The Americans swept down from Normandy and then east past Paris and north into Belgium, badly outflanking the Germans, while the English just stayed at Caen. Then the BBC reports about a terrific British victory! Nuts!!

The Australians and the New Zealanders won the war for the British in North Africa, and the Canadians are doing more good than them in the invasion now. I'll take the French any day to the blasted English. I read in one of our magazines, "The English are the only people that brag about their modesty." Well, that's a load off my chest, and about enough for now.

During their AWOL jaunt, Don and Jerry discovered that the ancient city of Chartres had suffered extensive damages from both the Germans and the Allies. But the beautiful Gothic Notre Dame Cathedral of Chartres Don wrote about somehow escaped the ravages of war, appearing much as it had in the Middle Ages. Parishioners stored away several of the church's famous stained glass windows for protection; otherwise, it was as if the war had simply passed it by. That wouldn't have been the case if it weren't for Colonel Welborn B. Griffith, Jr., an operations officer with Patton's Third Army.

As Allied troops closed in on the city, they came under heavy artillery fire. Suspecting the Germans were using the church tower to locate and target approaching Allied forces, Command issued an order to shell the historic basilica. Troubled by the looming destruction, Colonel Griffith challenged the order, volunteering to go behind enemy lines to ascertain if the Germans were actually occupying the cathedral. Under cover of darkness, he stealthily approached the church and climbed the bell tower. Relieved to find it empty, he safely sneaked back to his unit. Based on the colonel's new intelligence, Command rescinded the order, sparing the cathedral. Shortly after his return, the battle to liberate the city began. On the outskirts of Chartres, within sight of the ancient cathedral he'd just saved, Colonel Griffith was killed.*[95]

Although Don's impatience with his non-participating role in the war continued to grow, he hadn't lost his sense of humor:

> *Well, your hubby is still living the life of a country gentleman! It's quite dull, but easy to take—kind of like a pilot's rest camp! I don't even know if there's a war going on. I hear rumors to that effect, but as yet I haven't been able to confirm them. I'm still waiting around to go on my first mission.*

> *When our kids ask, "Daddy, what did you do in World War II?" I'll just blush and say "Well, I played a lot of pinochle, and flew over Paris and dropped gumdrops to the poor kids in the city." Won't I be embarrassed? I didn't even drop gumdrops!*

> *I never told you about our good friends the bees, did I? You remember how I wrote to you about the cockroaches in Texas? They were fairly good sports, and didn't insist on eating from the same plate and at the same time we were eating. But these damn bees are another story. I wouldn't care if they'd stand on the edge of the plate and eat toward the center like gentlemen. Instead, they insist on getting right in the middle and taking the choicest food, of which there's very little! Believe me, honey, you really have to eat fast to get your share. Competition—there's always competition!*

> *It's an unusual day—warm and sunny for a change. Reminds me of early autumn in the Rockies. I'm down at the line sitting on an old broken-down sofa with the rest of the boys watching the French people go by—walking, riding bicycles,*

---

* After learning of Colonel Griffith's brave act, Chartres citizens placed a plaque on the street near where he was killed. Confused which name on his dog tags was his first and last, they guessed wrong, putting it backward on the marker. Over fifty years passed before a local historian discovered the mistake and informed Griffith's surviving family members of his heroic deed. The Army later awarded Colonel Griffith both the Silver Star and the Distinguished Service Cross.

and a few in cars. I'm studying the Army French booklet they gave us and learning a few words and phrases, but my French isn't too good yet. We have a hilarious time trying to make the little French kids hanging around the base understand us.

We don't have much recreation over here. Our Ping-Pong table is broken, and playing football is too much work. Sounds like a lazy outfit, huh? Kenny still gets us to play catch quite often, though. I think he sleeps with his mitt on. You could probably put me in my place quite easily 'cause I'm getting kinda soft. Of course, I wouldn't succumb without a slight struggle, but then I'd be at your mercy.

———————

Patton's push across Western Europe placed too much distance between his Third Army and the 368th Fighter Group, forcing another move closer to the frontlines. After receiving relocation orders from Allied Command, the 368th prepared to move again.

Top to bottom: Jerry, Bob, Kenny, Pat, Don

FOURTEEN

Laon, France

Laon is an ancient city perched on a rocky hill overlooking the sandy plains of northern France, first settled more than 3,000 years ago. The Romans controlled the strategically located city for several hundred years until the Goths overthrew the Roman Empire in the fifth century. Its medieval buildings, cathedrals, and abbeys reflect the architectural influences of both occupations.[96]

Near the end of World War I, the Germans used a horseshoe-shaped, grassy military field, known as the Laon Aerodrome, as a makeshift airfield. During the Battle of France in World War II, the Luftwaffe seized the aerodrome, turning it into a major air base, launching night bombing raids over England and interceptor flights against RAF bombers flying missions deep inside the Rhineland. Beginning in 1943, the enemy airfield became a regular target for Eighth Air Force heavy bombers. However, the Germans stubbornly held on until unrelenting attacks by Ninth Air Force B-26 Marauders and P-47 fighter-bombers paved the way for Patton's Third Army to capture the strategic airfield.[97]

Before retreating, Luftwaffe demolition teams blew up nearly everything of value. In another remarkable feat, the Ninth engineers had Airstrip "A-69" ready for the 50th and 368th Fighter Groups to move into just four days later. Six fighter squadrons of 156 P-47 Thunderbolts made Laon-Athies a fighter-bomber attack base to be reckoned with.[98]

In less than three weeks, the Five had pulled up stakes three times, moving across France from Normandy Beach almost to the Belgium

border. Although they'd each flown training missions, none of them
had yet flown a combat mission. That was about to change. Several
flying slots had recently opened up, and not because any pilots
had returned stateside, like Don's tennis buddy Mark Boyle. There
were no more early releases, regardless of the number of missions
flown. The openings came from attrition, as tenured pilots in their
squadron ended their war early, permanently freeing up their place in
the lineup. The Ninth Air Force was losing a staggering 227 aircraft
each month—nearly 23 percent of its fighter force.[99] On September
11, Don wrote:

> *Things are really in a mess around here from another move,
> and we're just trying to get settled in again. Other than that,
> very little is happening that I can tell you about. Is that pin-
> up picture of you on its way yet, honey? I'm so damned
> discouraged with the mail system in the ETO! Sorry, please
> excuse the French, but I don't understand why we aren't
> getting any mail!*

> *In your last letter, you asked me about snooker and wanted
> to know if it includes gambling. So, you don't like it if I lose
> our money gambling, eh? Gee, honey, do I really have to tell
> you? Well, here's the dope. Snooker is a lot like pool, only
> it's played on a bigger table with smaller holes for pockets,
> so it's more of a game of skill. And yes, we gambled! But we
> just played for a shilling (about 20 cents), and I only played
> three or four games while I was in England. Anyway, you
> don't have to worry about your hubby gambling at Snooker
> anymore—'cause I'm cured! Pinochle is now my game!*

> *I had my weekly bath tonight in the coldest darn water—burr!
> When I get home, I want to lay in a nice warm tub full of
> water and have a tray filled of your delicious cooking in front
> of me…and if you can find a tub for two, so much the better.*

The next day, Special Services set up the outfit's mobile movie
equipment, giving the men a welcome break from the daunting tasks
surrounding a relocation move to a new air base:

> *I just returned from seeing a movie all about cowboys and
> rattlesnake murders, etc. And for a change there were several*

fairly nice looking cowgirls! Yippee-ki-yay! The picture strayed from the screen a couple of times, and as usual each reel ended just as something exciting was about to happen. Other than that—a wild time was had by all!

It isn't quite as nice here as at our last place. I rolled up the new mattress I found at the château and brought it with me on our move. It fits and feels darn good on my cot—but I think I could probably sleep on a cement floor, with no blankets, in the middle of winter, if I had to.

My laundry was really starting to stack up on me again, and you know how much I hate washing clothes! Now I just throw everything in a sack and some wonderful French people pick it up and do our laundry. Of course, it costs us plenty—but I'll pay anything to get out of doing it myself!

The pinochle games between Utah and Missouri continue to go on as our main pastime. And I might add that my unique and peculiar style of game seems to baffle our opponents. I'm not bragging—I'm just a good player, and that's all there is to it. Sharp and I won 4 out of 5 games today, and there was some real skill involved too. That's quite a way to fight a war, huh? I'm getting so I have to back up to the paymaster when I take my monthly wage! But I think I'll earn it before this is all over with.

The guys all said to tell you hello, so "hello." They also said that they'll kick me out of my own room, if I don't sign off and turn the "blankity-blank" lights out. So it's goodnight, my darling.

On September 15, the waylaid Army mail truck finally found its way from Normandy to the new air base at Laon, interrupting Don's card game:

Happy days are here again! I received seven letters today, and all of them were from the most wonderful little lady in the world. We were playing pinochle, as usual, when the mail clerk clobbered us with all kinds of precious mail. I haven't enjoyed myself so much for a long time. Now, I have lots of news, and a lot of questions to answer.

In your most recent letter, you said you're still having health issues. Darling, you've simply got to take better care of yourself and have the doctor find out what's causing all your stomach problems. That's an order!

Everything is fine with me. I can hardly wait for the homemade candy that you said is on the way. Sounds like you've been reading a lot of good books. And you and Kathryn are playing a bit of tennis, huh? Better get in good shape, because I'm going to challenge you when I get home.

Well, it looks like I'm heading to Paris in a few days! I can't wait. I'm going to buy you an anniversary present, although it probably won't get to you until a little after the wonderful day has passed. I had to tell you about it now so you'd know when the day arrives that distance and circumstances caused it to be belated.

Our rations are still the same. I don't think I'll be able to look at any hash [diced canned meat, potatoes, onions and spices all mixed] for quite some time after the war is over. We're living in a kind of shack or something, but it's dry and fairly comfortable. The days are getting shorter now, and it's starting to get a bit chilly.

Jerry became the first member of the Five to fly an actual combat mission, part of a twelve-plane-flight escorting B-26 medium bombers to Metz, France. Cloud cover was thick, forcing the Marauders they chaperoned to drop their bombs through the overcast, while Jerry and the other P-47 pilots flew protective top-cover. Their flight went on alert when Command radioed that German bandits had been spotted near their target area.[100] Jerry wrote:

I wasn't nervous when we took off, and I wasn't scared when we were flying over German occupied territory, but I was mighty scared when the guys in our flight called in bogeys!* My heart came up in my throat, and I about went blind trying

---

*   Bogey was a military slang word for unidentified enemy aircraft.

to see them. I was afraid that the Germans would climb on my tail, but they weren't in our vicinity. I never looked around so much in my life as I did that day.

There was no flak shot at us. Captain Gibson was leading my flight, and I was flying his wing. He said I did a nice job, so that made me feel quite good. I hope I get enough missions to earn the Air Medal before the war is over here.

In such situations, fighter pilots appreciated the long white silk scarves they wore when flying. While they *were* rather stylish, fashion wasn't the main reason pilots wrapped them around their necks in a Windsor knot. Their wool shirts had a tendency to scratch and itch, and the silk scarfs helped protect them from chafing against their collar, especially when they were looking for bandits and their neck was moving around like a bobblehead doll.

The rest of the Five took to the skies September 17 on their first combat mission, dropping bombs in a corridor the 368th pilots had sarcastically nicknamed "Happy Valley" because of its high concentration of anti-aircraft installations.[101] Kenny flew first, part of the early flight that morning. Following his debriefing, he told the guys:

Our mission was a bit rough. The flak was intense and accurate, and was exploding really close to us. I was pretty scared and just glad to get back home.

Bob took to the air next. After returning, he made the first entry into what became his unofficial and *unauthorized* mission report log, writing:

West of Koblenz, we ran into too much weather to fly through, so we did a 180. As soon as we started turning around, all hell broke loose. We were at 5,000 feet and the flak saw that we stayed there. I finally made a dive toward a train and dropped my bombs. I missed the train by forty or fifty yards, but I think I scared someone.

You just can't imagine the terror you feel the first time you fly over enemy territory and experience intense flak. I was one scared chicken.

On the last mission of the day, Don and Pat got their first crack at the enemy, bombing factory buildings and a railroad-marshaling yard, then flying an armed recce* on their return trip to the base. Don recounted:

We dropped our bombs on our assigned targets, then made several strafing runs on a train our flight leader had spotted. I was pretty nervous the entire mission—flak was light on our flight, but still scary. I just tried to do everything the flight leader was telling me to do and was relieved when I made it back home safely.

German anti-aircraft guns were the most dangerous enemy fighter pilots faced in the European Theater. Firing shells ranging from 20mm to 155mm in diameter, they claimed far more casualties than Luftwaffe fighter planes. The Wehrmacht** towed their mobile anti-aircraft guns behind a jeep, truck, or half-track, even horse-drawn wagons, while the biggest weapons were positioned in large, specially made concrete towers. But the biggest danger for the fighter pilots were the guns mounted on trains, often covered up, hidden from them as they attacked from the skies.[102]

The Germans called their anti-aircraft weapons and the destructive shells they fired *Fliegerabwehrkanone,* or *"Flak,"* for short. Exploding in violent puffs of black, greasy smoke with orange fireball interiors, flak shells didn't require a direct hit to be effective. If they detonated anywhere near their target, they sent enough destructive metal shrapnel flying in all directions to penetrate the hull of any size plane at altitudes up to 48,000 feet. Encounters with flak rattled the most seasoned pilots. Just seeing the black puffs of *ack-ack* was frightening enough—but feeling his plane lurch upward from a nearby flak explosion was something no pilot ever got used to.

---

* Short for armed reconnaissance missions, which often followed a bombing, or other specific mission, where fighter pilots were usually looking for targets of opportunity.

** Designation for Nazi Germany unified military forces from 1935–45.

On September 17, under the leadership of British Field Marshall Sir Bernard Law Montgomery, the Allies launched their largest airborne attack of the war, code-named *Operation Market Garden*. The mission objective was to capture a strategic bridge crossing the Rhine River at the Dutch city of Arnhem. Montgomery's plan called for 35,000 British and American Airborne paratroopers to be dropped near the bridge-crossing in a surprise daytime assault, while the British Second Army attacked eastward on the main road leading toward them. The endgame was to control the bridge and position the Allied armies for a rapid advance to Berlin, with the hope that it might hasten the end of the war. It was a complicated plan, layered with risks.[103]

The success of the operation depended heavily on the accuracy of British intelligence, and on Montgomery's ability to predict German Command's response to a surprise, daytime airborne attack. In addition, the plan relied on effective coordination of Allied air and ground communication and support. While most officers at SHAEF initially supported the plan, Eisenhower became concerned when Montgomery scoffed at his battle strategy suggestions and troop requirements. The ever outspoken General Patton also expressed reservations, questioning the operation's overall strategy and apparent lack of fighter-bomber support. Montgomery discounted their concerns and ignored their advice. Even worse, he downplayed his own intelligence reports about the size and experience of the German SS* Troops guarding Arnhem, arrogantly underestimating the enemy's strength and resolve to defend such an important military asset.[104]

The U.S. 101st and 82nd Airborne Divisions, along with their counterparts from the British 1st Airborne, were among the best-trained and most experienced soldiers in the Allied Army, making them an obvious choice for the operation. Airdropped on schedule, the crack troops parachuted safely to their designated locations, but after that, nothing went as planned. Badly outmanned, outgunned, and in over their heads, the paratroopers fought fiercely, turning back the German elite SS Troops attack after attack, struggling to hold on

---

*   *SS stood for Schutzstaffel, meaning Protective Squad in English.*

until the British Second Army could meet up with them. However, they also were under siege from all sides, unable to advance.[105]

Bad weather, faulty air-to-ground communications equipment, and inept coordination between the RAF and U.S. Army Air Forces kept Allied fighter-bombers grounded throughout much of the battle, further dooming the mission to failure. Poor planning and problematic execution during the battle led to a myriad of logistical problems, keeping the paratroopers and ground troops from getting the equipment, supplies, and ammunition they critically needed, even leaving them unable to evacuate their own wounded.[106]

After ten days of intense fighting and more than 16,000 British and American casualties, the SS Troops forced the last of the Allied survivors to surrender. The devastating loss at Arnhem validated Eisenhower's concerns and proved Patton's assertion that effective close air support was crucial in military operations against the Germans. Unwilling to acknowledge any of his planning or coordination failures, Montgomery called the operation "ninety percent successful." Others considered the outcome of his flawed plan an "utter disaster."[107] The failed operation gave Hitler a badly needed victory, along with additional time to try to turn the tide in his favor. The war against Germany wasn't going to end early.

———————

Command cancelled all 368th Fighter Group missions on September 18. Officers who had their trips to Paris nixed because of the group's unexpected move to their new base were given day passes to visit Reims. Considered "the next best thing to Paris." Going there was a welcome diversion for Don and Bob, especially after just surviving their first brush with German flak.[108] Don wrote the following after returning from their short leave:

> *Kelly is off to Paris on leave. He's only 20 and I think the Army took him right off his mother's apron strings, if you get what I mean. He's such a darn good kid, and as clean as they come, but not too well acquainted with the jesting ways of the ordinary Army man. I'm a wise old man of 21, and I understand everything! Can I help you with any of your problems?*

A while back, some of the boys were sharing ideas on moral standards that kind of riled him up, and he wasn't the least bit shy defending his principles—and he has plenty of 'em too. He didn't realize that they were intentionally egging him on, trying to get his goat, so to speak. There are some things that you have to get used to and learn to ignore in the Army. You live the way you believe you should, and pretty soon the guys respect you for your standards and outlook on life. Kelly understands that now and gets along great with the guys. In fact, most of them treat him like their kid brother.

Sharp and I got the day off and nearly walked our legs off seeing the sights in a nearby town. The old cathedral we visited today is an amazing piece of architecture. The park and the grounds were beautiful. Their different designs with various kinds of flowers and plants made a rather romantic spot to be walking with my favorite girl. I even mentioned that fact to Sharp, and he readily agreed. He's quite in love with a gal named Louise in Salt Lake, even though she doesn't know it. He's not too forward when it comes to women, and he'd just as soon she didn't know how he really feels. I guess he wants to wait until he gets back and can do something about it.

Just before we left, we heard a little French orchestra giving out with some real solid swing! They had a captain from the Air Corps playing the trumpet, and man was he ever good! The place was right on the sidewalk—half indoors and half outside. We enjoyed a few tunes, then took off for home.

The ancient basilica Don and Bob visited in Reims was the famous National Cathedral, constructed in the thirteenth century. Besides the remarkable architectural design and stunning gardens Don wrote about, the beautiful Gothic church played an important role in early French history as the site where thirty-three French monarchs were anointed and crowned.[109]

As fall arrived, the Five gradually worked their way into the 397th regular flight rotation, generally flying wing for one of the more experienced pilots in their squadron. Kenny Kalen became the first member of the Five to shoot down an enemy aircraft, a twin-engine Me-410 (Messerschmitt).[110] His score gave the new boys something to talk about that night between hands of pinochle.

On September 21, Don and Bob were back in the air again as part of a sixty-three-plane mission flying close air support for the 7th Army Corps in the Koblenz sector. Bob flew top-cover for some 47s while they destroyed six tiger tanks and damaged two others. Don's flight dropped their 500-pound bombs on the West Wall, causing significant damage, then attacked a nearby railroad, taking out four locomotives. It was a good day for the 368th—no flak, no casualties, and lots of damage to the enemy.[111]

Two days later, the Five flew with the second flight the 368th Fighter Group sent into the Rhineland, successfully cutting seven of the eight rail-line targets assigned to them.[112] Don wrote:

> I was flying wingman for my flight leader, Captain Russ O'Connell. We dropped our bombs on a railway trying to split some tracks. Later, we spotted a train and made several strafing passes at it. Captain O'Connell and I jointly strafed the locomotive until it ruptured in a cloud of steam.
>
> We ran into a Luftwaffe flight of a few Me-109s and Fw-190s on our way back home, but we didn't have enough gas left to chase after them. I was pretty nervous when we flew into enemy territory, but once our mission started I was okay. Flying was exciting, tiring, and scary all at the same time. Returning back home was always a big relief.

Since the American Civil War, railroads have been one of the greatest weapons of war. Germany recognized the importance they would play in the Second World War and built extensive railway systems to support its military—carrying everything from troops, tanks, artillery, guns, and ammunition, to food and medical supplies. Keeping these essential cargos flowing to their frontlines was crucial for the Nazis to win the war. And stopping them from getting there was one of most important duties of the Ninth Air Force fighter-bombers.

German trains were well defended by troops, artillery, and large anti-aircraft weapons positioned on specially made flak cars. Many of the toughest gunfighting battles of the war weren't the air-to-air combat kind made popular by the media, but rather the down and dirty fights between fighter planes and trains. P-47s weren't the only planes that bombed and strafed trains and railways, but the Thunderbolts did it best—and the pilots of the 368th Fighter Group excelled at it. Locomotives were hard to destroy, requiring fighter planes to fire their machine guns at perilously close range. Taking one out was a big deal. It stopped the whole train, leaving the rest of the rail cars and their cargo at the mercy of the fighter planes. Attacking trains, cutting rail lines, and dive-bombing railroad marshalling yards was dangerous business—the rewards were high, but so were the risks.

Between rainstorms on September 24, having just learned that Command had cancelled his upcoming leave again, Don unloaded his frustrations on Laura Jeanne:

All my plans for presents are shot—again! It makes me so darn mad. This is the second time that my turn came around, and I didn't get to go either time. With that news and getting no mail for so long, my morale is bucking a new low.

Today marks three long, painful, lonely months since I left you at the train station in SLC. Life is pretty rough when you go day after day with no mail. I write and write, but nobody answers me! I know you're writing, it's just that the mail delivery in this outfit isn't worth a darn! In fact—this whole outfit is messed up in many respects.

It's been raining off and on for days. Results?—lots of mud, cold, and no flying. We turned our watches ahead an hour the other day, so now it's dark about 7:30 p.m. The days are getting shorter and colder too. I keep plenty warm, though, so don't worry about me.

We have no PX and no rations either. About three-fourths of the outfit is going crazy because they don't have any cigarettes or candy. That, and the weather, kind of puts everyone in the dumps. And worse yet, I've been busy most of the day running to our little "outhouse." It seems that I have a slight case of dysentery—commonly known over here as the "G.I.s"!

Sorry I'm complaining so much, but it makes me feel better— well, not really. But don't worry, your hubby will get along fine and try and get what he can out of his stint in the Army.

After sleeping in the following morning, the Five decided to go exploring to break the monotony. After returning, Don wrote:

Well, it's another dreary dismal no flying day! We didn't have anything to do, so we've been trying to find "Jerry" souvenirs this morning. They seem to be maniacs for underground installations. They were still digging when we rooted them out of here. They left behind quite a bit of food and stuff—not very tasty. Got a patch from a jacket and enclosed it in this letter. I think all members of the "Luftwaffe" wear this insignia. I'm going to try and get some German pilot wings too.

I've had a good look at the Germans' best two airplanes—the Me-109 and the Fw-190. They're both single engine fighters and pretty smooth-looking jobs, but don't compare to the P-47.

Just before lunch, Command released the entire fighter group for the rest of the day, not requiring them to return until the next morning. The Five, like most of the guys on base, took off for Reims. That set back a propaganda mission originally scheduled for the day. Periodically, the air forces dropped leaflet bombs over enemy territory urging German soldiers to surrender. The flyers read almost like a travel brochure, portraying the Wehrmacht situation as hopeless and painting an optimistic picture of becoming a POW—promising excellent food, good medical services, pay for work, and for some, an expense-paid trip to the United States.[113] While some German soldiers decided this was a better option than living in a foxhole, slogging around in the mud, most remained loyal and unswayed. Ironically, Hitler was much better than the Allies at the propaganda game, convincing most of his troops they were winning the war.

A new cold front, accompanied by strong winds and rain, moved across Belgium and Western Germany, keeping the entire 368th grounded the next several days. Don spent most of his free time answering questions from Laura Jeanne's last letter:

So you're wondering if I have a plane of my own, huh? Well, the answer is "nope." Only about half of the guys have one they can call "theirs." The rest of us just trade around. I'll have to work my way further up the ladder before I'll have my own. Then I'll get a paintbrush and go to work painting "Torchy" on her!

When we do fly, we're mostly dive-bombing and strafing. You might say we're the "ramrod" for the infantry and the tank corps! But when we're on the ground, we're mostly arguing over a pinochle game!

I paid a visit to Reims again yesterday and got pictures of the cathedral and some other interesting sites of the city. I'm still studying my French Language Guide, but after stumbling all over myself in the city, I'm about ready to give it up for a bad job.

After two weeks without mail, Don received a record nine letters— one from his mother, seven from Laura Jeanne, and a newsletter from BYU, rescuing his spirits from an all-time low.

I sat down at the line and read a couple of letters, then went up to our shack, lay on my sack, and enjoyed reading the rest. I have to admit that a few tears crept into my eyes while I was reading your precious letters. I just can't explain what they do to me. You're without a doubt the best letter writer in the world! I wish I could put my love for you in words like you do. If I could, then you'd tingle from head to toe.

I'm relieved to hear you're feeling better. Keep going to the doctor until your stomach trouble clears up, OK? Now to your questions and comments: You wrote, "Have you made very many friends? Are the women attractive over there?" And my favorite, "Well, my sweet, you be very, very, careful. I hear quite a few tales about those French women, and I don't want you to go getting involved!"

I couldn't help but laugh, honey! Yes, I've made some very good friends. The English women aren't nearly as attractive as the French gals. And yes, I'm a faithful hubby. I might whistle at some curvaceous gal (like my lovely wife) under my breath, but that's as far as it goes. You might call me the "Wolf with a bark and no bite." Sharp and Kelly belong to the same club!

Sorry, but after being away from civilization for some time, we find that an occasional "bark" might come out! Don't ever worry about me being true to you. I saved myself for twenty years for the right girl, and now there isn't anyone else but you—and never will be.

French moral standards seem to be lower than those we're accustomed to back home. There are brothels in all the cities—generally with long lines of soldiers. Someday I'll tell you more, but right now, I've said enough to give you an idea of what goes on. But don't worry, honey. I would never do anything to threaten the faith and trust you have in me. Just remember…I'm loving you always.

A few days later, Don was able to talk a few of the boys who'd been on leave to Paris out of some "Chanel" perfume—for the right price. He boxed it up with a scarf purchased on his last trip to Reims, then shipped it off to Laura Jeanne as a belated birthday and anniversary present.

While the men in the 368th were stuck in their barracks waiting for the weather to clear, an advance-engineering group from the Ninth Air Force struggled in muddy weather conditions to rebuild what they thought would be their next air base at Le Culot, France. Then, in midstream, Air Command changed its mind, redirecting them instead to the recently captured airfield at Chièvres, Belgium, where the runways were in better condition. The 368th would soon be on the move again.[114]

Back home, Laura Jeanne was trying to fill the huge void left in her life when Don went off to war. Separated from her husband and saddled with an uncertain future so soon after being married was a lot for a nineteen-year-old girl to handle. Still, she had no regrets, and given a second chance, she would have done the same thing again. Reflecting on that challenging time, she wrote:

Our routine at 90 North Center Street didn't vary much from when I used to live there. Mother was still teaching school, giving piano lessons, and directing the Lehi Chantante Ladies Chorus. Daddy was still working the graveyard shift as a railroad telegrapher and running the DR&G Railroad station in town.

Lehi War widows Club. Laura Jeanne on top row, 4th from right

Staying as busy as possible helped the time pass more quickly for me. When I wasn't working, I did a lot of sewing and knitting and even started taking piano lessons again. I also taught young girls in our church YWMIA.* Eventually, I

---

* The Young Women's Mutual Improvement Association (YWMIA) was the name of the Church of Jesus Christ of Latter-day Saints' young women's organization set up to teach moral values and provide wholesome activities for girls ages 12–18. Laura Jeanne was close to the same age as the girls she taught, having been a member of the organization the year before.

joined what we called the "War Widows Club," a group made up of twenty ladies whose husbands were off fighting in the war. During the time we were together, six of our members lost their husbands defending our country's freedom.

But my favorite pastime was writing to my beloved husband. I lived for Don's letters and news of his whereabouts. He couldn't tell me very much about his flight missions, but I followed the war closely in the newspapers, magazines, and newsreels. Each letter I received from my "Mr. Lt." renewed my hope and faith that he was still alive.

I loved him so very much, and felt as though I wouldn't want to go on living if anything happened to him.

Laura Jeanne constantly worried about Don's safety, easily seeing through his attempts to convince her he was seldom in harm's way, that he usually just flew "milk runs."* The weekly movie newsreels showed fighter planes shot down over Europe, descending in flames, and crashing before the pilot could parachute to safety. Imagining the same fate for her husband kept her awake at night—worrying and missing him most during that state between wakefulness and sleep.

Living with daily apprehension likely contributed to the intestinal disorder she developed. Her struggle with pain and discomfort became a serious worry for Don. After several doctor visits, a brief stay in the hospital, x-rays, and a number of tests, her doctors finally diagnosed her with ulcerative colitis.

---

*   World War II Air Force slang meaning an easy bombing mission.

Adolf Hitler

FIFTEEN

Hitler and the Rise of the Third Reich

Adolf Hitler was born into a poor, dysfunctional Austrian family on April 20, 1889. Although he had a close relationship with his overprotective mother, Adolf grew distant and combative with his abusive, alcoholic father, who died when he was thirteen years old. He made few friends at school, and most of his teachers considered him just an average student. Uninterested and underachieving in many of his classes, he dropped out of high school to pursue his dream of becoming an artist. With his mother's encouragement, he applied to enter the prestigious Vienna Academy of Art, but the admission board rejected him when they learned that he'd left school early. At age sixteen, Adolf Hitler appeared destined for mediocrity.[115]

Three years later, his mother died of cancer while under the treatment of a Jewish physician, leaving him orphaned. The distraught Hitler held the Semitic doctor responsible for her premature death. The following year, he reapplied to the Academy, this time presenting a portfolio of his artwork as evidence of his talent. Bitterly disappointed when the art school again refused admission, Hitler blamed his rejection on a Jewish professor sitting on the acceptance committee who disliked his drawings, further inflaming his growing indignation for this "non-Aryan inferior race." Despite his Academy rejection, the future Nazi leader still pursued an art career, living on the streets of Vienna for four years with little financial success. His passion for art continued throughout the rest of his life. During World War II, he built an unrivaled art collection by stealing thousands of the greatest pieces of artwork ever produced.[116]

Shortly after Germany invaded France to begin World War I, Hitler enlisted in the German Army. He fought for four years, was wounded twice, and was awarded the Iron Cross (Germany's second highest military honor) on two separate occasions. Embittered by German leaders' lack of courage and willingness to surrender, Hitler joined the swastika-waving National Socialist German Workers Party (Nazis) after the war. He became their rising star and traveled across his homeland, giving public speeches and rallying support for the radical movement. Impatient with the party's slow progress, he spearheaded the Munich Putsch in an attempt to take control of the German state of Bavaria, hoping to incite a national revolution. Following the failed coup d'état, Hitler was sentenced to serve five years in Landsberg prison as a dissident. During his incarceration, the Nazi leader reinvented himself, dictating his autobiography, *Mein Kampf,* and transforming his political tactics. Surprisingly, after serving only nine months, German authorities released him early for good behavior.[117]

Post-World War I years were a time of great discontent among the German people. Like the rest of the world, they suffered economically from the effects of the Great Depression. In addition, the Allied nations had burdened them with harsh financial terms as part of the Treaty of Versailles, which ended World War I. Germans were required to pay crushing punitive reparations, which pushed the country deeply into debt and hopelessly in default. Germany predictably remained at odds with its enemies from the First World War, creating a perfect storm for a radical idealist to rise to power. With his charisma and spellbinding oratorical skills, Hitler convinced Germans that he was the leader they'd been looking for. Finding his rhetoric and promises appealing and inspiring, most Germans accepted his racial and ethnic policies and methods.

In 1934, Hitler gained absolute power and appointed himself the Führer and Supreme Military Commander. Rallying support to re-establish Germany's fallen empire, he convinced his people that it was their destiny to take back control of their European neighbors, using any means necessary. German-speaking Austria became the Nazis' first target. Hitler annexed his homeland in the spring of 1938 without even firing a shot. The world watched and did nothing, reacting as it had to the Japanese invasion of China in the Pacific. A year and a half later, Hitler made a much bolder move, this time invading Poland. No longer willing to just stand by and watch, Britain and France jointly declared war against the Nazi Third Reich on September 3, 1939.

The German Army dominated the early battles of the war, surging across their Western European neighbors, conquering them one after another, appearing unstoppable. America watched from across the ocean, letting the Nazis have their way, just as they'd done with the Japanese, naively hoping they could sit on the sidelines and not get involved.

Before invading Poland, Germany entered into a nonaggression pact with the Soviet Union, agreeing to divide the rich spoils of Europe while not attacking each other. It was only a ruse on the Führer's part. Once most of Western Europe was under his control, Hitler succumbed to greed and turned his gaze east toward Russia and the asset-rich countries lying between them. Ignoring the advice of his key generals, who warned that waging war on two battlefronts simultaneously was reckless and unsustainable, Hitler broke his pact with Russian leader Joseph Stalin. On June 22, 1941, Germany launched *Operation Barbarossa* and attacked the Soviet Union with more than three million troops. The betrayal became the largest land invasion in the history of the world—and Hitler's biggest mistake of the war.

The Führer predicted a swift and decisive victory over Stalin's Red Army. But he greatly underestimated the strength of the Soviet Army and the will of the Russian people to protect their homeland, just as Napoleon had done a century before. In the beginning, although outnumbered nearly three to one, Wehrmacht forces rolled across Russia, just as they'd done in Western Europe— plundering, murdering, raping, and scorching towns and villages as they advanced. The well-trained German armies slaughtered millions of untrained and poorly equipped Soviet soldiers and citizens, taking more than five million prisoners as they advanced toward Moscow. Then, just when Russia was teetering on the edge of defeat, fate intervened. Japan bombed Pearl Harbor and awakened a sleeping giant. America entered the war, forging an unlikely alliance between the Allied Nations* and the Soviet Union. That pact, combined with the timely arrival of brutal Soviet winter weather conditions, enabled Stalin to mount an effective defense, halting Hitler's infantry and tank battalions. Now, after three years of intense fighting, the massive Red Army had turned the tables and was winning more and more of the bloody battles fought on the Eastern Front.[118]

On the Western Front, the tide had turned against the Third Reich as well. The British and Americans had captured Italy, and the Americans were advancing across France and Belgium, driving the Germans back toward their own border. Hitler's key generals had little influence on his decisions, and most had lost confidence in his military leadership. Fearful of incurring his wrath, however, few disagreed with him, at least in his presence. Those who did generally suffered the consequences. The behavior of this once charismatic idealist who had captured the hearts and minds of an entire nation had turned unpredictable, irrational, and troubling. A few senior military officers in Hitler's inner circle feared he was losing his grip on reality, even his sanity. Seeing no other options, they began secretly plotting against him to try to save their homeland. On July 20, 1944, they made an attempt on his life.[119]

Around noon, the Chief of the German Army Reserve entered a high-level meeting being held at Hitler's "Wolf's Lair,"** carrying a bomb concealed in his briefcase. He placed it underneath the large wooden table near Hitler's seat, then quietly left the room. In a quirk of fate, a Nazi staff officer pushed the briefcase out of the way, moving closer to Hitler for a better look at the map he'd unrolled on the table. A few minutes later, the device exploded, killing four Nazi leaders—but Hitler wasn't one of them. Though seriously wounded and badly burned in the explosion, he eluded death.[120]

Consumed with vengeance and an extreme sense of paranoia, the Führer vowed to end the conspiracies against him. Under his orders, Nazi SS Troopers arrested more than 7,000 Germans suspected of taking part in plots to overthrow him. Many of the accused were

---

* The Big Three Allied Nations were the U.S., England, and Russia. Other Allies included Free France, Canada, China, the Netherlands, Norway, and Yugoslavia. The Axis Powers were composed of Germany, Italy, and Japan.

** Hitler's secret military headquarters located deep in the forest of northeast Poland.

innocent, but it didn't matter—nearly all of them ended up dead. Most were executed; others were forced to commit suicide. Even the legendary and idolized war hero Field Marshall Erwin Rommel, aka the Desert Fox, was implicated in the botched assassination attempt. Out of respect for his military service, authorities gave him the option of taking cyanide to avoid the embarrassment of a public trial. He agreed and the German press reported that he died from a brain seizure, covering up his suicide. Convinced he'd been saved by "an act of providence," Hitler boldly predicted, "Nothing is going to happen to me....The great cause which I serve will be brought through its present perils to a good end."[121]

Between June and September 1944, German military casualties exceeded 1.2 million dead, wounded, or missing in battle. In the five years since they invaded Poland to begin the war, German casualties numbered an astounding 3.3 million. To counter the catastrophic loss, Germany dropped its volunteer age to sixteen, increased the conscription age to sixty, and lowered the physical standards for frontline duty. The Third Reich's once unstoppable war machine was bogged down, under siege, and in retreat. And the German people, like the besieged Londoners on the other side of the English Channel, were now subjected to constant day and night bombing attacks. Under such desperate conditions, only a leader completely bereft of sanity could believe he was still capable of victory.[122]

Instead of focusing his efforts on defending his homeland from invasion, or trying to negotiate an end to an unwinnable war, Hitler opted to do just the opposite, believing that the course of the conflict might be reversed by a stroke of military genius. At a gathering of his military advisors and chief of staff that September, he revealed his *inspired* reversal strategy: "I have just made a momentous decision. I shall go over to the counterattack." Then, while their Führer unrolled the map on his desk, his stunned leaders watched in disbelief as he pointed to a marked spot and said, "We will attack here, out of the Ardennes, with the objective of Antwerp."[123]

Hitler was convinced that a surprise counteroffensive, striking at the heart of the Allied forces, would either cause them to surrender or force them to accept a negotiated peace accord. He detested the Western Allies, especially the Americans, considering them militarily inferior to his own armies and less of a threat than the Red Army advancing from the East. Even if the Allies didn't buckle under pressure of a surprise counterattack, Hitler believed such a move would buy him additional time, still making the risky attack worthwhile. Given enough time, he was completely certain that German scientists and engineers would develop enough super weapons to bring him victory on both fronts of the war.[124]

Nazi weapon development programs were further advanced than their American and British counterparts, causing great concern among Allied leaders. The Germans had been designing and developing amazing weapons at Peenemünde, a secret, futuristic research facility located on the Baltic Coast. The installation housed hundreds of Germany's top research scientists and physicists charged with developing superweapons, including the creation of a nuclear device.

Many of the weapons designed at the facility were decades ahead of their time. One of those was the Me-262, the world's first operational jet, a revolutionary new aircraft capable of flying 540 mph. Hitler could have used the Messerschmitt jets to defend his people against the Allied bombing raids now decimating cities throughout Germany. Instead, hell-bent on going on the offensive, he gave orders to convert them to fighter-bombers—a huge mistake that further delayed their production and kept them out of the air when they were desperately needed for defense. Only three hundred of the jets ever made it into combat.[125]

The Peenemünde scientists also developed a devastating new supersonic rocket, one much more accurate than the V-2 flying bombs they were launching on London. In addition, they developed the Taifun, the world's first anti-aircraft missile. Traveling at speeds in excess of 2,200 mph, this space-age weapon was capable of shooting down even the highest-flying Allied bombers in ten seconds or less. In another unbelievable strategic blunder, Hitler delayed its development, viewing the missile as defensive in nature. [126]

In August 1943, British pilots discovered Peenemünde. Subsequent RAF bombing attacks leveled the facilities, killing many of Germany's elite research scientists. The Nazi secret weapon development programs moved underground and resumed, but never fully recovered from the setback. Unrelenting Allied bombing, dysfunction created by the extreme secrecy and isolation of the weapons programs, politics, and Hitler's poor decision making all combined to keep Germany from mass-producing their most advanced, deadly superweapons. Had they done so, it might have changed the outcome of the war.

The Siegfried Line, or West Wall, was a defensive line extending along the German border for more than 390 miles, interlaced with more than 18,000 bunkers of all types and sizes. Huge ramparts had been constructed in certain areas along the wall, consisting of permanent forts, flak towers, and heavy concrete pillboxes. These massive structures had outside concrete walls up to eleven feet thick and were heavily fortified inside as well. Attacks from Allied aircraft—heavies, medium bombers, and fighter-bombers—generally resulted in only superficial damage to the fortifications. German propaganda depicted the West Wall as indestructible, and so far, it had been. The Germans were now fighting with their backs to Berlin in defense of their homeland and were no longer retreating. Dug in, standing their ground, the Wehrmacht had turned the battle at the Siegfried Line into a stalemate.[127]

The Five—Don (Far left), Jerry, Bob, Pat, Kenny

SIXTEEN

Chièvres, Belgium

The Gauls settled the ancient city of Chièvres, Belgium, in Gallo-Roman times. For centuries, people made pilgrimages to visit a fountain and shrine known as Our Lady of the Elder, made famous by miraculous healings that reportedly took place there. Parishioners later built a chapel to house the beautiful Gothic-style statue and legendary spring, but the sanctuary was destroyed in 1789 during the French Revolution. Worshippers later found Our Lady hidden in the ruins and placed her in the Church of Chièvres for protection.[128]

During their occupation of France during World War I, the Luftwaffe started constructing a military air base near the town, leaving their partially completed airfield behind when they lost the war. Neglected and unused, it reverted to farmland until the late 1930s when the Belgian government resumed construction on the abandoned airfield. The Germans recaptured the airfield during the Battle for Belgium, this time finishing their project—constructing runways, hangars, barracks, and several massive anti-aircraft blockhouse towers. Chièvres wound up eight times larger than the Belgians originally planned and became one of the major Nazi air bases in Europe.[129]

Following the Normandy Invasion, Chièvres became a main target for the Allied Air Forces, undergoing relentless attacks from Eighth and Ninth Air Force heavy bombers for nearly two years. In late September 1944, P-47s from the Ninth delivered the coup de grâce and forced the Luftwaffe to abandon the airfield. German demolition crews blew up and destroyed everything of value as they retreated. Undaunted, the Ninth engineers moved in and took over—reconstructing buildings, patching airstrips, filling in bomb craters, and making the base fully operational within a week.[130]

"Fully operational," however, didn't include heated living quarters, electricity, indoor plumbing, or hot water for showers.

——————

On October 2, the 368th Fighter Group completed the final leg of its move north to Chièvres Airstrip "A-84," putting the pilots 125 miles due west of Aachen, just minutes from the German border. The guys were back to living in a tent, using flashlights, and bathing out of their all-purpose helmets. But they didn't complain, knowing they had it far easier than the boys on the frontlines, who were often stuck sleeping in the same muddy trenches they fought from.

Our tent — fourth on the left

The Five flew together that morning, part of a thirty-six-plane mission targeting a double-track railroad used to transport German troops to the West Wall. Thick clouds covered their initial target area, so the P-47s orbited, waiting for the skies to clear. After half an hour, control gave up and vectored them to a secondary target site.[131] Bob recorded what happened next:

We flew through the weather—assigned to cut some railroad tracks west of Bonn. It was a messed up mission from the start, but our bombing results were good. We strafed two trains that steamed a good deal, and we cut the tracks up in eight places. One of my bombs hung up, then my tach went

bad as I pulled off my bomb run. Luckily on the way home,
I safely dropped my other bomb. I don't know if it was over
friendly or enemy territory.

Whenever bombs didn't drop after a pilot hit the release button, he tried his best to shake them off. If that failed, he went into a steep dive, then sharply pulled back up, hoping that gravity would help the bomb work itself free. Sometimes nothing worked—forcing the pilot to land with the bomb still attached to his wing—hoping it wouldn't jar loose during landing. When it did, the bomb generally exploded, nearly always killing the pilot.

The following day, the weather took a turn for the worse, forcing Command to recall the only flight that got in the air. The Five spent most of the day laboring in the mud, helping get their new base organized, and setting things up in their tent. After Don returned from mess that evening, he wrote Laura Jeanne the following short letter:

It's night and very dark, except for a small beam of light
coming from my flashlight. We've moved again and have no
lights at our new base. I do get around, don't I?

The Five—Kelly, Sharp, Kalen, Patrick, and I—are all in the
same tent. It isn't like a room in the Waldorf, but there's
something over our heads, and we have a good hard cot to
sleep on. And I have the nicest sleeping bag. It surely is cozy
and warm. It would be kind of crowded for the two of us, but
I wouldn't mind.

I understand they have good ice cream here in Belgium, and
I'm all for trying some. Remember when we used to go for
ice cream after a dance or a show? Those were the days. Have
to let Sharp use the light now—so it's goodnight, sweetheart.

Jerry spent that night in the operations trailer, taking his first turn as "officer of the day" (OD). Generally, the radios were quiet at night and there wasn't much to do. Staying awake was usually the hardest part of the assignment. To pass the time, the guys ate whatever they could find in the officers' mess tent, listened to the radio, and wrote letters using the staff typewriter. The manual machine hadn't fared too well in its three moves from Normandy Beach to their current makeshift airfield, as Jerry soon found out:

Operations trailer

....

dear mom,

it's pretty darn cold here at night. last night i slept with seven blankets over me, and i also had my wooly jacket thrown over my feet, and still wasn't too warm. if you have trouble reading this it's because the typewriter in here isn't working the way it should and won't make capital letters.

i'm prepared for the cold tonight with woolen socks, heavy winter woolen flying boots, and my winter flying suit. kalen tells me that i'll need every bit of it. he was od last night. sharp, kalen, evans, patrick, and I have been working on our tent all day, and with everything we've done, it ought to be quite cozy. we put in a wooden floor, and kalen and patrick found an old stove that we can make very good use of. they're over putting the thing in working order now. it won't be so bad once we get a stove in.

it's dark outside now. i've been typing by flashlight ever since the first paragraph and eating some of the pilots candy ration while i've been sitting here. there's a bit of fudge—not good—

and some sort of hard candy that tastes pretty good, and i don't get any pimples from that kind of candy. my mail still hasn't come through—of course i don't blame you. you've been wonderful about writing, but our mail system is so poor that nobody gets any. i have no mail from later than september 8.

i sure hope this war won't be a winter campaign. it will be awfully cold over here for boys in tents. i sure hope i'm not one of them.

On October 4, the 368th targeted railroad systems located east of the Ruhr River in Western Germany. Four flights of P-47s from all three squadrons took off late in the afternoon, flying through soupy skies with limited visibility.[132] Don wrote the following about his toughest mission to date:

Captain William Gibson from the 397th Fighter Squadron was leading the way in the center—flying his first mission as a group leader. The 395th flew on the left, and the 396th flew on the right, making forty-eight aircraft. I was flying wingman for 1st Lt. Pat Murphy, the element leader of our flight and a good friend.

The group entered low clouds at about 3,000 feet and started climbing. By the time we reached 6,000, the visibility wasn't more than a few feet. In dangerous situations like this, we flew close formation, trying to stay within sight of our flight leader. It was his job to do the instrument flying and navigating. At 10,000 feet, still in near zero visibility, we encountered a thunderstorm and severe turbulence. Making matters worse, German radar detected our flight group and started pounding us with their anti-aircraft flak guns.

The strong winds in the thunderstorm were bouncing us around pretty good, making it nearly impossible to stay in close formation, especially for those of us flying wing position. Several planes had to abort and headed back home. The rest of us kept climbing—trying to get above the turbulence and the dense clouds.

At about 15,000 feet, I watched as a strong gust of wind pushed Murphy's plane nearly on top of Gibson's. Murphy had to slide to the right to avoid colliding with him. Instinctively, I pulled to the right to give Murphy enough room to get out of the way, barely avoiding a collision with him. Then I peeled away and dove downward into the overcast toward the ground. Murphy later told me that Gibson's wingman couldn't hold formation and his propeller cut into the Group Leader's aircraft right behind his cockpit, causing them both to go down.

The crash triggered a chain reaction, forcing other planes to peel off from the group like I'd done to avoid further collisions. I held my breath as I continued diving more than 11,000 feet down toward the ground, praying that I'd soon break into the clear. At about 3,500 feet, I finally came out of the clouds and leveled out.

A few minutes later, Murphy radioed for us to fly counter-clockwise and regroup above the clouds. Around 20,000 feet, I finally broke through into clear blue skies and located part of our Squadron. Murphy told me he couldn't believe it when I reappeared next to him. After dropping our bombs through the soupy weather below us, we turned around and headed home.[133]

Captain Gibson died in the crash. His wingman fared better, safely bailing out, but landed behind enemy lines and spent the rest of the war as a POW. Don demonstrated an ability to keep a cool head when things happening around him were "not as briefed," showing some heady flying skills during the unnerving incident.

The Five loved to fly and got excited every time they climbed into a P-47 cockpit. However, flying combat missions also elicited other emotions, ranging from preflight jitters to being, as Bob wrote, "one scared chicken." Although most fighter pilots experienced anxiety at some point during their missions, they had more than enough bravado to cover it up. These audacious twenty-somethings flew alone, operating not only as pilot, but also as navigator, bombardier, machine gunner, and radio operator. It took dedication and bravery to report to the line each time their name was called, dive at every target they were assigned, and fly their plane through intense flak. Besides being fearless, fighter pilots had to control their emotions in the heat of battle to do their job and stay alive.

Going fast and being aggressive seemed to be part of every fighter pilot's DNA, as proven by their crazy antics in the air and on the ground. Early in training, they sought out mock dogfighting opportunities and played combat with Air Force heavies. Then there were the crazy bicycle firing passes and crashes in England, followed by the tank and motorcycle races on Normandy Beach. Even now, they still buzzed the tower, knowing beforehand that it would get them a reprimand—or worse. Bob summed it up best, writing:

I firmly believe that fighter pilots are a different breed. Those that couldn't handle the dangers and risks and fear that come with combat missions had long ago been weeded out. There were no cowards among us. I didn't know of any case where someone failed to take off, or aborted, or came home early because they were cowards. Our guys only came back early when they had engine trouble or had been shot up. Then one of us would be assigned to fly back to the base with them, since we tried to stay together in twos as best we could for our protection.

We were almost like Kamikazes—full ready to take the risks that came with being a fighter-bomber pilot. Were we ever scared? Yes, but very focused. The adrenaline level got very high when you were engaged in combat with an enemy fighter or on a dive-bomb run or coming in low and fast on a strafing pass. When you're pulling five Gs with full power and munching thru the tops of trees, you're breathing hard and sweating, and things happen fast.

We just tried to stay alert to every surrounding and focused on the task at hand. Seeing a plane get hit by flak and blow up in a cloud of white smoke or watching one of the guys in your squadron hit a telephone pole while strafing and just plain crash and die made that hard to do—but you had to do it to stay alive. Did we take risks? Yes, lots of them—but most of us didn't seek them out.

Those who did seek them out acted as if they were invincible, facing risky situations with a "why not?" attitude, believing they were probably going to die sooner or later in the war anyway. That mentality either earned them medals or got them killed, or both. Fighter pilots required lightning-quick reflexes and instincts to do the right thing in the heat of combat. Both were innate abilities that couldn't be taught, but they *could* be enhanced with enough experience and training. Experience was the big variable. All fighter pilots would get some experience—but it was elusive and required Lady Luck to get very much of it.

A few days later, it was Don's turn in the operation's trailer, which fortunately now had both heat and lights. Off and on throughout the night, he gave Laura Jeanne a play-by-play account of his all-nighter in the wheelhouse:

It's almost midnight, and you're probably wondering why I'm up so late? Well, I'm in a warm, cozy, little hut surrounded by beautiful women, and I have food an arm's length away. And I'm the only man here with all these women—wow!! Some of them are dressed in rather daring apparel too, such as negligees and swimming suits. Should I go on?

You're probably going to hate me for this, but I felt it was only right that you should know what your hubby does in his spare time. So here goes! I'm OD tonight, and I'm in our operations shack. The beautiful women are pin-up pictures, and yours heads the list! The food was secured from the pilot's kitchen nearby—on the sly, of course. Aren't I mean?

It's 2 a.m. now, which is far later than I've stayed up the last three months, and I'm getting pretty sleepy. I just took time out for a cheese sandwich and some canned grapefruit. A little earlier this evening, I had some sardines and pineapple juice, and enjoyed it immensely.

It's 4 a.m. now, and I'm sooo tired and sleepy! We had a pretty rough mission yesterday, but I got home safe and sound, so don't worry. It's clear and beautiful outside right now, and the moon is shining brightly—quite romantic in a sleepy sort of way. Surely makes me lonesome for my Jeannie.

My hands are kind of sore with a few slight burns here and there. We've been having a little trouble with our tent stove, so this morning—I guess yesterday morning now—I took out the hot coke and went to work on it. I finally conquered the situation, and now we have a fine working stove again! You probably didn't know I was such a handyman, huh? You'd be surprised, my sweet!

Please keep a stiff upper lip, honey, and don't let your lonesomeness get you down. I know exactly how you feel 'cause I'm in the same boat. And to make matters worse, I've only received mail three times since a week before I left England. And do I miss it? You bet your life I do!!

The Five's luck turned the next day. The weather cleared and the Army mail truck finally delivered, as well as picked up, the mail for a change. That afternoon, Bob and Jerry were part of a thirty-five-plane fighter sweep targeting the Düren-Düsseldorf area, near the western German border. Bob wrote the following in his secret mission log:

Our flight flew top-cover at 20,000 feet as the medium bombers blew the heck out of the whole area. A lot of bogeys were called in, but we didn't see any. The Germans threw up an awful lot of heavy flak at us and the B-26 Marauders— intense flak.

While Jerry's squadron was flying over their assigned patrol zone, the controller called in bogeys and vectored them to an area east of Bonn, where they engaged several German fighter planes in air-to-air combat. Jerry wrote:

I was flying Lt. Soo's wing when he shot down a Me-109. Mom, remember when I told you that we fight in pairs? Well, I kept Soo's tail clear of enemy fighters while he shot this guy down.

When we got back, Soo was happy, and I was happy, and everybody in the 397th was happy. I sure hope I can be an element leader in a couple of months or so. A wingman, if he

*does his job right, doesn't get much chance to shoot at any
enemy planes.*

The 396th squadron leader was flying near the same sector as
Jerry that afternoon when he saw a German plane slip through the
overcast, land, then taxi to a dispersal area. Dropping down to check
things out, he stumbled across more than fifty Me-109s and Fw-190s
parked on the field. The Thunder Bums made several strafing passes
and attacked the German aircraft with everything they had. By sunset,
the 368th had its biggest day ever, destroying or damaging thirty-five
enemy planes while suffering no losses of their own.[134] After missing
another battle with the Luftwaffe, Don wondered if he'd ever set his
sights on an enemy fighter plane:

> *I've been having pretty long hours as of late—up at 5 a.m. for
> briefing and breakfast when I fly an early mission. Everything
> is going well, except for the ache in my heart to be with you.*
>
> *I only have eight missions to my credit, which isn't much for
> the length of time I've been here—but I think things will pick
> up soon. I haven't seen too much of the German Luftwaffe
> yet, but some of the guys in our unit had a great day against
> them yesterday. I'm still waiting for the chance. And don't
> worry, honey, when I do, I'll be good and plenty careful.*
>
> *I like Belgium more than France. It seems to be quite clean,
> with lots of farming and patches of forest here and there,
> and a little more modern than France or England. They even
> have jukeboxes in their cafes playing good old American
> recordings. Sharp, Kelly and I are going into town one of
> these days to sample their famed ice cream and pick up a
> few souvenirs.*

At mail call on October 8, Jerry hit the jackpot. After reading
his long-awaited letters, he pulled out his fountain pen and began
writing to his mother:

> *Hooray! I got six letters from the States today, and they
> were full of questions. First, I can't tell you much about the
> missions I go on. I was over Germany yesterday, quite a ways
> inside too. I had some serious engine trouble and was pretty*

scared, but I finally got my T-Bolt running smooth again by the time I got back to the field. I love that plane. When I have one of my own, which I don't yet because there are quite a few more pilots than planes, I think I'll name it ZZZZT [the sound of bees].

I'm having lots of fun now. No kidding, Mom, you'd have to go a long way to find a bunch of guys that have more fun than the boys of the 397ᵗʰ FS.

I'm going to a briefing in a little while. Evans and I are on the mission this afternoon. And just so you won't worry, I'll leave this letter unsealed till after I get back, and add a line when I do, just to let you know I'm OK.

P.S. I'm back safe and sound.

Don and Jerry were part of the second mission that day, bombing strategic targets the VII Army Corps controller had marked with smoke near the Hürtgen Forest in western Germany, where a major ground battle was raging. After successfully dropping their bombs, they conducted a fighter sweep, searching for enemy airfields and plane dispersal areas. They were unable to locate any enemy aircraft, but they did find a German supply train and destroyed the locomotive and a dozen railcars in strafing attacks. The Germans threw up a lot of flak during their attack, but it wasn't accurate and there were no casualties. It was a good day for the 368th; all the 47s made it home safely.[135]

Back home in the States, campaign elections were one month away. On October 9, the 368th Fighter Group set their postal tent up as a voting site and encouraged the men to fill out absentee ballots. The turnout was great, as you'd expect from men who were putting their lives on the line to defend their country's freedoms.[136] President Franklin D. Roosevelt, affectionately called "Uncle Frank" by many of the servicemen, was running for an unprecedented fourth term. His continuing struggle with polio was taking its toll, now causing him to lose weight and appear haggard in public appearances. From somewhere deep inside himself, he found the courage and stamina to lead the nation through the stressful days of a world war.[137]

Roosevelt's ascension to the pinnacle of government in the United States seemed even less likely than Hitler's meteoric rise to power in his homeland. Born into New York aristocracy and graduating from Harvard Law School, Roosevelt seemed destined for success. But at age thirty-nine his crippling disease forced him to drop out of the public eye and begin a lengthy rehabilitation process. In the 1920s, society looked down on paraplegics, seldom employing them, even placing them into asylums. The president was determined that would *not* be his fate. Resolute in overcoming his disability, he vowed to walk again, something no one thought possible. Revitalized from his therapy and energized with newfound purpose, Roosevelt rose to power on a timetable remarkably similar to that of his German nemesis, Adolf Hitler.[138]

In 1933, Americans were still reeling from the Depression years and were as desperate as the Germans for a different kind of leader, one who understood them and could feel what they were going through. Roosevelt met both needs. Unlike Hitler, he wasn't a powerful and spellbinding public speaker. In stark contrast to the Führer, President Roosevelt spoke to the people as a friend, becoming famous for his Sunday night radio "fireside chats." There was little doubt he'd be re-elected for a fourth term, especially with the country in the midst of a world war. As expected, he soundly defeated Thomas E. Dewey that November in a landslide victory.[139]

Used to waiting weeks between letters, Don was surprised when his name came up again at mail call two days later. He wrote back to Laura Jeanne that same evening:

I'm glad that you're doing so well on your new job at the OPA, honey. Sounds like your brother is getting settled in after his new assignment. I was glad to hear that his eyesight won't allow him to go overseas, even though he wants to get over here. The war is different than I thought it would be—I wish none of us had to be here.

Our chow is a little better now. We even have hamburger or roast once in a while. I think it's horsemeat—but it's meat, and better than what we've had. Reminds me of what I recently read in the ETO magazine, "Boy this is such a good piece of meat! It's so tender you can cut it with a knife!" Ha, ha!—wasn't a very good joke, was it?

For the second time that week, Jerry struck the mail mother lode, receiving eight letters, causing even Bob to raise an eyebrow. Some of them were dated as far back as August:

Mom, we don't get many missions like you thought. I only have six missions to my credit, so you can see that we don't do very much flying. I expect another one tomorrow morning or afternoon.

It's raining now, and we have a nice warm fire going in our little stove. Sharp is already in his sack sleeping, Evans is writing a letter to his wife, Patrick is out in the latrine, and Kalen is in England on a Five-day flak leave—so that's where our little household is. We've all had OD in the past week— so our tent is fairly well stocked with food now. Evans and I are going to split a can of grapefruit in a little while.

The following day, despite socked-in skies, Jerry flew with the 397th on a combination bombing and ground support mission, followed by an armed recce. After nearly destroying a small town just outside Cologne with their 500-pound bombs, they provided close air support to Patton's VII Army Corps ground troops, wreaking havoc on some nearby rail lines, where Jerry was credited with taking out several railcars.[140]

Crossing the Siegfried Line

SEVENTEEN

Battle of Aachen

Rumors of thermal hot springs with healing powers attracted first-century Romans to the North Rhine area of Germany. Finding the spas and beautiful river valleys to their liking, they founded the ancient city of Aachen, which later became home to Charlemagne, the "Father of Europe" and former Emperor of the Holy Roman Empire. In the late seventh century, he oversaw construction of the famous Aachen Cathedral, where more than thirty German Emperors and Kings were crowned. Besides enjoying its spas, Europeans admired the city's Gothic architecture, prestigious universities, and beautiful fountains. While it didn't hold any great strategic value, the city was an important symbol to the German people—one worth fighting, even dying for.[141,142]

The Third Reich propaganda machine assured Aachen residents that the impenetrable German West Wall and the garrison of troops stationed inside the city would safely protect them from the Allied armies gathered along the Siegfried Line. Aachen's 165,000 citizens were shocked when the U.S. First Army unexpectedly broke through, triggering a chaotic mass evacuation of the city, with Nazi government officials leading the way. By early October, fewer than 20,000 remained inside the city walls.[143]

Under duress, the German commander at Aachen chose to negotiate terms of surrender, rather than see the beautiful ancient city destroyed. Hitler was incensed when he learned of his leader's decision and what he perceived to be the cowardly exit of the city's Nazi officials. In a fit of rage, he had them arrested, stripped them of their rank, then sent them all to the Eastern Front as privates—a virtual death sentence.[144]

The Führer hastily reinforced his garrison with experienced *Panzer* and *Waffen-SS** soldiers, making it clear to his new commanding general that "Aachen must be held at all costs."[145] The reinforced German Army dug in and began aggressively defending the city—even launching successful counterattacks against the invading Allies. Thousands of casualties mounted up on both sides as the bloody urban conflict raged on, with neither side gaining much of an advantage. On October 10, the First Army finally had the city surrounded and gave the Germans an ultimatum to surrender, or they would destroy the city. Knowing that Hitler would never agree, the new Nazi commander refused the capitulation offer and prepared for the worst.[146]

On the morning of October 11, more than 300 Ninth Air Force planes dive-bombed and strafed the historic city, carrying out the previous day's threat. While Jerry was leading a training mission with some of the new boys who had recently joined their squadron, the rest of the Five flew with the 368th in the air attack against Aachen. After dropping over seventeen tons of bombs on roads, buildings and houses, they strafed line after line of Wehrmacht and SS ground troops, leaving their entire target sector in flames. Thousands of terrified German soldiers tried to flee the burning city to escape the devastation.[147] Bob recorded the following in his mission report log:

This was just my fifth combat mission. The group flew to Aachen to help beat up the city. Our ground troops marked our targets with red smoke. Some Germans gave up and tried to surrender just before we went down—but our orders were to attack—so we did. We strafed on our bomb runs to reduce the morale of the enemy. No flak. Aachen was given 24 hours to surrender, but didn't, so this was the result.

After safely returning from Aachen, Don wrote to Laura Jeanne:

I had a pretty good mission today, but can't tell you much about it—only that it was successful. On a brighter note, I received three more letters from my wonderful wife while I was gone!

---

* Military arm of the Nazi Party.

I bought myself a Xmas present the other day while on a pass to Mons—a silver-metal wristwatch band. It's pretty good looking, and it only cost 200 francs (about $4). I couldn't leave without getting something for you too. What did I get? Oh, I can't tell you 'cause that would ruin the surprise.

It sounds as though you keep pretty busy, honey. We do a lot of waiting around for missions and stuff. I finally sent my laundry out again. Which reminds me, will you please send me a couple of washcloths and soap so I can keep my face clean? And we could use a couple of pinochle decks too— we've about worn out the ones we've got!

While "pretty good" and "successful" were accurate descriptions of Don's mission that day, they fell far short of the whole truth and in no way portended the effect the Aachen incident would have on him. Twenty years later, sitting around a campfire in the mountains with his sixteen-year-old son and a few close friends, Don opened up, answering questions about his wartime experiences—something he'd rarely done since returning from the war. Staring into the fire, he spoke somberly:

On one mission, we were ordered to destroy an entire city, and we killed a lot of German soldiers defending it. After that mission, I better understood how men on the frontlines must have felt when they set their sights on an enemy soldier—up close—and then had trouble pulling the trigger.

On my strafing runs that day, I could see the panic in the soldiers' faces. We were ordered to fire on them, even after they'd given up and were trying to surrender. It was a bloodbath. We were trained to destroy things, and so that's what we did. You didn't kill people—you just destroyed things. You had to think that way.

Nothing in Don's training prepared him for the death, destruction, and bloodshed he faced in the war. Targets bombed from thousands of feet in the air weren't difficult to view as "things." Even in close-support strafing attacks on tanks, trains, and railways manned by soldiers, he was able to look at his targets as "just things to destroy." But strafing terrified soldiers at close-range with .50 caliber machine gun fire while they were attempting to surrender was something altogether different. They were human beings, with wives, girlfriends, and families—and most weren't sociopaths like Hitler and his radical SS Troops.

Following orders justified Don's war actions but did nothing to help him forget them. Somehow he was able to push the horrific images from experiences like Aachen into the back of his mind, but they were never completely forgotten. He was haunted by occasional flashbacks of traumatic war experiences the rest of his life.

Struggles with killing and bloodshed weren't isolated or uncommon among soldiers. Killing one's own kind doesn't come naturally to any normal human being. However, with effective indoctrination and intense mind conditioning, soldiers can be trained to dehumanize their enemy. Killing without remorse follows next.[148]

Hitler was fanatical about mind conditioning and indoctrination techniques, identifying boys and girls with the greatest potential, then entering them into his infamous youth training camps as early as age ten. By age sixteen, most of them were ready and willing to obey any order they received without question, even to sacrifice their lives. Hitler was equally fixated with indoctrinating his elite Waffen-SS Troops, training them to respond as predictably as Pavlov's dogs.[*][149]

Don dealt with the increasing stress and violence of the war by immersing himself in his letter writing. The endless hours he spent hunched over his wooden writing box allowed his mind to drift back to more pleasant times and contemplate a brighter future.

———————

Admittedly a slow letter writer, Don spent the morning of October 13 finishing a letter to his parents that he'd been working on for most of the week while waiting for the rest of the Five to return from an early morning mission:

---

*   Russian Nobel Prize winning physiologist Ivan Pavlov's experiments allowed him to provoke a salivation response from test trial dogs through conditioning. He placed a ticking metronome near the dogs, starting it at the same time that he gave them food. After enough repetitions, the familiar sounds provoked a conditioned response, causing the dogs to salivate, even when they weren't given any food.

Today is my first wedding anniversary, and it's just my luck to be spending it alone far away from home. I miss Laura Jeanne so very much and can hardly wait to get back home and settle down.

Sounds as though you have most of your fruit put up now, Mom. That must be quite a relief! Mother Nature's hand-painted leaf that you sent me reminds me how beautiful the canyons and the mountains must be right now! The leaves are turning colors over here too. While we were buzzing back from a mission the other day, I noticed how pretty the hillsides were getting.

I guess by now that you probably have a deer to your credit, Dad. Get one for me too! Doggone, I surely do miss hunting season. I wish I could tramp the hills with you, but I'm a little busy at present with an even bigger game hunt! Hope I can get my limit soon and finish up this worldwide tour.

Throughout the day, the 368th Fighter Group continued pounding Aachen and the railways supplying the city. German flak seemed to be getting worse now with each mission, and the group's pilot casualties were mounting. The 395th Panzer Dusters lost their captain and two lieutenants that day, one the men remembered as Black Friday.[150] Waiting down at the flight line later that morning, Don was relieved as he watched each of his buddies touch down safely on the tarmac.

At 3:00 p.m. that afternoon, sitting on the edge of his cot positioned between his two best friends, Jerry filled his fountain pen with fresh ink and began composing the last letter he would ever write:

13 October 1944

Belgium

Dear Mom,

I was out over Germany again this morning, but I can't tell you much about it. The flak was thick, though. I'm back safe and sound—so no need to worry about that one.

There's not much to write about today. The snapshots I told you about will probably be ready tonight or tomorrow, so I'll send them as soon as I can. I'm very tired now. We were up at 5:00 this morning to be in time for the briefing. I'm going to snooze a while after I finish this letter.

Oh, I forgot—when we don't fly, we mostly just sit. We have a few duties like censoring some mail each day and eating chow and going to the show at night, but most of the time we're free to snooze if we want to. That sounds good, doesn't it? It is. I usually go to bed around 10:00 p.m., and get up at 8:30 a.m., so you see I'm getting enough sleep—except when I'm on an early mission.

I'm sorry for this wretched letter. I'll do better next time, I hope. All my love, Jerry

Jerry filled his fountain pen for the last time

Later that night, on the eve of his first wedding anniversary, Don struggled to keep his emotions in check as he started writing to Laura Jeanne. Taking his time, he deliberately considered each word before putting pen to paper:

One year ago today, at just this time of evening, I entered the small church in San Angelo, took you by the hand, and we walked down the aisle together. What a perfectly wonderful evening, night, and morning! True, the ceremony was quiet and not very elaborate. But, aside from the day we were sealed for time and eternity in the temple, it was the happiest day of my life! And after that, each day seemed to bring even more happiness than the previous ones.

It's because of you that life means so much to me. I'm ever thankful to the Lord that I've been blessed by the companionship of one so lovely, faithful, trusting, and with such high standards and ideals. There isn't one single thing in the world that I wouldn't do for you, sweetheart, or break my neck trying! You mean that much to me.

I'm so terribly lonesome and miserable tonight because I'm not with you on our first anniversary. I lay on my sack dreaming and reminiscing of days gone by and my heart just about breaks. I guess I sound quite depressed, but I'm not, it's only that I want so much to be with you. Thinking about what the future holds gives me the courage and strength to carry on.

During our first few months, we were robbed of many of the joys of married life by Army regulations. When I get home, it's going to be almost like starting all over again, isn't it, honey? We have so much to make up for, and I think a honeymoon would be an ideal place to start.

I'm a one-woman man, Laura—always remember that. I've pledged my life, body, and soul to you, and I'm living the best I can, expressly for the purpose of returning to you. I pray that we may never have to spend another anniversary away from each other. God bless you, my darling, and take care of yourself. I'll love you forever.

Far across the ocean, Laura Jeanne experienced similar emotions:

My first wedding anniversary was a lonely day spent remembering past events. Don had written there were still a few shops left where the soldiers could buy perfume, lace

*collar and cuff sets, and silk scarves in cities near his air
bases. I was the recipient of all these for our first wedding
anniversary. Since then, Chanel No. 5 has been my favorite
perfume.*

—————

As the autumn leaves began to fall in the ancient woodlands
surrounding Chièvres, the temperatures dropped as well. The Five
stoked their stove up at night, but by morning, the fire had often
died out, leaving their tent chilly from the cold, humid night air. Bob
explained their relighting process, writing:

> *First, we filled up the pot-bellied stove with coke or coal and
> wood. Then we poured some 130-octane gas in the top. After
> that, we stood a safe distance away by the tent door, and
> threw matches at the lower opening of the stove, until one
> hit inside. There was a loud "swoosh" sound when it finally
> lit, then fire would burst out the front of the stove, shooting
> high out of the pipe at the top of the tent where it was vented
> to the outside. It made for quite a sight every morning. We
> were all crazy.*

Grounded again by rainy weather and overcast skies, the guys
passed time writing letters, playing Pinochle, and hanging around
camp shooting the bull. In another attempt to assuage Laura Jeanne's
fears, Don tried to convince her how *safe* he was while flying armed
recces against the enemy:

> *Honey, you have the wrong opinion of what the Ninth Air
> Force is doing. The escort missions you worry about me being
> on are almost always taken care of by the Eighth Air Force.
> We usually do close support work for the ground troops. Of
> course, we have fighter sweeps and stuff, but it's mostly just
> bombing and strafing, nothing for you to worry about. I'll be
> fine—I promise.*
>
> *You sounded quite lonesome and down in the dumps in your
> last letter. Keep your chin up, honey, and don't let yourself
> get into those moods. I know how you feel—I get into them*

myself. But, things are what they are, and that's all there is to it, huh?

Following their first devastating air assault on Aachen, the Ninth Air force continued flying strategic bombing and close air support missions over the city, playing a key role in the outcome. Final victory came at a high cost in men and planes, including several from the 368th Fighter Group. In late October, the last Wehrmacht unit in Aachen surrendered to the Americans, making it the first large German city captured by the Allies during the war.

The defeat at Aachen devastated Hitler and shocked the German people. In one of the bloodiest battles of the war, each side suffered nearly 5,000 casualties. In addition, the Allies captured 11,637 German prisoners. The few remaining inhabitants of the city stared in disbelief as they watched their Allied captors march thousands of German POWs through the streets to prison.[151] The once-beautiful city—Charlemagne's legacy—with its ancient cathedrals, spas, fountains, and universities, now lay in ruins. One American observer wrote:

> The city is dead…; burst sewers, broken gas mains, and dead animals have raised an overpowering smell in many parts of the city. The streets are paved with shattered glass; telephone, electric light, and trolley cables are dangling and netted together everywhere, and in many places wrecked cars, trucks, armored vehicles and guns litter the streets."[152]

In a memorable speech delivered in Aachen early in his political career, Hitler made a prophetic statement: "Give me five years, and you will not recognize Germany again." [153] For Aachen—in the most ironic of ways—his prediction had come true.

After packing his bags, Don began writing his nightly letter to Laura Jeanne, sharing news of his upcoming leave and answering more of her questions:

Well, I'm finally scheduled for a short leave tomorrow. Instead of the usual flak leave to London, we're going to Paris! It looks as though I'm finally going to get a look at the famous capital of France after all. I wish you were going along. I'll write and tell you all about it as soon as I get a chance.

You asked quite a few questions in your last letter. Yes, I got to France the way you asked. No, my sweet, PT isn't part of our routine anymore. The only physical exercise I get is walking around the base, or playing catch with the guys. And about our shower…it's outdoors and is practically useless in this cold weather, so most of our bathing is done from water heated up on our stove in our all-purpose helmet. Can't you just see me trying to bathe in a little helmet that only holds a couple of quarts of water—ha!

On the morning of October 20, Don climbed aboard a canvas-covered Army troop transport truck, excited to begin his long-awaited leave in Paris. As promised, he started writing to Laura Jeanne about his stay in the famous city the day after he arrived.

Well, honey, here I am in gay Paree, staying at a hotel run by the Red Cross. I arrived yesterday afternoon pretty tired from the long truck ride. After a nap, I walked around the city a bit, seeing a few sights, then had supper about 8:30 p.m. I talked with some of the guys from RTU back in Nebraska that I ran into, then hit the sack. What a wonderful sack it was, too—a big, thick mattress with springs and even a pillow! Everything was perfect, except that you weren't there with me.

After completing the introduction to his travel log, Don stopped writing and emptied the ink from his fountain pen, screwed the cap back on, and carefully placed it back into his travel bag. He planned to tell Laura Jeanne all about his trip to Paris in one long letter, but decided to finish writing it after he returned to Chièvres, since Army regulations required the men to post all mail from their base.

Jerry Kelly before last mission

EIGHTEEN
....

"Kelly Didn't Return"

About the same time Don's troop transport truck was taking off for Paris, Bob and Jerry reported to the flight line, part of a seventy-plane mission flying close air support for the 9th Infantry Division fighting in the Hürtgen Forest battle. Their targets were marshalling yards and locomotive roundhouse turntables near Vossenack, nineteen miles southeast of Aachen. Bob wrote the following about their mission:

> The operations officer placed Jerry in Flight Red 2 and me in Flight Blue 2. We were still considered "new boys," so we were assigned to fly with more experienced pilots. We were parked side by side when we started up our engines. We waved at each other as we taxied out to our designated spots and got ready to take off. Jerry moved out to fly wing with Major Hendricks, and I moved out somewhat later as wing for Lieutenant Driscoll.

> My flight was top-cover for the other two flights on our mission. Ground control shot red smoke onto the target, which was in some woods southeast of Aachen. Both flights bombed perfectly, completely disintegrating the smoke. After bombing, my flight got vectored around by the controller, but didn't see anything.

> Jerry's flight found and destroyed three trains and shot up some train turntables. Just as we were ready to start home, Major Hendricks spotted another train with some vehicles on it. He took his flight down, with Jerry at his side and a little behind flying wing, and they both got shot up bad. Hendricks took flak through a prop blade, which also knocked off the

rocker box cover on the top of a cylinder. This threw a lot of oil, made his engine sound bad and cut out, forcing him to return to the base. Before he started back he told Driscoll, "Take over what's left of the squadron and go get that damn train!"

Meanwhile, Kelly had called in saying, "I've been hit, and there's smoke in my cockpit!"

My flight made two more passes at the train, and then started home. The Germans threw up an awful lot of flak and small arms stuff at us. I got hit on the trailing edge of my left flap, but had no trouble making it back home. Control said our bombing was very, very good, and that we did a lot of damage with our strafing. It was a good mission from that standpoint.

When we got back to the base, we just waited around to see who came back and who didn't, and tried to get information about missing pilots and planes. Hendricks made it home. Kelly didn't return.

Major Randall Hendricks was the 368th Fighter Group's most experienced flight leader and a recent recipient of the Distinguished Flying Cross and Distinguished Service Cross medals, two of America's highest combat flying awards. Conversely, Jerry Kelly was one of the "new boys," barely twenty years old, flying only his tenth combat mission of the war. Bob later lamented:

Major Hendricks was known for being aggressive and taking chances, qualities that undoubtedly contributed to earning his two newest medals. He was quick to drag Jerry, an unseasoned wingman, into a dangerous situation. But such were the risks of being a P-47 fighter pilot—all of our missions were dangerous, and flak was no respecter of a pilot's experience or skill.

Don returned from his leave in Paris on October 22 to bad news, first learning that his friend, Lt. Pat Murphy, was missing, forced to bail out over enemy territory after his P-47 was hit by flak. Then Bob stunned him with even worse news—Jerry was MIA, last seen disappearing into the clouds over the small German town of Stadtkyll two days earlier. The guys hoped and prayed that Jerry would surprise them and just show up one day, as other missing pilots occasionally did. But based on the accident reports, they feared it might be a fool's hope. Bob recorded the following additional details surrounding Jerry's disappearance:

> Jerry was close to the ground, going around 400 mph, and only had a few seconds to respond after he was hit by flak. I think the smoke in his cockpit made visibility so bad that he didn't know if he was right-side up or upside down, unable to see anything outside, or even see the instrument panel inside.

> Going so fast within a few hundred feet of the ground, and not knowing which way was up, Jerry probably didn't have much of a chance. Although there was no sight of him bailing out, we didn't know for sure that he hadn't, so that gave us a reason to hope.

The mood in their tent that night was somber. None of them wanted to talk about what had happened—their emotions were still too raw. Bob continued:

> Jerry Kelly was my best friend at that time, and maybe forever. Even though we were both from Salt Lake, I had only met him about April or so. After that, we were inseparable, and possibly insufferable. He was one of the cleanest, most moral, honest guys I've ever met.

> We were together as Kelly's "Five" for about six months. In that time we played a lot of catch, a lot of pinochle, did a lot of talking, flew our assigned missions, and tried to stay out of trouble and stay alive. We all saw what happened to Kelly coming for us too—we just didn't know when.

> We were sad, but as guys didn't come back from a mission, there wasn't crying or memorials. You just got back in your airplane when you were scheduled, did what was expected of you, and hoped you weren't next.

In his memoirs, Don talked about the effect Jerry's disappearance had on the 397th Fighter Squadron:

As the youngest member of our squadron, Jerry was heckled by most of the other men as "a kid away from his mother too soon." But he took their chiding good-naturedly, never lowering his moral standards. The guys knew he was a Mormon, and even though they ribbed him constantly, they looked up to him for sticking to his principles—and even looked out for him like a kid brother.

Seldom did a mission go by but what one or two of our men failed to return. Of course, there was always sadness on these occasions, but in Jerry's case, there was a time of mourning and respect, the likes of which had never occurred before—even when squadron commander Captain Gibson went down.

The Jabo Angels flew several rescue missions trying to find Jerry's plane, but it remained lost, seemingly swallowed up by the rugged, dense Schnee-Eifel woods. The details of his fate would remain a mystery until years after the war ended. His disappearance weighed heavily on the minds of the remaining members of the Five, spurring them to make contingency plans and decide who would take care of their personal belongings and write to their families back home—just in case.

The Ninth Air Force experienced one of the highest casualty rates in World War II. Death surrounded fighter-bomber pilots. In the short time the Five had been together in the 368th, they'd seen pilots in their fighter group die from fire and flak in the skies, from crash landings, and from hitting trees, telegraph poles, and flying into the ground on strafing runs. They'd also witnessed their own troops on the frontlines accidently killed as well, inadvertently caught in friendly fire during close air support missions.

Attempting to escape the sad events he'd returned to, Don aimed his attention at Laura Jeanne, and finished telling her about his recent trip to Paris:

I got up bright and early Saturday morning. Incidentally, "bright and early" was about 10:30 a.m. After breakfast, Captain Krause (he's one of our flight leaders) and I went to town to do some shopping and sightseeing. We decided to go together since we're both married, and have a little more in common. My buddies are all in different flights than I am, and so it's hard for us to get passes at the same time.

There were lots of pretty gals! Paris has far more women than men. But they're getting back to a more normal life now, and didn't come running to our truck and shower us with love and kisses like they did right after being liberated. The women are a little more bashful now, and you have to give them that "come hither" look before they grab you. Don't worry, honey, I left all my "come hither" looks at the Salt Lake train station four months ago.

Paris 1944

Back to the subject, Paris is quite a city. The subway is very modern, although crowded, and it saved us a lot of shoe leather. The city is still blacked out at night and the streets run every which way, making it easy to get lost. I visited the Notre-Dame Cathedral, Arc-de-Triomphe, and saw the Eiffel Tower, and many other things and places. I also visited the Louvre Museum, which is very famous for its sculptures and ancient Egyptian relics—such as mummy cases, mosaics, statues, etc.

I got some more perfume and a box of powder for you. I thought you might like a sample of what the French women use. I also bought bottles of perfume for our mothers and sisters. Tell them that's my Christmas present, OK?

We had dinner that night at the hotel and sat around and talked with some of the boys, then hit the sack. The next day we started back home.

Several lines had been blacked out in Don's most recent correspondence to Laura Jeanne. She knew that all overseas mail was censored during the war, but the thought that someone had violated their privacy still upset her. Military postal workers, whose motto was "loose lips sink ships," were often overzealous in their protection of national security. It was highly doubtful that Laura Jeanne's returned graduation photo or the words blacked out in Don's letters would have been of any value to the enemy. Servicemen were frustrated with restrictions the Army placed on what they could write about and what pictures they could send back home, especially when they found out censors had redacted their letters. Family and friends were keenly interested in finding out what their soldiers were doing in the war and repeatedly asked questions the military wouldn't allow the men to answer. Displaying his ire, Don retorted:

So the censor has been sticking his nose in our correspondence again, eh? Well, that's his privilege, so we'll just ignore him, OK? I'm sending you some pictures I had taken while we were in England.

NOTE TO CENSOR—leave these pictures alone 'cause everything is legal!!

Don and his buddies were excited when an article featuring the 368th Fighter Group appeared in one of the national magazines, telling Americans back home what they were doing. He wrote to Laura Jeanne about it in his next letter:

Try and find the October 21 issue of "Colliers Magazine" and read the article about the "Thunder Bums of the Ninth

*Air Force." It reports things we can't write about and has
pictures we aren't allowed to send—and you'll get an idea of
what goes on around here.*

*But you needn't swallow it hook, line, and sinker! You
see, my dearest, the "Thunder Bums" are just one of three
squadrons in our fighter group. Some of our "Jabo Angel"
guys were mentioned in the article too, but most of it was
about the "Bum" squadron. All three squadrons fly missions
together and live on the same field, so in reality, the article is
about our whole group in general. It seems that the "Bums"
cornered the Collier's correspondent first and took the whole
cake themselves!*

It was obvious from Don's letter that there was competition
going on among the 368th Fighter Group squadrons. None of the
flyboys who were interviewed by famed war correspondent W.B.
Courtney was shy, each relishing the reporter's attention. And in all
likelihood, given the same chance, Don's Jabo Angels would have
tried to monopolize the correspondent as well. However, the 396th
Thunder Bums did hold an edge over the other two squadrons worth
bragging about.

One of the "Bums" was the first fighter pilot to figure out how
to take out the biggest German Tiger Tanks with strafing. Before
then, fighter pilots considered rockets and bombs the only effective
weapons against the oversized tanks. After running out of both,
and with ground troops pleading for help, Johnny Baer, a tractor-
driving farm boy from Idaho, followed a hunch and strafed a Tiger
Tank at point blank range. His .50 caliber bullets hit the road
directly underneath the tank's belly, ricocheted up, and penetrated
the Tiger's weaker undercarriage. It wasn't a safe maneuver—but
it worked. His squadron leader, Capt. Joe McLachlan, described
what happened next:

The Tiger started popping little red puffballs and white tracer
streams out her sides and finally split apart like a Chinese firecracker.
The idea was flashed all over the air commands, and since then,
P-47 fighters have been strafing the hell out of Tigers and Panthers,
as well as bombing them, and believe me, we have clobbered plenty
that way.

When asked about dive-bombing, the squadron leader answered:

We try and let go with the thousand-pounders at no less than a thousand feet, and at seven hundred and fifty feet with the five-hundred-pounders. Any lower, the blast of your own bombs is apt to get you. One kid hit a railroad yard pretty low, and the air in front of him was full of rails and ties. When he got back he found a big piece of rail embedded in his fuselage. Another thing about going low—you come into the range of small arms and automatic weapons, which adds to your flak troubles.

Flak has no respect for experience. Any of us would rather face a couple of Messies or FWs [German fighter planes] any day than have one good flak battery hammering at us.

Then Capt. McLachlan talked to the reporter about flying close air support missions, explaining:

Sometimes we come back with dirt on a wing tip. You see, we won't strafe unless we're awfully sure it's the enemy. When the fight is confused, as it gets in a swift battle, identification is tough. We've got to know the outlines of not only the German tanks and vehicles, but allied types as well. From the window of a train going sixty miles an hour, try to call off the various makes [of car] you pass on a highway. Then imagine you are going seven times faster. How many would you be sure of?

Next, Courtney inserted part of a communication he'd just listened to between a 368th flight leader and a liaison radioman on the ground:

Flight Leader to Potato: "Here we are, son. Got anything for us?"

Potato to Flight Leader: "I will stand on top of my tank. Are you the one on my right?"

Flight Leader to Potato: "Yes."

Potato to Flight Leader: "I'm going to turn on a spotlight. Tell me if you can see it."

Flight Leader to Potato: "Yes, I can see your damn light. What do you want to do – flirt?"

Potato to Flight Leader: "I'm going to shine it on a building three hundred yards ahead on my right.

There's an eighty-eight hidden in the building and he's holding us up."

Flight Leader to Potato: "Dearie me! Why didn't you say so? Will fix."

There is a few minutes silence, during which we all strain our ears. Then we hear:

Flight Leader to Potato: "Betcha can't find any old building to shine your spotlight on now."

Potato to Flight Leader: "Nice bombing, now we can go ahead. Thanks pal."

Flight Leader to Potato: "Don't mention it. Call on us anytime."

The *Collier's* war correspondent ended his article with the following tribute to the P-47 flyboys:

They live in tents pitched over slit trenches in which the boys put their cots or bedding rolls. Some, who are squeamish about sleeping in a grave-like hole, bed down beside it and just roll in when there is an alert. These fighter-bomber kids...live, eat and sleep close to the front...only a matter of minutes from takeoff to target.

As proud as they are of what they do, they won't tell you that they or the Air Force have won the war. Generals Bradley and Patton commended them saying the infantry couldn't have achieved what they had if it weren't for the fighter-bomber pilots of the Ninth Air Force.

However, their heroes are the kids slogging on the ground...lads who have to fight without 2,000-horsepower motors and eight machine guns apiece. They comment, "Those boys can't slide for home base at four hundred miles an hour or bail to safety in a parachute if things go wrong for them. And the guys that drive those tanks—now that's a dangerous business. They sure got guts!"

A few minutes later, their flight is streaking over the trees in the distance at the end of the runway, off to pay a visit—not friendly— to some tanks—not ours. Every man to his own guts, you think.[154]

Optimistic about the outcome of the war, security officers at SHAEF set up a series of informational meetings to discuss "Conduct in Occupied Germany." They told the men there would be a "non-fraternization policy," meaning any social life with the Germans would be off-limits. They further explained that for security reasons, travel would be restricted to squadrons, and base personnel would be required to carry weapons with them at all times. At the end of the meeting, Command distributed their second War Department introductory series Language Guide, entitled *German: A Guide to the Spoken Language.*[155] Don ignored the new language booklet, finding the German language harsh and ugly, and chose instead to continue learning French.

Near the end of October, Major Leary began training the 368th pilots to fire rockets from their planes at a target range the Ninth engineers had set up on Lake Virelles, about fifty miles south of the base.[156] The newer P-47s could now carry ten High Velocity Aircraft Rockets (HVARs) mounted under their wings. Nicknamed the "Holy Moses," the HVARs were fifty-two inches long, five inches in diameter, weighed 134 pounds, and had an explosive force nearly equal to a 130mm artillery shell. Powered by a solid propellant motor, the rockets traveled at speeds up to 950 mph,[157] but without a built-in guidance system, they weren't very accurate. However, when the HVARs did connect, they could easily take out even the biggest German Tiger Tanks.

With wintertime approaching, the men of the 368th were excited when the engineers finally finished renovating their barracks. It was a relief to pack up their tents, move into heated rooms with electricity, and have access to indoor latrines and a washroom with indoor showers.

During a temporary break in the weather, the sun reappeared and warmed things up a bit, allowing the men to set up a large tent that would serve as their new PX. Don was glad for a break in the monotony. The last few days had been difficult, especially for him and Bob. Jerry's B-4 bag,* stuffed with all his belongings, and his vacant cot still set up between them were stark reminders that he

---

* Canvas luggage carried by WWII pilots that converted to a hangar type bag when they had a closet to hang it in.

was MIA. His disappearance was still too painful to talk about—so they didn't. And there were no grief counselors on base to help the men cope when friends failed to return from a mission, which was now a regular occurrence. Don dealt with the loss of his friend the only way he knew how, immersing himself in his letters to Laura Jeanne:

> *Bonjour, Mon Cherie. That means "hello," or "good day, my darling," and it's the better part of my French vocabulary. I still look at my little French book of words and phrases put out by the Army, just in case I ever get in a tight spot and really need to speak the language.*

> *To answer your last question, I haven't been doing anything but our daily routine. There's really no place to go, except a café (beer joint) in a small town nearby. And our group picture show hasn't been running very often of late. I haven't flown for almost two weeks now. The weather's been bad, and missions are scarce and hard to get on. I don't imagine we'll get much flying time in this winter.*

> *The sun disappeared again after a one-day stand. Guess I'll be putting my "long handles" back on pretty quick. I'll surely be a lot happier when I have you to keep me warm instead of having to resort to wearing long underwear.*

> *There's a big beautiful moon out tonight, the air is crisp and fresh, and the sky is filled with endless miles of contrails left by our heavy bombers as they pass over on their way to targets inside Germany. Hope they make it back okay.*

Don seldom skipped a day without writing to Laura Jeanne. And when he did, he usually came up with a witty excuse. The one on Halloween Eve 1944 was clearly his best so far:

> *Last night, the boys coaxed and begged me to join them in a game of pinochle. I had good intentions to write to you, but my resistance was low, and there were fresh doughnuts too—so I just couldn't say no. Sorry. Captain Krause and I trounced Kalen and my flight leader Lt. Olden. I just can't be beat!*

After a trying night of pinochle and walking all the way back to our room (about 20 feet), I was completely exhausted, too tired to write. Those doughnuts "were" pretty heavy. The Red Cross makes them in the kitchen at the end of our building, so we have them quite often. The Officers Club is down there too. They have a few easy chairs and a radio, so we hang out there and enjoy the music.

We have our "Homesick Hovel" (that's the name we gave our room) fixed up pretty good now. It's just a plain square room with plastered walls and a wood floor. Our sacks are placed around the room near the wall, and we have a clothes rack, a couple of little round tables in the center we "hooked" from another building, and two boxes we use for chairs. I also have a little box on legs for my toilet articles, and of course, the top is reserved for pictures of you.

Top to bottom: Pinochle cards, Kenny and Pat playing catch, and a landing gone wrong

NINETEEN

"Boredom Interrupted by Periods of Sheer Terror"

On November 1, 1944, the Chièvres Air Base was abuzz with unexpected news that Lt. Colonel Gilbert Meyers, commander of the 368th Fighter Group since its inception, had been appointed head of the Ninth Air Force air combat operations. However, disappointment of his departure quickly vanished when they learned that Lt. Colonel Frank S. Perego would become their new CO. Don liked Col. Perego and had been his wingman on several missions. It was Father Cleary's birthday as well. Rarely passing up a chance to throw a party, the 368th flyboys celebrated all three events that night in the Officers Club. Even a visiting countess and the head of the Red Cross joined in.[158] Later that night, when the party turned into a chug-a-lug contest, Don and Bob walked back to their room at the other end of the building for a nightcap of Pinochle instead of alcohol. At about midnight, unable to sleep with the ruckus still going on down the hall, Don reached for his fountain pen and a few sheets of stationery, positioned his writing box next to his cot, and began writing:

Oh, how I miss you at night! The days aren't so bad because I usually have something to do, even when I'm not on a mission— which is most of the time, since they're still scarce. I might only have a dozen in by the time you get this letter. Pinochle sums up my recreation, and I'm still the best partner in the squadron. Boy, am I good! Did I hear you say at ease, Lt.?

I'm sad to report that the Red Cross is moving their "doughnut factory" to another building. Oh well, it was nice while it lasted. I guess we'll start getting a little more exercise now, since we'll have to walk all the way to another building for doughnuts.

I finally got another mission in, but the weather was poor, and the mission wasn't successful as a result. The Eighth Air Force bagged over 200 "Jerries" yesterday, as you've probably already read about. Those guys are really "fat" when it comes to enemy aircraft! We're lucky if we even see the "Luftwaffe" once in five or ten missions—and don't think that we wouldn't give a month's pay to tangle with them once in a while! We just plug along doing the dirty work, bombing, and strafing our assigned targets—and giving our frontline troops whatever support they happen to need. Oh well, let them have their fun, and we'll have ours.

By the way, I had another chance to go to Paris for 2 days on a short leave—but refused it. The next time I see Paris...I want to have you by my side.

Bob and Kenny were part of the early flight on the morning of November 3, targeting an oil and gas dump northeast of Düren. Bob recorded the following in his mission log:

We dropped our bombs on the target and started some good oil fires. Before we bombed, our squadron encountered heavy flak, and Preston got hit. The flak tore a hole about two feet in diameter in his wing and blew a lot of it off. He turned back for the base and kept his plane flying until he got over our lines, then bailed out over friendly territory. They later found a P-47 and a dead pilot in the area where Preston had last been tracked. They're certain it was him, since he was flying a new bubble canopy model. Apparently, he bailed out at too low an altitude, and his parachute failed to open in time. He was a good guy.

On our way home, we saw another vertical contrail down by Koblenz. It must have been one of the German's infamous V-2 rockets headed for London.

Kenny had his first real scare that morning, coming home "on a wing and a prayer:"*

---

* A phrase originating in the 1942 World War II movie *The Flying Tigers*, starring John Wayne, later made popular in the 1943 patriotic song *Coming in on a Wing and a Prayer*, sung by Anne Shelton.

We spotted a German convoy on a road near a pine forest. We made our strafing run with the sun at our backs, hoping for a surprise attack. However, the Germans had already spotted us and moved into the forest. When I pulled up, my plane got riddled by small ground fire, and all of my flight instruments went out—the port control surface was sticking up in the air, and fire was trailing past the tail assembly.

I decided to bail out and opened my canopy, then suddenly the flame went out. Calm came over me as I realized that the oil pressure and manifold pressure were normal, so the engine wasn't damaged. I decided to try to keep the plane flying a little longer and headed towards the sun, which would take me over friendly territory before bailing out. Holding the control stick with both hands to the left and forward, along with using the rudders to fly in a crab position, I was able to return to home base and make a wheels-up belly landing. The flight crews removed the radio and a few instruments, then picked the plane up with a crane and carried it to a nearby dump.

Our flight surgeon met me as I climbed out of the cockpit and asked if I was injured. I told him, "I'm just fine now that I'm on the ground, but by chance would you have a shot of bourbon?" He loaded me in the ambulance and took me to the first aid tent, where he provided me with the requested medication.[159]

Don's flight took to the sky later that day, assigned to dive-bomb a power plant east of Aachen. They encountered dense overcast before reaching their target area, forcing the group leader to scrub their mission and turn for home with their bombs and rockets still attached. Fortunately, they landed safely without dislodging any weapons.[160]

The following day, Don flew an armed recce in the area around Schmidt, Germany, where the Hürtgen Forest battle was still raging. After the Jabo Angel squadron dropped their 500 pounders on fifteen enemy tanks, bad weather cut their mission short, forcing them to return home.[161]

The Hürtgen Forest Battle was turning into the longest and bloodiest battle of the war in Europe. The First Army had now suffered more than 4,500 casualties in the first month alone, and it was far from over. In early November, the Americans launched a new offensive, increasing their infantry to more than 120,000 men in an attempt to drive the Wehrmacht troops from the forest. After limited initial success, the close-contact fighting in the dense forest turned into a bloody stalemate, with each side experiencing horrific losses. Ground troops on both sides were forced to live in the same cold, wet foxholes they fought from and suffered from shortages of food and medical supplies. Cases of pneumonia, trench foot, frostbite, and exhaustion were commonplace, contributing to a staggering death toll.[162]

Ninth Air Force fighter groups provided some air support in the Hürtgen battle, but the extreme weather conditions and denseness of the forest limited what they could do, leaving the troops dependent on infantry weapons and close-in man-to-man combat. By the end of the three-month conflict, U.S. forces would suffer a shocking 33,000 casualties in one of their worst defeats of the war—all for control of fifty square miles of forest, with no real strategic value. It was a battle that probably never should have been fought.[163]

———————

After being stuck on the ground for more than three weeks, Don had now flown three back-to-back combat missions. His spirits were lifted now that he felt he was finally making a meaningful contribution in the fight against Germany:

This is your pilot husband and ETO correspondent once again spilling his love to his sweet adorable wife—via way of the pen! I'd so much rather show my love via the "touch and feel" system. But, I'll have to settle for just looking at a picture of my favorite pin-up girl. What a lovely eyeful—that's my Torchy!

I've flown three days in a row, and I'm scheduled to fly again tomorrow. I've been dive-bombing and strafing, cutting railroad lines, knocking out bridges, and blowing up "Jerry" Tiger tanks. It was late last night when we came from the field, and I was pretty tired, so I tumbled into my little sack in our "Homesick Hovel" without even going to chow.

Earlier today, I talked with some infantry boys back from the front. Those boys really love us—or rather, they really love our "Thunderbolts." When we're flying overhead, they're able to climb out of their foxholes and eat chow, bring in supplies, and do numerous other things.

One day they called in from the frontlines and wanted four of our 47s to come out and fly over the lines a few times, just so the "Jerries" would climb back into their holes, and give our artillery and infantry a chance to open up on them. Once either our artillery, or theirs, gets the other's position and keeps firing, the one being fired upon has to stay dug in. So when our planes come over, "Jerry" gets scared and hops into his hole. Then our boys climb out of theirs, open fire, and have the upper hand! That's why they love us so much.

Earlier that day, November 5, Don was part of a thirty-six-plane mission targeting the Green System railroad network located near the town of Hoff. They blew up rail lines and turntables and started oil fires throughout the target area with their 500-pound bombs. While the Thunder Bums flew top-cover, the Jabo Angels strafed a train, taking out close to twenty boxcars. It was a good mission—no flak was encountered, and no planes were lost.[164] After giving the field a good buzz, the 47s settled onto the field and rolled to a stop.

Flying for the fourth consecutive day, Don's squadron returned to the Green System, bombing and strafing the target rich railroad network. As the flyers regrouped, control radioed their flight leader, reporting that Me-110s had been spotted in the area over Aachen. They were vectored the location, but by the time they arrived, the German twin-engine heavy fighters had vanished. Too low on fuel to go looking for them, the squadron returned home.[165]

———

The 368th was experiencing another long mail drought. The men grumbled, struggling to understand why it took the Army so long to deliver their letters from home. Don was no exception:

Still no mail!!! I could swear, but I'll be a good boy, and see if I can't extend my patience instead. I guess our mail is being held up in the Christmas rush. I had another mission today and everything went well. From all reports, it sounds as though Uncle Frank has been re-elected. Did you vote for him, honey? I hope he'll help end this darn war soon, so I can get back home to you.

We had our first taste of snow today. Remember what fun we used to have sleigh riding and ice skating? Every day and every season brings back so many pleasant memories. I'm realizing more and more, as time goes by, how happy I was back then. When life comes too free and easy, I guess we're inclined to take things for granted, and don't fully appreciate how fortunate we are.

Honey, please try not to worry so much about me. There's really very little time that I'm in the least bit of danger. Things aren't nearly as bad as you read about or your imagination might make them. Sorry about the spots on the stationery. I'm eating another Red Cross doughnut, and they're a bit greasy!

It took over a month for Don to receive the letter telling him that Laura Jeanne's digestive disorder had been successfully diagnosed and wasn't as serious as he'd feared. The Army's slow and erratic mail delivery made it difficult to keep up with family life back home. It was frustrating for troops serving near the frontlines, especially when the letters arrived out of sequence:

I'm so relieved that the x-rays disclosed the cause of your health problem. I was worrying plenty about you, darling. Please follow your doctor's orders, take your prescriptions, and stick to that strict diet. All I care about is that you get well, sweetheart. So promise me, OK?

Those cokes, hot dogs, cheeseburgers, and malts you've been getting at the corner drugstore surely make the boys over here homesick—and I'm one those boys! Too bad they aren't on your new diet, ha! I drew my rations for the week, which consisted of just two candy bars, a bar of soap, and a couple of razor blades. So you can see why we miss the treats you wrote about so much.

A severe storm and poor visibility on November 8 forced Don's flight to abandon their primary mission objective and search out targets of opportunity instead. After dropping their bombs on

Nettersheim near the German West Wall, the 397th flew top-cover while the 395th bombed and strafed some marshalling yards. Before turning to go home, the Jabo Angels took out two locomotives, putting a few more dents in the Boche's rail transportation system.[166]

The 368th Fighter Group had flown missions for seven consecutive days, far exceeding their expectations for that time of year. Don's number had come up five times, placing him a few missions up on his tentmates. The flying streak ended the following day. Don's squadron got into the air, but control quickly scrubbed their flight. Extreme overcast skies forced them to turn toward home without getting credit for flying a mission.[167] Monotony followed on the heels of another foul-weather stretch, and the guys quickly grew bored, as illustrated in Don's next letter to Laura Jeanne:

> *Ho-hum, nothing to do but throw my old beat up pocketknife into the floor. When we get a place of our own, you'll have to watch me closely, or I'm apt to ruin the floor doing this unconsciously. It's the same old thing every day. We're up in the morning (usually not very early anymore), go to the flight line, and stay there waiting out the poor weather until after chow at night. What a life, huh?*

> *We've been listening to "Hit Parade"*on the radio tonight.[168] How do you like the new song "I'll Walk Alone" by Dinah Shore?…"I'll always be near you wherever you are. Just whisper, I'll hear you, no matter how far. So close your eyes and I'll be there. Please walk alone, but send your love and your kisses to guide me. Till you're walking beside me, I'll walk alone. Darling—all by myself—I'll walk alone." The words strike right at home, huh?*

An old war adage states: "A soldier's life is 90 percent boredom interrupted by periods of sheer terror." The troops fought boredom by listening to music on America's Top Ten Hit Parade countdown and to the other Armed Forces Radio Services programs.

---

*   One of the most popular radio music programs produced by the Armed Forces Radio Service (AFRS) during World War II. AFRS Hollywood studios pre-recorded the programs using A-List singers, who performed for the troops free of charge.

Bogart and Bacall on Armed Forces Radio Service (AFRS)

On November 11, 1944, Armistice Day, Don wrote:

How's my little honey feeling on this historic day? Seems somewhat ironic to celebrate the "war to end all wars," by fighting in a war, huh? I finally flew another mission earlier today, then got in a little extra time flying around the field. The latter doesn't count as combat time, but it keeps me in flying trim!

The sun never seems to shine in Belgium during the winter. The only time I ever see it is when we fly above the clouds. It's really a beautiful sight to see the soft, snowy-white bed formed by the clouds. They appear so dark and dreary when viewed from the ground—but fleecy white from on top.

That morning, Don and Bob were part of a twenty-one-plane mission that targeted railways east of Aachen. Thick overcast concealed their primary targets, forcing them to drop their 1,000-pound bombs from above the cloud cover. The results were disappointing. Worse yet, their friend Lt. Joseph R. Burney was hit by flak, forcing him to bail out for the second time in just a few months. This time he wasn't as lucky. He mangled one of his feet when he landed behind enemy lines, requiring doctors at a German hospital to amputate. Following his recovery, he spent the rest of the war as a POW.[169]

Heavy rains returned the next day and shut down the 368th Fighter Group for an entire week. Sequestered in their barracks, Don and his buddies slept late and laid on their bunks playing cards, writing letters, and snacking on goodies they'd recently received from back home. At night, they gathered at the Officers Club, watching a show whenever Special Services had their movie equipment working—or just shooting the bull, listening to the radio when it wasn't.

On November 15, the 368th Fighter Group attended their first USO* show since arriving on the Continent. The performance took place in a theater that the Germans had remodeled in Chièvres while they occupied the base. It even had a balcony.[170] Late that night, Don wrote:

> *I just returned from a USO show held at the Red Cross Theater. Roscoe Ates (an old-timer) was master of ceremonies. The performers included a tap dancer, a magician, and a twin sister duet with guitar accompaniment.*
>
> *The entertainment troop ate dinner at our officer mess, and Sharp and I were sitting right next to them. We both "barked" a couple of times, since they were the first real American beauties we'd seen in quite some time. I had to use brute force to get Bob out of the mess hall! During the show, they cracked a few rather "raw" jokes that were a bit disgusting, since they were directed at the gals in the show. Still, it was quite entertaining, and I really enjoyed it!*

After a late breakfast the following morning, Don finished his letter to Laura Jeanne:

> *Would you like to read a little more about the Ninth Air Force P-47s? It's in the "Air News" magazine for October. And if I were to write half of what they printed, the censors would cut it out without a doubt!*

---

* The United Service Organization is an organization formed in 1941 by President Franklin D. Roosevelt to help support America's troops by providing entertainment and emotional support.

That's one of the funny things about this war. Kalen had some pictures of P-47s sent to him from the U.S. showing guns, bomb racks, and rockets. But we can't send you pictures from here showing any of those things. Please tell my mom about the magazine article, OK? She keeps asking me a lot of questions I can't answer, and the article gives a good idea of what we're doing over here.

We still haven't been flying much due to the dense atmosphere. The birds have even been walking lately because the stuff is so thick. Visibility is less than zero, and we hate to go outside for fear of stepping on those poor "grounded" birds. Honest, I'm not making this up! We cut a path through them to the mess hall, though—to keep a direct line open to our chow. See, we're not so dumb!

The October issue of *Air News* was replete with stories about the Ninth Air Force, its planes, and the men who flew them. Don wanted Laura Jeanne and his mother to read a story entitled "Republic Thunderbolt." It began by quoting Solomon 5:21 from the Old Testament: "Then shall the right aiming Thunderbolts go abroad; and from the clouds, as from the well-trained bow, shall fly to the mark." The piece continued:

The P-47 Thunderbolt fighter stands unchallenged as the world's best dive-bomber...attacking at angles exceeding 60 degrees...dropping demolition and incendiary bombs. Clusters of anti-personnel fragmentation bombs are also used...each wing shackle carrying three, each one capable of devastating an area sixty feet in diameter.

With its high altitude speed and extra power in the clinches, the P-47 can throw more lead than any other fighter plane in the world...and simultaneously, it can absorb more punishment than anything it has yet come up against, making it pre-eminent as an air fighter and strafing plane. Its eight .50-cal. machine guns, with 6,400 rounds, fires 688 pounds of lead per minute...one bullet in each round of five is a tracer, two are incendiaries, and two are armor piercing incendiaries.

Naturally, the enemy fires back. Strafing planes get shot up—and badly—but somehow the P-47 brings its pilots back with amazing regularity. It has been said that the Thunderbolt can take more lead in proportion to its size than any plane in the skies.

———————

Responding to inquiries from his friends and colleagues about when he'd be coming home, Father Cleary wrote the following in his next newsletter:

> *What about the end of the war? We, like you, had been over optimistic as General Patton and his tanks and the Infantry swarmed across France. It looked like a matter of weeks then, and everyone was saying, "We'll be home for Christmas!" Then came the German border and, as you know from the papers, this began another story. The Germans are fighting with their back to Berlin, and it is going to be hard going from now on. They hope by so doing, I think, that we'll be as war weary as they are, and that our unconditional surrender ultimatum will be changed to a peace plan.*
>
> *It's a shame that the slaughter has to go on, but go on it must, until every German has tasted the bitter herbs of defeat,... has seen and felt just what the peoples of Belgium, France, Poland and Greece have seen and felt. I never thought I'd feel this way a year ago, but cemeteries and hospitals have a way of changing one's viewpoint.*
>
> *As I write, the boys are taking off on another mission. In a few hours, they'll be back and we start counting... "sweating it out," hoping and praying that each one comes thru safely.*
>
> *I find that the hardest part of my job is being unable to answer the pleas I get from anxious mothers, wives, and sweethearts, for further details about their missing boys. When I write, I give them all the information that regulations permit, and yet know the hundred and one questions, which the laconic telegram from the War Department must raise in their minds. Is he dead? If so, how did he die? Where is he buried? Was he shot down? Did his plane burn? Is he a prisoner of war, etc., etc.????*[171]

Jerry's letters to his mother, Violet, were her lifeline, each one increasing her hope that she might yet see her son again, despite the foreboding feelings she experienced when he went off to war. Late in the afternoon, a week after receiving Jerry's letter dated October 13, the doorbell rang, and the postman handed Mrs. Kelly a telegram from the War Department. As she stared at the first few words, her heart sank. "We regret to inform you…" Her worst fears had come true—Jerry was missing in action.

A week later, the Kellys received a follow-up letter from the Adjutant General's Office confirming the telegram, expressing regret and sympathy, and explaining:

> The term "missing in action" is used only to indicate that the whereabouts and status of the individual isn't immediately known. Experience has shown that many soldiers reported missing are subsequently reported as prisoners…Every effort is being exerted…We wish to assure you…Permit me to extend…In the meantime, if no additional information is received, we will communicate with you at the expiration of three months.

Shortly afterward, a letter arrived from Father Cleary. As the 368th chaplain had written in his most recent newsletter post, he was unable to provide many details to Jerry's parents, and struggled to provide comfort and convey hope that their son might still be alive. The Kellys also received an awkwardly worded letter from Herbert B. Maw, Governor of Utah, expressing gratitude for their son's service, "sincerely wishing them every possible comfort and happiness."

On December 8, 1944, the War Department sent the follow-up letter promised by the Adjutant General and released details from Jerry's "Missing Air Crew report:"

> Further information has been received indicating that your son, Second Lieutenant Gerald B. Kelly, was the pilot of a P-47 (Thunderbolt) fighter, which participated in a dive-bombing mission to an area west of Koln, Germany, on October 20. The report states that about 11:50 a.m., as our planes were strafing a train, a radio message was received from your son stating that his aircraft had been hit. It then dropped out of formation, headed in the direction of its base, and was last

observed to disappear into a cloud. No additional details pertaining to the loss of this fighter have been received in this headquarters. There were no other persons in the plane with your son.

The letter ended with the boilerplate promise:

Please be assured that a continuing search by land, sea, and air is being conducted to discover the whereabouts of all our missing personnel.

None of the letters brought the Kellys much comfort. How could they when the letters were clouded with uncertainties and contained so few details about what had happened? Still, the family held out hope Jerry was alive and would yet return home. They prayed for him constantly, anxiously awaiting more news. As days, weeks, then months passed without any further word from the War Department, their hopes dampened, except those of Jerry's mother. Convinced that her son was still alive—a belief she clung to for many years—she refused to succumb to her earlier premonition, even leaving food on the kitchen table, in case he returned home late at night or when the family was away.[172]

Bob wanted to write to the Kelly family, but couldn't bring himself to do it. What could he say? What he knew wouldn't provide them much hope, and Army regulations prohibited him from disclosing details of the incident. Worst of all, his last words to Jerry's mother still lingered in his mind: "Don't worry, Mrs. Kelly, I promise to take care of him and bring him home safely." He wondered how he could ever face her again. None of what happened was his fault, and he couldn't have done anything to change it. But it did happen—and his unfulfilled promise now haunted him.

APO 595, c/o Postmaster,
New York, New York,
10 December 1944.

Mrs. Laura J. Evans,
90 North Center Street,
Lehi, Utah.

Dear Mrs. Evans:

I have just had the honor of presenting the Air
Medal to your husband, Don. He received this decoration
for meritorious achievement while participating in missions over enemy territory. In all those missions, Don
displayed courage and skill which reflected high credit
upon himself and the armed forces of his country.

I take a great deal of pleasure in notifying you
personally of his success and to congratulate you, his
wife, upon having such a fine husband, who is doing so
much for his country.

With warmest personal regards, I am

Very truly yours,

E. R. QUESADA,
Major General, U S Army,
Commanding.

Air Medal

TWENTY

Holidays, Medals, and Close Calls

Holidays away from home were hard on the troops, and the days leading up to Thanksgiving were no exception. While the special meal the Army provided filled their stomachs with good food, it failed to assuage their homesickness and melancholy on the most American of holidays. On November 23, Don wrote:

Today was Thanksgiving. We got up about 11:00 a.m. and went to chow at noon. We had a very delicious dinner consisting of turkey, mashed potatoes and gravy, dressing, carrots and peas, cranberry sauce, mashed sweet potatoes, and peaches and cake. Not bad, huh? It was the best meal I've had since I left home!

I have so much to be thankful for this Thanksgiving, especially for such a wonderful wife. Sweetheart, you mean everything to me. I can't wait until next Thanksgiving when you'll be the one cooking the turkey and making the pumpkin pies with whipped cream.

They're having a big Thanksgiving dance in the Officers Club right now, with about thirty plus "beetles" they imported from Brussels. The girls are being chaperoned by a local Baroness so things don't get out of hand! It's pretty noisy down there, and they seem to be having a good time.

Well, it's about 1:00 a.m. now, and we just got rid of the last of the drunks. They like to come in our room and talk on their way back from partying at the club, lucky us. I'm signing off for now and hitting the sack.

On the other side of the world, Laura Jeanne reminisced:

That Thanksgiving, our family felt a rich outpouring of the Spirit as we counted our many blessings. Howard, Duane, and my beloved husband were all still alive and safe. But, without any of them with us, it was far from a happy occasion.

In addition to our prayers of gratitude that Thanksgiving, we pleaded with Heavenly Father to watch over and protect our loved ones and all the other brave men fighting in the war. I don't know how I could have gone on living if anything had happened to Don.

Bad weather conditions left the 368th flyboys with too much time on their hands, creating an environment ripe for boredom:

Morale is at an all-time low around here! There's so much time when we aren't doing anything—especially since this rotten winter weather blew in. We're grounded again on another wet, dismal day. I haven't flown for two weeks, and still only have fifteen missions to my credit.

All we've done today is loaf and mess around. This afternoon we painted some "Thunderbolts" on the back of our leather flight jackets. I fussed over mine for quite a while, then just when I had it looking good, I lost my painter's grip and messed up on part of it. I felt so bad I went over and cried on Bob's shoulder. After drying my eyes, I fixed it up the best I could, and it actually turned out pretty good. And that's how my career as a great painter came to an end!

The weather cleared on November 25, allowing seventy-two Thunderbolts to fly close air support for the First Infantry. The primary targets for Don's flight were located near Stommeln and Echtz, forty-eight miles east of Aachen. Some of their planes carried 500-pound general-purpose bombs (GPs), and others carried 260-pound fragmentation bombs (frags). GPs were usually fitted with a time-delay fuse, so the bomb wouldn't explode until after it hit its target. Frags, however, exploded into a mass of small, fast-flying metal fragments. They were especially lethal against infantry concentrations and were generally dropped at lower altitudes to maximize their damage. Don's flight bombed and strafed an artillery munitions cache and fuel dump, creating large explosions and fires from direct hits. They ended their mission strafing and dropping frags on a concentration of German ground troops.[173] Don had the following sobering experience after he landed:

> *My crew chief took me out with him to inspect my airplane after I reported in, saying he had something to show me that he thought I'd be interested in seeing. In the narrow protective lead plate located in the cockpit right behind my head, there was a one-inch hole with a large bullet still embedded in it, which didn't quite go all the way through the metal plate.*
>
> *The leading edge of the bullet had hit the back of my head, but in the heat of the battle, I didn't even feel it. If it had penetrated just a fraction of an inch further, it would have passed through the plate, killing me. This was another of the many little miracles I experienced during the war.*

Air Force crew chiefs took great pride in caring for their assigned planes and the pilots that flew them, often developing close personal relationships. Thirty-six-year-old war correspondent William Randolph Hearst, Jr., heir to the publishing empire established by his father, flew himself to different Allied airfields in an AT-6 Texan, writing exclusive stories for the *Hearst Newspaper*. In an article published that week, he wrote about the 368th crew chiefs he observed and interviewed:

> They think their own particular pilot is the best in the business and work and fuss over his plane like a mother chicken. They lie flat on their stomachs on the wing of a plane as it taxies out to the takeoff on each mission and meet it again as it rolls to a halt on its return, once more taking their prone position while it taxies back to its nest. After each flight, the pilots tell their chief if anything needs their attention. The gloom and tragic heartbreak when a pilot does not return is beyond my power to describe.[174]

Since Don was on the last mission of the previous day, he slept in, showing up later than usual at the mess tent. Breakfast at Airstrip "A-84" was his favorite meal. That morning he downed four hot cakes, a large sausage patty, a fried egg, and a glass of grapefruit juice, then walked back to his room to get his pen and stationery and joined his buddies down at the flight line:

> *Here it is Sunday again, and I wouldn't have known it if the radio hadn't mentioned it. A while back, Mom sent me the LDS Service Men's Edition of the Church News. Even though I haven't been able to go to any church services these past few months, I feel that my testimony of the Savior has increased many times. I think about Him more than I ever did before. That, and my love for you, makes it easier for me to ignore the temptations over here. Know that your faith and trust in me haven't been misplaced.*

> *In answer to your question, I've had the "Air Medal" for quite some time, but they're just presenting them tomorrow. I'll send it to you as soon as I get it. In fact, I even have a couple of "oak leaf clusters" to put on the medal. The Army Air Corps awards the clusters instead of giving additional air medals. Sharp, Kalen, Patrick, and Kelly have the same, and most of the boys in our outfit have clusters on their air medal. I'll write more about it tomorrow night after the presentation.*

> *Some of the guys are talking about applying for a commission in the Army after the war—but not me. I have too much to make up to my "Torchy," and I don't need any more interference from the Army!*

> *We're going to get an education, find a nice cozy place we can call home, and then concentrate on filling it up with some little Evanses, OK?*

That night, Don learned he was flying the early mission the next day, which would put him in the air during the medals ceremony. After spending all morning at the line waiting for takeoff clearance, Command finally scrubbed his mission due to bad weather, minutes before the ceremony began:

> *I quickly changed clothes and made it to the big show after all. The commanding general of the Ninth Air Force [General Quesada] made the presentations. A lot of guys got the "Air Medal." And a few "DFC"s [Distinguished Flying Cross] and "Purple Hearts" were also awarded. Quite a few of our*

crew chiefs got the "Bronze Star" for their good work and efficiency in caring for the T-Bolts we fly. It was pretty cold outside on the airfield, and everyone was rather numb by the time it was over.

The General himself pinned the medals and shook everyone's hand. He asked me how many missions I had, and how long I'd been over here. I said sixteen, and was just about to say that I'd been over here too damn long, but I guess those "stars" on his shoulders changed my mind, ha!! Oh, it was all so very dramatic! In fact, my heart almost beat an extra thump!

To get an "Air Medal" you have to fly ten missions without bombs, or fly half as many with bombs. That's why I already have two clusters to the medal—understand? Anyway, I'll send it to you presently.

Kelly's mother was notified a short time ago that he was missing in action, but I'm pretty sure he's OK. Maybe next time you're in Salt Lake and have a little spare time, you might drop in and talk to his folks. I've never known a finer fellow. I can't tell you any more about it, since doing so is a court-martial offense.

Please don't worry, darling. I wasn't going to tell you about Jerry for that very reason, but I thought that maybe you'd already seen it in the paper. I'll be safe, honey. Our old T-Bolts take more punishment than anything else in the sky—and I wouldn't want to fly anything else. Keep "sending your love and kisses to guide me."

Knowing that additional details of Jerry's incident would cause Laura Jeanne to worry even more, Don was relieved that Army regulations prohibited him from writing about it. After more than a month, there were no more clues to his disappearance—but Jerry was far from forgotten. The remaining members of the Five clung to the hope he might still be alive.

On November 29, Don flew with thirty-six Jabo Angels as they escorted three-dozen B-26 medium bombers from Nancy, France, to their bombing targets at Karlsruhe and Baden, near the southern part of the West Wall. The P-47s flew top-cover while the Marauders dropped their bombs, then safely chaperoned them back to Nancy without incident.[175] Don's seventeenth mission actually *was* a "milk run," his only one of the war. After returning, he felt sick to his stomach, skipped dinner, and went to straight to bed:

I didn't feel well and couldn't sleep. I got my all-purpose helmet out and placed it in a good spot near the head of my bed—just in case. I ate something that didn't want to stay down, and it definitely didn't! Kalen emptied my helmet twice during the night. I owe him a big favor.

Bob had one of the medics look in on Don the following morning. Since there were no other reports of food poisoning on the base, the medic suspected it was the flu. He told him to take it easy for a few days and officially grounded him. The guys stayed unusually quiet the rest of the day, trying to let him rest. Don slept fitfully and was awakened mid-afternoon by mail call:

Two back letters finally caught up to with me this afternoon, which made me happy. What's this about a sensational dream you had on October 29? So I "wooed" the socks off you, huh? That's exactly what I'd do, if I were there now. Well, maybe not right now in my current weakened condition.

Late on December 2, all three 368th squadrons gathered at the Officers Club, excited to listen to the Army-Navy football game— one of the most highly anticipated football contests in sports history. Besides the usual bragging rights, this time the Cadets and Midshipmen were ranked No. 1 and No. 2 in the nation, respectively, and a national championship was on the line. Touted as the "game of the century," the contest was moved from Navy's home field in Annapolis to the Baltimore Municipal Stadium, which had nearly triple the capacity (67,000 seats). The government was using the game as a fundraiser for the war effort and required fans to buy a war bond with every ticket purchased. The game sold out within 24 hours, and the War Department raised more than $58 million.[176]

Americans all across the country had a stake in the highly publicized game, since nearly every family had someone serving in the Army or the Navy. And they badly needed a diversion from an unending war that was experiencing too many setbacks in both Europe and the Pacific.

Leading by the score of 9-7 at the end of the third quarter, Army pulled away in the final quarter, winning 23-7 in a game that more than lived up to its hype. The raucous crowd at Chièvres cheered so loudly that they drowned out the radio announcer even with the volume turned up full blast.

Most American soldiers loved sports and continued to throw, shoot, kick, or catch whatever kind of ball they could get their hands on. The men followed their favorite sports teams back home on the radio and read about them in the newspapers and magazines that made their way to the base. Don especially missed being on a tennis court. After playing in England, he wasn't able to pick up a racket again in Europe. Even though the "sport of kings" originated in France, not far from his base, the game was seldom played during the war. Instead, he had to settle for heated Ping-Pong matches with Bob.

The pilots and aircrews played sports with their squadrons whenever they had a chance and the weather allowed. Mostly, they played a lot of catch. Kenny was always wearing his baseball glove and bugging someone to throw with him. He and Don looked forward to playing on the Jabo Angel basketball squad, scheduled to begin rivalry games against other fighter-group units in January.

December 5 was another big day at Chièvres; "The Yankee Doodlers" were putting on their Christmas holiday show for the 368th Fighter Group. Their troupe consisted of seven G.I.s and a four-piece band, but no American Beauties were on the stage this time. The show featured skits, impersonations, jokes and song, which raised the men's spirits, despite the absence of showgirls.

Feeling better, but still grounded, Don slept late the following morning. After stuffing himself at breakfast, trying to regain the weight he'd dropped from the flu, he headed to the Officers Club. He turned on the radio, sat down in one of the big easy chairs located in front of the fireplace, then fell asleep while waiting for his buddies to return from their early-morning mission. He woke up when a boisterous crowd of pilots entered the club.

The guys surrounded Bob and Pat, goading them into giving a play-by-play account of their dogfight that morning. More than happy to comply, the two pilots recounted that after dropping bombs on Zulpich, their twelve-plane-flight conducted a fighter sweep, searching for enemy aircraft that another flight had seen in the area—then the controller called in bogeys.[177] They explained in detail everything that took place after that, continuing to answer questions as they left the club and walked to the mess hall. After chow, several of the pilots followed them back to their room. Unable to concentrate with everything that was going on, Don finally gave up trying to finish a letter he was writing to Laura Jeanne and joined in the celebration.

Late that night, Bob took out his taboo mission log and recorded:

I flew No. 4 on Baker's wing in Major Leary's flight. The controller called in bogeys heading west from Koln at about 1,000 feet. Major Leary saw them immediately and took his wingman under the clouds for a look, while Baker and I stayed on top. Patrick and the other flights stayed even further up. Leary and his wingman ran right up the tail of 10 Me-109s. Leary fired and they broke. Then he had two on his tail, and his wingman ended up with two on his. The Major's wingman got shot up bad and had to head home.

Meanwhile, the rest of us tried to find a way down to join the fight. Before I knew it, I had two 109s on my tail, and so did Baker. I went around a couple of times with them, but didn't get anywhere—so I did a split "S" and headed farther down.

As I was headed for the deck, a 109 came through my sights. I gave him a short squirt, then cruised around on top and saw three P-47s chasing a 109. I climbed on his tail and got in a lot of hits until he went back into the clouds. Then about 30 Fw-190s came down on us from above, but we soon had them on the run.

I shot at five or six planes. The squadron got three and damaged six—not bad—since the odds were twelve of us to

40 of them. I think I shot down two aircraft because of the hits I saw on the wings and the fuselage, but had no camera film or eyewitness to confirm the kills. At first, I had a rough time, wondering if I should fire, but that feeling passed in a hurry, and from then on, I wasn't a bit afraid, even though I was sweating and breathing quite hard. It was sort of fun in a weird way.

After finally finishing his letter to Laura Jeanne, Don lay on his cot, listening to the sound of B-17 heavies going eastward on bombing runs deep inside Germany, glad that P-47s didn't have to fly night missions. As he drifted off to sleep, he wondered when his first chance to engage enemy fighter planes would come—hoping that when it did, he'd fare as well as his buddies had that day.

On December 9, the Air Corps medical staff finally cleared Don to return to the air. However, his excitement quickly faded when he was informed that he wouldn't be inserted back into the flying rotation for another four days. He recapped the end of another no-fly day, writing:

It snowed a little bit tonight, and some of the boys had a snowball fight out in the hall after we got back from seeing a show at the theater. I'm not quite up to that yet, but I'm feeling okay now, and I'm no longer grounded.

I finally received one of my mom's Christmas packages. It was pretty beat up when it arrived, but the contents were in good shape and tasted great. I suppose I'd better extend my heartiest Christmas wishes to all at home, if it isn't too late already due to the Army's slow mail delivery service. And please pass a "Happy New Year" on for me too. Hopefully, the coming New Year will be a happier one for all of us.

Christmas is going to be so very lonesome without you. It's just like you said in your last letter—my missing you and loving you so much is one of my weakest points. But on the other hand, it's what gives me strength and determination to live, fight, and look to the future. I'm all yours, darling, and always will be—and no German Army, or anything else, will keep me from returning to you.

Laura Jeanne was captivated as she read about her husband's adventures in France and Belgium, treasuring the postcards and photographs he sent her, hoping more than ever they'd be able to travel together someday. Sensing the longing in her letters, Don wrote:

> *Glad you liked the postcards of Paris and those snapshots of me. I didn't realize I was such a devastating character. Sorry it caused you to shed some tears. I'll probably shed a few myself when I finally receive that long awaited picture of you in your swimsuit. And I'll definitely bawl my eyes out, if I don't get it soon!*

> *Your plea that we someday take a trip together "somewhere" pulled at my heartstrings. I'm looking forward to visiting Paris and some of the other places I've been again—but this time with you. I didn't have "one grand and glorious trip to Paris" like you wrote, because you weren't with me.*

> *I've read and reread that huge seven-page letter that you sent to make up for the days you didn't write. It's a wonderful letter, honey. I wish I could have been there with you that night you were so lonesome and discouraged, to take you into my arms, and tell you how desperately I love you.*

The arrival of Christmas packages triggered mixed emotions among the men. Many of them had never spent the holiday season away from home and were feeling melancholy. In his next letter Don wrote:

> *I received a very nice Christmas package today from home, and Pat and I immediately went to work on it. I just can't seem to wait until Christmas to open anything that might taste good. Sounds just like me, huh?*

> *Today has been long and dreary with a little drizzle now and then and a cold breeze that goes right through you. Sharp and Kalen are away on a flak leave in Southport, England, for a few days, leaving Patrick and me here alone. It hardly seems like the same place without Bob here—he's such a crazy fool.*

And naturally, when he and I get together—well, there's never a moment's peace.

I feel so lost tonight. I can't keep my mind on writing this letter—it just drifts—and the first thing I know, I'm reliving precious holiday memories from the past. Then my heart and brain go spinning, and my pen stops writing. Guess I'm in pretty bad shape, huh?

Bob and Kenny each flew a new P-47 across the English Channel on their return trip to the base. After they arrived, things heated up in the Jabo Angel barracks—literally. In his nightly letter to Laura Jeanne, Don wrote:

Sharp got back tonight and brought us a case of quart cans of grapefruit juice. We're getting quite a stock of goods and snacks to carry us thru a long winter. He also returned with some red and green flares. Consequently, our hallway is now full of smoke!

Tonight's show at the Club was a Hopalong Cassidy thriller from the Wild West with heroes and villains. The crowd cheered and hissed at various intervals throughout the movie, and a good time was had by all. Walking back, I noticed what a clear, cold, beautiful night it is. I'd give anything to be strolling with you thru the park under the millions of bright stars shining in the sky tonight. I guess that I'm still a dreamer at heart, huh?

While we were away, I received another package from my "li'l pigeon." It's the one with all the nuts, candy, and tuna fish. Thank you so very much! We're enjoying ourselves immensely!

How about that?—I finally wrote a letter without complaining about anything. Bet that was a relief for you.

Since the skies were too thick on December 12 for the pilots to sight-bomb their targets, Command scheduled a radar assisted "blind-bombing" mission instead. Don flew with twenty-three P-47s from the 397th and 395th squadrons, dropping bombs through the clouds on targets over Euskirchen, an important transportation hub in Germany's North Rhine area. Afterward, control vectored the planes west of the city, where they cut several rail lines. The mission went off smoothly—no flak and no casualties.[178]

The Allied air forces had been plagued for months by overcast weather and poor visibility in the skies over Germany. As a result, medium and heavy bombers, as well as P-47 fighter-bombers, were now flying more and more blind-bombing missions using radar equipment. This method was safer than sight bombing in clear skies, since it allowed the pilots to bomb from higher altitudes, using cloud cover for protection. On the downside, blind bombing wasn't as accurate. To compensate, the Allies often used incendiary "firebombs." Filled with extremely flammable materials, these destructive bombs exploded on contact, taking out their targets with scorching fires. They also used firebombs when attacking concentrations of ground troops.[179]

At the beginning of the war, the Germans dropped incendiary bombs on London, indiscriminately killing and injuring tens of thousands of civilians, causing the city to burn out of control. Later, the British RAF retaliated in kind, using the same terror weapons. They copied Hitler and "area-bombed" major German cities in daytime and nighttime air raids, believing as he did that such ruthless tactics would eventually break the will of the people and hasten their surrender.[180]

During the early years of the war, American air forces adhered to daytime "precision bombing" policies, focusing on pinpoint airstrikes to minimize civilian casualties. But with bad weather scrubbing so many of their missions, the war-weary Americans had now joined the RAF in their indiscriminate area-bombing tactics and were ready to use anything and everything at their disposal to end the war. Although the Army avoided using the term "blind-bombing" for public relation reasons, they were now regularly doing just that, dropping the controversial firebombs on German cities and troop concentrations, as well as on strategic targets.[181]

The Officers Club was starting to show signs of the holiday season. Glen Miller Christmas tunes were blaring from the loud speakers, and a few of the pilots had cut down some evergreens they'd found in a Belgian farmer's pasture and propped them up in the clubhouse. Although the men were creative in their efforts to trim the trees, colored lights and traditional ornaments were noticeably absent. But even with their Spartan decorations, the Christmas trees added greatly to the spirit of the season. Unfortunately, the holiday reminders had an unintended side effect on the men as well, fanning the flames of homesickness.

Don didn't have to fabricate a witty excuse for not writing to Laura Jeanne on December 14—Mother Nature took care of that for him. Following a successful armed recce in which the 397th took out a train with twenty-five to thirty cars and cut several rail lines, bad weather diverted their sixteen-plane-flight to the Florennes-Juzain airstrip, forty-three miles from Chièvres.[182] Their hosts, the 430th Fighter Squadron flying P-38s, didn't exactly roll out the red carpet that night:

We had to sleep in a tent without a stove. I went to bed at 7:30 p.m. and didn't sleep more than about 30 minutes all night because it was freezing cold—burrr! When the skies cleared this morning, we finally came home. After getting back, I've had to work down at the line all day.

Now, I'm sitting on the edge of my cot with matchsticks holding my eyelids open while my pen moves along aimlessly. I haven't been so tired for a long time. I've started letters to my folks and yours, and after four days, they're still unfinished. I'm really off the ball.

Even with the decorations in the Club and the Christmas music they're playing on the base, I don't have much Christmas spirit, and I doubt I'll get it this year. I'll surely be glad when we can play Santa for our kids—of course, that's looking ahead quite a ways! But I can dream, can't I?

It's early, but I think I'll say goodnight for now and hit my little old sack since my brain is already asleep.

PART THREE

German Panzer Armies

VS.

US Third Army   US First Army

The chessboard is set

TWENTY-ONE

The Ardennes

In August 1944, General Omar N. Bradley assumed command of the entire 12th U.S. Army Group. Composed of four field armies numbering more than 1.3 million men, it was the largest and most powerful United States Army ever to take to the field. Frustrated with the stalemate at the Siegfried line, Eisenhower and his generals were planning a major offensive to break through the West Wall and invade the German heartland. The First Army, under General Courtney Hodges, planned to attack in the north, with the Lower Rhine as its objective; and the Third Army, led by General George S. Patton, in the south, toward the Saar and the Palatinate regions. By mid-December, both armies were in place, poised to attack.[183]

In early December, Allied Command received scattered intelligence reports that the Germans were building up strength along the Siegfried Line in the Ardennes Forest region. Preoccupied with their own upcoming assault plans, they paid little attention, assuming the German activity was defensive in nature. To encourage the Allies' flawed assumption and further mislead them, enemy radio traffic code-named the buildup "Watch on the Rhine."[184] Additional sightings by fighter-bombers of increased enemy activity in the thickly wooded Ardennes Forest and in nearby villages were discounted or ignored by SHAEF as well.

Myopically focused on their own upcoming offensive, Allied leaders gave little thought to what the enemy might try to do to them. The only intelligence officer who was alarmed by the influx of warning signs pointing to a German buildup was General Patton's Third Army G-2, Colonel Oscar Koch, who boldly predicted on December 9 that the Germans would soon launch a major new offensive at the Ardennes.[185]

General Eisenhower's top G-2, Major General Kenneth Strong, reported Koch's prediction as merely a warning to the General's chief of staff, Bedell Smith. However, Smith took it seriously, sending Major Strong to personally meet with General Bradley. Bradley discredited the reported threat, pointing out that the German situation was much too hopeless to launch a serious attack. Making light of the G-2's prediction, he scoffed, "Let them come," then abruptly dismissed Strong and did nothing.[186] Bradley's complacency and overconfidence, combined with his failure to heed credible intelligence reports, was reminiscent of Pearl Harbor—and about to become one of the Allies' costliest mistakes of the war.

The Ardennes plateau region crosses over Belgium and Luxembourg, extending into France and Germany. Its mountains and ridgetops are picture-postcard beautiful, blanketed by trees and rivers. However, its deep ravines, gorges, swamps, and marshy areas made it the most difficult terrain to traverse on the entire Western Front. In many places, its secondary dirt-road systems resembled trails more than roadways. It was through this same, remote, rugged territory that Germany had invaded France in 1940. Naively ignoring recent history, Allied military leaders were convinced that geography, winter weather, and its limited road network made the Ardennes region an improbable location to launch a large, armored military operation.[187]

For some time, the Wehrmacht had weakly guarded their side of the Siegfried Line along the Ardennes Forest. The Allies felt safe doing the same, deploying a combination of green troops sent there for training, along with battle-weary seasoned units stationed there to recuperate. It was here in the Ardennes, at the least guarded and most unlikely location on the Western Front, that Hitler planned to launch his counteroffensive.[188]

An entire month of bad weather and the dense cover of the Ardennes Forest, combined with the Allies' failure to act on their intelligence reports, allowed Hitler to mobilize massive numbers of troops, tanks, vehicles, and supplies. The Germans went virtually silent, limiting their radio communications to protect the secrecy of their mission. Even the secret code breakers at England's Bletchley Park failed to intercept details of the upcoming attack. Concerned that the Allies might detect a buildup of smoke in the area as their troops gathered, German leaders issued orders to substitute charcoal for wood in their fires, further reducing risk of discovery. By the middle of December, with his ground and armored military forces now assembled along the Ardennes frontline, Hitler was ready to launch his attack.[189]

The Führer's battle plan was simple: Nazi panzer armored tank divisions would advance through the Ardennes as fast as possible, splitting American and British forces in two as they moved westward, then take control of the bridges crossing the Meuse River. From there the terrain opened up, allowing them to race to their final objective, the Allied supply port of Antwerp, Belgium. Hitler could then starve the divided Allies of vital supplies and reinforcements and force them to sue for peace.[190]

The Germans delayed the attack until their meteorologists could forecast at least ten days of bad weather accompanied with enough poor visibility to keep Allied aircraft grounded. Mother Nature had cooperated so far, cloaking their initial buildup. Hitler gambled that his military could overcome these same extreme weather conditions and move their panzer tank divisions rapidly through the rugged Ardennes terrain. Germany's next biggest risk was their inability to transport enough fuel for their tanks and armored vehicles to reach the Meuse River, forcing them to capture gasoline along the way at Allied fuel dumps. Whether the overall plan was "a stroke of military genius," as Hitler believed, or "reckless and doomed to failure," as some of his top military leaders feared, one thing was certain: Germany was about to launch a major counteroffensive, and the Allies didn't see it coming.[191]

Amassing a large military force in the Ardennes was an enormous logistical challenge. It required the German armies to relocate troops, tanks, and weapons from the Eastern Front, leaving their residual forces vulnerable to attack from the Soviet Army. Hitler was taking a huge strategic risk in an attempt to reverse the consequences of his reckless decision to wage war on two fronts simultaneously. The fighting had to end on one of the two fronts or Germany would soon be finished.[192]

Hitler's contempt for the Americans and their "decadent democracy," and his view that they were "militarily inferior," made his choice of which foe to eliminate first an easy one. After a quick and decisive victory in the West, he could then focus his entire military forces on the much larger and unrelenting Red Army attacking from the East, an enemy he feared far more than the Allies.[193]

Irrationally, the Führer reasoned that Stalin would wait to see the outcome of his new counteroffensive against the Americans before continuing his winter offensive. But with memories of German butchery still fresh in their minds, the Soviets had no intention of watching and waiting on the sidelines. Hitler badly misjudged them— just as he did the Americans he was about to attack.

The Führer turned to his trusted SS to choose men for leading roles in the counteroffensive. Although entry into the SS was voluntary, it was restricted to men who could prove they were of pure Aryan German ancestry, as far back as their grandparents, assuring they were part of Hitler's superior master race. These elite units had to swear an oath to Hitler and the Nazi Third Reich, pledging total loyalty and obedience to orders, even to the point of death.

The *Waffen-SS* became the formidable military arm of the Nazi party. Their units weren't actually part of the Wehrmacht, but the two operated in tandem. Indoctrination and commitment to achieve their objectives, regardless of the cost or the methods required to do so, separated the SS from the rest of the German Army. Trained and conditioned to be ruthless in their tactics, they fought fiercely in battle, no matter the odds. As a result, they experienced a much higher casualty rate than the other German military forces.[194]

Hitler feared that once the Allies became aware of his strategy to capture Antwerp, they might destroy the Meuse River bridges before his panzer armies could cross them, dooming the mission to failure. To counter that possibility, he masterminded a plan called "Operation Greif," named after a mythical bird—and knew just the man to lead the special operation.[195]

Otto Skorzeny, Austrian-born like Hitler, tried to enlist in the Luftwaffe at the age of 31 when the war first broke out in 1939. The

German Air Force rejected him for being too old and too tall (6-foot-4). Instead, the military assigned him to one of the thirty-eight Nazi Waffen-SS units. A renowned fencing expert, Skorzeny was easily recognized by prominent scars on each cheek received during unsanctioned saber duals while attending the University of Vienna.[196]

After fighting the Soviets for several years on the Eastern Front, Skorzeny was promoted to captain and awarded the German Iron Cross for bravery. Impressed by his exploits, Hitler ordered him to form a special German commando unit, modeled after the famous British Commandos. Fluent in English and French, Skorzeny extensively interrogated captured British and French operatives, extracting the information he required to train his unit.[197]

Otto Skorzeny

The commando team's first undercover mission was to rescue Hitler's friend and deposed Italian dictator, Benito Mussolini. After flying in silently on gliders, they landed undetected on a mountaintop near an isolated hotel where the new government held the ex-dictator as a political prisoner. They stormed the building, extracted Mussolini, and escaped without even firing a shot. Hitler was so impressed with the daring rescue mission that he promoted Skorzeny to the rank of major and presented him with the Knight's Cross, the highest award a German military officer could receive.[198]

A year later, Hitler invited Skorzeny to his famous Wolf's Lair, promoted him to lieutenant colonel, then unveiled his plans for Operation Greif. In a disruptive false flag operation, the Führer wanted Skorzeny-led commandos to infiltrate enemy lines, capture one or more of the bridges over the Meuse River, and hold them until the German Army could cross. Hitler gave him free rein to handpick his special forces from any of the English-speaking elite Waffen-SS Troopers. His orders were to turn them into American soldier doppelgängers, who could speak American slang, smoke cigarettes like Humphrey Bogart in *Casablanca,* and look the part dressed in American uniforms, carrying American rifles. As the German counteroffensive moved westward, the commando teams would infiltrate American lines, marching alongside captured American tanks and jeeps.[199]

Operation Greif would be payback for Hitler, who was still reeling from the success of a similar American commando attack in Aachen. Dressed in German uniforms and driving captured German Panzer tanks, the Americans infiltrated German lines, driving right into the city. Hitler foresaw Skorzeny and his task force creating even worse disruption, confusion, and fear as they gave false orders, changed road signs, cut telephone wires, upset communications, and misdirected Allied troops. The Hague Convention of 1907 allowed the execution of spies captured wearing enemy uniforms, making this a dangerous operation, one carrying a death mark. Unwilling to see that fate for his favorite commander, Hitler ordered Skorzeny: "I forbid you to pass beyond the front line in person. In no circumstances must you let yourself be taken prisoner!"[200]

Joachim Peiper

Hitler's next decision was to select a battle commander to lead the key spearhead unit assigned to recapture the Port of Antwerp. He again turned to the Waffen-SS and chose another of his favorite officers, Joachim Peiper, who was also a recipient of the Knight's Cross. At age twenty-nine, he was the youngest regimental colonel in the German Army, distinguishing himself in battle many times on the Eastern Front. Far less imposing in stature than Skorzeny, Peiper was five feet eight inches and weighed only 140 pounds—but he was every bit the radical Nazi.[201]

The press had closely followed Peiper's combat exploits and made him a hero in the eyes of the German people. High Command considered the young colonel an outstanding leader, and his troops were fiercely loyal to him. In the war against the Soviets on the Eastern Front, he'd developed a reputation for using brutal battle tactics— attacking Russian villages at night without warning and setting everything left standing on fire with flamethrowers, seldom sparing civilians and rarely taking prisoners. Known as the "Blowtorch Battalion," they proudly painted their feared moniker on the side of all their armored vehicles and tanks. Colonel Peiper had repeatedly demonstrated his willingness to achieve battle goals, regardless of the cost or methods required, making him a perfect choice to lead Hitler's key spearhead division.[202]

By nightfall on December 15, 1944, Wehrmacht and Nazi SS forces, under the leadership of Field Marshal Gerd von Rundstedt, were concentrated in three main groups along about ninety miles of the Ardennes Forest. With more than 200,000 combat troops, five armored divisions, twelve and two-thirds infantry divisions, 500 tanks, and more than 1,900 artillery guns, the German armies were nearly three miles deep.[203]

The unsuspecting American forces in the Ardennes sector were now outnumbered nearly three to one in troops and weaponry. Composed of four and two-thirds divisions totaling about 83,000 men, the Americans had fewer than half as many tanks and only a third as many artillery guns as the Germans.[204]

With the chessboard now set, von Rundstedt was ready to make the opening move. Ironically, Eisenhower had positioned his First and Third Armies to the north and south of the Germans. The Allies were looking away from the Ardennes battleground lying between them—and had no clue what was about to happen.

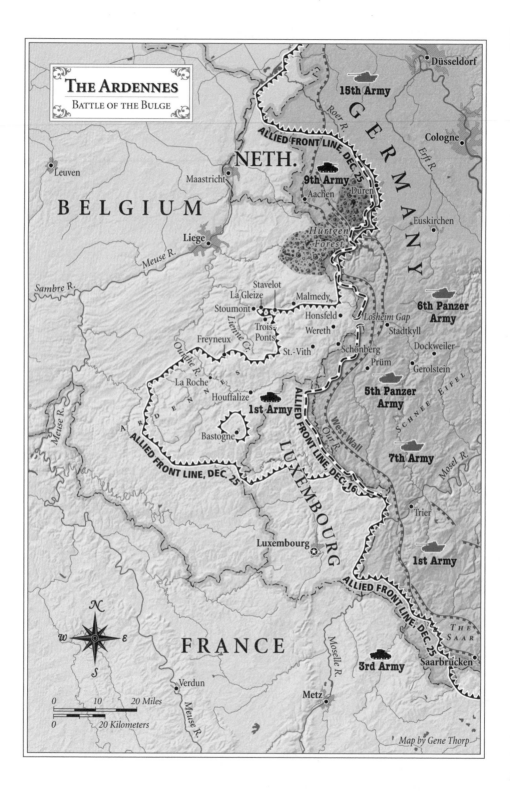

THE ARDENNES
BATTLE OF THE BULGE

Düsseldorf

15th Army

GERMANY

Roer R.

ALLIED FRONT LINE, DEC. 25

Cologne

NETH.

9th Army

Aachen

Düren

Eifl R.

Euskirchen

Leuven

Maastricht

BELGIUM

Hürtgen Forest

Liege

Meuse R.

6th Panzer Army

Sambre R.

Stavelot

La Gleize

Malmedy

Stoumont

Honsfeld

Losheim Gap

Stadtkyll

Dockweiler

Lienne Cr.

Trois-Ponts

Wereth

Schönberg

Gerolstein

Freyneux

St.-Vith

Prüm

Ourthe R.

SCHNEE EIFEL

5th Panzer Army

La Roche

ARDENNES

Houffalize

1st Army

ALLIED FRONT LINE, DEC. 16

West Wall

7th Army

Bastogne

Our R.

Mosel R.

ALLIED FRONT LINE, DEC. 25

LUXEMBOURG

Trier

1st Army

Luxembourg

ALLIED FRONT LINE, DEC. 25

THE SAAR

Meuse R.

N
W E
S

FRANCE

Moselle R.

3rd Army

Saarbrücken

0   10   20 Miles

0   20 Kilometers

Verdun

Metz

Map by Gene Thorp

TWENTY-TWO

Battle of the Bulge

Day 1

The Germans launched their counteroffensive early on the morning of December 16, 1944, catching the Allied armies completely by surprise. Hitler entrusted the Sixth Panzer Army, Germany's best-equipped armored unit, with the primary objective of capturing the Port of Antwerp. Composed of five infantry and four panzer divisions of about one hundred tanks, the Sixth was assigned to attack a twenty-five-mile section in the north sector of the Ardennes. The elite Waffen 1st SS Panzer Division, one of only two units bearing the Führer's name, spearheaded the attack. Led by Joachim Peiper, the 6,000 men and seventy-two tanks of the 1st SS had orders to advance to the Meuse River on a strict timetable and secure its bridges—at all costs.[205]

The battle began in the north as the Sixth Panzer Army hit the Americans with a massive artillery barrage, opening the way for German combat troops to begin their advance west across Belgium. The Sixth's assigned route led through the Losheim Gap, directly to the extensive fuel dumps and supply depots at Liège and Verviers, and from there to the coveted port at Antwerp. First, however, they had to cross the snow-covered hills of Elsenborn Ridge. Expecting little resistance, they were staggered at the tenacity of the battle-hardened U.S. 2nd and inexperienced 99th infantry divisions defending the area. One platoon of only eighteen new recruits from the 99th held off an entire German battalion for ten hours, denying them passage through the Gap. Their incredible feat bought time for American troop reinforcements to move into critical defense positions and further delayed the Sixth Panzer advance.[206,207]

The arrival of reinforcements made matters worse for the Germans, creating a huge bottleneck as their tanks, transport vehicles, and horse-drawn artillery became mired in the muddy, snow-covered roads. *Kampfgruppe* Peiper's* spearhead regiment was stuck in the congestion and forced to wait while the traffic jam blocking the main road was cleared.[208] During the delay, Skorzeny dispatched six of his eight commando teams to begin infiltrating American lines. Each of his Special Forces teams consisted of a demolition crew, a communications unit, and a lead group charged with cutting telephone wires, disrupting communications, and changing road signs.[209]

After waiting all day in the traffic jam, Peiper received orders to take an alternate route to the south. Frustrated and already more than a half day behind schedule, he left the main Sixth Panzer Army, skirting around the battle at Elsenborn. Attempting to make up for lost time, Peiper's detoured unit traveled all night, trudging ahead on nearly impassable secondary roads. As dawn broke, his spearhead regiment had fallen even further behind schedule.[210]

In the south sector, the German Seventh Army attacked a fifteen-mile front with its four infantry divisions. Their chief mission was to establish a defensive line and protect the flanks of the armies to their north as they advanced westward. The German Seventh, surprised at the resistance they encountered, were only able to travel four miles before divisions of the U.S. VII Army Corps held them in check. Although still a serious threat, the German Army in the south was without armored vehicles and proved to be the easiest of the invaders to contain.[211]

In the center sector of the Ardennes offensive, the legendary German Fifth Panzer Army, spearheaded by its Second Panzer Division, attacked a thirty-mile front with two infantry and four panzer divisions. Their initial targets were the towns of St. Vith and Bastogne, where road junctions critical to the success of the German counteroffensive were located.[212]

The attacks caught American regiments across the center sector of the battle by surprise. Hopelessly outnumbered, they fled the

---

*   A German multifaceted combat group consisting of tanks, infantry, and artillery organized
      for a specific operation.

frontlines in disarray. At Schönberg, in the heavily wooded Schnee-Eifel region, the Fifth Panzer Army utterly surprised and cleverly out-maneuvered the U.S. 28th and 106th Infantries, surrounding them both by the end of the day—and no reinforcements were on the way.[213]

Bad weather grounded the Allied air forces on the first day of the German battle. SHAEF had no idea a massive assault was even taking place. General Bradley was still clinging to his belief that the German situation was hopeless and dismissed the reports coming in from the frontlines as merely localized attacks. Inconceivably, even after his First Army intelligence officers captured a copy of von Rundstedt's orders, Bradley failed to respond, still unwilling to accept that the attacks were part of a major counteroffensive.[214]

As Don began writing to Laura Jeanne that night, he couldn't possibly have imagined the life-changing impact that the events taking place 125 miles away in the Ardennes Forest would soon have on him:

Here I sit with my legs wrapped around our little table, just about as happy as my heart will allow. Sharp, Kalen, and I just got back from the show and found mail galore, four letters from my adorable wife, and one from my folks, and a package from my mom, too!

I'm happy that you were so thrilled with the scarf and the perfume. True, it did cost me quite a bit, but you're well worth it—all I ask is that you save a little for when I get home, OK?

I got up bright and early this morning, but didn't fly 'cause of bad weather all day. I've just been sitting here looking at the pictures you sent, rereading your letters, and reminiscing in general. I'm so lucky to have you, and to know that you're mine and mine alone. When I get home, you can bet that I won't ever leave you again.

Honey, please don't worry so much about me, OK? They take care of us well enough. I'll be okay, I promise. I love you and miss you ever so much.

Day 2

On the morning of December 17 in the north sector of the Ardennes, the Sixth Panzer Army continued to meet dogged opposition from the Americans at Elsenborn Ridge. Although outnumbered five to one, the 99th Infantry Division held on to the high ground, refusing to budge, stubbornly blocking the German advance through the Losheim Gap.[215]

Peiper's 1st SS passed through several small Belgium villages during the night and early morning hours of Day 2. Although they met little resistance from American forces, they did lose five tanks to mine explosions along the way. As they approached Honsfeld, the Germans found the roads filled with retreating American vehicles and infantry, all scattering as their panzers approached. The town was easily taken and about 150 captured American prisoners were turned over to Peiper's 9th Parachute Battalion while he led the rest of his forces westward. Next, they surprised an American platoon stationed at Büllingen. After executing fifty U.S. 2nd infantrymen who were attempting to surrender, they forced the seventy survivors to fill their Tiger tanks with gasoline from fuel stores located there. By late morning, Peiper's division had destroyed twelve American planes, killed dozens of civilians, and murdered at least sixty-nine American soldiers—one of them deliberately run over by a tank. Peiper mistakenly believed his breakthrough of the American lines was now complete.[216]

At about noon, Peiper's spearhead division approached the Baugnez crossroads. Five Points, as the Americans called the junction, was located near the tiny village of Malmedy, Belgium. Elements of the 285th Field Artillery Observation Battalion, armed only with rifles and small arms, were traveling south on one of the five roads intersecting at the crossroads on their way to reinforce American troops at St. Vith. As fate would have it, they both arrived at the same time. The 1st SS immediately opened fire, killing around fifty men from the 285th. The Americans panicked, broke ranks, and scattered as they tried to evade the gunfire. Some were able to escape into the woods, but most took cover in nearby ditches and were quickly captured.[217]

Malmedy Massacre

In too big a hurry to cope with so many POWs, Peiper left them at Five Points with a small contingent of SS Troopers, watching as they stripped the prisoners of their cigarettes and valuables and marched them into a nearby field. The colonel then returned to the front of his tank division and started down the road toward the heights of Stavelot. There are conflicting stories about what happened next between the 150 or so POWs and the SS left behind to guard them. In the German version of the story, when a few of the prisoners tried to escape, the guards fired warning shots over their heads to stop them, then the situation escalated. In the American version, surviving soldiers claimed that an SS Trooper deliberately took aim and shot one of the prisoners without any provocation. Then someone yelled an order to kill them all. What followed next, however, is indisputable.[218]

Two panzer machine guns opened fire on the defenseless group of POWs while they still had their hands on their helmets as a token of surrender. Panic erupted. Stunned prisoners fell to the ground, then scattered, trying to flee the onslaught. A few escaped into the woods. Twelve Americans ran into the nearby Café Bodarme, trying to take cover from the barrage of machine gun bullets. The 1st SS Troopers lived up to their Blowtorch reputation, setting the café on fire and forcing the POWs to choose between being burned alive or shot while trying to escape the inferno. Some of the prisoners attempted to survive by dropping face down into the cold, muddy ground, pretending to be dead. Having seen this tactic before in similar massacres of Soviets soldiers on the Eastern Front, the SS walked back and forth among the bodies for the next twenty minutes, kicking groins and shooting anyone that appeared to be alive, reportedly laughing as they did so. Miraculously, more than a dozen G.I.s survived, lying lifeless on the bloody ground, pretending to be dead for more than two hours until the last of the SS battalions had passed. Peiper's SS killed at least eighty-six Americans at Malmedy, many shot in the head at point blank range.[219,220]

The Waffen-SS Troopers removed the dead prisoners' dog tags, then abandoned the bloody field in a hurry to catch up with their lead unit. Whether Peiper actually ordered the bloodbath remains uncertain. Regardless, his decision to leave the POWs in the hands of soldiers fresh from the brutal battles fought on the Eastern Front, where killing civilians and prisoners was commonplace, made him directly responsible for the massacre.[221,222]

By evening, Peiper's forces were bogged down on a muddy Belgium backroad near Stavelot. They had only advanced five miles from Malmedy and were running low on fuel. German intelligence reported vast stores of gasoline on the other side of the lightly defended town, which seemed easily within his grasp, but bad luck continued to follow Peiper. As his tanks crawled down the steep, winding road leading to Stavelot, they encountered mines laid by the U.S. 291st Engineer Battalion. The normally aggressive Peiper stopped and postponed the attack. Exhausted from nearly forty hours without sleep, he chose to wait for his infantry to catch up with him, a decision he'd soon regret. Hitler's tight timetable had Peiper's spearhead unit taking control of the bridges crossing the Meuse River that night. Instead, they were stuck outside Stavelot, forty-two miles away, less than half the distance to their first objective.[223]

The second morning started badly for the Americans in the center sector of the battle. The Fifth Panzer Army launched a brutal attack on regiments of the 28th and 106th Infantry units they'd surrounded in the hilly forests of the Schnee-Eifel region the previous night. The 333rd Field Artillery Battalion, one of two segregated black artillery units fighting the Germans, courageously defended the infantry forces, but the battle quickly turned one-sided. Seriously outnumbered and outgunned, the 422nd and 423rd Infantry Regiments of the 106th were forced to surrender. It was a crushing defeat—the worst suffered to date in the war against the Germans. Between eight and nine thousand men were lost, along with their arms and equipment, with estimates of those killed running as high as one-third. The five to six thousand Americans captured in the battle joined long columns of POWs being marched east to German prison camps.[224,225]

Eleven of the men from the 333rd escaped capture and headed south, trying to get back to American lines. After walking cross-country for hours through deep snow, the hungry, freezing soldiers cautiously approached a farmhouse on the outskirts of the small Belgium village of Wereth. Luckily, the occupants weren't Nazi sympathizers and provided the men with food and shelter. But others in the village informed the next German patrol passing through Wereth of the Americans in hiding. Waffen-SS Troopers serving under Major Gustav Knittel captured the eleven black artillery gunners later that morning. After stripping the prisoners of their coats and belongings, the SS forced them to sit on frozen ground the rest of the day. Then, under cover of darkness, the troopers marched them to the corner of a snow-covered cow pasture, where they were tortured and executed.[226]

SS Troopers had committed three POW atrocities within a matter of hours and within a few miles of each other. Even though Germany had signed the Geneva Convention Treatment of Prisoner of War Rules, Hitler had long since abandoned disciplinary action against soldiers failing to follow them. The Waffen-SS considered the Geneva Conventions more like guidelines than rules, adhering to them only when it was convenient or didn't interfere with their mission. The regular German Army treatment of POWs was better—but not by much. Reports of the Malmedy massacre and the murder of the Americans attempting to surrender earlier that day reached Command within hours. The eleven 333rd POWs executed at Wereth, however, lay buried in the snow-covered cow pasture for two months before the Army discovered them.[227]

After defeating the Americans at Schönberg, the Fifth Panzer Army advanced to the small Belgian town of St. Vith, overlooking the beautiful Our River Valley. Although it had fewer than 2,000 residents, six roads and three railways intersected there, making the town a key transportation hub. Taking control of the crossroads was crucial for the Germans to keep their supply lines flowing as they advanced west toward the Meuse River.[228]

The Germans launched a vicious attack on St. Vith, expecting a swift victory over the greatly outnumbered Americans defending the town. Although surrounded and under heavy bombardment, remnants of the badly beaten up 28th and 106th Infantries, along with recent reinforcements from the U.S. 7th and 9th Armored Divisions, foiled the Nazi plan for a quick and decisive victory. Just like Peiper at Elsenborn, the Second Panzer Division's spearhead unit skirted the battle—leaving the fight for St. Vith to the main Army forces—and raced toward Bastogne.[229]

Throughout Day 2 of the battle, reports flooded SHAEF Command Headquarters from all over the Ardennes. Although von Rundstedt's first move caught General Eisenhower completely off guard, he and most of his staff were now convinced that a major counteroffensive, not localized attacks, was taking place across the entire region.[230]

After intercepting radio communications confirming that the Allies were in disarray across most of the battlefront, Hitler gloated, confident it would take several days before Eisenhower could get approval from his superiors in Washington and Great Britain to deploy additional tanks and troops into the Ardennes to block their advance. By then, it would be too late. However, Eisenhower wasn't micromanaged by President Roosevelt and Prime Minister Churchill, as von Rundstedt was by Hitler. He straightaway pulled his chair up to the chess table, ready to make his first countermove. Within hours, instead of days, General Eisenhower ordered reinforcements to the Ardennes and scheduled an emergency strategy session with his key generals in Verdun, France. Despite his quick response, the Allies were under serious threat, and German armies were advancing toward Antwerp.

In his first major countermove, Eisenhower ordered the 101st Airborne Division to Bastogne to reinforce the meager American forces defending the town's pivotal crossroads. Having recently returned from combat in Holland, the 101st "Screaming Eagles" were resting and recuperating at Camp Mourmelon, located near Reims, France. Many of the men weren't at the camp. Some were on leave in England, but most had passes closer to the base in Paris and Reims and were rounded up throughout the night of December 17. Although ill equipped and surprised that the Army had called them back into action so soon, the battle-tested 101st Airborne nonetheless rose to the occasion. Brigadier General Anthony C. McAuliffe gathered his men that night, telling them, "All I know of the situation is that there has been a breakthrough, and we have got to get up there."[231] The race was now on to see who could get to Bastogne first—the 101st or the German panzer armies.

On the second morning of the battle, the Luftwaffe sent up more planes in support of their ground troops than they'd put in the air since D-Day. Between 600 and 700 German fighter planes attempted to disrupt Allied air attacks all over the battlefront. The Eighth and Ninth Air Forces matched their move, sending out 647 sorties of their own. Both sides packed the overcast skies with fighter planes, and a major air battle took place above the Ardennes Forest. The Germans' decision to support troops from the air that day worked. They succeeded in diverting Allied air attacks by luring fighter planes into air battles, forcing them to jettison many of the bombs and rockets intended for Wehrmacht and SS ground forces. But it was a costly strategy. Luftwaffe aircraft losses in the dogfights with American fighter planes were catastrophic—sixty-eight German planes to sixteen American, more than four to one.[232]

The 368th Fighter Group sent out fifty-two P-47s on Day 2 of the battle to provide close air support for the 28th and 106th Infantry

Divisions defending St. Vith, and to conduct armed recces fifty miles to the south around Trier near the West Wall.[233] Bob took off that morning in a flight of sixteen Thunderbolts, each armed with four rockets. After returning from his mission, he made the following entry into his mission log:

> Our group, led by Major Leary, was sent to help stop the new German counterattack. Our flight went out at about 5,000 feet. We missed our point and slipped into enemy territory. We knew this because we got the worst flak I've ever seen. We flew out, then made it to our target area and stooged the enemy. There was a lot of German activity everywhere.
>
> I flew over some trucks and shot up three of them. They fired back, hitting me in the rudder, and the tail of my fuselage, and in the prop spinner. It made me mad, so I flew back over and fired all four of my rockets in their vicinity, badly damaging them. Weinstein was flying with me and he mushed into some tree on a strafing pass that dented his wings, but he was able to keep flying. The flak, with those red balls and tracers, and that white puffed stuff, was really rough.

The controller relayed a radio message from the troops defending St. Vith, pleading, "If you can knock out the leading tank and slow them down, we may be able to hold the town tonight." Major Leary responded, making eight solo passes through heavy flak, single-handedly destroying several tanks and vehicles. His feat earned him a Silver Star, America's third highest military combat medal.[234]

Don's flight group of twelve planes, carrying a combination of bombs and rockets, targeted enemy road traffic coming into St. Vith. In a combat statement filed that evening, Don reported the following details of his mission:

> I was flying Tropic Blue Four on a ground support and armed recce mission. We were flying at about 12,000 feet in the vicinity of Prüm [just east of St. Vith on the German side of the West Wall] when we were attacked by about 22 Fw-190s and 15 Me-109s.
>
> The enemy aircraft came from above us at about 15,000 feet. We were forced to ditch our bombs and rockets, and then we

immediately began to climb in their direction to meet their attack. Four or five of the 190s started down on us from 11 o'clock high. One of them made a head on pass at Lt. Frederick Stoll, my flight element leader. Both aircraft were firing at each other, and I observed hits on the 190, as well as on Lt. Stoll's plane. His aircraft burst into flames and began to spin at about 13,000 feet as the enemy aircraft broke away.

I don't know if he was able to bail out or not, since another aircraft was demanding my full attention at the time, but Lt. Stoll did inflict damage on the Fw-190 that attacked him. I had trouble getting the other 190 off my tail. He fired at me, shooting up my prop hub, canopy, wing, and tail section. I was finally able to get in position to fire back and got several hits, seriously damaging the airplane. I was pretty shot up, but was able to return to the base. I was low on fuel and had a difficult landing due to strong wind gusts and the beat-up condition of my plane.[235]

Bob's touchdown wasn't a picture-perfect, three-point landing either:

Coming home, I landed in a crosswind and ran off the side of the rain-slicked runway—and then went over a sand pile, ran over some 6 by 6 logs, and finally came to a stop.

Lt. Stoll wasn't as lucky as Don and Bob and suffered serious burns and injuries as he bailed out of his fiery plane behind enemy lines. A month later, he died in a German POW hospital from his wounds.[236] Kenny and Pat entered the fray that day as well, having their own confrontation with enemy planes. The guys huddled around their pot-bellied stove until late that night, musing over their close calls, feeling lucky they'd made it back home safely from their toughest mission to date. Sitting next to the warm fire burning in their stove, they couldn't imagine how awful it must be for their ground troops—stuck in foxholes filled with snow and mud, trying to survive sub-zero temperatures on one of the coldest nights on record in the Ardennes.

In air skirmishes like those Don and his buddies were in that day, there frequently wasn't any photo taken or other pilots present to confirm and document the results of the air battles. Don's written statement regarding Lt. Stoll's fateful mission was entered into the official war records of the 368th, while his own mission results went unrecorded. Although later describing his first aerial battle as "a white-knuckle affair he barely escaped," Don remained eager for his next encounter with the Luftwaffe. But fate dictated otherwise. This would be his only dogfight of the war.

While his bunkmates took off to see a movie at the Officers Club, Don reluctantly headed to the operations trailer. Fully briefed, with first-hand experience about the new German counteroffensive, he was in a quandary about what to include in his next letter to Laura Jeanne. Knowing that she followed the war in Europe closely, he couldn't ignore the alarming turn of events, but he didn't want to worry her either. Concerned more about the latter, he kept his letter that night as witty and upbeat as possible, hoping to waylay her fears about the abrupt escalation in the war:

> *It's about midnight, and I feel pretty dopey, which naturally means I'm OD again. I flew another mission today, and it was really a rough one. Someday I'll tell you all about it. The weather has been "stinking" all day (rain, wind, drizzle, and fog) but we flew nevertheless.*

> *It's now a couple of hours later, and I just finished eating a very delicious steak, along with a fried egg. It was undoubtedly the best steak I've had since I left the States. The sergeant of the guard and I cut out two thick steaks from the best piece of beef we could find in the pilots' kitchen and cooked them on a little stove we have here in the operations trailer. I think I could go right to sleep now.*

> *Remember how tired I used to get when I first started RTU at Bruning? After a mission over here, I feel even more knocked out, even though the mission may only last for 2 ½ to 3 hours. Sorry, I just dozed off for a few seconds and almost fell off my chair! It's now 5:19 a.m. About three more hours to go, then I'm going to hit my cozy little sack all day long. I've been informed my name has been approved for promotion to first lieutenant, but I'm still waiting for the paper work to come through.*

According to the radio reports I'm getting tonight, the Jerries have started hitting us with about all they have in an effort to stop our advances and prolong the war. Our boys on the frontline got beat up pretty bad the past two days. You're probably listening to the same thing right now on the radio.

I still haven't developed much Christmas spirit, but we're all chipping in to get the orphans in a small town nearby a few things for Christmas. Sharp, Kalen, Patrick and I are also donating candy from our Xmas packages to help out. I guess it's been a long time since these kids have had anything like that. I hate to part with what I get so little of, but if it will make these kids happy, then I can stand it. So I guess I do have a little Christmas spirit after all.

The telephone is ringing quite frequently now, so I'd better sign off. Take care of yourself, honey, and I'll do the same. I'm loving you always.

Eisenhower received a distressing phone call that night from General Patton, reporting alarming news coming from the frontlines: "Ike, I've never seen such a goddamn foul-up! The Krauts are infiltrating behind our lines, raising hell, cutting wires, and turning around road signs!"[237]

Skorzeny's commando teams were wreaking havoc on Allied ground troops, just as Hitler had foreseen. One unit directed an American infantry division down a wrong road, and the unit was lost for three days. A different team blocked off a key road junction, disrupting traffic by marking the roads with minefield warning tape. Others jammed or completely cut off Allied communication lines. But as successful as that part of Skorzeny's mission was, Kampfgruppe Peiper's setbacks forced the commandos to delay and eventually abort their original mission of infiltrating American lines and capturing key Meuse River bridges.

101st Airborne in Bastogne

TWENTY-THREE

"Hold the Bastogne Line at All Costs"

Day 3

General Bradley's First Army was struggling to hold back the German Sixth Panzer Army in the north sector of the battle. Even with four of his divisions in full retreat, he remained unconvinced that the Wehrmacht had mounted a major attack. Worse still, when General Courtney Hodges, First Army Commander, realized the magnitude of the counteroffensive, he came unglued, closing himself up in his office, refusing to take any calls. Two days later, he emerged in a panic and haphazardly evacuated his command post, leaving secret maps and classified documents scattered all over his office— apparently more concerned about properly packing his Pinks-and-Greens and liquor cabinet than he was about his command. Hodges remained dysfunctional for several days, providing little leadership to officers serving under him. His behavior caused Eisenhower and Bradley to consider relieving him of his command. Instead, they temporarily replaced him with other capable officers, hoping he would regain his previous gravitas, which he reportedly did the following week.[238]

The small town of Stavelot lay in the beautiful Amblève River Valley, surrounded by high wooded bluffs. Most of its 5,000 residents lived on a hillside on the north bank of the river. A single bridge, located at the bottom of a steep, winding road provided the only access to the town. Early on the morning of December 18, after his infantry finally caught up to him, Peiper attacked the town, eager to refuel his tanks and armored vehicles. During the night, however, the small First Army unit defending Stavelot took advantage of the delayed attack, evacuating most of the fuel supplies and bringing in reinforcements. What would have been an easy victory the previous night now turned into a fierce battle as the Americans doggedly defended the bridge accessing the town.[239]

By late morning, the Americans realized they couldn't hold back the 1st SS Panzers much longer and decided to blow up the bridge. The demolition attempt failed, but the First Army unit wasn't yet ready to give up. They repositioned on top of the hill overlooking Stavelot, dug in, and prepared to make another stand. After crossing the bridge, the German tanks started climbing the hill in pursuit of the Americans. Armed with three puny 57mm anti-tank guns, the Americans' situation didn't look good against an entire column of Tiger tanks. However, their quick-thinking platoon leader ordered his men to commandeer gasoline from the remaining fuel stores and dump it into a deep gully located in a narrow section of the road between them and the Germans. As the tanks advanced close to the dug-in First Army, the Americans lit up the pool of gasoline, creating a massive, flaming, anti-tank barrier that blocked the Tiger advances. In control of the high ground above the town, the undaunted platoon continued holding back the German advance. The 291st engineers then redeemed themselves by blowing up the remaining fuel stored at the dump. Peiper watched in frustration as more than 124,000 gallons of gasoline went up in flames.[240] For the first time, the "Blowtorch" battalion was on the receiving end of firestorms.

Eager to make up lost time, Peiper left most of his regiment at Stavelot to battle the Americans and led an advance group to the next bridge crossing at Trois-Ponts (Three Bridges), four miles to the southwest. The secondary roads the 1st SS had traveled so far had been muddy, snow-packed, and in places, not much better than trails. However, the main road west from Trois-Ponts, all the way to the Meuse River, was a good highway. Once across the next bridges, Peiper was confident he could drive to the Meuse before the day was over.[241] Two of Trois-Ponts' three bridges crossed the Salm River, and the other crossed the adjacent Amblève. About 140 men from the First Army 51st Engineer Combat Battalion, armed with only eight bazookas, ten machine guns, and no anti-tank weapons, guarded the crossings.[242]

Earlier that morning while passing through Trois-Ponts, part of an artillery column of the U.S. 7th Armored Division became lost. They decided to stop and wait next to a railroad underpass located in front of the first bridge that crossed the Amblève, hoping someone from their unit would return for them. For no particular reason, they positioned their only anti-tank weapon, an undersized 57mm gun, in the middle of the narrow, muddy, snow-packed road coming from Stavelot.[243]

About noon, Peiper's advance guard of twenty Tiger tanks came rolling down the road and ran into the small artillery unit. The gun crew might have been lost, but they were still quick on the draw and got off the first round. One lucky shot from their anti-tank gun crippled the lead Tiger tank, bringing it to a halt on the narrow muddy road. The Germans immediately fired back, destroying the 57mm gun and killing four members of the gun crew. As a direct result of the brief mêlée, two remarkable things happened. First, the disabled lead tank blocked the entire Tiger column, keeping the other tanks from advancing the last hundred yards to the bridge. And second, the noise from the brief cannon fire exchange warned the bridge guards and engineers of an impending assault.[244]

The resulting delay bought the 51st Engineers enough time to blow up the first bridge—right in Peiper's face. Then the alert engineers retreated to the second bridge crossing over the Salm and blew that one too. Peiper was reportedly furious, yelling curses at the American engineers blocking his advance with their timely explosions. Now there was only one direction to go—north to La Gleize, where one of the few remaining bridges strong enough to support the 1st SS heavy tanks was located.[245]

Peiper's lead unit slowly advanced north along another muddy, snow-packed backroad, winding its way through the steep, rocky, walled canyons of the Amblève River Valley. Eventually, they found a bridge near La Gleize, crossed over the river, and headed back toward the main highway. Just as Peiper's luck appeared to have changed, the thick overcast skies that had been shielding him from air attacks suddenly cleared. A squadron of P-47 fighter-bombers flying an armed recce spotted the exposed Tigers and attacked. Dropping bombs, firing rockets, and strafing with their .50 caliber guns, they took out three tanks and destroyed seven halftracks, forcing the battalion to halt.[246]

The delay was another costly one. It took Kampfgruppe Peiper several hours to clear off the road and get the tank column moving again. Anticipating Peiper's next move, an opportunistic squad from the 291st Engineer Combat Battalion beat him there. As the Germans approached the bridge crossing their final obstacle at Lienne Creek—within sight of the main highway, only a few hours from the Meuse River—the engineer crew waited patiently for the first Tiger to drive onto the bridge, then blew it up.[247] Peiper reportedly cried out in frustration, "The damned engineers! The damned engineers!"

Peiper, running out of options, turned around and headed north again. After traveling all night in the dark, his unit reached the outskirts of Stoumont, where the Americans controlled the only remaining bridge strong enough to support the heavy Tiger tanks.[248]

Bastogne, Belgium, is an ancient town situated atop the high Ardennes plateau near the Luxembourg border. Founded in the early days of the Roman Empire, the town is best known for its Gothic churches, which date as far back as the Middle Ages, and for its agriculture and cattle fairs.[249] The Germans were only interested in the small town's high-capacity road network. Seven hard-surfaced highways converged there, including the main roads leading west through the Ardennes Forest. Capturing Bastogne was critical to the success of Hitler's counteroffensive, and holding on to it was equally crucial for the Allies. On Day 3 of the battle, German intelligence intercepted careless American radio traffic, confirming that Eisenhower was sending reinforcements to Bastogne. The German Seventh Army from the south and the Fifth Panzer Army from the northeast hurried to get there first.[250]

Usually the 11,000 paratroopers from the 101st Airborne Division airdropped into their combat zones, but this time they were trucked.[251] One of the 101st officers, Colonel Edward Shames, later wrote the following about their 107-mile truck ride to Bastogne through rain and snow flurries and freezing temperatures:[252]

We ended up in 10-ton open tractor-trailer trucks without a top, freezing our tails off. We had no good clothing and some of the men even had no weapons. We saw hordes of hysterical soldiers [retreating] and watched them throw their weapons and equipment to the ground to lighten their load, yelling: "Don't go up there! The Germans are going to kill everyone!" One good thing...we were able to retrieve equipment, clothing, and ammo scattered all over the area.

When we offloaded the trucks that morning, [we] didn't have the foggiest notion where we were... and it was cold as hell.[253]

The 101st paratroopers arrived from the west at midnight, minutes before the Germans reached the outskirts of the town from the north and east. The Americans had won the race to Bastogne, but they still faced a greater challenge—retaining control of the town while greatly outnumbered and seriously outgunned.[254]

Bitter fighting continued in the battle for St. Vith on day three of the counteroffensive. That the Americans were still holding onto the important crossroads surprised Allied Command as much as it did Wehrmacht leadership. Part of their success was due to disagreements and miscommunication among the advancing German armies concerning priorities and strategy. Neither the Fifth nor Sixth Panzer Armies seemed interested in taking ownership of the battle to capture St. Vith, located on the boundary line of areas assigned to each army. The Sixth passed it by, advancing west as fast as possible—and the Fifth underestimated the resources required to defeat the resolute Americans defending the strategic town.[255]

The German advance in the center section of the Ardennes gained momentum on Day 3, the counteroffensive's greatest success to date. The Fifth Panzer Army, spearheaded by its 2nd Panzer Division, picked up speed, pressing forward unchecked toward the Meuse River.[256] Despite setbacks in the north and south, where fighting was at a stalemate, Hitler was ecstatic at the success experienced in the middle sector and believed his strategic gamble was paying off. The 2nd Panzer spearhead unit's rapid advance had created a growing protrusion in the Ardennes frontline, giving the German counteroffensive its best-known name—the Battle of the Bulge.

———————

Bob, Kenny, and Pat took part in a dangerous, eighty-five-plane "volunteer only" mission on December 18. Virtually unflyable weather forced thirty-six P-47s to abort and return to the base shortly after takeoff. The rest managed to provide close air support for the 28th and 106th Infantries, which were struggling to hold on at St. Vith. The 396th Squadron attacked the troops Peiper had left behind at Stavelot, destroying fourteen tanks and severely damaging another thirty, helping the Americans retain control of the town.[257] Bob recorded the following:

> *I flew in Major Leary's flight on Baker's wing, Red No. 4. We tried to stay under the clouds, but finally had to go up one layer. It turned out to be solid overcast, instead of a layer, and we got separated. We finally broke out, and circled for about half an hour until the rest of the squadron joined us, then headed for Düren.*

> *There were a lot of Spits* and P-38s in the area. Red flight broke away from them and went down to get rid of some of our rockets. I damaged a building and a truck with my two rockets, then destroyed three armed vehicles and damaged one more with my strafing.*

> *Top-cover got jumped by 30 plus Me-109s. I jettisoned my other two rockets, and we started to climb. Leary followed a diving 109 and shot him down. Baker and I just circled, trying to get altitude to get up to the fight. Potter and Clary each got one destroyed. I saw one 109 explode. It was a pretty sight.*

> *Fauley got hit by three cannon shells and started burning. Luckily, the fire went out. We lost Conant, who was flying in Green Flight. The P-38s that were there with us didn't shoot down anything.*

———————

*   Slang for British Spitfire fighter aircraft.

When the boys returned home that afternoon, they found Don asleep on his cot, pulled close to their pot-bellied stove. They roused him, eager to share details of their air battles with the Luftwaffe. He started feeling a little guilty for sleeping all day while his buddies were in the air putting their lives on the line. But he had a good excuse, having spent the previous night on O.D. Besides, his crew chief was still patching up his plane from his skirmish with an Fw-190 the previous day. In his letter that night to Laura Jeanne, Don wrote:

The weather was "lousy" again, raining all day, but the guys flew anyway and ended up tangling with the Luftwaffe. I got a pass due to my all-night assignment. I think I'm beginning to understand why the French and Belgians are such great wine drinkers—it rains so darn much over here they hate the sight of water!

Not much doing around here. Sharp and I played a few games of Ping-Pong, and that took care of the entertainment for the evening. I'm munching on some popcorn Mom sent in the last package. It's "Snacks" by name and tastes very good. Why don't you send me some more, okay? There was a show tonight, but the guys saw it last night while I was on OD, and I didn't want to go alone, so here I am.

I just read a brief fashion note from the ETO magazine you might find of interest, "As in '42 and '43, young ladies will be wearing the same thing in sweaters again this season." Wish I could see you in one right now. I'll probably go "looney" before that happens, though!

Day 4

In the north sector of the battle on December 19, Peiper's main forces at Stavelot captured the town from the Americans, following a fierce all-night tank battle.[258] When a few townspeople threatened their German captors with shotguns, the elite SS Troopers killed them on the spot, then took retribution against the entire town. Going door to door, they randomly dragged 130 terrified residents from their homes, accusing them of harboring American soldiers. After lining them up in the street, the SS Troopers executed them all. Included in the atrocity were sixty men, forty-seven women, and twenty-three children—the oldest a seventy-eight-year-old woman and the youngest a nine-month-old baby.[259] Once they'd secured the town, the Germans left a small rearguard behind, then quickly moved west to catch up with their lead battalion.

Earlier that morning, Peiper launched a surprise attack on the Americans guarding the tiny village of Stoumont. Following a two-hour tank battle, the 1st SS captured the village, then headed west toward the final bridge between them and the Meuse River. As their first Tiger started across, a tank battalion from the 30th Infantry Division ambushed Peiper's lead unit and knocked out three of his tanks. The rest retreated from the bridge crossing. It was the closest Hitler's favorite battlefield leader would get to the Meuse River.[260]

Peiper anticipated that the German divisions behind him would reinforce his rearguard at Stavelot and quickly catch up with him. Instead, the Americans unexpectedly retook control of the town that night, effectively cutting Kampfgruppe Peiper off from the rest of the Sixth Panzer Army. After receiving news that Stavelot had been lost, the colonel ordered SS Major Knittel's Waffen-SS battalion to return and recapture the town. However, the reinforced Americans repelled the attack and forced the SS to retreat, leaving Peiper completely cut off. Too low on fuel to advance farther, he had no choice but to dig in and hold out until reinforcements arrived. Loss of communications with the main Sixth Panzer Army left him unaware that the fighting to his rear had hit a stalemate, blocking their advance.[261] The Blowtorch Battalion was now isolated and in serious trouble.

———————

In the south sector, battles were taking place all around the outskirts of Bastogne. Even with the arrival of the 101st Airborne Division, General Anthony McAuliffe's forces remained greatly outnumbered. A battle-hardened leader who was revered by his troops, the general remained resolute in following his orders to "hold the Bastogne line at all costs." However, to do so for very long would require additional reinforcements and supplies, and neither was yet on its way. Sensing impending doom, the residents began fleeing the town in droves.[262]

———————

In the center section of the battlefront, the Fifth Panzer Army and its 2nd Panzer Division spearhead battalion encountered limited opposition on Day 4 and extended the bulge closer to the Meuse River. So far they'd been unstoppable, remaining the Allies' most serious threat. With Peiper's spearhead unit in trouble, German Command had now charged them with primary responsibility to capture and secure bridges at the Meuse, the most critical piece in the Führer's strategy to recapture Antwerp.[263]

Mother Nature continued her adversarial role in the Ardennes region, not only keeping the 368th out of the sky, but the entire Ninth Air Force as well, grounding them with her cloud cover. Don expressed his frustration, writing:

The visibility has been near zero all day long. What fog! As a result, we've just been sitting around at the line waiting for the weather to break up, but to no avail. Our troops on the frontlines need us, and we can't get up in the air! Are the home-front strategists still optimistic the war is about over? They ought to make those "crackpots" get a taste of what's really going on over here.

Late that night, Don picked his fountain pen back up and ended his letter on a better note:

We've had about 10 guys in our room all night just gabbing and doing nothing in general. As usual, we're eating again. Sharp got some more crackers from home, and we opened some of my tuna fish—it makes a very tasty nighttime snack before hitting the old sack.

We've really been enjoying all the Christmas goodies we've received lately, but I don't feel the Christmas spirit much. I just feel lost and a million miles from home. I'd give anything to be with you when the New Year comes in, but it looks like we're going to be pretty busy over here for quite some time with this new German offensive.

Generals Eisenhower and Patton

TWENTY-FOUR

Eisenhower and Patton

On December 19, U.S. Generals Eisenhower, Bradley, Patton, Devers, and Smith, along with British Air Marshall Tedder, met in Verdun, France, in an emergency strategy session. Eisenhower traveled there secretly in an armor-plated Cadillac while a security detail was driving around the streets of Versailles in one of his Jeeps with a look-alike decoy wearing Ike's hat and overcoat.[264]

During interrogation, recently captured members of Skorzeny's commandos divulged a plot to kill or kidnap the supreme commander. The fabricated conspiracy propagated by the clever special operatives advanced the mission of Operation Greif and forced Eisenhower to remain under guard and in seclusion. Fuming over the disorder, confusion, and rumors that Skorzeny and his special forces had created, Eisenhower finally ordered a manhunt and plastered "wanted" posters with the commando leader's picture and description all over Allied-occupied territory.[265]

During the SHAEF strategy session, the Allied Generals not only discussed how to halt the German drive west, but also deliberated a counterattack of their own to exploit the spread-out German armies. British Field Marshall Montgomery was conspicuously absent from the meeting. Once again offending the Americans, the arrogant commander refused to attend when he discovered there would be officers of lesser rank at the meeting. In his stead, he sent his deputy, while he remained safe, far behind enemy lines.[266]

Eisenhower made clear his first objective in dealing with the new threat, stating, "The enemy must never be allowed to cross the Meuse." So far, reports confirmed that the Sixth Panzer Army was being contained in the north sector of the battle. But the Fifth Panzer Army, led by its 2nd Panzer Division spearhead unit, was rapidly advancing in the center front, where the bulge had expanded dangerously close to the Meuse River. Eisenhower faced two major challenges: First, he had to halt the spearhead division that was creating the bulge and deal with the main Fifth Panzer Army that followed them. And second, he had to retain control of the vital road network at Bastogne. Doing so would choke off vital supply lines to the battlefront and bring the advancing German armies to an abrupt halt—the same strategy Hitler had devised in his drive to capture Antwerp.[267]

After evaluating input from his generals, Eisenhower gave General Bradley orders to move his troops farther north to reinforce the Allied defense in that sector. Then he ordered General Devers and his Seventh Army to move into position from the south to halt the German advance in the Bulge. For the most problematic mission, Eisenhower turned to General Patton, ordering him to go on the offensive with his Third Army and attack the southern flank of the Bulge, all the way to Bastogne. In total, Eisenhower's second countermove would send more than 250,000 troops to the Ardennes battle sectors. His response was quick, big, and decisive—and neither Hitler nor von Rundstedt saw it coming.[268]

Aware the Americans defending Bastogne were running out of time, Eisenhower's first question to General Patton was how soon he could get started. In typical fashion, Patton blurted out, "As soon as you're through with me. I can attack the day after tomorrow and be in Bastogne by Christmas Day." The others in attendance looked at Patton with raised eyebrows, some reportedly even laughed, skeptical of his claim. Eisenhower spoke for them all, saying, "Don't be fatuous, George; if you go that early you won't have all three of your divisions ready, and you'll go piecemeal. Start on the 22nd or even the 23rd if it takes that long to get ready. I want your initial blow to be a strong one." But Patton didn't waiver, sticking to his original reply. However, he failed to divulge that he'd already met with his staff and initiated plans to mobilize the Third Army. Fearful that Bastogne would fall to the Germans if it weren't rescued by Christmas Day, Patton knew he had to take action before the meeting. Realizing what had to be done, and how critical the time frame was, the general had already set the wheels in motion, confident that Eisenhower would concur—if he ever found out. Unlike the other leaders that had come to Verdun, Patton arrived with a well-devised strategy, consistent with his motto: "Lead me, follow me, or get out of my way."[269,270]

The weather had turned terribly cold. Sleet, fog, snow, and mud now plagued the entire Ardennes region. Mobilizing 100,000 men, thousands of supply trucks, tanks, and other vehicles to move 125 miles over muddy, snow-packed roads in only two days did sound "fatuous." But Patton, possibly the most brilliant battle commander ever produced by any military in history, was up for the challenge and eager to prove himself one more time.[271]

George S. Patton was one of a kind. Born into a wealthy family with a proud military heritage, he grew up listening to stories about his ancestors, who had fought in the Revolutionary, Mexican, and Civil wars. Patton graduated from West Point, receiving a commission as a second lieutenant in the Army at age twenty-four. An exceptional athlete and master swordsman, he was selected by the Army to represent the United States at the 1912 Stockholm Olympics in the first modern Pentathlon. The events included pistol shooting, sword fencing, swimming, horseback riding, and cross-country running. He dropped out of the medals to fifth place after a scoring controversy in the pistol shooting competition. In typical Patton fashion, he shot a powerful .38 caliber pistol, which made much larger holes than the tiny, non-recoiling .22 caliber used by the other contestants. The judges docked him for a miss when his target was short one bullet hole. He contended, however, that one shot passed cleanly through one of the other holes tightly grouped on his target.[272]

Patton saw his first military action in the Spanish American War, fighting against Pancho Villa. During the conflict, Patton observed the newly created 1st Aero Squadron provide air support to Army ground troops and cavalry, knowledge that would serve him well in future wars. In 1918, during World War I, he led his men to victory in the Army's first major tank battle. He demonstrated his lead-from-the-front strategy, placing himself in harm's way to better direct his tanks from the frontlines. After the battle, the Army awarded him the Distinguished Service Cross for Heroism for his brave leadership during the battle—and for getting himself shot in the process.[273]

Shortly after America entered World War II, General Eisenhower gave Patton command of the Western Task Force, where he invaded North Africa and defeated Germany's most famous Nazi general, Field Marshall Erwin Rommel. The following year, while leading the Seventh Army, he invaded Sicily and took it back from the Germans. Then in 1944, he assumed leadership of the Third Army in France, where he drove the Germans 600 miles back across central France, right up to the West Wall, while the armies of Bradley and Montgomery struggled to keep pace with him.[274]

Far from a role model, Patton was repeatedly embroiled in controversy. He was hard on his men and intolerant of failure, his language was colorful, he was frequently brash and outspoken, and his impulsive behavior landed him in trouble on a number of occasions. While being attacked by fighter planes during the Allied invasion of Sicily, the Seventh Army was prevented from crossing a bridge by a cart being pulled by a pair of stubborn mules. Patton was livid that the cart driver couldn't move the mules, so he shot both animals and pushed them off the bridge so his troops could advance. When their owner angrily confronted him, he started beating the muleskinner with his walking stick—and might have pushed him off the bridge too, if his men hadn't intervened.[275]

Patton regularly visited wounded soldiers at medical aid stations and evacuation hospitals to commend them for their bravery in battle. On two separate occasions, he interviewed G.I.s who were recovering from what doctors had called "battle fatigue." Patton disagreed and diagnosed the soldiers' condition as "cowardice." He slapped them, gave them each a tongue-lashing, and sent them back to the frontlines—then issued orders to his commanders to discipline any soldier making similar complaints.[276]

Word of the "slapping incidents" eventually reached General Eisenhower. He severely reprimanded Patton and insisted that he personally apologize to the two soldiers and all others who had witnessed the incidents. Reluctantly, Eisenhower felt compelled to take away his command of the First Army and reassigned him to England. Patton smoldered inside when he was kept out of the D-Day invasion—but was lucky his friend Ike hadn't sent him home over his unseemly behavior. Even with all Patton's flaws, Eisenhower still considered him his best battlefield general and couldn't afford to lose him.[277]

Most overseas news reporters were aware of the slapping incidents. They chose not to report them because they were more concerned about the success of the war effort than airing salacious stories that might get the general sent home. However, war correspondent Drew Pearson, one of the last reporters to hear about the incidents (over three months after they took place), couldn't pass up the notoriety he knew would accompany the story. Claiming the revelation as his own inside scoop, he reported the details of Patton's foibles on national radio. He also implicated Eisenhower, accusing him of trying to cover up the incidents, even though he knew that to be untrue. It all made for good press.[278]

Back home, Americans were stunned by the actions of their favorite war hero. Former military leaders and members of Congress harshly criticized Patton, many calling for his resignation. Earlier in the war, his picture had graced the covers of *Time* and *Life* magazines. And in one of his press conferences, President Roosevelt had praised him as "America's greatest fighting General," comparing him to Lincoln's General Grant in the Civil War.[279] But even the president was troubled by the slapping incidents.

In the end, the scandal blew over. Recognizing that Patton's win-at-all-costs leadership style was exactly what America needed against the Nazis, Roosevelt took no further disciplinary actions against him. After a cooling off period in England of several months, Eisenhower finally gave Patton another command—the newly organized Third Army. The rest is history.[280]

Patton cast a long shadow and enjoyed basking in his own limelight. He was seldom seen without one of his flashy ivory-handled pistols. His favorite, a silver-plated Colt .45 Peacemaker, had a 4.75 inch barrel. Sometimes he wore his Smith and Wesson .357 Magnum, the most powerful handgun in the world. And on a few occasions—mostly for photographers—he strapped on both pistols.[281]

Now age fifty-nine, Patton was called "old blood and guts" by many of his men, while others affectionately referred to him as the "old man." He often stopped his open-air Jeep on rides around the battlefront to talk to his men and learn how they were doing. In contrast, his counterparts usually received their battle reports in safer, more comfortable locations, miles behind the frontlines. Still leading from the front, as he'd done in World War I, Patton was considered reckless by many of his peers, but to his men, he was courageous.[282]

German High Command respected and feared Patton more than any other Allied commander. According to Eisenhower, "His name struck terror at the hearts of the enemy." Hitler couldn't figure him out, referring to him as "that crazy cowboy general!" Patton was America's answer to Skorzeny and Peiper, equally fearless with a sword or a tank, and he backed them up with his six shooters. In his own words, "May God have mercy upon my enemies—because I sure as hell won't!"[283]

———————

The stage was set for General Patton's finest hour. German intelligence had pinpointed his Third Army 125 miles south of Bastogne and considered him too far away to disrupt their attack. His response, if successful, would come as a complete surprise, considering the terrible weather and near impassible road conditions—and the fact he would have to break through German lines to get there. Patton was determined to succeed, however, convinced that only the weather or God could keep him from achieving his mission. In desperate need of clear skies to allow the air forces to resume their bombing, strafing, and close air support, that's exactly where he turned.

Before beginning his campaign, Patton asked his senior chaplain to compose a prayer, pleading with God to "restrain these immoderate rains...grant us fair weather for Battle that...we may crush the oppression and wickedness of our enemies, and establish Thy justice among men and nations." Third Army head chaplain James O'Neill initially struggled with the idea of praying for clear weather to kill his fellowmen, but Patton persisted, reminding him God had intervened in many Old Testament battles. A devout Episcopalian, Patton was convinced that God *did* take sides when good and evil were at odds, and fervently believed that Deity would side with the Allies against the "Godless Nazis." The general had 250,000 wallet-sized cards printed up with the "Chaplain's Prayer" on one side and a "Merry

Christmas" holiday greeting on the other, giving one to each officer and soldier in his command.[284] George S. Patton paid attention to every battle detail—and having God on his side wasn't one he was about to overlook.

Patton's Third army trudging toward Bastogne

TWENTY-FIVE

Bad Weather and Bad News

Day 5

Dense overcast hovered over the entire Ardennes Forest on December 20. Unexpectedly, the day's first gray light revealed the outnumbered U.S. 7th and 9th Armored Divisions still holding on at St. Vith. The Americans' stubborn defense not only safeguarded the fuel and supplies stored there, but also forced the Germans to detour onto nearly impassable secondary backroads, creating traffic bottlenecks and further slowing the panzer armies.[285]

Further to the west, Peiper's forces were defiantly holding on at Stoumont, exchanging cannon fire with the 505th Parachute Infantry Regiment of the 82nd Airborne Division. That afternoon, the 1st SS Panzer Grenadier Regiment, carrying reinforcements and supplies for Kampfgruppe Peiper, fought their way west, intent on fording the Amblève River near Trois Ponts.[286]

Forty miles to the south at Bastogne, General McAuliffe and the 101st Airborne Division received encouraging news that General Patton's Third Army was on the way with reinforcements. Until they arrived, however, the 101st had their hands full. Outnumbered and outgunned, they were running low on food, supplies, and ammunition. Panzer tank columns now had the Americans nearly surrounded, and additional Wehrmacht troops were on the way. Although the 101st faced a tenuous situation, McAuliffe remained undaunted, determined to keep his pledge to hold the town at all costs. One of his greatest challenges was finding his men enough shelter from the elements to keep them from freezing to death in the bombed-out, mostly abandoned town.[287]

In both the north and south battle sectors, American resistance forces continued holding the Wehrmacht and SS attacks in check, buying time for the Allies to organize defense lines along the Meuse River. Eisenhower was determined to blunt and narrow the bulge, and contain it to the area between Bastogne and St. Vith, short of the Meuse River. The central bulge area was the only sector of the battle going completely in Germany's favor. Having advanced to the Ourthe River, the 2nd Panzer Division was now only thirty-five miles from the Meuse. However, like Peiper's stranded lead division to their north, they too had outrun their fuel supplies. After traveling all day in fits and starts, the 2nd Panzers, including their spearhead battalion, ran out of gas and were forced to halt and wait for reinforcements.[288]

Exaggerated rumors about Skorzeny's elusive commando teams were running wild from the frontlines all the way to Paris. The commandos posed a serious threat the Allies couldn't ignore, even though the hysteria created by their acts of sabotage far exceeded their actual damages. Everyone traveling across bridges or between towns was now required to show IDs. G.I.s developed code words, used slang expressions, and even asked American sports-related questions, trying to trip up the disguised German Special Operatives. While the creative questioning was only intended to expose Skorzeny's infiltrators, it had unintended consequences as well, creating delays and mix-ups among the Allies.

No one was exempt from questions and scrutiny, not even British Field Marshall Montgomery. Annoyed that security stopped his vehicle at a checkpoint, he ordered his driver to ignore the command and keep driving. American MPs shouldered their rifles and shot out his tires, forcing his driver to stop. The guards then dragged the field marshal out of his car and into the guard shelter, demanding identification. Montgomery was incensed and threatened to court-martial the Americans if they didn't immediately let him go. After several hours, the MPs confirmed his identity and released the peeved general, who apparently was more insulted that no one recognized him than he was for being roughed up as a suspected German spy. When Eisenhower learned the details of the Montgomery episode, he reportedly smiled and thanked Skorzeny "for at least one worthwhile service."[289]

Although surrounded by war, Don and his buddies still found ways to have a little fun, scuffling and pulling pranks more reminiscent of boys at a Boy Scout Camp than men at war. In his letter to Laura Jeanne that night, Don wrote:

Another foggy, lonesome day is drawing to a close. There was less than fifty yards visibility again today, making it impossible for us to fly.

Sharp wouldn't leave me alone, and we've been going the rounds all day. We have a lot of fun messing around together. Anyway, it seems to take the pressure off our weak brains. He got the best of me this time. I came out of the conflict with a skinned shin and a pair of red ears! No serious battle scars, though.

I sit here in a dreamy mood, and everything I want to write seems to be just out of my reach and not getting on paper. Maybe it's because of all the chatter and confusion around me. All the boys seem to pop in and out of our room—either to read Sharp's comic books or to get something to eat. Right now, we're eating the fruitcake that Beth sent, and it's delicious. Please thank her for me. We went to the show earlier tonight and saw an English picture. It was undoubtedly the worst show I've seen—a typical "Limey" picture—oh boy, their humor really stinks!

Even the strong, brave fighting men over here admit their homesickness around Christmas. We don't sit in the corner and sulk, or anything like that. It's mostly at night, when

*one's thoughts are more or less to himself, and the pleasant
memories of the past go drifting thru your mind.*

*Sharp's getting ready to hit the sack. I tied it in a knot to
get back at him for my earlier beating today—so I'd better
prepare for a counterattack.*

The impenetrable fog kept the entire Allied Air Force out of the
skies on day five of the battle, allowing the German panzer divisions
in the bulge area to advance without fear of attack by American
fighter-bombers.[290] Mother Nature still seemed to be on Hitler's side,
in spite of Patton's prayer cards.

Day 6

The fierce fighting in the north sector at Stoumont escalated the
morning of December 21 as the U.S. 119th Infantry Regiment joined
other American forces in the battle against Kampfgruppe Peiper.
Early that morning, the 1st SS Panzer Regiment, in an attempt to
reach Peiper, built a bridge across the Amblève River near Trois-
Ponts. After their first few heavy tanks crossed the river, the makeshift
bridge collapsed, leaving the Germans exposed and vulnerable. As
their combat engineers worked frantically in the river's freezing water
to rebuild the bridge, the 505th Regiment from the 82nd Airborne
attacked the boxed-in Waffen-SS Grenadiers. Supported by forty U.S.
Sherman tanks, the Americans forced the rescue regiment to retreat,
leaving Peiper's unit still cut-off and isolated.[291]

Under massive bombardment, Peiper's men suffered horrific
losses, and his Tigers started to fall back. Enraged, he sent a warning
to each tank commander that he "would personally destroy them if
they retreated so much as a meter." His loyal, battle-hardened unit
responded and defiantly held back the American assault the rest of
the day. Then after dark, they used the last of their fuel and retreated
four miles to La Gleize, leaving their dead and dying behind.[292]

The 7th Armored Division and the 14th Cavalry Group, assisted
by elements of other American troops, had unexpectedly withstood
the German siege at St. Vith for six days. When the Germans initially

attacked, the Allies feared the town would quickly fall into enemy hands. Defending the valuable crossroads until December 21 seemed out of the question. Frustrated by the stubborn American resistance, the Germans launched a massive attack on the town, intent on capturing it before the day ended. Late that night, after a devastating barrage from their heavy artillery, Tiger tanks and panzer troops rolled into the town, finally forcing the Americans to retreat.[293]

Keyed up after their long-delayed victory, the Germans raced haphazardly into St. Vith from all directions, creating congestion and tying up traffic on the town's muddy roads. In the midst of all the confusion, the American troops safely slipped away. The Germans won the battle for St. Vith—but at great cost and five days later than planned, making their victory a hollow one. More than 3,400 Americans gave their lives in defense of St. Vith. Their sacrifice bought the Allies valuable time to regroup and bolster their defenses against the enemy onslaught.[294]

The Germans shifted their focus from St. Vith to Bastogne. Conditions for the Americans defending the town were growing worse each day. Food and medical supplies were scarce, and they were running low on ammunition. However, following two days of attacks that failed to break through Bastogne, there was a brief respite while the Germans built up their troops to the west and the south. To General McAuliffe's credit, he kept the morale of his men incredibly high, even after overcast skies had again postponed desperately needed airdrops of food, supplies, and ammunition. Having survived the D-Day invasion and Montgomery's Operation Market Garden debacle, the general had long since proven himself in battle, but he knew his force's staying power was diminishing each day. That evening, McAuliffe reported to command that they could hold out for at least forty-eight more hours—and maybe longer.[295]

Patton's Third Army rescue divisions continued fighting their way toward Bastogne through German lines, trudging day and night over nearly impassable roads covered with snow, ice, and mud, but they were still more than forty-eight hours away. After hearing McAuliffe's report that night, Patton apologized to General Eisenhower for his slower-than-expected progress, and worried that he might not get there in time.[296]

In the center sector of the Ardennes, the 2nd Panzer Division remained stranded, completely out of fuel, waiting throughout the day for elements of the Fifth Army to catch up with them at the Ourthe River. Late that night, they received a fuel allotment, but it was only enough gasoline to refuel their Reconnaissance Battalion spearhead unit, forcing the main 2nd Panzer Division to remain behind while their lead battalion pushed forward. It was enough to keep Hitler's hopes for victory alive.[297]

Competing fog, rain, and snow from the polar air masses hovering over the Ardennes kept the entire Ninth Air Force grounded again on Day 6 of the battle. Their inability to provide the American infantry battalions close air support, combined with their long mail drought, demoralized Don's entire fighter group. He complained to Laura Jeanne, writing:

> If I don't hear from you soon, I think I'll go crazy—and I already have a good start! I miss you so very much, honey, and when your letters are so far between, it kinda puts me in the dumps.
>
> It's pretty rough up on the frontlines right now, and we can't do anything to help out. Well, at least I finally have an airplane of my own! Now, I just have to christen her and paint "Torchy" on the cowling, then hope for some good flying weather.
>
> We slept in this morning and missed getting our rations, except for a couple of candy bars. The stuff that's scarce usually goes quick. They had some toothpaste today for the first time since I've been on the Continent, so we really missed out. Maybe Santa will send me some for Christmas; he's already been pretty good to me.

Sharp is preparing our before bedtime nightly snack—Vienna sausages, olives and crackers. He's heating up the sausages over a candle!! They say, "Where there's a will, there's a way!"

A feeling of uneasiness engulfed the Chièvres Air Base as wild rumors of Skorzeny's SS Commando infiltrations reached the men of the 368th. They also received reports that German panzers were heading their direction. As a precaution, guards were posted to protect the HQ area, and the pilots were instructed to keep their Colt .45s loaded and strapped on at all times.[298]

Day 7

A blizzard raged over most of the Ardennes on the morning of December 22. Peiper had concentrated his remaining fifteen hundred men and twenty-eight tanks on the southern edge of La Gleize, ready for a showdown with the Americans.[299] A church and a small school were located in the center of the tiny Belgian village, and thirty or so houses lined its two narrow streets—all abandoned now that the threat of battle was looming. Peiper gave orders from the schoolhouse basement as the opposing forces exchanged cannon fire throughout the day.[300]

American tanks and artillery battered the entrenched 1st SS Panzer Division, knocking out several Tiger tanks and causing heavy casualties. By the end of the day, the bombardment had reduced La Gleize to rubble. Now as low on ammunition as they were on fuel, Peiper requested permission to retreat and rejoin the main Sixth Panzer Army. Instead of granting his request, German Command sent twenty-two airplanes at about midnight, airdropping ammunition, gasoline, food, and supplies. However, it was a bad drop, and the Waffen-SS were able to recover only a few cartons of cigarettes, a few bottles of schnapps, and a case of luger semi-automatic pistols. The Americans happily gathered up the rest.[301]

Early that morning, two German officers (one English speaking) and two enlisted men approached Bastogne carrying a large white flag. Guards escorted the German envoys to a nearby command post, where the two enlisted men were detained. The two officers were blindfolded, then led over a hill to another command post. Calls went up the chain of command to 101st Battalion HQ that some German officers were there with a paper outlining surrender terms. After his staff informed him what the message was about, General McAuliffe wadded it up into a ball and threw it into the wastebasket unread. Not one to use profanity, he laughed instead, then said, "Aw nuts!"[302]

Although nearly out of food, medical supplies, and ammunition, McAuliffe was determined to hold on at Bastogne until Patton arrived, or die trying. His men reportedly felt the same way. Unsure how to word his reply to the Germans, he asked his staff what they thought. One of his officers replied, "That first remark of yours would be hard to beat." Seeing the general's perplexed look, he reminded him, "You said 'Nuts!'" His entire staff applauded—and that's how the response went out.[303]

One of McAuliffe's bilingual officers then delivered the soon-to-be-famous, one-word reply to the German envoys. Noticing that the English-speaking officer was puzzled by the response, he helped him out, explaining in German, "If you don't know what 'nuts' means, in plain English, it's the same as 'Go to Hell.'" Then he sent the four Germans packing down the road with their white flag, baffled by their interaction with the Americans. The rest of the day was quiet. That night, however, the Luftwaffe bombed the town and things started heating up again.[304] If the Germans took control of Bastogne—which appeared imminent—they would be able to open their supply routes in the center sector, allowing reinforcements, fuel, and supplies to flow freely to their 2nd Panzer Division and powerful Fifth Army that followed.

In the center sector, the 2nd Panzer Division's spearhead battalion cleverly slipped through an opening between two American Infantry Divisions, pushing to within three miles of the Meuse River. Just as the bridges crossing the river were within sight, they ran out of fuel. Stranded painfully close to their target, they spent the rest of the day waiting for reinforcements and fuel supplies that would never arrive.[305]

Discouraged by reports that St. Vith had been lost and Bastogne was ready to fall, the men of the 368th were in a dour mood. Don responded to the bad news in his usual way. He penned a letter to Laura Jeanne—the last one she'd receive from him until after the end of the war:

22 December 1944
Belgium

My Darling Jeanne,

And still another day of bad weather goes by. I hope it clears up soon. We have a war going on over here, and must have a little good weather for flying once in a while. Instead, we just sit around, sweatin' out the weather, unable to fly. As you're probably reading back home, things aren't going too well over here right now.

I get so lonesome when I go so long without hearing from you. You'll simply never know how desperately I miss you. I look forward to every letter you write—they're really priceless. I love you and wish I could show you how much. If I could just take you into my arms and kiss you and...perhaps I better get a hold of myself.

I've been kinda busy writing recommendations for awards for various men in the squadron. Went to a show tonite, "Make your own Bed," with Jane Wyman and Jack Carson, and it was quite entertaining. I'll be glad when you're making "my" bed again. That sounds almost too good to be true, huh? Or maybe you're thinking I could still make my own bed? Anyway, we're all getting along fine, and we aren't losing any weight with all the Christmas packages we've received!

The New Year will probably be in by the time this letter arrives. Nevertheless, I'll extend my heartiest wishes for a year I pray will bring us back together—never to be parted

*again. I worry about you, honey, so please take very good
care of yourself for me—and I'll look out for Mr. Lt., OK?*

The skies cleared long enough for the Ninth Air Force to fly a
few sorties between Aachen and Trier, but bad weather scrubbed all
other air operations over the Ardennes, including another promised
airdrop to Bastogne. Now caught between the advancing Germans
and their objective at Antwerp, Air Command decided to relocate the
368th Fighter Group to a safer location. Disappointed with the news
of another move, the men reluctantly started packing. They'd been
stationed at Chièvres for nearly three months, their longest stay at
any air base since arriving on the Continent, and no one was looking
forward to relocating. The weather was awful, and even worse, their
upcoming move was in the wrong direction—away from Germany,
instead of closer to it.[306]

Rain, fog, snow, and blizzards alternated during the first week
of the Battle of the Bulge; the only constant was the record-breaking
cold. At 5:30 a.m. the day the battle began, the temperature was
14 degrees Fahrenheit. After that, it got much colder—especially at
night, when temperatures fell well below zero.

The Allied Air Forces had only been able to fly 1,800 sorties
inside the Ardennes battle area since the fighting commenced, and
most of those were on December 17 and 18.[307] The success of the
Allied march through France and Belgium was owed in no small part
to the close air support the Ninth Air Force fighter-bombers provided
the infantries and armed battalions. Unless they could get back in
the air and resume their bombing and strafing, the German panzer
units would continue to expand the bulge and eventually capture the
Meuse River bridges, paving the way west to Antwerp.

P-47 REPUBLIC THUNDERBOLTS

Back in the skies

TWENTY-SIX

"The War's Most Beautiful Sunrise"

Day 8

In the twilight hours before morning on December 23, the vanguard of Patton's Third Army advanced to within twenty miles of Bastogne, but terrible weather conditions, with visibility near zero at times, greatly hampered their progress. The ground and sky often appeared the same off-white color, making it difficult to tell where one ended and the other began. Hours before sunrise, Patton entered an ancient Catholic chapel in Luxembourg City. After removing his helmet, the general fell to his knees and prayed to God, pleading:

> *Give me four clear days so that my planes can fly, so that my fighter-bombers can bomb and strafe, so that my reconnaissance may pick our targets for my magnificent artillery. Give me four days to dry out this blasted mud, so that my tanks can roll, so that my ammunition and rations may be taken to my ill-equipped infantry.*
>
> *I need these four days to send von Rundstedt and his godless army to their Valhalla.* I am sick of this unnecessary butchery of American youth. In exchange for four days of fighting weather, I will deliver you enough Krauts to keep your bookkeepers months behind in their work. Amen.*[308]

An unnamed doughboy** was credited with calling that day's dawning "the war's most beautiful sunrise."[309] It ushered in a seldom seen weather condition known as a Russian High (an eastern high-pressure system). Unpredicted cold, dry winds blew from the east,

---

*   The mythical Asgard hall where the souls of those who die in battle are received by Odin.

** Nickname given to American infantryman dating as far back as the Revolutionary War.

bringing with them the clear skies Patton had prayed for so fervently. The strong winds that accompanied the unexpected weather caused snow to drift in the hills west of the Rhine River, bringing traffic on German supply roads nearly to a halt. Up to this point of the battle, Mother Nature had been the Nazis' staunch ally, but now she abandoned them, abruptly turning into their worst nightmare. The Allies were finally able to bring the full weight of their superior air forces to bear against the German panzer tank divisions, which the dense overcast had been protecting for almost a week.[310]

Supplies to Bastogne

One of the Air Force's first missions was to airdrop desperately needed food, supplies, medicine, blankets, and ammunition to General McAuliffe's Army in Bastogne. Eighty-two P-47s, eager to do more than just chaperone, escorted 241 C-47 Skytrain cargo planes making the delivery. Following the supply drop, the fighter-bombers took out their bottled-up wrath against the Germans surrounding the crossroads, dropping bombs and napalm, then strafing with their .50 caliber machine guns. In a follow-up mission later that day, a courageous group of surgeons flew into Bastogne in a military glider, operating on and attending to badly wounded soldiers who had been without adequate medical care for days.[311]

The Luftwaffe sent out more than 800 fighter sorties on Day 8 to defend their panzer tank divisions, which were exposed and vulnerable from the air for the first time since the Battle of the Bulge began. The Eighth and Ninth Air Forces countered, sending thousands of their heavy and medium bombers, fighters, and fighter-bombers into the skies all across the Ardennes. It was a record-setting day for the 368th Fighter Group in air combat against the Luftwaffe. And their bombing and strafing assaults on German supply locations, locomotives, transport vehicles, and ground troops forced nearly all German motor and armored transports off the roads during daylight hours, virtually cutting off their flow of reinforcements and supplies.[312]

Deprived of their protective overcast, the German 2nd Panzer Division stranded at the Ourtheville bridgehead became sitting ducks for Allied fighter-bombers and lost more than half of their tanks and armored weapons by the end of the day. And unknown to the 2nd Panzer Spearhead Battalion, which was waiting for fuel within sight of the Meuse River—Hitler's best remaining hope to capture and control its bridges—14,500 infantrymen and 400 tanks from the U.S. VII Army Corps were closing in on them.[313]

Farther to the north in La Gleize, combined American infantry, tank, and artillery continued to bombard Peiper's diminishing forces. Except for those in tanks, the 1st SS soldiers experienced catastrophic losses and were forced to take shelter in underground cellars. Late that afternoon, the Americans moved their Sherman tanks toward what they thought was an utterly defeated enemy. Instead, they were taken by surprise—first running into a minefield, then taking heavy fire from Peiper's remaining Tiger tanks and 20-mm flak guns. After quickly losing two tanks, the Americans retreated, resuming their artillery assault on La Gleize from a safer distance. Command sent in Allied fighter-bombers to deal with the German tanks, but they mistakenly bombed Malmedy instead, killing dozens of civilians and setting the town on fire. Kampfgruppe Peiper continued to fend off nearly insurmountable odds, refusing to give up. That evening, after learning that the battalion sent to rescue them had been destroyed near Trois-Ponts, Peiper decided to try to make it back to German frontlines near the outskirts of Stavelot.[314]

The Allies had now captured sixteen of Skorzeny's commandos, executing them as spies for masquerading in American uniforms. Another thirty-five were killed before they could reach the Meuse River. [315] Most of the rest abandoned their original mission soon after Peiper's spearhead battalion bogged down and rejoined other SS panzer units. But a few of the commandos still posed a danger. They infiltrated well behind American frontlines and continued their acts of sabotage. SHAEF took the fictitious threat circulated about killing or kidnapping Eisenhower seriously and kept the general under twenty-four-hour protection, forcing him to spend an unhappy Christmas Eve as a prisoner of his own security forces. Despite the Allies' best efforts to apprehend him, Skorzeny and several of his operatives avoided capture and returned to relative safety behind German lines.[316]

Don flew late that afternoon in his new plane—named but still unpainted—as part of a sixteen-plane-sortie from the 397th Fighter Squadron. His flight didn't encounter enemy planes, as earlier flights had that day, allowing them to provide close air support for Patton's Third Army as they advanced toward Bastogne and to search for targets of opportunity between Trier and the Rhine River. With their sixteen bombs, sixteen rockets, and .50 caliber strafing firepower, Don's flight group destroyed twenty-five freight cars and badly damaged sixty-seven more, as well as wiping out a marshalling yard, leaving several strategic buildings in ruins. On their way back, they caught up to forty C-47 transport planes and escorted them home.[317] Don later wrote:

This was the first time in over a week that many of the men on the frontlines had been able to stand up in their trenches and move around. As we flew over them, we could see them waving to us, like a cheering section in a ball game. The ground troops kept calling us on the phone, giving us orders, specifying coordinates, and telling us what was in their way that needed to be taken out.

Our squadron leader finally said, "Guys, we've got to get out." The ground troops pleaded, "Can't you make a couple more passes?" Even with our gas tanks now reading "low," how could we not respond to them? We made one more pass and then had to return to base. It was one of several times that we made it back home on not much more than fumes.

It was another record-setting day for the 368th Fighter Group. They shot down twenty-nine enemy planes and devastated enemy ground targets across the battle zone with their bombing and strafing attacks. Several P-47s took flak during the day's air skirmishes, forcing them to land at other airfields, and a Panzer Duster pilot was killed when his plane crashed.[318] For every success, there was a price to pay, but Day 8 of the battle was a lopsided one, solidly in favor of the 368th flyboys.

With the benefit of just one clear day, the Allies had unleashed the fury of their superior air forces on the Germans, turning the tide in the Battle of the Bulge. Patton believed God heard the prayer he'd uttered before first light that morning in the ancient Luxembourg chapel and had faith that God would deliver the additional three clear flying days he had petitioned for as well.

Don's buddies didn't fly that day and were waiting at the line to welcome him back as he landed, eager to hear his report. There was excitement and talk everywhere about how successful the missions had been for all three squadrons. That night, however, the mood changed as they started packing for their upcoming move. Don intended to write to Laura Jeanne, but when he found out he was flying the early mission the next morning, he hit the sack instead, promising himself to write her a long letter the next night, Christmas Eve.

At about 1:00 a.m., under cover of darkness, Peiper and some 800 of his men sneaked down the hill on the south edge of La Gleize toward the heavily wooded Amblève River, leaving 300 wounded Germans and 130 American prisoners behind. Shortly after they slipped away, a small rearguard he left behind blew up their remaining tanks and equipment, then quickly caught up. Supplied with only a few hard biscuits and a bottle of cognac, the defeated storm troopers crossed over the river on a rickety wooden bridge and began working their way southeast through the Salm River Valley back toward Stavelot.[319]

After slogging miles and miles through deep snow and surviving several skirmishes with Americans, the gritty 1st SS Troopers swam the icy waters of the Salm River. Cold, wet, and exhausted, 770 survivors from the once mighty spearhead regiment of nearly 6,000 men finally reached the German frontlines east of Stavelot, where their SS Panzer comrades welcomed them as heroes.[320]

PART FOUR

Last mission

TWENTY-SEVEN

Shot Down

Day 9

D awn broke on Sunday, December 24, to mostly clear, bitter-cold skies, granting Patton the second of the four flying days he'd prayed for. That morning, he radioed General McAuliffe, promising him a Christmas Eve present. The general's response, although cleverly worded, troubled Patton: "It's getting rather sticky around here. We only have one more shopping day." The men of the 101st Airborne, again running low on fuel, ammunition, and food rations, were in need of immediate relief. The German Fifth Panzer Army intensified its attack, fully aware that Patton's Third Army was approaching Bastogne and that time was running out to take control of the crucial road network. Patton pushed his troops to their limits to prevent that from happening, but intermittent skirmishes, coupled with horrible road conditions, delayed his advance unit from arriving that night, failing to deliver on his promise.[321]

Don's buddies were half-asleep when he lit the lantern in their tent and started getting ready for his early morning mission. The 368th Fighter Group would send eighty-six P-47s into the skies over the Ardennes Forest before the day ended—his was the first of six armed recce operations flying close air support for American ground troops inside the Bulge. As Don closed the tent door flap, the guys thanked him for stoking up the fire, wished him luck, then turned over on their cots and went back to sleep.

Don joined a few other pilots who were also heading to the briefing room for final mission instructions, but none of them said much as they walked across the airfield. It was dark and cold outside, adding to an eerie feeling that seemed to hover over the base. Their CO considered scratching the mission because of conflicting weather reports for southeast Belgium between La Roche and Stavelot, but he realized how badly the ground troops needed air support. Following their briefing, the sixteen Jabo Angel pilots quickly threw their parachutes into the back of the Jeep-pulled-pilot trailer and hopped in for the ride to the flight line. Don's crew chief made a final check of the plane, gave him a thumbs up, then watched him climb into the cockpit of the last P-47 he'd ever fly.

About thirty minutes later, the squadron was flying over the target area. The mission went according to plan as they bombed and strafed German tanks and armored vehicles. They were ready to turn for home base when they got a call via ground forces radio asking them to make an ill-fated staffing pass to take out a tank that was bedeviling them.

Don made one last pass, waiting until he was about 1,000 feet from the target before he pulled the trigger. He felt the shudder of his machine guns through the plane's airframe as the .50 caliber bullets fired at the rate of 106 rounds per second. After passing over the tank, he pulled up hard, skimming the treetops as he leveled out and began gaining altitude. Then he rolled his plane a little left, which enabled him to look back over his shoulder and see the Tiger belching black smoke.

At that exact moment, a German flak gunner pulled the lever on his anti-aircraft weapon and rocked Don's plane with a cannon shell. His wingman was yelling in his headset that he was on fire and telling him to bail out. But it wasn't that simple. Traveling at 400 mph and less than 200 feet off the ground, he was too low for his parachute to deploy. As he saw the engine explode and the plane burst into flames, Don offered a quick prayer for help and it became clear in his mind not only what he should do, but in what order he should do it.

He rolled his plane over on its back and flew upside down.

It was a counterintuitive maneuver, but it positioned him to bail out in the most efficient manner—at the last possible moment.

The curvature of a P-47's wings was relatively symmetrical, which made it aeronautically possible for the plane to fly inverted, but its fuel system was gravity fed and stopped draining gas into the main tank when it was upside down. This made sustained flight impossible. Like most airplanes, Thunderbolts were designed with some positive angle between the wings and the fuselage (they tilted slightly upward), which enabled them to fly horizontal during level flight. When flying upside down, the pilot had to compensate for the built-in angle by keeping the nose up. As in regular flight, the angle of attack* had to be steep enough to generate an upward force on the wings and create lift for the plane to gain altitude.[322] However, if the angle was too steep, it could generate more drag than the wings were able to bear and cause them to fall apart. In addition, when flying inverted the ground is above the pilot, requiring him to push the stick forward to gain altitude, the reverse of flying upright.[323]

Pilots caught in sticky situations—the kind not addressed in their training or flight manuals—had to rely solely on their instincts, without time to think about what to do. Don later stated that his guardian angel must have been flying with him that day and superseded his instincts. Otherwise, he wouldn't have responded the way he did. His altimeter confirmed that he needed more altitude before he could safely escape his burning plane. He tilted the nose skyward and continued to climb, praying that his plane would hold together for just a few more seconds.

Paratroopers in World War II were able to jump out of C-47 transport planes as low as 250 feet, but they used a static line to pull their ripcord as they exited the jump door, giving them the three to four seconds they needed for their parachute canopy to open and slow their descent. But at that altitude, a fighter pilot could seldom eject from his aircraft in time for his chute to open—almost always hitting the ground before it deployed.[324]

Following the inspiration that came to him as he prayed, Don pushed the stick forward and chose the correct angle of attack. His plane held together, but the cockpit was filling with smoke, making it nearly impossible for him to see anything. At the last possible moment, he pulled the canopy ejection lever (which instantly blew off its tracks), tore off his headgear, hit the quick release seat belt, and struggled against the G-force as he tried to stand up in his cockpit

---

* The angle between the oncoming air or relative wind and a reference line on the airplane or wing.

seat. Once he did, the slipstream sucked him out of his plane. The Air Force manual said to count to three before pulling the parachute ripcord, but Don knew he was too close to the ground to wait and pulled it as fast as he could.

He cut it close. After just one swing of his parachute, Don crashed into a snow-covered side hill, just missing a stand of trees. He hit the ground hard, sliding and rolling down through the snow and bushes. The slope of the hillside, the snow, and the undergrowth all combined to break his fall. That he survived was a miracle. No one in his squadron saw his parachute in the air during the few seconds it was open. On his first few flyovers, Don's flight leader, Major Leary, spotted the chute on the ground, but failed to observe any activity around the crash site. On his final flyover, he could no longer see the chute. Someone had gathered it up.

Leary's post-mission report gave Don's buddies reason to believe that he'd survived the crash and was still alive. Although it had now been more than two months since Jerry had gone missing, they still held out hope for him as well. The odds of seeing them both again weren't good.

Day 10—December 25, 1944

Huddled under his protective pine tree deep inside the Ardennes Forrest, Don shivered as he waited for daybreak. Phosphorous bombs were no longer exploding, leaving the skies above him dark and speckled with stars. Lost, cold, and hungry, he'd never felt more alone. He longed to be home with Laura Jeanne and his family on his favorite holiday of the year. Instead, he was stranded in the middle of the Ardennes Forest, surrounded by German SS Troops. Although disheartened by his predicament, he knew he was lucky to be alive, and his determination to stay that way kept his mind focused on escape. After a long sleepless night, Don watched the sun rise on a cold, clear Christmas morning:

At first light, I started searching again for a way back to our frontlines. Slipping from pine trees to hedge lines and ditches, back and forth, I tried to find an opening for escape, but I kept running into Germans every direction I went. It seemed as if there was no way out. About two o'clock in the afternoon, groups of German SS soldiers began coming toward me from all directions. I stopped moving and hid in the trees, remaining motionless.

Ardennes Forest near Don's crash site

German anti-aircraft guns were constantly going off now. I watched as several B-17s returning from bombing runs in Germany were shot down. It made me heartsick to look up and see some of our airmen falling hopelessly through the sky with their parachutes on fire—and even sadder watching others, still descending in their parachutes, shot down before they reached the ground. The Germans, especially the SS Troopers, seemed to have no regard for life. They thought they were winning the war and that there would be no repercussions for their inhumane actions. I now had even more motivation to get away and not get captured.

After the SS passed by, I started moving again. My instincts told me I was going south toward Bastogne, but without a compass, I wasn't sure. It seemed hopeless—German soldiers were everywhere.

The airmen that had bailed out near me had attracted a lot of attention, and German troops were combing the area for survivors. Late in the afternoon near dusk, a group of them started coming right at me, forcing me to stop and hide again. I crawled into a shallow ditch, hoping they'd pass me by, and drew my .45 from the holster—just in case. While at our base, I'd painted a colorful picture of a P-47 on the back of my flight jacket. That turned out to be a mistake. I could hear the Germans talking as they came closer to me, and even though I couldn't understand German, I heard them say "Jabo," and knew they were referring to the picture on my jacket.

I was lying on my stomach, and I don't think they knew whether I was alive. As soon as they got close enough for me to see their boots next to me, I rolled over with my .45 automatic in my right hand. There were twenty SS Troopers standing above me—all with their guns pointed my direction. I didn't want to get shot. And since there was no way I could shoot all of them with only seven shells, I laid the .45 to my side, relying on some greater power to help me. My miserable day of wandering in the woods had just got a lot worse.

After picking up my .45, the SS Troopers motioned for me to stand up, then they had a little fun knocking me around a bit. They took my A-2 flight jacket, hat, and gloves—my only sources of warmth in the bitter cold—then took my watch, the bracelet Laura Jeanne had given me, even my fountain pen. I had no other personal belongings, having lost them all when I bailed out. What worried me most was what they took next—my dog tags.

A few of the SS Troopers nudged me forward about twenty feet into the woods at gunpoint, then stood guard over me. The officer in charge sent two men a short distance away to a little clearing in the woods and then returned to his troops. The two soldiers pulled out their backpack shovels and started digging a hole about two and a half feet wide and six feet long. It was pretty obvious what they were digging the hole for—and I started praying for my guardian angel to show up and rescue me again.

I tried to tell the soldiers guarding me that I had to talk to the officer in charge, but they didn't understand any English, and the only German words that I knew were "achtung" (attention) and "ja" (yes). Suddenly, other German words came to my mind, and as I repeated them to the guards, they understood whatever it was I said. I experienced a modern-day version of the biblical Gift of Tongues—my second miracle in as many days. The two guards then prodded me to move, taking me to see the officer with the most stripes on his uniform.

I received a strong impression to start up a conversation with the SS officer in French, and was greatly relieved when he started speaking back to me in the same language. The officer spoke about as much French as I did and we were able to understand each other well enough to converse.

The two guards must have told him what I'd said to them, because he already understood that I had some valuable information and was willing to share it. I made a plea for him to take me to his commanding officer. I knew if I stayed where I was much longer that it would become my final resting place. He thought about what I'd told him for a few moments, then hollered down to the two men digging the hole (it was about two feet deep by then) and told them to stop. They placed me in the center of their group and started marching.

The troopers moved at a fast pace, making it hard for me to keep up. I ached all over, and my feet hurt with every step I took in the deep snow—and I was freezing since they'd kept my flight jacket, hat, and gloves. After marching through the woods for about fifteen to twenty minutes, we came to an old barn-type structure serving as a temporary German field headquarters. It was almost dark when we finally arrived.

A guard forced me to sit on a little board bench about three feet long and a foot wide while the unit leader reported to his commanding officer. I couldn't understand anything they said. After a brief interrogation attempt (I only told him my name, rank, and serial number), the officer in charge of the Advanced SS Headquarters lost interest in me and left the room.

A while later, one of the guards offered me a dried piece of German black bread smeared with oleo* and some blood sausage.** Even though I hadn't eaten for two days, I could hardly force myself to eat it. I spent the rest of the night on the bench, cold and tired, taunted by my guards, only able to sleep for a couple of hours. Not my best Christmas—but at least I was still alive.

———————

Bastogne was a bleak, uninviting place to spend the Christmas holiday for McAuliffe and his men. The situation had worsened after Patton failed to keep his Christmas Eve rescue promise, leaving them to face the upcoming German assault without the reinforcements they desperately needed. The German Fifth Panzer Division was about to launch an all-out attack, promising their Führer victory as a Christmas present.

Fearing this might be their final day of fighting, McAuliffe issued only ten rounds of ammunition to his paratroopers, telling them not to fire "until you see the whites of their eyes." Early that morning before the battle began, the officers shook hands, saying what they thought would be their last goodbyes. But the American troops turned back every barrage the enemy threw at them that Christmas Day, although they experienced heavy casualties.[325]

———————

The air base at Chièvres wasn't a happy place on December 25, either. Decorations hung in the mess hall and music was blaring through the base loudspeaker system, but no one thought much about

———————

*   An artificial substitute for butter, similar to margarine.
** Dried blood with a filler, usually fat, potato, or cornbread, cooked thick enough to congeal when cooled.

Christmas. The 368th Fighter Group had orders to retreat to the airfield at Juvincourt, France, away from the now volatile frontlines. Don's tentmates spent the holiday packing, lamenting his loss. Since his plane went down behind enemy lines, more than a hundred miles from their base, they knew he was certain to be captured by the Germans—assuming he'd survived the crash. The guys could only hope that was the case.

Later that day, Major Richard E. Leary, flight leader on Don's last mission, filled out the previous day's *Missing Air Crew Report*. The official report, submitted to Ninth Air Force Command, read:

Destination: Malmedy & SW area
Type of mission: Dive-bomb
Plane was lost as result of: Enemy Anti-Aircraft
Basis of Report: Saw Crash.
Attachment to the report:

I was flying Tropic Leader, strafing targets one mile northeast of Freyneux on 24 December 1944, when I saw Lt. Evans pulling off the target. He was burning. I called for him to bail out. He had already bailed out. I saw the plane crash and his chute on the ground. His chute had opened, although he was very low. I circled the spot (P-532876) and saw no movement. However, on about my fourth orbit, the chute had been gathered up. I still saw no activity. The snow and mud, brush and trees made it impossible to see if he was the one who picked up the chute or not.

American prisoners

TWENTY-EIGHT

Don's Band of POWs

Day 11

D on was awakened early on the morning of December 26 by the sound of the SS Field Headquarters' creaking barn-style door and the rush of bitter-cold air entering the room. As he sat up on the narrow wooden bench where he'd spent a nearly sleepless night, he was caught by surprise as SS guards prodded seven captured Americans through the door—four from the 101st Airborne Division, and three from the First Army infantry units. Their arrival lifted his spirits. It gave him hope that the SS commanding officer—the one he'd refused to give information to the previous night—might have more in store for him other than another hole two and a half feet wide and six feet long:

> *The other POWs immediately recognized that I was a pilot from my flight gabardines and an officer by the stripe on my shoulder. They all looked relieved to see me and said, "You're the only officer in the group, so you're in charge."*
>
> *An older German guard was initially assigned to our eight-man group and directed us to start marching east down a snow-packed road just outside Freyneux. The guard changed several times along the way as we marched toward the Belgian town of Houffalize. By now, the cuts and bruises I experienced during my landing were very sore, my lips were cracked and swollen, my feet were killing me, and I was cold—having no coat, no hat, and no gloves—only my flight gabardines.*
>
> *We were marching in the mouth of the bulge, and the Ninth Air Force was dropping bombs all over our area, forcing us*

to stop and take cover several times during the day and sweat out the attacks from flights of P-47s. I began to understand why the German people hated Jabo pilots so much. It took us all day to march the 17 miles to Houffalize. We arrived around 5:00 p.m. and were met just outside town by a "Bomb Disposal Committee."

The guards marched us inside a compound, similar to the one where we spent the previous night; only this one had more buildings, troops, tanks, and equipment around it. My American flying buddies had been busy throughout the day and had dropped some 250-pound time bombs* that hadn't yet exploded. The Germans had three of the bombs laying right in the middle of the courtyard next to their headquarters, not knowing if or when they were going to explode, afraid to go anywhere near them.

Dropping time bombs wasn't uncommon. I'd dropped plenty of them and knew the settings on the bombs could be anywhere from 45 minutes to 4 hours. We heard the last P-47s fly over us a few hours earlier in the afternoon, so I knew time was running out for them to detonate.

The commanding officer was standing a safe distance away from the bombs, surrounded by six SS Troopers. In good English, he ordered the enlisted men with me to take the bombs to a nearby gully about 75 yards away. As the officer in charge of our little band, I reminded him of the Geneva Convention Rules of War and refused to have the men obey his order. Then he had his troopers chamber a shell in their rifles and gave the same order to "my" men a second time.

The guys were getting a little nervous by now. The German commander then asked, "What are you going to do, lieutenant?" I held my ground and again refused the order. Having now lost patience with me, he ordered his men to point their guns at our heads and in a loud voice gave me an ultimatum, "Now move!

---

* General-purpose time bombs, equipped with delayed detonation fuses, were used either to harass an enemy, or to prevent them from passing through or remaining in the location of the bombing raid.

I give you thirty seconds to start getting those bombs out of here or my men will shoot."

I hadn't been trained how to do anything like this, but all of a sudden I was prompted to ask the officer for some G.I. type blankets. He understood what I'd asked for and sent his men racing after them. After getting us the blankets, the troopers forced us over to where the bombs were laying and then quickly moved a safe distance away.

The guys were now real nervous. I told them, "Don't worry. The bombs aren't going to go off right now. Let's just carefully roll them on to the blankets and carry them over to the gully and roll them in." Of course, I had no idea when the bombs were set to go off and was just as scared as my guys were.

We each grabbed a corner of the blankets and carried the bombs one at a time over to the gully, tipped them out, and let them roll down the hill into the bottom of the creek bed— hoping it wouldn't set them off. While we were carrying the third bomb toward the gully, I received another strong impression that we'd run out of time and yelled, "Guys, hurry, hurry! Run like hell! We've got to throw this thing in the gully right now!"

As we were dumping the last bomb, I shouted, "Race back a few paces, then hit the deck as fast as you can!" Just as everybody's nose hit the ground, all the bombs went off. The downward side of the gully was steep enough that even though we were still close to the edge, the blast was directed upward and away from us. I'd just experienced another miracle.

The Germans, including their commanding officer, were so grateful we got rid of the bombs that they gave us each a little package of crackers and cheese to go along with our evening meal of black bread and oleo. They placed us in one of the unheated compound outbuildings, with no bedding or mattresses, so we had to bed down on the dirty floor. It didn't matter much anyway. The delayed response to the events of the day, combined with the cold conditions, made sleep impossible.

Momentum in the Battle of the Bulge had now turned in favor of the Allies. In the north, Peiper's spearhead battalion had been wiped out, and the Sixth Panzer Army was contained well short of the Meuse River bridges. The Americans' valiant defensive stands at Elsenborn Ridge and St. Vith had bought valuable time for the Allies to reinforce key defensive areas all along the battlefront.

In the center sector, the German 2nd Panzer Lead Battalion—stranded within sight of the Meuse River—was surrounded by the U.S. VII Army Corp. The spearhead unit Hitler had rested his hopes on would be destroyed before day's end, leaving the German Fifth Panzer Army in disarray.

Further south, Patton's Third Army advance division finally reached Bastogne. Although the struggle at the critical crossroads was far from being over, the arrival of reinforcements and supplies would allow General McAuliffe to fulfill his orders, "to hold the Bastogne line at all costs."

Day 12

On December 27, the weather took a turn for the worse, temperatures dropped, and heavy fog rolled into the Ardennes Forrest. The Germans postponed the prisoners' march, giving them another work project instead:

> *While the guys started to work, I had another brief but unsuccessful discussion with the German SS commander about the Geneva Convention Rules. We worked until about noon, when our road detail was interrupted by a visit from my flying buddies. Then our guards took us back to the building where we spent the previous night.*

Partial clearing that afternoon allowed waves of Ninth Air Force B-26 Marauders and P-47 Thunderbolts to resume bombing raids on the Belgian towns of Houffalize and La Roche, setting the towns on fire and forcing the residents to flee for safety in nearby forests and neighboring villages:[326]

> *Bombs exploded all around us and caused the ground to shake violently. We joked that if the Germans didn't kill us, our own planes would.*

The building we were in had been occupied by U.S. advance forces just a few days before. I had one of our guys, Staff Sgt. Gallagher, scrounge around to see if he could find any food or anything else of value. He came back with a few cans of stew our boys had left behind—real American beef stew in a G.I. can. I had him cook it up, and I can't even begin to describe how wonderful it tasted.

Later that day, after the bombing stopped, more American POWs showed up at the compound in Houffalize. Exhausted from working most of the day, we ate a supper of black bread spread with oleo and tried to get some sleep. It was too cold to sleep much, and we had to get up and move around most of the night to keep from freezing.

———

The clear skies Patton prayed for continued, which enabled the Ninth Air Force to fly 2,343 sorties in two days, bringing the total number flown by Allied Air Forces since the Russian High blew in to an incredible 12,000 sorties.[327] Their air onslaught had eliminated nearly all German supply movements during daylight hours and put the Americans in position to take over the offensive.

Day 13

Don's band of POWs left the bombed-out Houffalize compound at 7:00 a.m. on December 28 and resumed their march toward a gathering station located in Gerolstein, some fifty miles to their east:

We were now over forty strong, and I was still the ranking officer of our group. We arrived at Luxembourg about 4:00 p.m. Our guards fed us watery soup, cheese, and hardtack,* and I had my first drink of water in five days that wasn't out of a ditch. My lips were cracked and swollen and my feet were killing me, but I was determined to keep going no matter what.

---

* Hard, dry bread or biscuit made from flour, water, and salt.

I worried that no one had seen my chute open, since I bailed out so close to the ground, and that I might have been reported as killed, rather than MIA. I wondered how Laura Jeanne and my loved ones at home would handle not knowing what had happened to me. I knew if I made it to a prison camp, word would eventually get to them through the Red Cross that I was still alive, and that helped keep me going.

After a few hours rest, we started marching again through cold, snow-covered, mountainous country. Whenever we stopped to rest, I started to shiver uncontrollably and had to keep moving around so I wouldn't freeze. Several times during the night we passed through artillery barrages from isolated elements of our own troops still holding out behind enemy lines.

Hours later, we came to another field headquarters building and stopped for the rest of the night. The Germans had a stove in the building, and I got warm for the first time since I was shot down. We were given no food or water and got little sleep—but at least we were warm and still alive.

By the end of the day, the seesaw battle at Bastogne had finally tipped in the Americans' favor. The 101st Airborne's heroic defense of the town had disrupted the German drive west in the mouth of the bulge, just as the U.S. armored divisions' stubborn defense had done in the north at St. Vith. The Germans would never recover from their failure to capture Bastogne's vital road network. While casualties in the siege for the small town numbered in the thousands, an exact count remains unknown.

Foreseeing the inevitable, von Rundstedt informed Hitler that their counteroffensive attack was failing all across the Ardennes and tried to convince him to retreat before they experienced further losses. The Führer's most astute and competent field marshal was now looking in the opposite direction, fearful that the Soviet offensive would soon be on their Eastern doorstep. Convinced there was still an outside chance for victory, Hitler ignored his advice, adding another mistake to his growing string of costly errors.[328]

Day 14

The weather improved slightly on the morning of December 29. Sixty-eight planes from the 368th Fighter Group were part of the 949 sorties the Ninth Air Force flew that day. They executed bombing attacks and armed recces all over the mouth of the bulge,[329] including the north central Luxembourg area where Don's POW group was located:

We couldn't move during the day due to the danger of being strafed by Allied fighter-bombers. Some of the Jabo bombs hit close enough to shake the walls of the building we were in so violently that it caused the windows to fall out.

We were given some soup and black bread at noon—our only meal for the day. It was a relief to be able to rest all day in a warm building, even with all the bombing that was going on. I was worn out and weak from lack of food and sleep.

After dark, we started our journey again and marched until about 2:00 a.m. When we arrived at Prüm [a small village just inside the western German border], we were put up in an old distribution warehouse. It was getting colder and colder each night, and I didn't know how I was going to survive much longer without a coat or hat. I started to scrounge around and search the area for anything that might help keep me warm.

Over in a far corner in some straw, I found what appeared to be an old, discarded, linen tablecloth or bedspread. I tore it up into long strips, dropped my gabardines, and wrapped my upper body like a mummy. When I zipped my flight suit back up all the strips stayed in place.

I was miserable and hungry, but a little warmer now and grateful to be wearing good, sturdy, G.I. field boots, especially with my injured feet. It was too cold to take my boots off at night, and I was afraid if I did, I might not be able to get my swollen feet

*back into them. But I was better off than some of the guys who
were suffering from more serious physical injuries.*

Day 15

Thanks to unflyable weather conditions on December 30, the
POWs received a welcome reprieve from Allied bombing and strafing.
They left Prüm about 7:00 a.m. on empty stomachs, and trudged
along a snow-covered back road that wound its way east through
the Eifel Mountains. When they came to a marker pointing north
to the small town of Stadtkyll, Don's thoughts turned to Jerry Kelly.
Pondering his own survival against all odds gave him hope that his
missing friend might still be alive as well:

*As we marched, and whenever we stopped to rest, "my guys"
positioned themselves around me. The people could tell I was
a pilot from my flight suit, and the guys tried to protect me by
keeping me in the center of the group.*

*The people of the towns we passed through hated pilots.
Whenever they identified I was one, many would yell
"Teufelsengel" [Devil's Angel], while others would spit
or make angry gestures at me. So far, nothing else had
happened, but we'd heard stories of pilots being gouged
with pitchforks—and even beaten to death with clubs. I was
grateful to my guys for their protection.*

*We marched all day without food and were forced to eat
snow or drink from ditches. At dusk, we arrived in Gerolstein
[thirteen miles east of Prüm], and received a cold reception as
we entered the town. Some of the townspeople identified me
as a pilot and tried to get to me, but the guys pushed them
back and told me, "Evans, walk in the middle of our group!"
We were put up in the third story of an old warehouse and
given soup and drinking water.*

*The Germans were collecting thousands of POWs in Gerol-
stein to process and send to internment camps. We had to
lie on 3' x 3' warehouse racks or on the dirty straw-covered
floor—either one was cold, hard, and nearly impossible to
sleep on. The guards taunted us and treated us like we were*

animals. My feelings toward the German soldiers and even the German people had turned from resentment to hatred.

Bombs rocked the town the rest of the night, but none struck our building.

Day 16

The town of Gerolstein served as an important railway junction in support of the German panzer divisions fighting in the Ardennes. A Dulag, or transit camp, was also located there that temporarily housed thousands and thousands of Allied prisoners waiting to be relocated to permanent prison camps. The POWs were usually processed within a day or two, then shipped out in boxcars to their assigned camps. However, on December 24–25, the Americans bombed the town and badly damaged the railroad marshalling yards. With few trains now running, the constant influx of prisoners quickly exceeded the town's limited housing capacity, causing POWs to stack up in the rail yards. Enraged by the Allied bombing and the overflow of prisoners, the townspeople attacked and stoned the next group that marched into town.[330]

The situation was still tense when Don's band of POWs arrived in Gerolstein five days later. They were anxious to get out of the angry town, even if it meant leaving on foot. They got their wish the following day and began a brutal odyssey toward Frankfurt, Germany, 140 miles east:

We were up at 8 a.m. and given a bowl of watery soup and ersatz coffee. * *Later that morning, we were combined with another group of POWs that included two bird colonels, one from the tanks and one from the infantry. They had quite a few wounded men that were in worse shape than we were.*

Since the two colonels outranked me, I was no longer in charge, but our guys stayed together in a group, and they still looked to me as their leader.

We were given some cheese and hardtack for lunch and issued rations that were supposed to last us for the next four days.

---

*   An inferior substitute for coffee usually made from roasted grain, acorn, or chicory.

There were rumors floating around about a train ride, but that's all they were—rumors. Around 2:00 p.m., our walking wounded group started marching again.

We walked on winding mountain roads through a blizzard the rest of the day and continued for several hours after dark. We finally arrived at a small gathering station [near the village of Dockweiler] at 9:00 p.m. where "rations" were divided and a Mosquito [British combat night bomber] paid us a visit.

Even though we were on cold, hard, dirty floors, I was so tired that I got some sleep that night anyway. One of our guards wished us a Happy New Year.

Weather over the Ardennes region improved slightly on the last day of the year, allowing the Eighth and Ninth Air Forces to fly 703 sorties, bombing and strafing the bulge salient. During the final week of the year, the Ninth Air Force flew more than 10,000 sorties, dropped nearly 7,000 tons of bombs, and destroyed 207 German tanks, 173 gun positions, 20 railroad cars, 45 locomotives, 333 buildings, and 7 bridges—paving the way for Patton's Third Army to go on the offensive.[331]

Day 17

Mother Nature started the New Year off by again siding with the enemy. Heavy snow, icy roads, and overcast skies slowed Patton's Third Army to a crawl as they pushed north and gradually narrowed the bulge. General Eisenhower ordered Montgomery, who was now in charge of the First Army, to drive south toward Patton no later than January 1 in an effort to trap the German armies in the collapsing bulge. Instead, he grew cautious and delayed his departure for three days, frustrating both Eisenhower and Patton.[332]

Don's fighter group back at Juvincourt was packing again, this time for a move to Metz, France. His buddies spent New Year's Eve in their tent, none of them in a mood to celebrate. It was the same all over the base. An advance air echelon arrived at Metz early on New Year's morning, just as the airfield came under attack by Luftwaffe fighter planes. All hell broke loose as thirty Me-109s attacked at deck level, making strafing passes for fifteen minutes at parked aircraft and the vulnerable base facilities. The German bandits destroyed more than twenty P-47s parked on the ground and wounded eighteen men. Smoke filled the sky over Metz as bombs and munitions exploded and planes burned.[333]

The Luftwaffe's last-ditch air raid, known as Operation Bodenplatte, included more than 800 planes and targeted sixteen Allied air bases in France, Belgium, and Holland. Although they destroyed 150 Allied aircraft and seriously damaged another sixty, the operation proved costly for the Luftwaffe, which lost 234 of their own planes. The surprise attack delayed the 368th move to Metz for several days while the Ninth engineers cleaned up the base and made it operational a second time.[334]

That same day, the Wehrmacht also launched a final desperate ground offensive, known as Operation Nordwind, attacking the U.S. Seventh Army south of Saarbrücken. While it caused the Americans to withdraw in the north salient and prolonged the Battle of the Bulge, the ground operation was ultimately a failure.[335]

The New Year started out badly for Don and his band of POWs:

A four-day, near starvation march to Limburg officially commenced at 7:00 a.m. on January 1, in a snowstorm, with our two lt. colonels leading the parade. Besides having to survive the cold, snowy weather, we now faced rationing what little food we had left for four days. Rationing food to oneself creates a problem when you're really hungry.

We marched all day through a blizzard, finally stopping a few hours after dark. We were miles from the nearest town and forced to spend the night outdoors, unprotected from the elements. We huddled close together to try and keep warm and got up and moved around often to keep from freezing. No one got much sleep.

Day 18

January 1945 was the coldest month on record in the Ardennes region, with nighttime temperatures dipping as low as 13 degrees below zero. It felt much colder to Don's POW group due to the wind chill factor. The previous day's blizzard let up on January 2, but the skies remained overcast, giving the POWs a temporary reprieve from both the storm and the Allied bombing:

> *We were up at sunrise, following a long, uncomfortable night. After dividing up the last of our black bread and cheese for breakfast, we started walking toward Koblenz, about 20 miles away. We were now completely out of rations.*

> *We marched all day on snow-packed roads, finally stopping at an abandoned schoolhouse west of Koblenz. We spent the night inside the old school building, which gave us some relief from the freezing temperatures outside. Our guards refused to get us any food or drinking water. Exhausted to the point that I didn't care about anything, I lay down on the filthy floor and fell asleep.*

Day 19

Hindered by deep snow, ice, and bitter-cold conditions on January 3, Patton's Third Army Corps plodded to the north, slowly narrowing the bulge. German opposition was as fierce as the brutal weather, making every mile of ground won costly for the Americans, who still bore the brunt of the Allied battle casualties.[336]

The Eighth and Ninth Air Force fighter groups were active that day in the Koblenz area, except for Don's old fighter group. The 368th was still stuck in Juvincourt, mucking around in awful weather conditions as they waited for their engineers to make repairs to the bombed-out airfield at Metz.[337]

––––––––––

It was difficult for the POWs to resume their march that morning. Hunger pangs and rampant dysentery—caused by drinking water out of ditches—were taking their toll. Prodded at gunpoint by their guards, the prisoners started marching toward Koblenz shortly after first light. The 2,000-year-old German city was built on both banks of the Rhine River. Before the war, it was renowned for its Romanesque architecture, early Christian churches, and beautiful gardens.[338] Now it lay in ruins, nearly destroyed by Allied bombing:

> *When we arrived at Koblenz, the streets in town were lined with hundreds of German Army supply trucks parked next to buildings and housing projects where they couldn't be so easily seen by our planes from the air. While we were marching through, the city came under heavy attack by Allied fighter-bombers.*

> *Our guards forced us right next to the supply trucks targeted by our planes—likely in the hope they could get rid of us. Luckily, the P-47s skipped over our end of the truck convoy they were strafing after completely destroying the other end. Being on the receiving end of bombs, machine guns, and rockets was a scary experience. It made it easier to understand the hatred the German people had for our planes and pilots.*

> *Then something completely unexpected happened to me— something that forever changed my life. As I stood next to a rundown apartment building for protection against the bombing and strafing raid, I stepped back into a little doorway. Suddenly, the door opened. My first impression was that someone was going to shoot me. Instead, a little old German lady, dressed in several layers of old, tattered and torn clothing to protect her from the cold, held out her hand and put some hard rock candy into my hand.*

> *There she was, in ragged clothes, in a war-torn city, somehow surviving in a partially destroyed apartment without heat or electricity, bombs blasting all around her, having no doubt had family members killed in the war, with every right to hate me, her enemy. Instead, she shared part of her precious Christmas candy with me. Then, she looked into my eyes and said, "Gott segne dich" (God bless you).*

> *Up to that moment, my heart was full of hatred for my enemy. This little German woman's compassion for me, her enemy, exemplified the principle of "Love thine enemies,*

and do good to them that hate thee." Her example softened my heart and provided me with one of the greatest learning experiences of my life—one I'll never forget. And I can't even begin to explain how good those little pieces of candy tasted.

When the air raid ended, the guards rounded up the surviving POWs, marched them through the bombed-out city, then turned east toward Limburg, still thirty-four miles away:

We passed through Koblenz to a small village [Neuhäusel] about 6 miles to the east. When we arrived, the townspeople gathered around us—but they didn't bring pitchforks or clubs. This time the people fed us.

I walked the rest of the day in humility, confusion, and guilt. The hatred I had in my heart for all Germans at the beginning of the day was gone. I'd experienced rare kindness twice that day from war-torn German people.

We marched until after dark, then spent another night outdoors in freezing weather. We had some ersatz coffee, but no food.

Day 20

Dreadful weather continued across the Ardennes battlefront on January 4, freezing at night and muddy during the day from alternating rain and snow. Movement on either side of the battle line was nearly impossible. The conditions at Juvincourt were awful as well. Overcast skies and snow limited visibility at the base to less than 100 yards, grounding the 368th Fighter Group again and further delaying their move to Metz.[339]

Don was now more than 250 miles east of his fighter group. The POW's next destination, Limburg, was still some twenty miles away. The Luftwaffe had built an air base there to protect the city's railroad marshalling yards from Allied bombing raids, and lately, it also served as a way station for prisoners marching to Frankfurt:

We marched all day. No food. We arrived at an airfield outside town around 9:00 p.m. The guards fed us black bread, oleo, some soup, and ersatz coffee, and then put us up for the night in an old military warehouse.

Our four-day starvation march was finally over. Not all our men made it. Several guys died along the way, and we left some of our badly injured men behind at a hospital in Koblenz for medical care.

Day 21

On January 5, despite lousy weather and limited visibility, Don's old squadron conducted its final armed recce mission from their base in Juvincourt. One hundred miles south, the 397th dropped sixteen bombs on a 40-car train, then landed at their new base in Metz.

Before sunup, Don's prisoner group began the last leg of their forced march—Limburg to Frankfurt—over forty miles to the southeast:

We were given some soup, a slice of black bread, and a cup of ersatz coffee, then started walking toward Frankfurt. Our guards pushed us harder than usual, since they wanted us to march halfway there that day. Flights of Allied bombers flew over us several times during the day, and we could hear the bombs going off near Frankfurt. Fortunately, no attacks took place on the road we were traveling.

After marching all day, we stopped at an old, vacant, unheated warehouse and were given some soup and black bread. Then we bedded down on a cold, straw-covered, dirt floor and tried to get some sleep.

Day 22

The following day, the 368th Fighter Group completed its move to Metz, negotiating the last half of the journey through the steep, slippery hills of eastern France in the dark. The men's spirits picked up after their arrival—they were once again within a few miles of the German border, and their new base had barracks instead of tents.

However, the skies were so socked in that all flight briefings were cancelled and no missions were flown.

―――――――

Overcast skies again came to the aide of Don's band of prisoners, providing protective cover from Allied bombing raids on the final day of their march to Frankfurt:

Early that morning, our guards forced us to start marching again. Three or four hours after dark, we finally arrived at a warehouse outside Frankfurt that was being used to house in-transit prisoners. We were given some watery soup and a slice of black bread, then spent the rest of the night huddled together on the warehouse dirt floor trying to keep warm.

Day 23

As Patton moved north to trap the Wehrmacht and SS Troops in the narrowing bulge, Hitler finally conceded that Germany was losing the battle and ordered his armies to pull back. Although forced to abandon hundreds of fuel-starved panzer tanks and armored vehicles as they retreated, the Germans fought tenaciously, barely escaping the planned Allied snare—thanks in part to British Field Marshal Bernard Montgomery. His late arrival left a back door open for the fleeing Wehrmacht, allowing them to escape what should have been a noose.

The Americans had succeeded in flattening the bulge and had put the Germans on their heels. But it would take another three weeks of intense fighting before each side would be back where they'd started, officially ending the Battle of the Bulge.[340]

At a press conference held on January 7, Montgomery startled reporters when he claimed full credit for saving the Allied victory in the Ardennes. The ensuing public outcry was so great that the arrogant, and, in many minds, incompetent military leader was nearly relieved of his command. Seldom constrained by facts, Montgomery had attempted to whitewash his record from Operation Market Garden all the way to the Battle of the Bulge. But this time he went too far.

Eleven days later, in an attempt to repair Montgomery's damage to the U.S.–British relations, England's Prime Minister, Winston Churchill, addressed Parliament stating emphatically, "This is undoubtedly the greatest American battle of the war and will, I believe, be regarded as an ever-famous American Victory."[341]

Early that morning, SS guards led Don's prisoner group to a gathering center in Frankfurt for processing, then, as expected, split them up. The Air Force officers boarded a train for the infamous interrogation center Dulag-Luft Oberursel and the enlisted men were sent to a processing center in Wetzlar, forty-five miles north. Despite the interrogation facing them, the officers were the lucky ones, eventually ending up in Luftwaffe-run prison camps. The enlisted men would likely end up in work camps and be subjected to worse conditions.

Don was saddened when it came time to say goodbye to his guys. The men from his original band of POWs had grown close during their ordeal. They'd marched more than 200 miles in twelve days, surviving freezing weather conditions, days with little or no food and only ditchwater to drink, lack of sleep, dysentery, cruel treatment by guards, and Allied bombs. Don had led them and they had protected him. He would never see or hear from any of them again.

Dulag Luft observed from watch tower

TWENTY-NINE

Dulag-Luft Interrogation

The 368th Fighter Group newspaper, *The Fortress Feature*, reported that Air Command held an awards ceremony on January 8, 1944 at the Metz airfield. Among those receiving air medals with bronze and silver clusters were Lts. Robert D. Sharp and Kenneth Kalen. At the ceremony, they learned that the Air Force had approved Don's promotion to first lieutenant. Miserable weather grounded the fighter group for the second day in a row, keeping the pilots holed up in their barracks with little to do.[342] Lately, Bob had been thinking a lot about Don and Jerry. He would have gladly traded all his medals, clusters, and pins just to know if they were still alive.

Interrogation Day 1

The Air Force officers entered the gates of Dulag-Luft Oberursel on January 8, dead tired, barely able to walk from the train station to the prison compound. Officially known as Auswertestelle-West, the Nazi intelligence and evaluation center was located about eight miles northwest of Frankfurt. The largest building, called the Stonehouse, served as the main interrogation center at the 500-acre complex. Three additional buildings served as barracks to house staff and prisoners.

The buildings had "Prisoner of War Camp" painted on their roofs in white letters. The Nazis also placed large, white rocks forming the letters "POW" on the front lawn. While the prominent markings *did* protect the POWs from bombing attacks, their true purpose was to safeguard Germany's high-value interrogation and intelligence operation.

Two twelve-foot fences, deep trenches, coiled barbed wire, guard towers, armed pillboxes, and even trained dogs surrounded the compound. After a failed tunnel escape in 1941 by RAF pilots, no more breakout attempts were made.[343] Prisoners entering the gates at Dulag-Luft Oberursel weren't going anywhere until their interrogators were through with them:

After entering the main building, I was stripped and searched and then processed [ID pictures and fingerprints were taken]. I hung on to my strips of cloth, in case I wasn't given a coat. One of the interrogators gave me a Red Cross form to complete. I filled in my name, rank, and serial number, but stopped filling out the form when it started asking questions like which fighter group I was in, where I was stationed, who my CO was, etc. The Red Cross clearly hadn't put this form together.

The interrogator assigned to me wasn't pleased with my unwillingness to complete the form or answer any of his questions. I reminded him that the Geneva Convention Rules only required me to give my name, rank, and serial number, and that was all I was going to give him.

I was put into solitary confinement in a room about 6' x 8' in size. It was just wide enough for an iron cot, which had a little straw tick mattress on it about an inch thick. There was one small, frosted glass window in the corner letting in a little light, but no electricity—so the room was quite dark. They gave me one blanket, which I kept wrapped around me to help keep warm.

The room was quite chilly. A steam heater clanged and banged as the steam came on. But as soon as the pipes echoed that steam was coming to the heater, the Germans turned it off before the heater could get warm. Every few hours, they turned it on and off again.

Notches were marked on the wall, supposedly by previous prisoners, showing they'd been imprisoned up to 28 days in solitary confinement. Like the heat manipulation, this was another of the psychological games the Germans played to break prisoners down. Instead of the 28 days notched on the wall, the average stay was usually no more than a week or so.

I was given one skimpy bowl of thin soup, a slice of black bread, and a can to relieve myself that I put in the corner of my room. Then I was left alone. I lay on my cot the rest of the day and slept better that night than I had for a long time.

It was unlikely that interrogators at Dulag-Luft could have extracted any information from Don that would have been valuable to them. As a 2nd lieutenant pilot, he wasn't privy to any future air attacks, strategic military plans, or new weaponry. Nevertheless, his interrogation continued for days, just as it would for thousands of Air Force prisoners that followed in his footsteps until Patton captured the city of Frankfurt and shut down the interrogation center two months later.

When the POWs entered the Oberursel Dulag, the Germans allowed them to fill out a prisoner-notification card. Whenever Red Cross representatives visited and inspected the interrogation center, they picked up the cards and mailed them to the prisoner's loved ones. Don addressed his card to Mrs. Donald N Evans. On the reverse side, he entered the day's date, his name, rank, and service branch. His pre-printed card read:

I have been taken prisoner of war in Germany. I am in good health– slightly wounded (cancel accordingly).

We will be transported from here to another Camp within the next few days. Please don't write until I give new address.

Kindest regards

Neither the "good health" nor the "slightly wounded" option on Don's notification card was "cancelled accordingly" by the Germans, suggesting that the condition of his feet and his other post-march ailments placed him somewhere in between. Laura Jeanne wouldn't receive the card until the end of February, nearly two months later.

Interrogation Day 2

Don wrote:

That morning [January 9], I was taken to an interrogation room. The interrogator seemed pleasant enough, and in perfect English, asked me to complete the Red Cross form

I'd started filling out the previous day. He told me they needed the entire form filled out before the Red Cross could follow up and notify my family that I was being held as a POW.

Seeing that I didn't buy his explanation, he started asking me questions like: "Where are you from? Which outfit are you flying with? Where is it located? Who is your commanding officer?" When I didn't answer his questions, he went on to tell me some things they already knew about me and my fighter group that surprised me. They were fishing around trying to make me think they already knew so much that talking about it wouldn't really matter—and doing so would get me out of there sooner. But I didn't take the bait and again gave him my Geneva Convention name, rank, and serial number spiel. This time, he got angry and said, "If you get hungry, and decide to talk, let us know."

I was taken back to my little room and left alone to count the notches on the wall and wonder how long I might be there and what was going to happen to me.

Some guys nearly went nuts being left alone all day in solitary confinement. The time passed slowly—but being alone didn't bother me that much. I just lay on my cot, remembering good times from my past, and dreamed about being with Laura Jeanne and my friends back home. Those who smoked were denied cigarettes and seemed to have the hardest time.

That night, the cold and hunger, and listening to the steam heater clanging and banging and shutting off just as heat started to come out was getting to me. I'd developed a sinus infection on our forced march that was now getting worse. I was feeling pretty lousy and knew the Germans weren't likely to give me any medicine. I started to worry about what was going to happen to me and prayed for help from a higher source.

That same night, more than 5,000 miles away and unaware of what had befallen her husband, Laura Jeanne lamented:

All of my body and soul aches and yearns for you tonight. I'm feeling so lonesome and lost I could cry—but that doesn't do me any good. Usually after I write to you and pour out my heart, I feel better. But that's not the case anymore. Sometimes I wonder if we will ever be together again.

I haven't heard from you for several days now—so I'm getting a little impatient. Now the Christmas rush is over, things ought to get a little better, so I'll be expecting some mail again but soon.

Please be careful, my dearest; your safety is always on my mind and in my prayers. This new German offensive has scared us all, but we seem to be holding our own now. Do watch your step. I'd rather die myself than have anything happen to you.

Bye for now, my precious, darling pilot. I love you always.

One month later, the letter was returned to her by the United States 1st Base Post Office stamped, "Return to Sender—Recipient Missing."

Interrogation Day 3

Don wrote the following about his final interrogation session at Dulag-Luft:

For the third day in a row, I was taken in to meet with my interrogator. He again tried to get me to talk, but stubbornly, I just gave him my name, rank, and serial number.

He could tell I was pretty sick. I was congested, coughing, running a fever, and my head ached from the sinus infection I had. For whatever reason, probably because I was sick, he gave up and sent me back to my room.

Don's interrogators faced a decision—they could admit him to their medical facility and continue his interrogation when he was in better health, or send him to the Dulag-Luft processing center in Wetzlar and get rid of him:

A while later, one of the guards told me they'd be moving me the next day. They gave me some soup, a slice of black bread smeared with oleo, and a cup of hot ersatz coffee. For some reason my interrogators decided to give up on me sooner than they did with most of the prisoners.

Dulag-Luft, Wetzlar

January 12

Following a fitful night of sleep, one of the guards roused Don and told him he was being moved. He quickly rose from his cot and followed him out of his cell without looking back—happy to be leaving the inhospitable Nazi interrogation center:

> *At the railroad station in Frankfurt I was put on a train bound for the collecting center in Wetzlar. Most Air Force POWs leaving Oberursel were kept there until being sent to a permanent prison camp. The train ride took a little over an hour. After arriving, I was processed and assigned to a prison camp located on the Baltic Sea.*

> *The Dulag at Wetzlar was crowded. Thousands of prisoners were being processed and waiting to be sent to German prison camps. I was housed in a prisoner barracks while I waited for the next train to Barth.*

Earlier in the war, when the Nazis processed prisoners through Dulag-Luft Wetzlar, the International Red Cross provided them with "Capture Kits." Toiletries, a sewing kit, cigarettes, chewing gum, a G.I. coat, a sweater, shirts, pants, underwear, pajamas, and a knitted cap were packed in a cleverly designed cardboard travel suitcase. However, by the time Don arrived at Wetzlar, the relentless Allied bombing attacks were blocking Red Cross supplies from getting to the Dulag. They were out of nearly everything, including the cardboard suitcases. Years later, underneath a watercolor painting by Lt. Colonel Ross Greening that depicted POWs marching into prison camp carrying Capture Kits, Don wrote:

Who was so blessed to have "any" belongings to carry in a suitcase! It would have been great to have even had a coat—I just had tablecloth strips wrapped around my upper body when I entered prison camp.

Back home that night, Laura Jeanne watched intently as the theater newsreel showed Gen. Douglas MacArthur triumphantly walking ashore to cheering Filipinos, after American troops landed on the beaches of Luzon.[344] As moviegoers erupted in applause at the news, Laura Jeanne's thoughts drifted from the Pacific to the European Theater of War on the other side of the world, where her soul mate was fighting in the Battle of the Bulge.

Laura Jeanne was no longer receiving letters from Don. She hoped and prayed that the interruption was temporary, just another glitch in the Army mail delivery system. But after a few more days, the awful premonition she felt on Christmas Eve began haunting her dreams again.

Stalag Luft-1 processing mug shots

THIRTY

Serial Number 7435

January 13

Without medication, Don's acute sinusitis worsened. After a miserable night at Dulag-Luft Wetzlar, he boarded a train headed for Barth, Germany, located nearly 500 rail miles to the northeast:

> *At 6:00 a.m., I, along with many other Air Corps prisoners, was taken back to the rail station in Wetzlar and put on an old broken-down train that had most of its windows missing. After a long delay, we began a three-day train ride to Stalag Luft I at Barth on the Baltic Sea.*
>
> *The boxcar I was put in was cold, drafty, and very crowded, with over 60 men inside. There weren't enough benches for everyone, so we had to take turns standing up or sitting down on the floor.*

Don and the other Air Force POWs were crammed into "forty and eight" railroad cars. The French designed the stubby cars during World War I to carry forty men or eight horses. They measured only 20.5 feet long and 8.5 feet wide. From late 1944 through the end of the war, the Germans used these "rickety, rough-riding, unheated, slow-moving boxcars" to transport Allied prisoners to German POW camps, sometimes packing as many as ninety men into each car:[345]

> *I don't remember very much about our train ride to Barth. I was really cold the entire journey, since I was still without a coat and hat. I was pretty sick and still running a fever, which was probably why I couldn't remember much about the trip.*

Sometimes, having no memory is a blessing that keeps our heart and mind free from the canker of hate.

The POWs took advantage of delays along the way, relieving themselves or emptying their bowels whenever the guards opened the boxcar doors. When the train was moving, the doors remained closed, forcing them to use slop buckets placed in the corner of their railcar. Many of the prisoners suffered from dysentery and soiled themselves when they were unable to get to one of the buckets in time.

January 14

While Don's train moved slowly toward Berlin, the 397th Fighter Squadron experienced its darkest day. In one of their final air attacks of the war, the Luftwaffe sent forty Me-109s and forty Fw-190s into the sky between Karlsruhe and Mannheim, about fifty miles south of Frankfurt. Major Leary headed a twelve-plane Jabo Angel Squadron on a bombing and armed recce mission, with Bob leading flight Blue No. 3, his first time as an element leader.[346]

After the Jabo Angels destroyed a truck depot and strafed some troop-carrying railroad cars, German bandits jumped them without any warning. Bob called the Topic Yellow No. 3 element leader to warn him that more than fifty enemy planes were coming out of the sun. But it was too late. Major Leary and the rest of the squadron didn't have a chance. Bob was one of only six 397th pilots that returned to the base.[347] He ended the report of his thirty-first sortie, writing, "This was the worst mission I was ever on."

On Day 2 of his rail journey, Don recounted:

The stench was awful in the cars. We had a lot of delays along the way and welcomed the fresh air whenever the guards opened the doors. I remember stopping at some marshalling yards in Berlin at the end of our second day, where we were finally able to get out and walk around.

We were given some black bread to eat each day, but very little drinking water, causing nearly everyone to get dehydrated.

January 15

Don's train left Berlin early that morning, taking the rest of the day to travel the final 175 miles of their journey. After dozens of stops and delays, the POWs finally reached their destination:

We arrived at Barth after dark and got off the train in the middle of a heavy snowstorm—tired, filthy, and hungry. We marched from the train station, through the center of town, and then about three miles to the POW camp, finally arriving about 9:00 p.m. The guards opened the outer gate, and we entered the place I'd stay until the end of the war.

After being "de-loused" and given a two-minute shower (my first in over three weeks), the guards looked at our papers and took us to a barracks room for processing. I was fingerprinted, had a mug shot taken (one side-view and one-front view), and given German dog tags. Mine were stamped with serial number 7435 and Stalag Luft I on both sides.

Prisoners of war arriving at train station in Barth

Next, I was given a washcloth, a bar of hand soap, a toothbrush, and an Army field jacket, hat and uniform, since I had none. I also received one thin wool blanket, a sheet and pillowcase for my bunk, and a small blue YMCA notebook and pencil. Then I was assigned to a barracks. Room 9, Block 309, North 3 Compound was my new home.

Searchlights from the guard towers followed me as I was taken to the barracks. The guard unlocked the door and took me inside a cold, dark building to my room. Some of the guys woke up and welcomed me, and pointed to an empty bottom bed of a 3-stack bunk. I thought they were being nice to me, but soon discovered that the bottom bunks weren't as warm, since heat rises. Still, it was the best deal I'd had in over three weeks, so I was happy.

I lay down on my bunk tired and hungry, but relieved that I was done with forced marches, interrogations, drinking out of ditches, and going days with little or no food. I was looking forward to being warm, getting my first Red Cross parcel, and eating something besides black bread and thin soup. Little did I know.

CLASS OF SERVICE

This is a full-rate Telegram or Cablegram unless its deferred character is indicated by a suitable symbol above or preceding the address.

WESTERN UNION

1204

A. N. WILLIAMS
PRESIDENT

SYMBOLS

DL = Day Letter

NL = Night Letter

LC = Deferred Cable

NLT = Cable Night Letter

Ship Radiogram

The filing time shown in the date line on telegrams and day letters is STANDARD TIME at point of origin. Time of receipt is STANDARD TIME at point of destination

H RO 44 govt

Wux Washington DC 904Am Jan 16 1945

Mrs Laura J Evans

90 North Center St

Lehi Utah ....

The secretary of war desires me to express his deep regret that your

Husband Second Lieutentant Donald N Evans has been reported missing

in action since twenty four December over Belgium if further details

or other information are received you will be promptly notified

Dunlop ,acting the Adjutant General

822Am

THIRTY-ONE

Missing

The following morning, Laura Jeanne walked across the street from her home and reported to work at the Lehi OPA office. Like every other day, she issued stamps for shoes, sugar, coffee, fuel, and other items that were being rationed, listening to the usual complaints from those disagreeing with recent decisions of the Price Administration Board.

Around 2:00 p.m., the jingle-jangle of the brass bell on the front door rang, and Laura Jeanne looked up as the Lehi mail carrier entered the office:

I knew the postman well, and he was always very friendly. As he approached me at the front counter, I could tell something was wrong. He had a serious look on his face, and I could see tears in his eyes. He handed me the yellow Western Union telegram he was awkwardly holding, then turned around and left the office without saying a word. I knew it was bad news.

I calmly put on my coat and followed him out of the office, and then walked across the street to my parents' home. After opening the front door, I started screaming—the telegram still tightly clutched in my hand.

My mother ran into the entryway and held me in her arms, unaware of why I was screaming and shaking. She walked me to my room, where I fell on my bed face down. Mother pried the telegram from my fingers and read it to me, as I lay there sobbing uncontrollably. Hysterical is the only word that begins to describe my state of mind.

Hours passed before she regained her composure enough to read
the telegram for herself:

Washington DC
Jan 16 1945
Mrs. Laura J. Evans

The secretary of war desires me to express his deep regret that your
husband second-lieutenant Donald N Evans has been reported
missing in action since twenty four December over Belgium if
further details or other information are received you will be
promptly notified

Dunlop, acting the Adjutant General

Laura Jeanne continued:

*I didn't sleep at all that night. Mother held me in her arms
for hours trying to comfort me, telling me that I needed to
have faith and pray for Don's safety. But I felt numb—like
my world had just ended.*

*For many nights, I couldn't sleep more than a few minutes
at a time. As soon as I'd fall asleep, I dreamed about Don. It
was always the same dream, his plane was on fire, and I could
never tell if he was able to parachute to safety. Then I'd wake
up in tears and nothing could calm my troubled heart.*

*I couldn't bring myself to go back to work, and I didn't want
to see or talk to anyone. My heart wanted to believe Don
was all right and that we'd be together again someday, but
my mind was unsure, causing my days and nights to be filled
with despair.*

A week later, she received another letter from the Adjutant
General's Office, confirming the telegram and expressing regret and
sympathy. It read like a form letter, which it was—identical to the
one Mrs. Kelly had received two months earlier. It was followed by a
letter from Father Cleary, the 368th chaplain. He wrote:

*I can appreciate, at least in some small measure, the grief this
has brought you. I'm also conscious of the fact that no words
of mine can in any way ease the burden of sorrow, which is*

yours at this time. I do, however, wish to express the sincere sympathy, which the officers and men in Don's squadron and the Group as a whole feel. He was very popular with the men, and we miss having him with us.

I hesitate to hold out any false hope, nor am I allowed to give you any details of the type of mission he was flying. The fact that there aren't any details to give is a cause for some measure of hope. Time alone will give us the answer.

Still another official letter arrived, this one an awkwardly worded form letter from Utah's Governor Herbert W. Maw that was identical to the one he'd sent to the Kellys. None of the letters provided much comfort, and Laura Jeanne remained haunted by the image of Don trying to escape his burning plane. A few days later, after an unexpected visit from Grant Ashe's mother, her life took an abrupt turn:

She suggested that if I read Don's patriarchal blessing, I might find the peace of mind I was looking for. Doing so was an answer to my prayers. As I read it, the words glared up at me as if they were in bold print: "The Lord will go with you and bless you in times of danger and guide your footsteps... and you will return home safely when the war is over." At that moment, I knew he was still alive.

I found my faith again and was able to get on with my life. I prayed a lot, went to church, read the scriptures, and was conscientious in striving to help others who weren't as fortunate as me. A number of the ladies in my "war widows" club had also received telegrams from the secretary of war. Six of them were later informed that their husbands wouldn't be returning home. I now had faith that mine would.

Both our parents were so supportive while I waited for news about what had happened to my sweetheart. Keeping busy at home, at church, and in my job helped with the lonely days. And something that Don did before he went off to war helped me to make it through my hardest times. He pre-arranged with his mother to have a gardenia corsage (my favorite flower) delivered to me every other Sunday, for the entire time he was overseas. I believe that was the kindest and most thoughtful thing anyone has ever done for me.

At the insistence of both mothers, Laura Jeanne visited the *Lehi Free Press* and the larger Salt Lake City newspaper offices and provided them with a picture of her missing pilot along with the War Department's notifications. The newspapers were full of similar pictures and announcements of soldiers reported MIA. The short articles mentioned their military branch, where they served, and commendations received, but contained few details about what had happened to them. The next articles printed about them would be more conclusive, reporting that they were either alive, held captive as a prisoner of war or killed in action. The newspaper stories expanded the support group that Don's loved ones badly needed.

The next letter Laura Jeanne received surprised her and gave her the hope she desperately needed. Fearing that the Army would keep her in the dark and reveal little about what had actually happened to Don, Bob decided to bend regulations and write to her:

18 February 1945
France

Dear Laura,

Last night I received a letter from my mother that told me you'd heard about Don. In fact, mother sent me two clippings from the papers about it. Gosh, I don't know exactly what to say. I wasn't on the mission that Don got hit, but we all felt certain he was ok and would show up in a couple of days. He hasn't arrived yet, however, but we're inclined to believe that he's OK.

You can never tell what will happen after you hit the ground and start looking for some place to go. There's one thing for certain about Don—everyone knows that he can take care of himself in any situation. He's one boy you don't have to worry about when it comes to keeping calm and cool in an emergency.

I don't know what else to tell you except that his plane was hit by flak and he bailed out. Don got hit the day before Xmas so you can see what a merry Xmas we had. Maybe next year Don and Jerry and I will be together again. I sure hope so.

The chaplain will probably write you a letter and I do hope he does a better job than he did with Jerry's. Later, the War Dept. will send you a letter that will explain in full detail almost exactly what happened. The one they sent Mrs. Kelly was a pretty accurate story. It lacked a few details—but then the gov't never does tell all it knows.

I have a picture of Don that I'll send to you as soon as I get the negative. We found a little book that Don had with a lot of dates and such, but I can't send it to you because he has a couple of missions written in it. I'll bring it with me when I come back home because I thought you might like it. Don probably wants it too. If I'm on the receiving end of some flak before then, I'll have Pat or Kalen get it to you. We made arrangements a long time ago so everyone knows just what to do with the other fellow's stuff—just in case.

You probably can't imagine how much we all like Don. I don't think we're as concerned as you are, but we don't miss it by far. Pat, Kalo, Jerry, and I respect, admire, and even love Don. He's one of the best friends I've ever had, and I hope he thought half as much of me as I think of him. He's a peach of a swell guy.

I feel rather guilty about what happened because I remember Jerry and I pleaded with him to come over here to the 9th with us. He was assigned to go with the 8th, but we finally won him over. I know he had fun while he was flying with us, but like everyone else, he got a scare now and then. It's a little late, but I'll say now that I'm sorry I pleaded with him so much.

I don't know if I should tell you how much Don loves you or not. No fooling—when he and I weren't fighting and having fun, I was always listening to him tell me what a wonderful girl you are, and I wasn't bored a bit. Yep, he talked about you all the time.

I better close now. As you can see, I'm the wrong person to write to you at this time. I never was much of a writer, and a subject like this is especially hard to write about. I hope you'll forgive me for any mistakes in judgment I've made. Please don't give up hope.

As ever, Bob

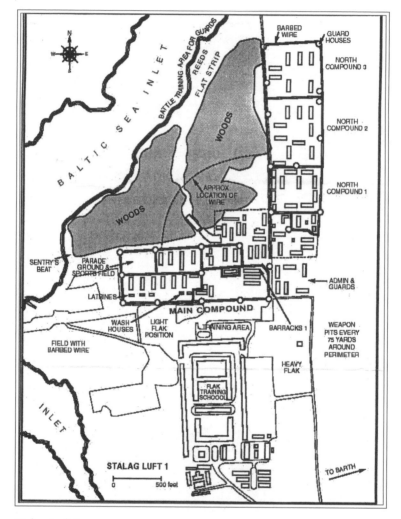

Stalag Luft 1

THIRTY-TWO

Barth on the Baltic Sea

The ancient German town of Barth lies on a lagoon of the Baltic Sea near the southern tip of Sweden. According to legend, Slavic tribes built the town on the site of a mythical sunken city named Vineta, known as "Atlantis of the North." Like Plato's fictional island, it, too, fell out of favor with the gods and was eventually taken to the bottom of the sea as punishment for its inhabitants' debased and corrupt lifestyle. There were still rumors that spoke of occasional reappearances of the lost city as a continuing warning to others.[348]

The townspeople of Barth suffered through centuries of wars, epidemics, fires, and storm tides. They were overrun by early Danish and Germanic tribes and warlords, then later struggled under successive occupations by Sweden, Denmark, France, and Prussia. The selection of Barth as a POW campsite was a godsend for the locals, serving as a protective shield against Allied bombing raids throughout World War II. A satellite operation of the infamous Ravensbrück women's concentration camp was also located at Barth. Nearly 7,000 women prisoners were forced to work in deplorable conditions as slave laborers in the Heinkel airplane factory. More than 2,000 died there before the war ended.[349]

The German Luftwaffe chose a sandy, forested inlet jutting into the Baltic Sea as the site for their first Stalag Luft prison camp. Besides its remote location, the lagoon's high water table also factored in its selection; it made digging escape tunnels more difficult. In November 1943, the Nazis relocated the non-commissioned prisoners at Stalag Luft I to a different camp and turned it into an officer-only POW compound. Soon after, U.S. Air Force officers joined the RAF officers already at camp. By September 1944, the number of prisoners had surged to nearly 6,000.[350]

The North 1 Compound opened in February 1944 to accommodate the overflow of prisoners from the West and South Compounds. Originally home to the Hitler Youth, North 1 was by far the best compound. Besides its communal mess hall, kitchen facilities, indoor latrines, indoor running water, and bathhouse with showers, it had a theater, church, library, and a recreation room. The West Compound also had indoor latrines, indoor running water, kitchen facilities, and a large mess hall, which also served as a theater and chapel. In addition, the North 1 and West compounds had full-sized football and baseball fields. The South Compound, however, was poorly constructed and nothing like the other two.[351]

Guard Tower

To accommodate the burgeoning inmate population, in late 1944 the Luftwaffe built two additional compounds, North 2 and North

3. Unfortunately for the prisoners, the Germans constructed both of the compounds using the South Compound as their model, with no running water and no communal buildings except for a mess hall. Latrines were located outside in a separate building, forcing the men to use a slop pail to relieve themselves at night after guards locked up their barracks. The parade grounds of the new compounds were small, and there were no buildings to gather in. North 2 and 3 prisoners were required to use the North 1 facilities for sports, church, and entertainment—if and when they could get permission from the kommandant.[352,353]

Double barbed wire fences

With the addition of the two new compounds, the camp took on a reverse L-shape look and followed the contours of the adjacent bay. The Germans built the barracks using rough-cut lumber, leaving two feet of open space exposed between the floor and the ground. Besides deterring tunnel digging, the space allowed enough room for guard dogs to roam underneath at night. The void also permitted air to circulate below the rooms, making the barracks cold and drafty in the winter.[354]

Two ten-foot-high barbed-wire fences surrounded each compound. Another double fence, with rolls of barbed wire placed in between, encircled the entire prison camp. Forty-foot guard towers, equipped with powerful searchlights and manned by guards armed with machine guns, were located on the corners of the camp. Escape attempts were common. Each compound had a well-organized escape committee. All escape plans required approval from the camp's senior POW officer and the blessing of the compound's leader—but after more than ninety tries, no one had made it more than thirty-six miles from Barth.[355]

Most of the breakout attempts involved tunneling. The Germans countered by installing seismographic equipment, which enabled them to detect underground noises. Once they discovered a tunnel was under construction, the Nazi secret police usually let the POWs continue to dig and painstakingly remove the dirt from their underground escape project, waiting to shut them down when they neared the outer fences.[356]

A much easier plan of escape was to cut through the barbed-wire fences, navigate the rolls of coiled barbed wire, and hide in one of the buildings located outside the camp enclosure until after dark. Several prisoners did just that and successfully bolted to the nearby woods and temporary freedom. However, without identity cards or travel permits (which Germans were required to carry at all times), capture was a near certainty. Once returned to prison, the escapees faced solitary confinement, relocation to a hellhole Gestapo prison camp, or worse. The high water table in winter caused escape tunnels to flood, and the white backdrop of the snow-covered ground made it nearly impossible to sneak through the fences undetected, leaving the compound escape committees little to do.[357]

All five compounds at Stalag Luft I were interconnected. Initially, the gates separating them were only locked at night, allowing the Kriegies* to mingle freely with other's barracks and facilities during the day. However, the Germans now locked them up during the day as well, denying prisoners in North 2 and 3 regular access to the communal facilities in the original compounds. The sports fields, theaters, libraries, and churches were restricted to "permission only" status—and Kommandant Oberst (Colonel) Willibald Scherer wasn't

---

* Nickname the POWs called themselves—short for *Kriegsgefangenen*, the German word for Prisoner of War.

a generous man, seldom permitting the men to leave their barracks, even to attend church services on Sundays.[358]

Earlier in the war, camp administrators allowed the barracks to organize teams and compete in softball and football games at the North 1 and West sports fields. They were also allowed to watch American films, take educational courses, and create variety shows, concerts, recitals, and other productions the prisoners put on at the "Kriegie Theater" in the North 1 Compound. The YMCA supplied most of the musical instruments and materials for costumes and stage props. The prisoners bribed the guards with American cigarettes in exchange for the rest of the instruments and props they needed. The musicians among the prisoners wrote music for the performances from memory and trained other prisoners how to read music and play instruments. With little else to do, the performers had endless hours to rehearse, giving attention to every possible detail in preparation for the concerts and stage productions. They starred talented singers, professional musicians, and accomplished actors.[359,360] The most famous, Donald Pleasance, later starred as the psychiatrist in the film series *Halloween*, the villain in James Bond's *You Only Live Twice*, and an RAF officer in *The Great Escape*.

Unfortunately, the last two major productions at Stalag Luft I took place before Don arrived. The kommandant lifted curfew on Christmas Day and opened the gates between the compounds, allowing the prisoners to socialize. The American POWs built a Christmas tree in the North 1 parade grounds using a broom handle and strips of wire cut from Klim dried milk cans for branches and decorated it with everything from toilet paper ornaments to tinsel made from thinly sliced strands of cigarette packaging. The Kriegie orchestra, several talented musicians and singers, and a few wannabe comedians put on a variety show on Christmas Eve. Then at midnight, one of the camp chaplains conducted Christmas services for an overflow crowd of prisoners in the North 1 mess hall, and a choir of 2,000 men sang Christmas carols.[361] A week later, on a bitter cold New Year's Eve, the Kriegie performers treated the POWs to a three-act performance of *The Man Who Came to Dinner*,[362] a comedy made popular at Chicago's Music Box Theatre two years before the war began. It was the last camp-wide performance the POWs enjoyed together. Even if the kommandant hadn't ordered them to stop, the brutal Baltic Sea winter weather probably would have ended the productions anyway.

    U.S. 8th Air Force ace pilot Colonel Hubert Zemke crashed his P-51 Mustang behind enemy lines on October 30, 1944. After a series of prolonged interrogations at Oberursel and Wetzlar, German intelligence sent him to Stalag Luft I a few weeks before Don arrived. As the highest-ranking POW officer in camp, Zemke became the new Senior Allied Officer, taking over leadership of more than 6,000 American and British prisoners. Being fluent in German greatly helped him in his new leadership role, eliminating the need for an interpreter and the inevitable misunderstandings that can

Colonel Zemke

engender. Room 21, Block 9, North Compound 1 became the new Allied POW Wing Headquarters, or as the Kriegies called it, the "Head Shed."[363]

Kommandant Scherer and most of his staff were ardent, hard-hearted Nazis and were despised by the POWs. Shortly after Colonel Zemke's arrival, camp administration unexpectedly changed hands. The new kommandant, Oberst von Warnstedt, was an older man, reportedly not as ruthless as his predecessor. However, that immediately came into question when he retained the previous henchman in charge of security police—the notorious Nazi Major von Miller zu Aichholz, who had no love for British and American flyboys.[364]

The new kommandant showed his true colors when he welcomed in the New Year with harsh regulations. Guards were given free rein to shoot prisoners at will for even inadvertent infractions, such as accidently touching the warning wire located near the barbed-wire fence during ball games or while doing exercises. Anyone caught outside the barracks during an air raid was also open season for the guards. Nearly as ominous were the food and supply reductions von Miller implemented—supposedly to accommodate the huge influx of new prisoners. Colonel Zemke, however, was convinced that "hunger was intentionally induced by the camp administration, or by a higher authority, with the aim of subduing the internees."[365]

The situation was further complicated by the difficulty of delivering food and supplies to the remote prison site in Barth. There were fewer railroad cars available because of the Allied bombing on the railways. Since the Germans gave higher priority to their own military needs than those of POW camps, food and supply deliveries suffered. Just as Don entered the prison gates, life had taken a sharp turn for the worse at Stalag Luft I.

———

Early on the morning of January 16, Don woke up to the sound of blowing whistles and German cursing, abruptly reminding him where he was. After the guards unlocked the barracks doors, he followed his new roommates across the parade grounds to a smaller building located in the northeast corner of the compound, where their washing shed and latrines were located. After waiting in line, Don washed his face with cold water from a washbasin, then relieved himself in the latrine—instead of outside, or in a slop bucket, as he'd done the last three weeks. Afterward, the men returned to their room to get ready for morning *appell.** It didn't take Don long, since he'd slept in his clothes, including his newly issued army field jacket and wool hat. His fever broke sometime during the night, and he felt better than he had in days.

Appell took place twice a day, at 6:45 in the morning and 4:30 in the afternoon, regardless of the weather. The Germans claimed they made the counts to determine food rations for the day, but it was obvious they were just checking to see if any POWs had escaped. Each of the POW barracks had a commander who was responsible for getting his men to the parade grounds on time, lined up five deep, ready to be counted under the direction of a Lager officer. The POWs were required to stand at attention until the guards had accounted for all of the prisoners. They hurried the counts, as eager to get out of the bitter-cold winter weather as the prisoners.[366] Years later, Don

———

*   German word for "roll call."

would mark his roll-call position in another of Lt. Colonel Greening's watercolor renditions: front row of his group, seven men to the left, directly in front of his barracks.

Appell — Roll Call

After roll call, the POWs in Room 9 walked to the mess hall to make their morning cup of ersatz. Stalag Luft I made their variety of the coffee substitute from barley. Its main redeeming virtue was that it was hot. Don was disappointed when he learned that breakfast was no longer being served at the camp—not even a slice of the black bread he'd grown accustomed to eating since his capture. The men were down to one hot meal each day.

After returning to the barracks, the Kriegie Kut-Ups, as Don's roommates called themselves, gave him a seat at the bench table located in the center of their room and egged him on to tell his story. All their stories were gripping and had a lot in common. Like Don, most of them had parachuted from a burning plane, survived their fall without serious injuries, been captured by German soldiers, forced to march (or transported by rail if they were lucky) to Frankfurt, booked as guests at the Dulag-Luft Oberursel interrogation center, then crammed into a forty-and-eight boxcar for a nightmarish train ride to Barth.

There were two other fighter pilots in Room 9. One, flying a P-51 Mustang, was shot down by friendly fire in southern Germany near Ulm. The other, flying a P-47 Thunderbolt, was hit by flak and bailed out in the snowy mountains of Italy. Another roommate, piloting a troop transport glider in Montgomery's disastrous Operation Market Garden, was shot down in Holland. Two other pilots flying C-47 Skytrain air cargo planes were hit by flak on December 23 while dropping supplies to McAuliffe's Army in Bastogne. Seven of the men in his room, all from the 100th Bomb Group, were flying in B-17 Flying Fortress bombers on a mission over Hamburg, Germany, on New Year's Eve. Heavy flak took down all four of their planes, killing twelve of their crew. Another B-17 pilot in the room, along with seven of his crew, bailed out of their exploding plane at high altitude over southeast Poland. Only half of their parachutes opened and four airmen died on impact. Don's other roommates were survivors from shot down B-24 Liberator heavy bombers or B-26 Marauder medium bombers.

German staff prepared the food rations for the POWs' one hot meal in a central kitchen, then divided them for distribution to the various compounds based on the number of prisoners. The German meals were supplemented with food from Red Cross parcels (when they were available) and allocated to each barracks. The meal generally consisted of thin barley soup with a few vegetables (potatoes, rutabagas, beets, or cabbage), and occasionally a small piece of horsemeat. Black bread was always on the menu. Cutting it into slices became a ritual. Don recalled:

With great care and precision, the guy assigned to KP duty that day in our room accurately cut the heavy, ten-inch long loaves into 48 thin slices—two slices for each man. Everyone stood around the table to make sure the crumbs were all saved into a little pile so they could be put in our soup before we ladled it into our bowls. It was the only fair way to divide them up.

*We got to choose our two slices of bread based on our length
of time at the prison camp, but I wasn't the last to choose—
that honor always went to the guy who sliced the bread. That
helped make sure he kept all the slices the same size. He didn't
want to short himself.*

After eating, Don lay down on his bunk, wrapped himself in his
thin wool blanket, and tried to keep warm. His mattress, straight
from 15th century Europe, was a rough burlap material stuffed with
wood shavings and straw. It wasn't comfortable, but he'd slept on
worse, and with his history of being able to sleep anywhere, anyplace,
anytime, he soon got used to it. The Germans had to triple stack
in order to pack twenty-four bunks into each North 3 Compound
room—six on each level on one side of the room (total of eighteen),
and two on each level on the other side (total of six).

Two wooden dressers with several drawers stood on the far end
of the room about two feet from the table, providing a spot for the
prisoners to store their meager belongings. Don didn't require much
space since he had less of everything than most of the guys in the
room, especially those who arrived at Stalag Luft I carting Red Cross
Capture Kits.

Wooden shutters were attached to the two-pane glass windows
located on the outside-facing wall of their room. Each night the
guards closed the shutters when they locked the barracks, tightly
sealing the rooms, then reopened them at 6:00 the next morning.
The rooms each had a small ventilator, but they didn't provide
enough air circulation for the overcrowded quarters, leading to
upper respiratory problems for many of the POWs. The ventilation
problems would have been worse if it weren't for the barracks' poor
construction, which left cracks and gaps in the walls and ceilings.
After dark, a single low-watt bulb dangling from the ceiling lighted
each room.[367]

A small stove, located in the far corner of the room, burned
briquettes made from coal dust. Used for both cooking and heating,
it failed miserably to do the latter, forcing the men to spend a lot of
time in their bunks trying to stave off the cold. The only time the
stove warmed up the room was when one of the guys on coal detail

was able to sneak a few extra briquettes back to their room without being noticed by the "Goons." *[368]

Late afternoon on his first day at camp, Don noticed several POWs gathered in the hallway outside his room. Curious, he moved closer to the group, listening as their barracks officer read from a one-page newsletter in a subdued voice. Everyone within hearing range became excited when he read that Patton's Third Army, attacking from the south, had met up with Hodges' First Army, fighting from the north, at the town of Houffalize, Belgium. The Americans had finally flattened the bulge, forcing the Wehrmacht to retreat toward the Siegfried Line.

As the officer finished reading, Don noticed a familiar face on the other side of the crowded hallway. When they made eye contact, they both smiled—it was his former Jabo Angel element leader and good friend Lt. Vernon Murphy. Pat was last seen bailing out of his burning airplane the same week that Jerry went missing. They hugged each other, then excitedly began catching up on what had happened since they'd last seen each other three months earlier. Lt. Murphy was just three rooms down the hall from Don in Block 309, Room 6.

———————

Earlier that day, after receiving the same war briefings as the Stalag Luft I POWs, Adolf Hitler entered a huge, self-sufficient bunker fifty-five feet under Berlin. He continued to manage his war operations, safely protected from the daily bombing raids that terrorized the German capital above him—still ignoring the advice of his military leaders. Everyone, except for the Führer, knew defeat was inevitable. Against all reason, Hitler was convinced that publicly announcing his decision to stay in Berlin would inspire the shattered German people and drive his retreating armies on to victory.[369]

———————

In December 1943, with the kommandant's approval, RAF leadership at Stalag Luft I started to produce a single-page camp

———————

*   Kriegies called their guards "Goons," after the simple-minded, oafish looking characters in the Disney movie Sleeping Beauty that Maleficent called, "Fools! Idiots! Imbeciles!"

newsletter, gleaning their news from German radio broadcasts and German newspapers and magazines. The editors carefully avoided printing anything that might offend their German captors or run the risk of censorship. In reality, the vanilla publication was a ruse used to cover up a secret daily war newsletter, which soon became the largest circulated underground newspaper in the war. News for the single-page, clandestine publication came from interviews with newly arrived prisoners, from the BBC, and later from the Voice of America* radio news broadcasts.[370]

The Kriegie news staff listened to the broadcasts on a radio set hidden in the West Compound. In exchange for American cigarettes, guards smuggled in parts for the original radio. Two inventive RAF officers built it using "pencil lead, shaving soap containers, toothpaste tubes, silver paper, greaseproof paper, and condensers made from Healthy Life Biscuit Tins."[371] The nails that attached the radio to the wall also served as terminals for an antenna and earphone cables. The device could run either off the camp's electrical system or by flashlight batteries when the power was off. North 1 Compound prisoners later smuggled in a second radio but couldn't get it to work. Concealing it in a large detergent box, they transferred the radio to the RAF gurus in the West Compound, who soon made it operational. The new radio could pick up nightly broadcasts from the Voice of America, as well as those from the BBC.[372]

The radio operators monitored the broadcasts, taking meticulous notes, then passed them to the security officer in the West Compound. He in turn hid them in a Klim can that had a false bottom. The next morning, they typed up their notes on wispy thin paper, and the North 1 liaison officer delivered them to the British senior officer in the West Compound. Finally, the Brits deftly concealed the tightly folded notes in the liaison's gutted wristwatch, redesigned so the watch hands could display the correct time when he passed through inspection. After delivering the broadcast notes, the British produced their newsletter, the *Red Star*; and the Americans published their version, the *POW-WOW* (Prisoners of War Waiting on Winning). Copies of each issue were typed up, then distributed to the POW security officers in each compound.[373]

---

*   The official radio broadcast station of the United States federal government

Delivering the newsletters to the compounds posed additional challenges. Every afternoon, a few of the prisoners gathered near the fences between each of the three north compounds. Appearing bored, with nothing better to do, they took turns throwing rocks at targets on the other side of their fence. Eventually, they mixed in a few stones carefully wrapped with the newsletters, nonchalantly throwing them over the fence. The prisoners on the other side caught the newsletters before they hit the ground and passed them on to the next barracks the same way. The guards didn't have a clue—never catching on to what happened every day, right under their noses. Passing the final copy to the West Compound was more complicated. The thin newssheet was folded into a small square, then wrapped in protective wax paper. The communications carrier from North 1, who entered the West Compound every day to pick up and deliver mail, concealed it in his mouth between his teeth and cheek, with instructions to swallow it if the Germans discovered the scheme. Once the barracks officers read the newsletters in each of the compounds, they threw them in a stove or incinerator.[374]

During a surprise search in the summer of 1944, the Germans discovered a copy of the *POW-WOW*, tipping them off that the Kriegies had a hidden radio, the only possible source for the information in the newspaper. Since they found the copy in the North 1 Compound, the security police assumed that the radio was located there as well. Search after search took place in North 1, diverting attention from its actual location—behind a false cupboard in the theater of the West Compound. The news staff at Stalag Luft I printed the secret newspaper nearly every day from March 1944 to May 1945. Amazingly, the Germans never discovered the hidden radios.[375,376]

The German-induced hunger and the relentless cold were taking their toll on the prisoners, especially those, like Don, who arrived at camp already weakened from lack of food and exposure to the elements. Over the next few days, he recorded the names and addresses of his new roommates on the first page of his YMCA notebook, along with their rank, flight position, and type of plane they flew. The Kriegie Kut-Ups came from twelve different states—from Oregon in the West to Massachusetts in the East.

From the beginning of Don's internment at Stalag Luft I, food was the main topic of discussion—nothing else even came close. The Kriegie Kut-Ups in Room 9 complained nonstop about the food reductions and constantly reminisced about the good old days when they received one Red Cross food parcel*[377] per man *every* week, practically drooling as they described the tasty meals they used to concoct. Then the reductions had begun. First, the Germans cut the parcels to bi-weekly, then monthly. Now they were lucky to receive even a partial box to divide among everyone in the room. His roommates described the contents of the coveted Red Cross parcels in detail, comparing them to the Jerry rations—then versus now—and speculated how many calories they were now surviving on.

Don filled in the second page of his YMCA notebook with the contents of the Red Cross food parcels and the current Jerry rations his roommates had so exactingly described to him:

Red Cross Parcel

2 "D" chocolate bars (Nestlé) or 1 "D" bar & 1 pkg. of M&M's
1 eight-oz. can of cocoa
1 one-lb. can of Klim (powdered milk spelled backwards)
1 one-lb. package of raisins or prunes
1 one-lb. can of oleomargarine
1 six-oz. can of jam
1 one-lb. can of spam
1 one-lb. can of liver paté or peanut butter
1 one-lb. can of meat & beans, vegetable stew, or corned beef
2 bars of soap
1 box vitamin tablets
5 pkgs. of cigarettes
1 twelve-oz. can of salmon, sardines, or tuna fish

---

*   Germany, as a signer to the Geneva Conventions, allowed the International Red Cross to visit POW camps with trained medical staff to check on prisoners' health and living conditions, and to send them relief packages of medical supplies and food. The Red Cross food parcels were a godsend to the nearly 1.4 million Allied POWs who received them during the war, keeping thousands from starving from the inadequate Jerry rations provided at the camps. The absence of the parcels for extended periods greatly reduced prisoner survival odds.

Jerry Rations (1,100 calories per day)

1/4 lb. oleo per week
1/6 loaf of black bread per day (two thin slices)
Cheese (twice a month)
Sugar
Marmalade
Potatoes (3 rations per week)
Cabbage (2 rations per week)
Rutabagas (turnip-like root vegetable, 2 rations per month)
Salt (1small ration per month)
Pea powder (same as above)

The Kriegie assigned to KP duty usually brought back the same thin soup and bread each day. Occasionally, the German rations included marmalade, instead of oleo, almost making their slices of black bread taste good.

After eating their one daily meal, the prisoners usually threw a few coal briquettes on the small fire burning in their pot-bellied stove and lingered around the table for a while shooting the bull. When the fire burned down, they climbed back in their bunks and tried to keep warm while they waited for afternoon roll call. Afterward, they hit the sack early to escape the freezing temperatures in one of the coldest Januarys on record along the Baltic Sea Coast.

Don's YMCA notebook

THIRTY-THREE

Post Cards, Letters, & YMCA Notebooks

Stalag Luft I prisoners were permitted to send three letters and four postcards per month. Outgoing POW mail not only had to pass German and Kriegie censors,* but also survive a mail delivery system that at best was unreliable—and, at worst, corrupt. The Nazis were meticulous record keepers and seldom discarded *any* correspondence. But they didn't always deliver or post prisoner mail, especially toward the end of the war.

Camp administration periodically issued preprinted letterforms to the prisoners called *Kriegsgefangenenpost* (Prisoner of War Post). They were nearly six inches wide x eleven inches tall with a fold-over flap on top. The outside of the letterforms included areas for addressing and processing, while the inside contained twenty-four writing lines. When completed, they neatly folded into a four-inch envelope. Prisoner *Postkartes* (postcards) were the same size as the folded up letters, but contained only seven writing lines. Each was efficient, well designed, and like nearly everything else in Germany, was in short supply.

Don carefully worded his first letterform to Laura Jeanne, heeding his roommates' warnings to write cautiously and even stretch the truth when it came to comments about prison conditions and his personal well-being, or his letters wouldn't get past German censors. Rumors were circulating around camp that they might not anyway:

---

* Kriegie camp leaders also censored prisoners' mail, concerned that they might unwittingly reveal information in their letters about escape plans or other confidential activities they didn't want the Germans to know about.

20 January 1945

[Letter 1]

My Beloved Wife,

I hope this letter finds you well and relieved from worry. I'm fine with nary a scratch, so please don't worry, darling. Take good care of yourself, have faith, and believe me when I say that all is well with me.

I'm not with any of Lehi's boys, but we have a swell bunch here. We do our own cooking and manage fairly well. Oh for the day when I can be surrounded by the luxurious life that you afforded me back home.

I love you with all my heart and soul and miss you desperately. My prayers are with you constantly, darling. I'm looking forward to the future, and I know you're doing the same. God bless you, my sweet, and keep your chin up.

Prisoner postcard

Two days later, Don wrote his second letter, this one to his parents:

22 January 1945

[Letter 2]

Dear Folks,

Well, I've added another country to my tour. I know you've been worried and anxious about me, but now there's no reason for further worry. We don't live like kings, but we're getting along OK.

I'm well and have suffered no injuries. We have 2 roll call formations a day. They're starting lectures on various subjects and we have an occasional show to occupy some of our spare time. We also have a fair supply of reading material.

I can write 3 letters and 4 postcards a month, so you and Laura can share the little news I have. When I get home, I'll tell you about all my travels. Have they heard from Kelly yet, and how is everyone else? It's snowing today and blowing a bit too, but we have a stove to keep us warm in our little room with [number blacked out by censor] occupants.

I miss you very much, and I'm anxiously waiting to hear from you again. You can write as often as you wish and figure 3 months for mail or any packages to reach me, so use your judgment in case it looks like the war is coming to a close! Again, I say—Please don't worry and let's look to the future with faith and high spirits.

Don's "nary a scratch" comment was for Laura Jeanne's benefit. His feet were still bruised and swollen, and the dark, hardened blisters on his toes exposed the frostbite he suffered during his forced march. His ability to survive bolstered his hope that Jerry might have also survived, as evidenced by the first question he asked in the letter to his parents.

The only thing censored in Don's first two letters was the number of prisoners crammed into his little room. It was comically ironic that the Nazis were worried that word would leak about overcrowded conditions in the Stalag when they were committing atrocities throughout Europe and the Soviet Union. If he told the truth, Don would have divulged that their little room had twenty-four prisoners packed in so tightly that they couldn't all stand up at the same time, and that their wooden shelf beds were stacked so closely together the Kriegies called them "the catacombs."

It didn't really matter what Don wrote because none of his letters was ever sent. Following orders, a mail clerk likely did the censoring and filing. But someone much higher up made the decision not to post prisoners' letters, choosing to stockpile them instead.

The next week, the Germans issued two postcards and one letterform to each of the Kriegies Kut-Ups, even though they didn't intend to post them:

28 January 1945

[Postcard 1]

My Beloved Jeanne: This may be short, but all my love and thoughts are with you. I'm well and doing OK. Please don't worry. Get word to Sharp that I'm OK. It will be around June before any mail gets to me. Hope you and the rest are well. Take good care of yourself. Hope to be seeing you soon. Don

———————

29 January 1945

[Postcard 2]

My Dearest Jeanne: I'm fine. Spending most of my time reading. KP comes once a week and it's an all-day job feeding the guys in our room. You should see some of the meals we scrape together! We get to shower once a week—ha! Wish you could do my laundry for me. Give the folks my love. Have faith, for all is well. Mr. Lt.

———————

29 January 1945

[Letter 3]

My Darling Jeanne,

Your long-haired hubby is still getting along OK. Haven't had a haircut in over 2 months so I look like a caveman. Getting sheared next week tho! I wish I knew how you're feeling. I'm hoping you're back to normal and that everyone else is well.

It's like living in a lost world here—quite a feeling! I heard that I made 1ˢᵗ Lt., but I'm not certain. If so, that means about $40 more per month for our nest egg. I receive no money here and need none since there isn't anything to buy. What few necessities we need are given us in Red Cross packages— when available.

There's snow on the ground and it's pretty cold. I'm constantly dreaming about how wonderful things are going to be when we're reunited. I pray that time might not be far off. It seems like a hundred years since I held you in my arms and told you how much I love you. I miss you desperately. Tell all "hello" and give my love to the folks. Please take care of yourself. I'm loving you always.

The Germans maintained a detailed medical record for each prisoner interned at Stalag Luft I. When Don arrived, the medical staff consisted of two British doctors and six orderlies. A month later, an American doctor arrived. Although extremely capable, the volunteer medical staff was much too small for the burgeoning prison population. They were further handicapped by poor facilities and a shortage of medical supplies. The biggest health risk facing the POWs was the poor sanitation at the camp. Initially, there was only one bathhouse containing ten showerheads for more than 4,000 American prisoners in the North 2 and 3 compounds.[378]

The bathhouses doubled as delousing plants in an attempt to control the endless outbreaks of lice that plagued the prisoners. These tiny, wingless, parasitic insects came in two varieties: head lice, which lived in the prisoners' scalp; and body lice, which proliferated in their infrequently laundered clothing and bedding. Both types thrived in the camp. After piercing the skin, they added a saliva mixture with their mouthparts to keep the host's blood from clotting, then sucked his blood with two tiny pumps located in their head. Little red bumps later appeared, along with intense itching. After Don arrived, the Germans added another bathhouse and delousing station, but ten additional showerheads didn't make much of a difference:[379]

> *We were promised a shower once a week, but even this privilege was denied us most of the time. We had to go to one of the other compounds that had showers, and they only gave us a couple of minutes to lather up and rinse off. Sponge bathing with cold water in the washbasins located in our outside latrines became our second best and only other option. That was also the only place we had to wash our clothes.*
>
> *Since I only had the clothes I was wearing, whenever I did my laundry I had to wrap up in a blanket to protect myself from the cold until my clothes dried. It was a real pain, so we didn't do it very often, which caused our room to smell pretty rank most of the time.*

Earlier in the war, Stalag orderlies changed bed linens once a month. By the time Don arrived, they'd stopped altogether, adding to the lice outbreaks in camp. Prisoners were confronted with sanitation issues everywhere. There was no garbage pickup at the camp—the 2,500 prisoners in North 3 were required to burn their trash in one of the three incinerators located around the perimeter of the compound. And the drains in the latrines and washbasins were sorely inadequate, often leaving the areas around their barracks flooded.[380,381]

Camp officials issued one letterform and no postcards to the prisoners in February. Don took his time, carefully choosing the limited number of words he could squeeze into his next letter to Laura Jeanne:

18 February 1945

[Letter 4]

My Beloved Wife,

How's my "li'l pigeon?" The mail situation has been screwed up, and I've been on KP all day—only have 30 minutes before mailing deadline. I'm feeling fine, honey, so don't worry about me. Maybe this mess will be over by the time you get this letter. [Next line blacked out by censor].

Today is Sunday and I attended a Mormon Church service along with 5 other fellows. We've started a little branch of our own and I really enjoyed it, altho the membership is small. I keep wondering how you and the folks are. Tell everyone hello and to have faith, for all is well. [Next line censored].

I love and miss you so very, very much, my darling. Faith and prayer are all that keep my lonesome heart consoled. A letter from you would be worth a million dollars. Love to all. You're always in my heart, Jeannie.

---

18 February 1945

[Letter 5]

Hello Again, Darling,

I have a few more minutes, and after drawing an "ace" from our card deck, I got another letterform! Rumor was that last month's mail didn't get thru, but I hope it did 'cause I know you're worried.

It's been thawing the past week, but it's still a bit chilly. I'm making a collection of "Kriegie" recipes so you'll be able to get a taste of what we have here. I'm doing a bit of cooking so I'll be right in shape to step into the kitchen and we'll have a contest, OK? I'll eat yours and you can eat mine (ha, ha).

Still haven't been able to find out if Grant is here since we aren't allowed out of our little section of the camp. I'm hoping for the end of hostilities soon so I can get back to civilization and the sweetest, most wonderful wife in the world. We may never make up for the time lost, but I intend to try—just thinking of that keeps me going.

Give my best to the folks and tell them I miss them very much. Please don't worry, and remember...I'm loving you always.

In a document labeled Top Secret Berlin 24.X1 1941, Herrs Mansfield and Moritz of the Food Ministry in Berlin published the recipe for World War II German black bread in its official records. It read:

50% bruised rye grain
20% sliced sugar beets
20% tree flour (saw dust)
10% minced leaves and straw

The grain should be sufficiently rotten to provide gasses to allow the bread to rise. The pieces of sugar beets provide sugar to supply the yeasty rye. Mix ingredients together to create dough. Shape into loaves and bake. A loaf should weigh 3 to 4 pounds.

Although nearly inedible and heavy enough to be used as a weapon, *Kriegsbrot* (German War Bread) was tagged "the POW staff of life" by Stalag Luft I artist/prisoner Lt. Colonel Ross Greening. In the same watercolor picture that depicted new prisoners carrying the Red Cross Capture Kits, Greening portrayed POWs pulling an uncovered wagon loaded with black bread to the camp food-distribution warehouse. The narrative accompanying his picture reads, "The new arrivals won't like it—but they'll eat it!"

Trying to kill boredom one day, the Kriegie Kut-Ups took the job of bread cutting to a whole new level. Don wrote:

Since the black bread we ate was hauled in on open, uncovered wagons, it didn't always arrive in great shape, sometimes bouncing off on to the ground, making it challenging to cut into equal slices.

We had a little contest going on one afternoon to see if we could get 72 slices out of our four loaf daily ration of black bread. We ended up with three thin slices each (instead of two), and a lot of crumbs for the soup.

The YMCA writing notebooks came in two sizes—one with thirty-eight pages, and a thinner version containing twelve pages. After a trade, Don ended up with one of each. Writing poetry was a popular pastime. For those who weren't good at it, the Kriegies freely circulated dozens of poems throughout the barracks, copying their favorites into their blue notebooks. While they covered a number of topics, including combat, planes, being shot down, capture and interrogation, and various versions of "For You Der Var Ist Over," most of the writing and poetry was about food. Don's best poem was a witty composition entitled "The Staff of Life or Black-Bread à la Kriegie." In the verses, he not only memorialized black bread, but also recounted his POW journey to Stalag Luft I:

I made its acquaintance on an S.S. Trooper first aid bed,
the purpose in mind was for me to be fed.
I'd just dropped in—was new in town,
and politely refused the stuff with a frown.

But later, when I got back on my feet,
I craved for the stuff, tho it was not made of wheat.
It was rumored that things like coal and wood,
and ersatz ingredients, made it so good.

I do not deny it was heavy as lead,
but please don't deny me my two slices of bread!

When Kriegies gather 'round, and stories are told,
the merits of Black Bread are exceedingly old.

There once was a guy who came down in a chute,
it was then that the tale of his journey took root.
He was taken by Jerries and brought to a shack,
given some water and the standard Kraut snack.

Two slices of Black Bread were given to him,
and also some pork fat was gladly thrown in.

The foreigners searched his person with care,
in hopes of finding some valuables there.
Satisfied with pawing, they left the abode,
next morning they had him marching a long, hard road.

They marched and marched until night finally fell,
bringing with it the food we all know so well.
Not disdainfully refusing what was previously fed,
he eagerly devoured that old Black Bread.

The next day found him walking some more,
his stomach just gnawing and his feet very sore.

When they finally reached a railroad line,
He lumbered on board and rolled along fine.

For three days they travelled, till Dulag did reach,
and the fare for that time was two slices each.
The time in solitaire had passed very slow,
and this gent was glad when the time came to go.

The mountains of food described by the guard
made the prisoner think life wouldn't be very hard.
But when he arrived at Stalag Luft I,
he found his problems had just begun.

Thousands of men awaited the call
for the new famous food, familiar to all.
As he told us the tale, he shook his head,
for all he had during that time, was "old Black Bread."

Ingenious methods were soon found out,
to make the most of such a small amount.
Cabbage, potatoes, rutabagas, and such,
were all boiled with water, so that "little" made "much."

A sprinkling of horsemeat and a few soiled hands,
made the stew so delicious that we had great demands.
But topping the list on our bill of fare,
was old king Black Bread, quite debonair.

We had it for breakfast with jam thereon,
and the room was in silence till the last crumb was gone.
Cole slaw at noon—and so it won't hurt,
with jam, I guess you know the dessert!

For supper of course, some stew was the thing,
with a wafer of Bread the width of a string.
But the eight o'clock snack was the boys' biggest glory,
and the result of their "sweet bit" is an old, old story.

With bread as a base, plus raisins and Klim,
sugar and oleo, according to whim.
They made some concoctions that put on the fat,
and I wonder what Laura would say about that!!

Yes, sandwiches, cereals, and cake a must,
were all derived from "Black Bread crust."
And now whenever a Kriegie shakes his sad head,
it's because he wants more of that "Old Black Bread"!

The unsavory German black bread later became part of a sacred, faith-promoting experience:

About a month after arriving at camp, I met three other men who were members of the LDS [Mormon] Church. We decided to get together and try to hold a church service. We posted a notice on the North 3 Compound bulletin board, inviting others to join us that coming Sunday at the mess hall.

We held our first meeting on February 18, 1945, with six from our compound in attendance. The first thing we did was to organize the group so that we'd be able to have a sacrament meeting every Sunday.

Our only source of scripture was an old Bible, which we used to prepare our sermons. We had to rely on our memory to record the proper wording for the sacrament prayers and to determine how we should conduct our meetings and business.

Allen D. Young, also imprisoned in the North 3 compound, kept detailed minutes of the meetings in his YMCA notebook, recording the names of those attending, their hometowns, and whether they were members of the LDS Church or visitors. The minutes noted that Don opened their first worship service with prayer. Don wrote:

Our church services consisted of an opening hymn, an opening prayer, any business or announcements, followed by administration of the sacrament. The bread for the sacrament was one day's ration donated by a member of the group. In the circumstances we were in, giving up your portion of bread for this ordinance was a humbling experience. The sacrament water was passed in a common cup.

One or two of us usually gave prepared talks, depending on the time we had. Many inspirational sermons were given and miraculous stories shared that strengthened our faith and gave us hope for the future. Most of us were convinced that

it was due to the grace of God that we were still alive. We
ended our meetings with a closing hymn and prayer.

After the second church service, the kommandant surprised the
men by allowing them to post information about their meetings on
the bulletin boards of the other compounds. Allen Young wrote:

Contrary to usual procedure, the Germans allowed LDS
prisoners (and interested nonmembers) to move from
one compound to another for our church meetings. Clare
Oliphant (branch leader) had arranged with the Germans for
the men to come over and join us, but I don't know how he
did it. Eventually, we had about twenty people attending.[382]

Clare and Don became good friends at Stalag Luft I. Clare was
a few years older than most of the men, a returned missionary, and
the closest thing the LDS prisoners had to a chaplain. On page 13
of his main notebook, Don listed seven *buddies* he made during the
war. Clare H. Oliphant, Jr. was the only one on his list who wasn't a
member of the Jabo Angel Squadron.

CLASS OF SERVICE		SYMBOLS
This is a full-rate Telegram or Cablegram unless its deferred character is indicated by a suitable symbol above or preceding the address.		DL = Day Letter
		NL = Night Letter
		LC = Deferred Cable
		NLT = Cable Night Letter
		Ship Radiogram

WESTERN UNION

A. N. WILLIAMS
PRESIDENT

1204

The filing time shown in the date line on telegrams and day letters is STANDARD TIME at point of origin. Time of receipt is STANDARD TIME at point of destination

KH RO 34 Govt

Wux Washington DC 427PM Mar 2 1945

Mrs Laura J Evans

90 North Center St

Lehi Utah .

Report just Received through the International Redcross States that

your Husband Second Lieutenant donald N Evans is a Prisoner of War

of the German Government Letter of information follows from provost

Marshall General

Ulio the Adjutant General

247PM

THE COMPANY WILL APPRECIATE SUGGESTIONS FROM ITS PATRONS CONCERNING ITS SERVICE

THIRTY-FOUR

"He's Alive!"

Friday morning, March 2, dawned chilly and overcast in Lehi, Utah. Noticing a light drizzle, Laura Jeanne put on a raincoat for her short walk across the street to the OPA office. Her job was a godsend, keeping her mind occupied with something besides her missing husband. Work had been busier than usual lately, requiring her to stay late to help her boss. She didn't mind. The extra money she was setting aside would come in handy when her husband returned. Laura Jeanne forced herself to be optimistic, focusing on *when,* trying not to allow *if* to enter her thoughts or conversations. It wasn't easy, especially at night when her dreams too often betrayed her.

Around 3:00 p.m., Laura Jeanne looked up as the mail carrier unexpectedly returned, having already delivered the regular office mail earlier that day. Seeing the yellow paper clutched in his hand caused a flashback to the afternoon of January 16—the most terrible day of her life. But this time, the mail carrier's face broke into a smile as he quickly approached her desk and handed her a Western Union telegram.

Tears filled Laura Jeanne's eyes as she read, then she let out a scream, "He's alive!" She beat the postman out the front door and raced across the street in the rain, her coat tucked under her arm, yelling her good news for all of Lehi to hear. By the time Laura Jeanne climbed the front steps, her mother had opened the door and stepped out onto the porch to see who was screaming. Hugging her mother tightly, she cried, "Mother, he's alive! He's alive! This is the happiest day of my life!" Then she rushed to the telephone to call Don's parents.

The next morning, Laura Jeanne and both mothers drove to the Red Cross office in Salt Lake City to find out how to get in touch with Don. The volunteer workers provided her with several German Prisoner of War Post letterforms, similar to the ones Don was using, along with the address of the International Red Cross. They also gave her a Post Office leaflet with instructions to write the words "Prisoner of War Post" and "Kriegsgefangenenpost" in the top left-hand corner of the envelope. Immediately after returning home, she rushed over to the OPA office to use their typewriter:

3 March 1945
Lehi, Utah

My Dearest Darling Don,

My prayers have been answered, and as I write, there's thankfulness in my heart. Knowing that you're alive is the most wonderful blessing I could ask for. Words cannot express my feelings.

Your main worry must be us here at home, but please, my beloved, do not. I assure you we are all in the best of health. Home is the same, darling, and so are we. I'm acquainted with the Kellys and the Sharps, and they are lovely people. Ruby, Mildred, Ashes, and I are all in the same boat.

We haven't made too good of a showing in basketball. Last night's game was against A.F. and we lost. People that saw me said it seemed good to see the gleam back in my eyes, which has been missing the past two months. All of us are so happy and relieved.

Mom is back teaching at school. Kay is a young lady now. Howard and Beth are still in Nevada and their daughter Patsy is walking now. I'm still working in Lehi. My days are more or less routine—practicing piano and vocal, club, trip to Salt Lake on weekends, sewing, helping Mom, visiting your folks, and missing my husband more than you'll ever know.

I pray that our future hopes and dreams will be realized. Will you still take me on a honeymoon trip? Just seeing you and holding you in my arms will be sufficient. Everyone rejoices and sends their love. Need I say that I'm worried about you?

Happy Birthday, darling. The cake will have to wait for another year. My mind is buzzing with questions that can only be answered when we're happily united again. Do write as often as possible. Take care and try to make the best of the situation. I realize to some extent how awful your conditions must be, and my humble prayers are constantly for you.

I love you with all my heart, body, and soul, and I'm eagerly awaiting news from you. God bless you, my sweetheart.

The following day, Laura Jeanne and both mothers returned to the offices of the *Lehi Free Press* and the two Salt Lake newspapers with a picture of Don in his Air Force uniform and the newest War Department telegram. Unlike their somber visit forty-five days earlier, this time the newspaper staffs met the three women with smiles, hugs, and best wishes.

Her second POW letter read:

5 March 1945
Lehi, Utah

My Darling Husband,

Everything here is rolling smoothly. Received word from New York that your baggage sent from your first base in England will be forwarded to me soon. Also, I received a letter from Bob Sharp a while back. Congratulations on your promotion. I'm very proud of you, darling.

Don Johnson and Dee Schow are both home on leave now and send best wishes. Dee is so thin. Their baby is sweet. Just wait till we have our little Don! I spent Sunday visiting with your folks and in church. It was Fast Day and all our testimonies, prayers, and blessings were in your behalf. All your friends send love and best wishes.

Both our families are fine—even your lonesome wife. Time goes by quite slow, but my work helps out. I pray our dreams will come true soon. My faith remains strong, and I didn't ever give up hope. Everything will turn out as it should, if we keep up our courage and faith, though it may take some time. We have so much to look forward to.

I know it must be hard for you there. I hope you have some ways of occupying your mind and time. When I'm able to I'll send you some packages, but until the Red Cross sends your permanent camp address that's impossible. As Bob said, though, you can take care of yourself in any kind of predicament. Still, my heart aches for you.

I feel and know that there's no end to our love—no matter how dark the picture may seem to us at times. Cheer up "Tough." I'm loving you always.

Your "li'l pigeon," Laura Jeanne

On March 24, she received a letter from the director of the American Prisoner of War Information Bureau stating that the German Government hadn't released the name or location of Don's POW camp. The letter went on to explain:

Experience indicates that his camp address may not be reported to this office until up to three months have elapsed from the time he was first reported a prisoner of war. Pending receipt of his permanent address, you may direct letter mail to him by addressing him through the International Red Cross.

Laura Jeanne never received notification of Don's prison camp name or location. She wrote to him almost every day, sending her letters to the International Red Cross address, but Stalag Luft I officials failed to deliver any of her letters to Don. Inexplicably, Laura Jeanne's first two letters were placed in his personnel file under *Gefangenennummer* 7435. The rest were either lost somewhere in the German mail system or intentionally destroyed by camp officials.

Gerolstein p30   Block 9   Room 9   7435 "
                          24 Man Room
"Oberussal — Wetzlar"   Outskirts of Berlin   Remegen Bridgehead
"Stettin"   What's He Pounding on Now?   Lubeck Aachen
Kriegie Nuts.   Large Charge   What's the Poop?
        More Volume   When I Get Home
Whatcha Makin'?   It "Was" Good   Zemke Says   Duren
Mess Hall Menu — Hot Water, Hot Water, Hot Water
Sign Me Up)   More Ruddies   Donnelly's "P" Poultry   Bowl
        Our Combine)   Delousing Party   North II clobbers
Gee the Stew's Thin   Parcels in Lubeck   He Won't Shoot
How's the Line?   Limburg   Two More Weeks Brrrrr
        Who's Going to Volunteer?   Koblenz   Barb Wire
His Own Wing Man Clobbered Him
Comin' Down   Frank Filled His Sack + Hadda Crawl Thru It!!
They're After Me!   Anybody Here From the Hundreth?   But
Who?   Round the Bend   He's Up Gettin' Wood   How
The Jerries!!
Are They Shootin'??   Horror Stories — Nix - Nix! P--Call)
No, But They Will — (Exit)
Who the Hell Was That???   Bring Back Some Water   AIR RAID!
C'Est La Guerre!   Where's Your Cup?   Stach It Away
(C'Est La Gray)   What's Your Number??   Hell + Dam
        Who's K.P.?
How's the Stew Look?   Jump Boots Recommended
Good Show)   Anyone Lit? Any Good Rumors:
You've Had It   Wanta Trade?
        Jerry Rations)   Don't Go Away!   Victory approach

Random comments from Don's YMCA notebook

THIRTY-FIVE
·····················

Boredom and the "Lean Days"

Time passed slowly at Stalag Luft I. Each day seemed like a repeat of the previous day. Boredom was a formidable enemy, second only to hunger. Having little or nothing meaningful to do allowed the infectious tedium of prison life to run rampant throughout the camp, driving many of the Kriegies to unusual or strange behaviors. More than a few counted the individual barbs on the wire surrounding their barracks. Many became listless and apathetic, spending most of the day in their bunks staring at the walls. The relentless boredom of POW life, combined with hunger, bitter-cold temperatures, and sporadic mail from home, pushed some prisoners over the edge, leading to severe depression and even suicidal thoughts. Others found ways to fight off what the prisoners called "barbed-wire disease" and were able to keep their spirits up by dreaming of better days ahead. Don's best remedy was to make meticulous entries in his YMCA blue notebooks:

Activity was limited for us, since it was too cold to go outside most of the time. Many of us tried to exercise in our rooms to keep in the best shape possible, but it was hard because the barracks were small and crowded. So our days were spent either sleeping in our bunks trying to keep warm, writing, or occasionally walking outside, weather permitting.

The miserable, record-setting winter dragged on into March. Adding to the prisoners' woes, Red Cross food parcel deliveries from Switzerland stopped—an unintended consequence of the Allied Air Forces destruction of the German railroad system. In his notebook, Don referred to this period as the "lean days":

Our food rations were cut back again during March. We weren't given any Red Cross parcels, and the German rations were reduced to thin rutabaga stew from the mess hall once a day, ersatz coffee, and 1/6 loaf of black bread per man a day with oleo, and jam when we got lucky. The leaders in our compound determined that we were consuming about 700 calories a day. Everyone was losing weight.

During those days, once in a while a black cat wandered along the fence line and then suddenly disappeared. We knew that some barracks would have protein in their soup that day.

An average-size, sedentary male between 19 and 30 years old requires at least 2,400 calories per day to maintain a healthy weight. During the month of March, the Germans reduced the prisoners' food rations to near-starvation levels, providing them with old, rotting, often worm-riddled vegetables to prepare a watery, meatless, stew— their only meal of the day. Colonel Zemke observed, "The POWs became increasingly subdued, and food was now more than ever the most frequent topic of discussion. It didn't take a medical authority to predict that the prison population would be reduced to skin and bone in a month or so."[383] Toward the end of the month, many of the men fell down when they tried to get out of their bunks, too weak to make it to the parade grounds for roll call. Some were so desperate they resorted to eating garbage scraps, making themselves sick and forcing Kriegie leaders to place guards around the camp garbage cans.[384]

On adjoining pages in the center of Don's larger YMCA notebook, he recorded amusing notes, phrases, and seemingly random comments, many of which crossed over from one page to the other. Most of the annotations were humorous or sarcastic, like *Old Kriegies never die*, *Delousing party*, and *One "D-Bar" for a quart of blood*. Others provide clues and insights into Don's life as a POW.

On the left-hand side of these adjoining pages, Don respectfully printed *Zemke says*, and on the right he underlined the name *Gabby*. Lt. Colonel Francis S. Gabreski was senior officer in Don's North 3 Compound, representing them at the Head Shed. Gabby, as the men called him, held the American record for shooting down German planes with twenty-eight to his credit. Unlike most of the pilots in Stalag Luft I, Gabreski didn't wind up as a POW because of flak. The P-47 fighter pilot dove so low on a strafing run that his propeller struck the ground.[385]

Near the entries *"Bowls up!"* and *"Mess hall menu…hot water, hot water, hot water,"* Don underlined *"Remagen Bridgehead."* The March 7–8 edition of *POW-WOW* reported the U.S. 9th Armored Division captured the key bridge crossing over the Rhine River before the retreating Germans could destroy it, opening the way for Allied troops to advance toward the heart of Germany. The news greatly lifted the prisoners' spirits.

Don's double-page section included a number of food-related comments, including: *"Gee, the stew's thin. Who's KP?" "Jerry rations. That's all we're getting then—huh?" "North II clobbers the black cat."* *"Gogan* (one of his roommates) *brings in two dead birds during starvation days!"* And the hopeful rumor, *"Parcels in Lübeck—two more weeks?"*

Another entry: *"Remember Gerolstein!!"* suggested Don hadn't yet suppressed memories of the inhumane treatment he experienced on his forced march. Other notations allude to events that put the prisoners' lives in danger: *"Horror stories." "Air Raid!" "Enemy up, Nix—nix!" "They're after me! Who? The Jerries!! Are they shootin'?? No, but they will."*

Air raid warnings had now become routine occurrences at Stalag Luft I. The prisoners had orders to remain in their barracks when they sounded and to wait for the all clear sign. Any POWs caught outside during an air raid alert were open season for the guards, thanks to Kommandant von Warnstedt's "shoot at will" regulations.

Rather than using an air raid siren, the alarms at Barth were mere whistle warnings blown by the tower guards. The warnings often weren't loud enough to be heard in the latrines, mess hall, or several other locations around camp. And the instructors at the nearby flak school were constantly blowing whistles as part of their training, further confusing the warnings. As a result, prisoners experienced several narrow escapes. As part of a warped game, tower guards took potshots at prisoners during air raids, sometimes even randomly firing at their barracks. Although Colonel Zemke registered loud complaints, the kommandant ignored them.[386]

On March 18, during a prolonged air raid by the 8th Air Force, a South African Air Force officer in the British Compound unwittingly left his barracks while the warning was still in effect. A passing guard shot him in the chest from about forty yards—shouting a warning and firing his 7.92 mm Mauser automatic rifle simultaneously. Ten minutes later, an unsuspecting American officer who had been waiting out the alert with friends in the South Compound started walking back to his room. Halfway there, he noticed the prison yard was empty and realized that the air raid warning wasn't finished. He turned and raced for the safety of his friends' barracks. The guard's bullet passed through his head just as he reached the doorway.[387]

The first shooting victim was rushed to the camp hospital, where one of the volunteer Allied surgeons saved his life. The second prisoner wasn't so lucky. Putting their own lives at risk, his friends dragged him inside their barracks, but they could do little else to save him. He lay there semi-conscious, bleeding to death, as they screamed and banged on the barracks walls for help. About twenty minutes later, one of the tower guards finally notified camp authorities that a prisoner had been shot and he was taken to the infirmary. By then, it was too late to save him, and he died that afternoon on the operating table. Although the kommandant conducted a superficial investigation into the shootings, nothing happened, and the open-season policy continued. Ten days later, there was another unprovoked shooting, but this time the guard missed his target.[388]

The shooting incidents fueled camp-wide loathing among the prisoners and elevated "Goon baiting" to a new level. The Lager officers understood little English, so even the vilest slurs, threats, and insults generally went over their heads, especially when the prisoners uttered them with a smile on their faces. In his random comments pages, Don included several guard taunts: *"Goons Up"* (warning that guards were coming). *"Who's on Goon Guard?"* And the most irritating insult, *"C'mon Joe,"* referring to Joseph Stalin and the avenging Russian Army rapidly approaching from the East. The guards understood that offensive chant well, and it brought a look of fear and anger to their faces whenever they heard it. When the Kriegies took their Goon-baiting antics too far, another of Don's entries was apropos: *"How long in the sweatbox?"*

The POWs actually liked a few of their guards. Don respectfully recorded *von Beck said* in his notebook adages. Senior Lager Officer Hauptmann von Beck was an Austrian baron and decorated World War I pilot. The affable, English-speaking officer took a liking to the flyboys in camp and occasionally even sneaked them food and contraband. He relished sharing accounts of his visits to England and America before the war, captivating the inmates with stories of his skiing and hunting trips. Later that month, von Beck disappeared—reportedly shot for failing to embrace the Nazi party and for undue fraternization with Allied officers.[389]

The day after the air raid shootings, the guards passed out a few letterforms and postcards to the prisoners in the North 3 Compound:

19 March 1945

[Letter 6]

My Beloved Jeanne,

Hello again. I traded a fellow a postcard for this letterform. I hope my idle gab doesn't bother you—there's very little information that I can write about.

Just read "A Tree Grows in Brooklyn" and thought it was OK. Still holding our Sunday service and membership has increased to about ten or twelve. I surely enjoy them. I'm continually living in the past—picturing us together. Oh, for the day when we can start making up for the time gone by. Can't you just see us in a little place of our own—living like real married people with no interference from the Army?

I don't know what plans are being made back in the States for POWs, but I'm definitely going to take advantage of any breaks. I still have hopes that this year will bring us to together again. It seems like years since I left you and the folks at the train station.

This is my sixth letter—hope you're getting all of them. Give my best to the folks.

Don filled most of the pages of his two YMCA notebooks with food menus and recipes:

One small bowl of rutabaga soup and a slice of black bread daily drive one to dream of and share his favorite foods with his buddies. Many hours were occupied taking turns telling each other how to fix our favorite dishes. All the time we did so I was saying in my mind, "I'll never miss another meal in my life when I get home."

In the smaller of his YMCA notebooks, Don entered nothing but food menus. Each meal—breakfast, lunch, and dinner—had an à la carte page, followed by full meal entreés with all the trimmings. The dinner menus were extensive, including sections for salads, breads, soups, pickles and relishes, vegetables, meats, fowl, fish and seafood, wild game, and various combination meals. Other pages covered foreign dishes, egg combinations, gravy and dressings, and desserts. He marked his favorite menu items with an asterisk and cross-referenced them to detailed recipes recorded in the larger notebook. The dessert section was exhaustive, filling several pages with recipes for pies, cakes, puddings, cookies, candies, sweets, and dessert "tidbits."

———————

The Third Army had come to a halt on the banks of the Rhine River at Remagen in desperate need of fuel and supplies. General Patton was chomping at the bit to cross the final barrier separating him from Berlin, eager to claim the coveted river-crossing honor for America. But for political reasons, General Eisenhower decided to give the crossing-over honor to Patton's nemesis, British Field Marshall Montgomery. Galled by the decision and hell-bent on stealing his rival's thunder, Patton ordered the U.S. 5th Division to quietly cross the Rhine during the night of March 22, just a few hours before Montgomery was scheduled to launch Operation Plunder ninety miles to the north. The American division became the first invading army to cross the Rhine by boat since Napoleon in 1805. It all took place in typical Patton fashion—in secret and against orders. His commander, General Bradley, didn't find out until after the crossing had successfully taken place and Patton's Third Army had captured more than 19,000 German troops.[390]

Patton crossed over the Rhine the following day on a makeshift pontoon bridge. Then, in full view of his troops and news cameras, the audacious general made good on a promise he'd made the previous week, engaging in another of the exploits that kept him in both the limelight and the doghouse. Immediately afterward, he sent the following communiqué to Eisenhower: "I have just pissed in the Rhine River. For God's sake, Ike, send some gasoline." General Eisenhower, likely as amused as most other Americans were with his stunt, complied. Refueled and resupplied, Patton's Third Army rolled across southern Germany, forcing the Wehrmacht to retreat and liberating POW and concentration camps as he advanced east toward Berlin. Incidents similar to the river-crossing episode became legend, adding to Patton's growing fame and popularity among his troops and back home.[391]

––––––––––

Stalag Luft I prisoners cheered wildly when they read about Patton's crossing in the daily edition of the *POW-WOW*, culminating a good week for the Kriegies. Several days of pleasant weather had allowed them to leave their barracks and move around the compound. And rumors that Red Cross food and supply parcels were on their way from the port at Lübeck finally came true:

> *On March 26, we each received ¼ issue of a Red Cross parcel. Two days later, we started receiving one parcel per week per man. That first week we ate baked potatoes with cheese inserted, "C Ration" loaf (black breadcrumbs plus klim, with oleo on top to form a crust), and fish loaf (cooked the same as the "C Ration" loaf).*

Red Cross parcels supplied to POWs in the ETO came from America. They were shipped across the Atlantic to International Red Cross locations across the neutral country of Sweden and from there to prison camps all over Germany. The parcels designated for Stalag Luft I were shipped across the Baltic Sea to the Port of Lübeck, then taken by train the final 115 miles east to Barth. But they'd been stuck at the port for months now, undelivered because the Allies had destroyed the railway system between there and Barth.

Colonel Zemke finally pressured the kommandant into accepting his proposal to man the camp's transport trucks with experienced Kriegie drivers, accompanied by armed Lager officers to retrieve the Red Cross parcels from Lübeck. The German food rations were running short and were of such poor quality that camp officials had no other choice if they wanted to keep the prisoners alive. The life-saving parcels arrived just in time and the starving prisoners started adding weight back to their emaciated frames. Most of the POWs in camp had lost more than a third of their body weight in less than a month.[392]

Kriegie Kook Book dessert recipes

After the first truckload of Red Cross parcels arrived, Don's Kriegie Kut-Ups' started making plans for an Easter feast:

The guys saved food up for 3 days for an enormous Easter dinner. Our menu included:

Breakfast

Cereal made with stewed prunes, Kriegie nuts, chunk of oleo, and thick Klim. Served hot with toast, jam, and p-nut butter whip.

Lunch

Toast (two pieces) with plenty of jam and p-nut butter whip, and ersatz coffee with sugar!

Dinner

Potatoes creamed with oleo (1/2 bowl), "C" Rations (1/4 bowl), ersatz with sugar, and cakes and pies of enormous size for dessert.

1st Snack

3/4 lb. of Kriegie Fudge per man (recipe, see notebook page 42) and ersatz.

2nd Snack

Toasted cheese sandwich and ersatz.

I lost a ten-dollar bet that one of the Kriegies couldn't eat all his huge cake within one hour! We all ate well and wasted not—everyone got full on Easter.

Since Don was one of the camp's better cooks, his barracks commander regularly assigned him to KP duty. With Red Cross food parcels now at his disposal, he tried out several of the creative recipes he and his roommates had dreamed up during their "lean days," including *Brown Bombers, Kriegie Cherry Pie, Snow Ice Cream, Fudge, Prune Bars,* and *Kandy Koated Kriegie Krunch.* The addition of canned meats, fish, jam, and oleo enabled them to spice up their Jerry rations of rutabagas, potatoes, cabbage, cheese, and black bread.

Just as one prisoner dilemma was resolved, however, another one arose. Rumors began circulating that the Nazis planned either to move or exterminate the Stalag Luft I POWs before the Russians could liberate them. The Head Shed took the rumors seriously, aware that the Germans had already relocated tens of thousands of Allied prisoners from other camps that winter, forcing them to travel by foot under horrible conditions away from Stalin's approaching armies.

The Germans had run out of postcards and letterforms. Don traded for one of the last letterforms in his barracks so he could write to Laura Jeanne on his birthday. One of his greatest worries was that she still hadn't received word he was alive. He longed to receive just one letter or card from her confirming that she knew:

28 March 1945

[Letter 7]

My Beloved Wife,

Today was truly a wonderful day, since the sun was out and it was nice and warm. Maybe spring is just around the corner— hope so! Loafing in the sun made me feel so lazy—what a life!

As I go into my twenty-second year, I look back, and it makes me realize how much valuable time has been lost because of this worldwide mess. We're compensating partially by having a big cake on the occasion—remind me to tell you how we made it!!

I'm still working on my specialty dishes and post-war snacks. It's going to be oodles of fun trying to fix some of these things I have in my little blue books!!! I'm pleased to report that we had twenty-three fellows at our church services last Sunday and a few more prospects that are interested in joining us.

My thoughts are continually with you, my darling. I'm praying that everyone is well and getting along fine. It's been four months since your last precious letter. I must confess I have a lonely heart—but still feel that you're actually with me every minute of the day.

At the Yalta Conference in early February 1945, Roosevelt hoped to entice Stalin to participate in the formation of the United Nations and join America in the war against Japan, so he made secret boundary and occupation concessions to Russia involving much of Eastern Europe. Churchill was devastated when he found out, viewing the behind-the-scenes negotiations as a betrayal. Although some feared that Roosevelt's siding with Stalin evidenced a loss of judgment brought on by his failing health, most Americans believed the president showed foresight and trusted him in his quest for a lasting multigenerational peace.[393]

By the beginning of April 1945, Western Allied forces had crossed the Rhine River and were pressing toward Berlin from all sides. In the Ruhr River area, the Americans captured more than 325,000 German soldiers, tightening the noose on the Wehrmacht troops west of the capital. Stalin's Red Army was racing from the East, determined to be the first to invade Berlin. Even though the collapse of the Third Reich was inevitable, Germany's military wasn't willing to concede defeat and prepared for one last stand in their capital city.

Patton and Montgomery finally agreed on battle strategy, both in favor of U.S. and British forces taking Berlin before the Soviets. Prime Minister Churchill strongly supported the plan as well. But it wasn't to be. In his most controversial decision of the war, Supreme Commander Dwight D. Eisenhower ordered the Allied troops to stand down at the Elbe River southwest of the German capital. Both Americans and Europeans severely criticized the decision to stop the Allied drive to Berlin. Churchill was furious, accusing Eisenhower of bowing to political pressure from Roosevelt, influenced by the president's recent capitulations toward the Soviets. Why he gave orders forbidding the Allies to halt short of Berlin remains a mystery. There is no direct evidence that Roosevelt issued him a political directive to stop for fear of offending Stalin, although it may have happened. But there are military considerations supporting Eisenhower's decision— the most persuasive being the projected 100,000 American casualties it would cost to seize Berlin.[394]

On April 12, 1945, while vacationing in Warm Springs, Georgia, President Franklin D. Roosevelt suffered a massive stroke and died. His death shocked the nation. One of America's most beloved presidents, he served a record four terms covering more than twelve years. He guided a grateful nation through the Great Depression and led the Allies to the threshold of victory in World War II. Vice President Harry S. Truman took over the difficult job of keeping the fragile alliance between the U.S., Great Britain, and the Soviet Union intact.[395]

The 368th Fighter Group was on the move again, this time to Frankfurt am Main Air Base, near the site of Don's interrogation. Bob, Kenny, and Pat were now element leaders, and with more than sixty combat missions under their belts, they regularly led bombing and strafing missions over Eastern Germany and Czechoslovakia. Their fighter group had recently set a new one-day record, flying 184 sorties in close air support of Patton's Third Army as they fought their way to the Elbe River. P-47 air combat hadn't changed much since Don was shot down, as evidenced by the following excerpts from Bob's mission report log:

> *The clouds were thick and low when we took off...It was a long flight...We carried fragmentation bombs and a 150-gallon belly tank...We took on a lot of heavy flak...It was so cold we all nearly froze to death...Gave chase to an Fw-190...Strafed three Do 217 Bombers...We lowered the seats, built up speed, and came out of the sun strafing an airfield...A strong crosswind and a rainstorm closing in on the airfield made for a rough landing.*

As the weather warmed that spring, the prisoners at Stalag Luft I were able to spend more and more time outdoors. Allied aircraft were regularly flying over the camp, increasing odds that the prisoners might be inadvertently bombed. Despite requests from Colonel Zemke, Kommandant von Warnstedt refused to paint Red Cross or POW signs on the prisoner hospital and barracks. Zemke speculated that the Nazis "would probably be only too happy to capitalize on the propaganda value of an Allied air attack on their own people, particularly if it were Soviet aircraft against a British-American camp."[396]

Yalta summit — Churchill, Roosevelt, Stalin

There were differing opinions among the Head Shed leaders about how to respond to the rumored Nazi relocation or extermination threat. Several of the leaders favored taking the camp by force, but Zemke feared that would give the SS an excuse for mass prisoner annihilation. Eventually, he persuaded the other leaders to pursue a peaceful takeover by negotiating what he hoped would be a bloodless power play. In plain sight where he knew the Germans would read it, Zemke posted a regulation on the Wing X Headquarters wall, outlining how cooperating Luftwaffe guards and administration would be treated when the Kriegies took control of the camp. Foreseeing this as a possible lifeline once the Russians arrived, the Germans didn't react at all, leading the colonel to believe his first step had succeeded.[397] If it hadn't, Head Shed leaders would likely have seen the inside of a sweatbox for the rest of the war—or worse.

Optimism among the prisoners continued to grow as they read each new *POW-WOW* edition. With Allied victory in sight, the men began to plan in earnest for life outside their barbed-wire home. Don dedicated an entire notebook page to *"Places to Go* and *Things to Do After the War,"* recording missed celebrations and events, and places he and Laura Jeanne would go to make up for lost time. Not surprisingly, each makeup occasion included dinner, with restaurant names and main menu entreés in notations. The Kriegie Kut-Ups also created a list of top restaurants, hotels, and places to go that spanned twenty-two different cities scattered across America.

Now that the prisoners were recovering from the effects of the bitter-cold winter, long periods of inactivity, and a month of near starvation, they were getting antsy, worrying Head Shed leaders that maintaining order and discipline would soon become an even greater challenge. As a countermeasure, they sponsored educational courses and organized sports again. Even Colonel Zemke joined in, agreeing to box any airman lucky enough to draw his name in the upcoming ten-card boxing match scheduled for April 18. More than fifty men entered the drawing for a chance to duke it out with their senior officer, who wasn't a bad fighter in his own right. Fortunately for him, he drew an opponent who was nearly his same size and age, instead of one of the younger camp bruisers, and won by unanimous decision.[398]

The atmosphere at Stalag Luft I had dramatically changed by mid-April. Surprise guard raids on the barracks had stopped. The Kriegies seldom saw the ruthless head of intelligence, Major von Miller. And the attitude of the German guards toward Colonel Zemke had taken a complete about-face. They now respectfully clicked their heels and saluted him and allowed him unfettered access throughout the camp. The guards even seemed to ignore the raucous chants sung out by the men: "Come on, Joe" and "Come on, Ike." Zemke remained committed to his no revenge, nonviolent tactics to take control over the camp, and it looked more and more like they were going to succeed.[399]

Once the Russians were within a hundred miles of Barth, Nazi leaders gave Kommandant von Warnstedt twenty-four hours to evacuate the camp and relocate the prisoners 150 miles southwest to Hamburg. The news circulated like wildfire, creating a somber mood among the men. Zemke immediately called Wing X and barracks leaders together and conducted a secret ballot to decide whether they'd obey the orders. They voted unanimously to stay put and notified the kommandant that their 9,000 prisoners would openly resist any attempt to move them. Fearing a prison uprising more than the consequences of disobeying orders from Berlin, the kommandant expressed a willingness to discuss a peaceful transition of control, eager to find a way to get himself and his men out of the Stalag without bloodshed. Most of the German officers and guards were terrified at the thought of facing the barbaric Russian hordes advancing from the East and were already making plans to flee west and surrender to the Americans.[400]

There was a lot of commotion around Stalag Luft I the last few days of April—sounds of Russian cannons echoed in the distance, air raid warning whistles blared day and night, and unusual Fw-190 activity took place at the nearby training airfield. The stressful atmosphere made the POWs jittery and tempered the excitement of their imminent liberation:

The Chaplain came into our compound with the typed POW-WOW news in his pocket and reported that the Soviets were getting close. The Germans and Russians fought an altogether different war. It was brutal. I heard some of the guards talk about it. Both sides were bloodthirsty. It was no holds barred—kill everyone and everything and burn anything that would burn.

When the Germans heard the guns of the Russians coming from the East and knew they were approaching the camp, they hauled tons of potatoes into a large fenced-off area for two days. Everybody kept looking at that compound, thinking about how easy it would be to just snip the wires and get into those potatoes. But we were still prisoners, and things were tense with our German captors.

On April 29, after hiding out in their underground bunker for 105 days, Adolf Hitler and his mistress of twelve years, Eva Braun, exchanged wedding vows. A few hours later, Hitler's staff informed him that Germany's last-ditch effort to defend Berlin from a Russian takeover was failing. Unwilling to face the humiliation of being captured, the Führer and his new bride swallowed cyanide capsules—after first trying them out on their "beloved" dog and her pups. Paranoid and impatient to the end, Hitler couldn't wait the few seconds it took for the cyanide to take effect and shot himself in the head.[401]

Kommandant von Warnstedt and Colonel Zemke exited the prison camp together through the main gate and walked down the road until they were safely out of hearing range. The kommandant finally spoke, saying, "Der Krieg ist jetzt über für uns" (the war is now over for us). He accepted Zemke's take-over proposal, with the stipulation that all German personnel be allowed to leave that night without incident, sealing the deal when he committed not to destroy any camp facilities before they left. The two leaders concluded their brief meeting by agreeing to keep their departure plans secret. Neither side wanted to risk the potential for chaos and bloodshed if word of their plan leaked out to the prisoners. After a perfunctory handshake, they turned around and walked back through the prison gate without saying another word.[402]

Nothing out of the ordinary happened the rest of the day. Evening appell and dinner took place as usual, and lockup that night appeared routine to the unsuspecting prisoners. The Head Shed leaders were sweating out every minute, crossing their fingers that the transition would go off without violence. At 11:00 p.m., Zemke and the other senior officers exited their unlocked barracks and met their German counterparts on the road leading out of the prison camp. After exchanging token salutes, von Warnstedt uttered, "Auf Wiedersehen," climbed into a little sedan, and drove off. Colonel Zemke had just inherited the largest command of his career.[403]

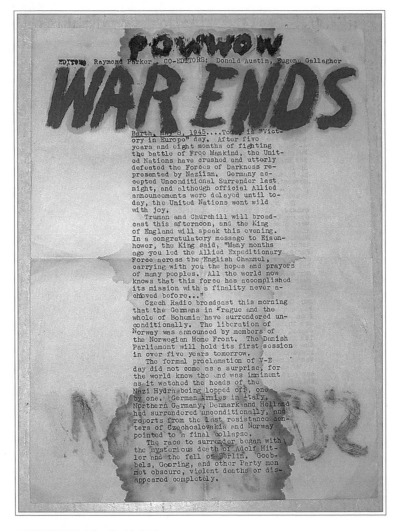

POW-WOW

EDITOR: Raymond Parker **CO-EDITORS:** Donald Austin, Eugene Gallagher

WAR ENDS

Barth, May 8, 1945....Today is "Victory in Europe" day. After five years and eight months of fighting the battle of Free Mankind, the United Nations have crushed and utterly defeated the Forces of Darkness represented by Naziism. Germany accepted Unconditional Surrender last night, and although official Allied announcements were delayed until today, the United Nations went wild with joy.

Truman and Churchill will broadcast this afternoon, and the King of England will speak this evening. In a congratulatory message to Eisenhower, the King said, "Many months ago you led the Allied Expeditionary Force across the English Channel, carrying with you the hopes and prayers of many peoples. All the world now knows that this force has accomplished its mission with a finality never achieved before..."

Czech Radio broadcast this morning that the Germans in Prague and the whole of Bohemia have surrendered unconditionally. The liberation of Norway was announced by members of the Norwegian Home Front. The Danish Parliament will hold its first session in over five years tomorrow.

The formal proclamation of V-E day did not come as a surprise, for the world knew the end was imminent as it watched the heads of the Nazi Hydra being lopped off, one by one. German Armies in Italy, Northern Germany, Denmark and Holland had surrendered unconditionally, and reports from the last resistance centers of Czechoslovakia and Norway pointed to a final collapse.

The race to surrender began with the mysterious death of Adolf Hitler and the fall of Berlin. Goebbels, Goering, and other Party men met obscure, violent deaths or disappeared completely.

POW-WOW, *May 8, 1945 Issue*

THIRTY-SIX

"The Germans are Gone! We're Free!"

On the morning of May 1, 1945, the POWs at Stalag Luft I were awakened by the usual sound of guards blowing their whistles—but after that, nothing was the same. At morning roll call, they were surprised when the tower guards chanted in English, "The Germans are gone! We're free!" The Kriegies cheered wildly, then stormed the front gates. Anticipating such a reaction, Head Shed leaders had positioned armed guards at the prison gates with orders to prevent the men from escaping. Temporarily deterred, the prisoners redirected their pent-up energy by dismantling the gates and fences that had restricted movement inside the camp. Then the rampage escalated as hundreds of POWs overran the guards, tore down sections of perimeter fencing, and escaped camp.[404,405]

The guards also struggled to stop the crowds of Germans gathered outside the prison gates from entering the compound. Many were seeking refuge from the Russians invading Barth, while others were trying to get their hands on the food and clothing the Germans had left behind. The locals successfully stormed the Stalag and carted off thousands of Red Cross parcels.[406] It was a wild and unforgettable day:

Freedom!! We were liberated May 1 at 1:00 a.m. After the Germans left, our camp officers organized groups of armed men to go into the big, barn-like warehouse at the nearby Flak School and take charge of the thousands and thousands of stockpiled Red Cross parcels that the Germans hadn't distributed to the POWs.* They took care of the distribution of the food in an orderly manner.

---

* Don and many other Kriegies, including Colonel Zemke, believed that since they found more than 60,000 Red Cross parcels stockpiled in the warehouse... (continued page 420)

A search group discovered a stockpile of mail that was never sent—thousands of letters dating as far back as December. I found the letters I'd written to Laura and my folks that were never mailed—the lousy Krauts!

I was able to get into the camp records office and discovered the file the Germans had set up under my prisoner number. It contained my pink Dulag-Luft prisoner identification card, which recorded the details of my capture and imprisonment, along with my picture, which they took when I first arrived at the camp. I obviously needed a haircut and looked very tired, but other than that, I thought I looked pretty good, considering the dreadful march I'd been on. My heart almost stopped when I found two letters from Laura Jeanne in the file. Reading them brought tears to my eyes.

That afternoon, the Allied Head Shed leaders upgraded their quarters from the Wing X barracks to the abandoned Luftwaffe administration building. In their first official act, they tore down the Nazi Swastika flag and raised the Stars and Stripes and Union Jack flags. Colonel Zemke sent out two officers, one German-speaking and the other Russian-speaking, in a jeep marked with stars, stripes, and a white flag, to make contact with the advancing Russian troops. His next priority was to locate adequate flour and vegetables to supplement the Red Cross parcels and the tons of fenced-off potatoes their captors had left behind. The kommandant and his cronies had secretly absconded with all of the POWs' cash, leaving a $60,000 I.O.U. in the camp safe in its place. The embezzlement left the prisoners no way to purchase food and supplies from the German people in and around Barth. Their only choice was to take what they needed, by force if necessary.[407]

[continued from page 419] ...at liberation, there must have been undistributed food parcels at the camp during the starvation period. While German pilfering of Red Cross shipments was a fact, and cruel treatment of prisoners wasn't uncommon, it isn't certain that they intentionally starved the prisoners during March of 1945. The Germans needed thousands of parcels to issue even partial rations to the POWs each week, and shipments from Sweden during that time had completely stopped. However, those facts failed to convince most Kriegies otherwise.

The Kriegies' first night of freedom started out a little bumpy. In an attempt to thwart the Russians, the fleeing Wehrmacht soldiers had cut the power lines leading to the prison, leaving the camp without electricity that was needed for lights and the well pumps. However, it took more than a night with no lights and backed up latrines to dampen the men's spirits. They burned candles while former electricians among them restored the power. About midnight, cheering echoed throughout the prison grounds when the first Russian soldiers showed up in a truck.[408]

Two days later, the commander of the first wave of Soviet forces to arrive at Stalag Luft I promised to provide food and supplies for the camp. That evening, Russian soldiers drove a herd of cattle, including milk cows, into the prison grounds. The POWs were elated at the prospect of eating real beef again. They butchered dozens of steers and barbequed them over open fires, feasting most of the night. And for the first time since they'd been incarcerated, they drank fresh milk instead of Klim.[409] The men were finally getting enough to eat—and for some, too much. Don later wrote:

Some of the men in our camp had been there for several years. An Englishman, who had survived prison life for over four years, took supplies from the Red Cross parcels and made a large, fabulous, chocolate cake, eating all of it by himself. His body was so weak and rundown that he was unable to digest such a rich dessert, and he ended up dying as a result.

It was a sad day for all of us. We learned it was important to control our appetites and not allow ourselves to overindulge now that there was so much food available to eat.

The following day, May 2, 1945, one of the bloodiest battles of the war ended when German General Helmuth Weidling finally surrendered Berlin to Russian General Vasily Chuikov. Stalin had raced to Berlin, determined to exact his revenge on Hitler by destroying the Nazi capital before the Americans and British could arrive. To get there first, the Russians employed an aggressive attack strategy, resulting in excessive casualties. But with the memory of more than twenty-three million dead Soviet soldiers and civilians still fresh on their minds, the Red Army troops didn't complain and were eager for retaliation against the Nazis, regardless of the costs.[410]

Although outnumbered more than eight to one at Berlin, neither the depleted Wehrmacht nor the shell-shocked German people were willing to give up. Nearly half of their remaining army consisted of Hitler youth, old World War I veterans, women, and children. German propaganda had left the people terrified, convincing them that fighting to their death was a better fate than falling into Soviet hands. And for many of them, especially the women, their fears proved justified.[411]

The undisciplined Russian soldiers committed barbaric atrocities, showing little mercy as they rampaged through the capital, plundering, burning, raping, and killing without restraint. More than 92,000 German soldiers died in the Battle of Berlin. German civilian losses were even more shocking—estimated as high as 125,000. Victory in the last major battle of the war in Europe also came at a steep price for the Russians. More than 81,000 Soviet troops lost their lives in the siege.[412]

Stalin had an even more important reason than retaliation to reach Berlin before their Allies. Russian nuclear scientists were trailing far behind their counterparts in the United States and Germany. Arriving in the capital city first enabled Stalin to take over the coveted Nazi nuclear program at the Kaiser Wilhelm Institute. In addition to seizing the facility and capturing many of Germany's top nuclear scientists, the Soviets found more than three tons of uranium oxide at the research center—enough to begin constructing their first nuclear weapon.[413]

Joseph Stalin, who was as ruthless as Hitler, followed the Führer's Machiavellian dogma: "The ends justify the means." The outcome of the war against Germany might have been different if America and Great Britain hadn't struck an alliance with the brutal Soviet dictator, but the union came with a price. Despite the coalition's success in defeating the Nazis, the relationship between the Big Three was about to take a turn for the worse, morphing from strange bedfellow status to adversary.

Like the Great War that preceded it, World War II would also fail to bring peace. Stalin was starting to show his true colors, setting his sights on new territory. The ever-outspoken General Patton argued for the fighting in Europe to continue, but against a new threat—the Soviet Union—believing the Soviets were an enemy to the entire free world. Although his fears proved visionary, Patton paid dearly for speaking his mind in his typical loose-cannon fashion. Eisenhower wasn't able to protect his four-star general this time from the backlash that followed. Patton's controversial comments and confrontational posturing created a political firestorm that forced Eisenhower to relieve him of his command and relegate him to a desk job.[414] Before the end of the year, Patton would die in a Heidelberg hospital from injuries suffered in a car accident. The suspicious circumstances that surrounded the accident still intrigue conspiracy theorists.

While German SS troops continued fighting sporadic battles the next few days, the Wehrmacht were finished and surrendered in droves. The country lay in ruins, its people utterly defeated. Starvation, disease, and homelessness were now their enemies. And the entire German nation faced worldwide scorn, wrath, and retribution following the discovery of concentration camps, where more than six million Jews and dissidents died from Nazi atrocities.

On May 4, Don and a squad from the North 3 Compound led by Colonel Gabreski made a shocking discovery. While searching the Barth airfield they found nearly 2,000 Greek and French Jewish dissidents locked up in three two-story barracks. SS guards had abandoned the barracks weeks before, leaving the prisoners without food or water. In their final act of unthinkable cruelty, the Nazis had charged the electric fences surrounding the buildings. The skeleton-like prisoners were now all dead or dying from starvation. The hands of decaying dead bodies still clutched the wire fencing that had electrocuted them as they attempted to escape. Before the gruesome discovery, the POWs were unaware such camps even existed. The stench of defecation and death was so strong at the airfield that anyone working there had to know about the atrocity—yet they chose to do nothing about it.[415,416] Don wrote:

> *About two miles away from Stalag Luft I, there was a concentration camp where political prisoners had been kept.*

That was something awful to behold! We took vitamin D pills and whatever else we could take from the Red Cross parcels to those who were still alive. Some of our medics tried to mix a solution for them to take, but they were so far gone their bodies couldn't absorb the remedy. None of them survived.

The hatred created by war and the brainwashing of the Germans by Hitler made them insensitive to human decency. I'm trying not to hate anyone. After that experience, we all felt grateful that the war was nearly over. We'd survived, and it wouldn't be too long before we'd be going home.

Don was appalled at the brutality of their Soviet liberators as well, describing them as "crude and reckless" in his YMCA notebook. The first few days after arriving, the Russian troops rampaged out of control, doing virtually anything they wanted. Hordes of drunken Siberian, Mongolian, and Ukrainian soldiers terrorized the German people by plundering, violating, and ravaging nearly every household. Barth and nearby towns were burning. Hundreds of locals were shot and killed, including women and children. Many, including the mayor of Barth, chose to commit suicide rather than succumb to the Red Army brutality. Displaced civilians from the Barth area showed up at the camp gates each morning, pleading for protection from Russian soldiers. At night, women and children huddled under the guard towers for safety. The Russian soldiers' behavior continued unchecked until Colonel T.D. Zhovanik arrived at Barth and restored order. The men at Stalag Luft I were also affected by Zhovanik's arrival. Any POW caught outside the camp without a pass would be locked up in a Russian jail.[417]

The men grew more and more restless as spring sunshine and warmer temperatures arrived at the Baltic Coast. Restricted to the confines of the camp, they still felt like prisoners. Head Shed leaders hoped the swing music blaring through the camp loudspeakers would pick up the men's spirits. Instead, it backfired, making them edgy and homesick, and drove even more of them AWOL. Education classes and sports activities no longer captured the Kriegies' attention. Many were too impatient to wait for their turn for a pass to leave camp and sneaked off without permission in search of souvenirs or a good time. Most of the fences had been pulled to the ground, so it wasn't hard for those willing to openly disregard orders to get past the guards.

POWs who went AWOL had become an embarrassing problem, especially for the Americans, who now had seventy men in Russian jailhouses and another 730 unaccounted for. Most were behind bars for looting or for being drunk and disorderly. Several escapades had ended badly. One night, three Americans left camp without permission, hijacked a car and went joyriding. After a few hours of drinking and partying, they lost control of the vehicle and crashed into a ditch. All three were killed. Others, too impatient to wait for evacuation, risked court-martial and set off on their own, determined to walk hundreds of miles to the Allied frontlines. A few even attempted to get there by boat.[418]

During the next few days, Don entered a list of "Things to Remember" in his notebook. They included finding a model P-47 like the one Jerry bought in Paris, buying Lt. Colonel Ross Greening's book of Stalag Luft I paintings he'd promised to publish, and discovering what happened to the rest of the Five. On the last page, he documented "Kriegie Exchanges" he had made with several of his Room 9 buddies. Not surprisingly, they all involved food items. Don put up Utah black cherries in exchange for New England maple syrup and maple sugar candy, Washington apples, Chicago Fannie Mae nut chocolates, and Texas grapefruit. Although the men intended to follow through with their food exchanges and to honor their card-betting markers and IOUs, they would soon forget about them.

On May 7, five days after the fall of Berlin, Germany unconditionally surrendered to the Allies in Reims, France, officially ending the war in Europe. But because the Russian general who had witnessed the signing didn't have approval from Stalin to sign documents, the Soviet premier demanded the surrender ceremony be repeated in Berlin. The following day, Soviet secret police arrested the general who witnessed the first signing, and he was never heard from again.[419]

As a concession to Stalin, the Allied leaders withheld news of the surrender for twenty-four hours, releasing it in the United States, Great Britain, and the Soviet Union on May 8, 1945, at exactly the same time. When they heard the announcements, millions of people danced in the streets of London, Paris, and cities all across America. Prime Minister Churchill spoke to cheering crowds in London, paying tribute to those who had "fought valiantly on land, sea, and in the air." President Truman, having served less than a month in the Oval Office, graciously dedicated the victory to the late President Roosevelt during a news conference. Stalin congratulated the Russian people, extolling their role in the victory over German imperialism. The communist dictator, still gloating after the surrender reenactment coup, was planning his next move against his former allies—to seize additional territory for Mother Russia. The war in the Eastern Theater of Operations may have ended, but the geopolitical conflict with the Soviet Union was just beginning.[420]

The May 8 edition of *POW-WOW* led off with the bold heading *WAR ENDS*. In addition to reporting the surrender details broadcast by the BBC and Voice of America, the two-page newsletter included thought-provoking editorial comments:

The news which thrilled the outside world was taken in stride by Stalag Luft I—for Nazism's death throes were almost anti-climactic to the frenzied excitement of liberation by Russians. Crowds were dancing in the streets...with excitement, but life had picked up its pulse best for us again on April 30th when our seedy, disillusioned Volksturm guards fled for their lives toward the Allied lines.

But now, with other free men, we turn our thoughts toward the world that is to be...thinking as well of the war against Japan, standing alone and doomed to fall. Victory in Europe has released vast forces for this task.

We at Stalag Luft I are ready to play our part in the events foreshadowed by this day. We came to Europe and learned to appreciate America. We fought and learned why we were fighting. We are proud of our share in bringing about this glorious occasion. Our planes brought the war home to the enemy. We were the vanguard of Victory.

Two days later, the Head Shed issued a single page of plain stationery to each POW to write their first letter home as free men—one they were assured would actually be posted and delivered:

10 May 1945

Barth on the Baltic

My Beloved Wife,

It's been a long time since I've written. I've been under censor restrictions for so long that I can't even remember what I used to want to write. Everyone here is of the opinion that we'll beat our mail home—maybe we will. At any rate, I still wanted to write to you. I have quite a horror story to tell about my experience as a POW.

I'm feeling fine, honey, so don't worry about me and be patient for a little while. I'm so homesick and lonesome for you that it's almost unbearable. Living in this fenced up "hell-hole" is bad enough, but being away from you for so long is a feeling that I can't even begin to describe.

We're still sweating out the C-47s and B-17s that are supposed to come in and fly us out to freedom. We're "supposed" to fly to England or France within another week. From there we're "supposed" to have Very High Priority on transportation back to the good old U.S.A. I have a picture in my mind of taking you into my arms, holding you ever so close, and hearing you whisper—anything.

I was so disappointed when your recording of "I'll Be Loving You Always" didn't arrive before I was shot down. Since entering Germany, I've lost all my prized personal possessions. My pilot bracelet, fountain pen, wristwatch, and even the setting out of my class ring are all gone, with no hope of recovery. That bracelet was precious. What's most important, though, I have my life—and I'm indeed grateful to the Lord for that. I don't want to be a slacker, but I have no desire to enlist for a tour of duty in the South Pacific.

We're only allotted one letter for now. Said letter is supposed to be taken to our lines and then to England, and then to the most wonderful wife in the world. Give the folks my very best. May God bless you and bring us together very soon.

Yours for eternity, Don

Stalag Luft I was now the only German POW camp the Allies hadn't evacuated. The Head Shed leaders were frustrated with Field Marshall Montgomery's inability to work out an evacuation agreement with Soviet leaders. Initially, the Russians proposed transporting the prisoners to the Port of Odessa (more than 1,200 miles away on the Black Sea), then shipping them to England. Colonel Zemke rejected their plan as totally illogical and petitioned to have the men evacuated by air transport. The Communists denied his request and refused permission to fly over Soviet-held territory. After an unproductive 10-day delay, a British captain on Colonel Zemke's staff finagled a secret meeting with the 65th Soviet Army general in charge of the area. Behind closed doors, they hammered out an agreement for a massive air rescue that was intended to be operational and executed before Moscow ever heard about it.[421,422]

On the night of May 11, Allied Command notified Zemke that "Operation Revival" was set to take place over the next three days. After getting the news, most of the men were too excited to sleep and stayed up all night, sitting around campfires, reminiscing, and singing. The following morning, they cheered as they heard the sound of B-17s. Colonel Zemke insisted that the British POWs be evacuated first, since they'd been there the longest. Next, six C-46 transport planes took the sick and the wounded. After that, thousands of Americans marched to the Barth airfield. More than 6,250 former prisoners were evacuated by the end of the day.[423]

Day 2 of the evacuation operation dawned with a beautiful sunrise. The men in the North 3 Compound eagerly assembled that morning on the parade grounds, then marched to the airfield. The engine roar of the approaching heavy bombers was sweet music to the ears of most of Don's roommates, since they'd served as pilots, navigators, or bombardiers in the massive Flying Fortresses. This would be Don's second trip in a B-17 and definitely the most anticipated flight of his military career.

To make room for more passengers, the Air Force stripped the B-17s of their guns, weaponry, and seats, except those in the cockpit for the pilot and copilot. They expanded the carrying capacity even further by installing wood flooring in the bomb bays and cutting down the normal aircrew size from ten to five. Most of the planes kept their engines running after landing, continuing to slowly taxi toward their takeoff area as groups of twenty-five to thirty men scrambled aboard. In a matter of minutes, ground control cleared the transports for takeoff. As the engines roared and the big bombers slowly rose into the air, the Kriegie Kut-Ups from Room 9 began cheering wildly.[424]

Operation Revival wrapped up on May 14. Among the last POWs to be evacuated were those caught going AWOL, many of whom had just been released from Russian jailhouses. They feared they might be court-martialed, but the worst punishment most of them received was being pushed to the tail end of the evacuation line. By 2:00 p.m., Colonel Zemke had signed over everything left in the deserted camp to their Russian liberators, including 45,000 Red Cross parcels. Only one B-17 remained on the Barth airstrip. True to his word, the colonel was the last of 8,498 prisoners to leave Stalag Luft I. With no desire for one last look back at the camp, he climbed aboard the final evac plane and headed for Paris with several other Head Shed leaders.[425]

The rest of the Stalag Luft I POWs were on their way to Camp Lucky Strike, located near Le Havre, France. Some of the B-17s flew directly there, but because of the large number of aircraft in the evacuation effort, many of the flights were directed to airfields scattered across Western France, from Bordeaux to Reims. Wherever they landed, the liberated Kriegies all received the same special treatment—warm welcomes, doughnuts, lemonade, and coffee—the moment they stepped off their planes. In Don's case, he was also welcomed with music. Blaring over the loudspeakers as he entered Camp Lucky Strike was the new hit song "Don't Fence Me In."

Shortly after landing, the freed prisoners, the pilots and aircrew, and even the evacuation aircraft itself were de-loused. Afterward, the men enjoyed their first long, hot shower since the day they'd become POWs. After eating a good dinner at the mess hall, Don went straight to bed. He later wrote, "Sleeping in a warm barracks, on a G.I. cot, with a real pillow never felt so good." The next day, the men who were unable to land at the airfield in Le Havre boarded buses, trains, and C-47 transport planes for the last leg of their journey, to Camp Lucky Strike.

Operation Revival

Tent City at Camp Lucky Strike

THIRTY-SEVEN

Camp Lucky Strike

L ocated three miles inland from the coastal fishing port of Saint-Valery-en-Caux, Camp Lucky Strike was one of eight "Cigarette Camps" the U.S. Army set up in the area of Le Havre, France. Earlier in the war, the camps served as staging locations for newly arrived Allied troops about to enter battle in the European Theater. The Army chose *cigarette names* for security reasons, enabling them to keep communications about the staging locations secret. Although the cigarette companies didn't sponsor the camps that bore their name, they did provide the soldiers stationed there with all the free cigarettes they wanted—their brand, of course. At the end of the war, Camp Lucky Strike became the main gathering and processing location for liberated prisoners in the ETO, housing as many as 100,000 men at a time. [426] The POWs from Stalag Luft I were the last to arrive at the camp, which placed them at the end of a long line of liberated prisoners waiting to get home. When he arrived, Don found the camp overcrowded and disorganized, with seemingly no one in charge. In his next letter to Laura Jeanne, he wrote:

I'm a free man! I'm awaiting "red tape" processing before being shipped to the good old U.S.A. And what's more important, I'm heading straight for home upon arrival!!! (Or so we're told.) I'm in good health, so have no fear about my condition. I'm so anxious to get home.

Since we discovered thousands of letters dating as far back as December that the Germans hadn't mailed to the States, you probably didn't receive any of the letters I wrote at Stalag Luft I, Barth, Germany. We were flown to France by B-17s on May 13. It took five months of POW life to make me

appreciate a G.I. cot and delicious G.I. food! The Red Cross
parcels were a Godsend while at the prison camp.

I have a million things to tell you about the events dating
back to last June 24 at 5 p.m. when we said goodbye. I have
very high hopes of being home within a month for a "60-
Day" leave. So keep your fingers crossed and remember…I'm
loving you always.

An article in *Stars and Stripes*, the official newspaper of the United
States Armed Forces, reported POW complaints of overcrowding,
bland food, poor sanitation, and growing impatience with the
slow process of returning home. Troubled by the reports, General
Eisenhower arranged to visit Camp Lucky Strike and check things
out for himself. After eating the food, the general agreed with the men
that it *was* plain and bland, but he explained that camp medical staff
believed it was necessary, given the men's weak digestive systems.
He told them he would try to improve the food, but he wasn't going
to overrule their doctors' recommendations. Eisenhower apologized
for the overcrowded camp conditions and for the processing delays
in getting the men home, then asked them for their patience. He
reminded them that as former POWs they were first in line, ahead
of millions of other G.I.s just as eager to get home. The men cheered
their popular commander as he traveled throughout the tent city,
even though he couldn't do much to improve their plight.[427]
Bored and tired of the delays, many of the ex-prisoners left camp
without permission to visit nearby cities, some traveling as far as
Paris. Although technically AWOL, few were ever reported missing
or court-martialed. Don wasn't willing to do anything that might
delay his trip home. He waited untiringly in lines for everything
from medical and physical examinations to in-depth intelligence
interviews, seeking every possible opportunity to move ahead in
the processing quagmire. He even concealed the severity of his foot
problems, fearful that their diagnosis and treatment might keep him
in the camp longer.[428]
On the afternoon of May 18, his second day at Camp Lucky
Strike, Don wrote:

Today finds me still impatiently waiting for my processing to
begin so I can get in line for a boat bound for the U.S. The

fresh eggs, fried chicken, roast beef, etc. are keeping me from swimming the Atlantic at present.

I have no officer clothes as yet, but I think we'll get a set of greens and a partial pay allowance of $80 before we leave here. I have no idea what happened to my belongings or the footlocker I sent home last August. At any rate, I'll probably be short on clothes when I arrive. I'm still not sure if my promotion to 1st Lt. came through, since I've had no "official" word or proof, nor do I know where to find same. About all I know for certain is that I love and miss you desperately, my darling.

I just had a very pleasant surprise when I ran into Grant Ash and Bob Wilson [also a former high school classmate and friend]. They've completed their processing and await shipment. Tell you more later.

The U.S. Army Medical Department reported that most POWs at Camp Lucky Strike were consuming in excess of 5,000 calories per day and rapidly adding weight to their emaciated bodies. That evening, Don inserted a few comments in the remaining pages of his YMCA notebook:

...turkey and dressing, fresh vegetables, all sorts of desserts, and ice cream, plus pancakes, bacon, and eggs—much better than black bread or rutabaga stew. I couldn't care less for the free "Luckies," but the G.I. cot and the delicious food at camp are really something! Seems like all we do is stand in line for chow.

I have a big appetite and we can eat as many times a day as we want. So we stand in mess lines that are about a quarter mile long for about an hour, eat for about an hour, and then get back in line again. I'm starting to feel like a balloon. It feels so good.

No word of Kelly yet. I'm anxious and impatient—can't wait to get home.

RAMPS Notice

....

Don and his two Lehi school buddies were inseparable the next
two days, catching up on what had happened to them since they'd
last seen each other before going overseas. Grant, whose plane went
down at the end of May 1944, had spent the most time as a POW.
Later that fall, after Bob Wilson's plane took flak, the two of them
were reunited at Stalag Luft III, located near the small town of Sagan,
southeast of Berlin. Allied prisoners considered it the best prison
camp in Germany. But that changed when the Red Army drew near.
At midnight on January 27, in snowy, bitter-cold conditions, Hitler
ordered the evacuation of all 10,000 POWs in the camp. Following
a brutal three-day march and three-day train ride in overcrowded

boxcars, Grant and Bob entered the largest and possibly worst German prison camp, Stalag VIIA, located in southern Bavaria.[429] After listening to their story, Don shared details of his own hellish ordeal.

While together at Camp Lucky Strike, the Lehi ex-Kriegies read an article in *Stars and Stripes* reporting that Hitler had twice issued orders near the end of the war to execute all POWs interned in the Stalag Luft camps. Fortunately, the Luftwaffe officers at the Stalags ignored the Führer's orders, providing further evidence how lucky the three of them were to be alive.

The next day, after waiting in line for hours, Don finally made it into the camp's main processing office and initiated the paperwork necessary to secure his travel papers. It was a bittersweet day. While Don was filling out the forms, Grant and Bob boarded a Liberty Ship and sailed for home before they could say goodbye. Don took solace knowing that Grant had promised to contact Laura Jeanne as soon as he arrived in the States to let her know he was alive and well.

Surrounded by ex-POWs in his tent, all of them trying to sleep, reminded Don of late nights spent with his Jabo Angel buddies. He was again sitting on the edge of his cot, writing to Laura Jeanne, while his tentmates begged him to turn off the lights. He missed the prized fountain pen the SS had seized when he was captured, and grudgingly printed his letter using the eraserless pencil issued to him at Stalag Luft I:

> Hello again, my lovely lady. I'm still very impatient. I don't mind waiting in the chow line or in the pay line, but sweatin' out the line for a ticket home to you is simply too, too much!!
>
> As I wrote before, Grant and Bob were here at Lucky Strike. They're about two weeks ahead of me in the line to get on a boat home. Both of them are looking swell, and they're as anxious as I am to get home. We tried to pull a few strings so that I could ship out with them, but to no avail.
>
> I've seen lots of fellows from my old squadron (POWs), but I haven't been able to locate any record of Kelly as yet. I'm still keeping busy at those "strings" trying to move myself ahead in the line. Grant and Bob left today for their ship—the lucky

stiffs! On the other hand, I was very happy to see them get on their way.

Later that week, the 397th Fighter Squadron received a letter from F/O Charles W. Vickerman, one of the thousands of POWs waiting in Le Havre to be shipped home. While he was at Camp Lucky Strike, the flight officer reported that he had seen several missing Jabo Angel pilots previously held as prisoners of war. Among them were Lts. Vernon (Pat) Murphy, Donald N Evans, Milton S. Bender, and William C. Olden, all alive and well.[430] The men in the squadron celebrated, relieved that a few of their close friends listed as MIA were still alive. The squadron had now accounted for every missing Jabo Angel pilot, except for Jerry Kelly.

———————

Don knew his letters to Laura Jeanne were one-sided and would remain unanswered, since he'd likely arrive home before they did. Still, the letters were the closest thing to a conversation he could have with her. Recording his experiences and feelings in his letters seemed to help him cope with his growing homesickness:

Hello again, my precious! Well, I finally got into the processing area where it takes three or four days to complete all the paperwork. There are dozens of forms to fill out, and Intelligence asks us endless questions. Now I wait a few more days, pending shipment from this camp to another one, where I again wait a few days for some old broken-down tub to take me home! And that may mean another ten to fifteen days.

Next, we stop at a camp in the States until they're able to route us on a troop train to Ft. Douglas, Utah. Then I wait there until I get my leave papers. Figuring all those delays, it will be about this time next month when I step off the train and take you into my arms—as you've never been taken before!!!

Since they're moving all "Kriegies" as a group on travel orders, that kind of knocks our hopes of meeting on the East Coast and seeing the country as you wanted to when I came back. Sorry, honey. There might even be more delays, since POWs no longer have shipping priority anymore.

The delays were longest for the Stalag Luft I prisoners, since they arrived at Camp Lucky Strike weeks later than those held at the other German prison camps. Worse yet, they got stuck in the middle of a policy change and lost the priority treatment afforded the other POWs. On May 24, Don made the following short entry in his YMCA notebook:

Waiting is terrible! Word is finally out that we're sailing on June 1ˢᵗ on a "cattle boat." Should be sent to Le Havre soon.

Don arrived at the port city of Le Havre three days later. Hopes of making it home by the middle of June buoyed up his spirits. At sunset, he sharpened his pencil and started writing again:

My Darling, I'm at another camp now and hope to get on a ship in a day or two. I'm about on schedule, but the days are dragging, and I'm getting more lonesome and impatient every day. This all still seems kind of like a dream and hard to explain, like I've been lost and forgotten with only your love and memories to keep me going for so long, and now, I don't know—it's too hard to explain.

I've been spending my free time seeing movies and eating doughnuts at the Red Cross Dug Out. We don't have any lights in our tents. This camp, like the last one, seems rather disorganized—but this is the Army, so I'm not too surprised.

We were issued a blouse, two khaki shirts, underwear, soxs, a pair of low-cut shoes, an overseas hat, a pair of green pants, toilet articles, and a few other odds and ends to hold us until we hit the States. It surely felt wonderful to get into some clean new clothes after wearing the same duds for so long. Some of my many ambitions or wants or whatever are to take a Swedish bath, have an alcohol rubdown, get a "good" haircut, have my teeth cleaned—just an overhauling in general, you might say!

I just returned from a lecture given by an Air Force colonel from Washington D.C., confirming the 60-day leave rumor. He *also said we'd be able to collect our back pay and allowances (all income tax-exempt) from the day we went down, but not until after our leave. That will be almost $2,600. Then he said that none of us POWs would have to go to the South Pacific. Pretty good news, huh? He also explained that we'd probably get assigned to a training base somewhere as an instructor, operations officer, or to some kind of desk job until we get our flying time in and get discharged.*

A 60-day leave sounds so unbelievable! I can't wait until I can actually wake up in the morning, after dreaming about you during the night, and find you still there next to me. Remember all the lumpy, saggy mattresses we've slept on? Any one of those would suit me after sleeping so long on wooden slats and a thin straw tick for a mattress. Real white sheets, a soft comfortable bed, and you—what a perfect dream!

On May 31, Don sent his final letter from Europe:

Hello, My Precious, I'm lying on my cot outside the tent trying to get a suntan. We're camped up on a hill in the woods near the city, so it's quite safe. Le Havre is pretty well beaten up, and the only things here of any interest are the G.I. theaters and the Red Cross Club where they serve coffee and doughnuts.

Prices are sky-high in town, but it doesn't really matter, since I only have five francs. We had to turn our money in to be converted to American currency before we could ship out. The catch is—that was eight days ago and it seems to be too much trouble for Army finance to give us any francs back now. Just stuck a fork in myself and decided I was well enough cooked for now, so it's back to my tent.

I've heard so much propaganda about how soon we'd be home that I don't believe anything now. All I know is when I do finally get home I'll have one year of your delicious cooking to catch up on, one year of dances, shows, picnics, etc. to make up for, and one year of loving to make up with my lovely little Jeannie.

Laura Jeanne celebrated V-E Day (Victory in Europe) with family and friends, later recalling, "There was dancing in the streets—even in the little town of Lehi, Utah." She was relieved when she read news reports that the Allies had liberated all the German POW camps and expected to hear from Don any day now. As the days turned into weeks without any word, she started to worry again, fearful something might have happened to her husband. Then, true to his word, Grant Ash sent a telegram to Laura Jeanne when he arrived in New York City. In her life history, she wrote:

What welcome news receiving that telegram was—to know for certain that my Mr. Lt. was alive and okay. When Grant got home, he told me all about their happy reunion at the relocation center in France, and about all the good food they were fed to "fatten" them up. However, he was concerned for Don, telling me he'd lost a great deal of weight, and that his feet were in bad condition.

A few days later, the postman delivered the letter that Don had written to her from Stalag Luft I. Shedding tears of joy, Laura Jeanne rushed across the street from work to tell her parents the good news, then immediately called Don's parents. The following day, she made one more trip to the *Lehi Free Press* and the Salt Lake City newspapers and reported that all three liberated Lehi POWs were on their way home.

Statue of Liberty

THIRTY-EIGHT

Home

America built a new class of merchant fleet cargo ships during World War II to haul food, fuel, jeeps, airplanes, tanks, and locomotives overseas. Medium in size (440 feet long and fifty-seven feet wide), they were slow movers with a top speed of only 12.5 mph, less than half the speed of large troopships. However, these "ugly ducklings," as President Roosevelt nicknamed them, could carry an impressive load—up to 10,800 deadweight tons.[431]

The first new cargo ship was the SS *Patrick Henry*, named after the Revolutionary War hero who coined the famous phrase "Give me liberty, or give me death!" The "Liberty" tag stuck, and each of the ships that followed kept the same handle.[432]

The United States opened shipyards all across the country to ramp up production of the new cargo ships. Using streamlined assembly methods, factories were able to build them in as little as forty-two days. But there was a serious shortage of skilled workers at the shipyards, since so many men from the former labor force were now serving in the military. Factories filled the void by hiring women to do work previously thought to be "a man's job," providing inspiration for the popular song and iconic Norman Rockwell poster featuring Rosie the Riveter.[433]

After Germany's defeat, The Merchant Marines converted 220 Liberty ships into transports to help bring American troops home from Europe. First in line were the wounded, then the POWs gathered at Camp Lucky Strike. From May 1945 through February 1946, Liberty ships carried more than three million American soldiers across the Atlantic Ocean, back to the States.[434,435]

On the morning of June 1, the SS *Sea Porpoise* steamed across the English Channel to the Port of Southampton to be outfitted. Three days later, Don and the other 449 POWs on board the Liberty Ship departed the harbor and began their transatlantic voyage:

> *At last, I'm crossing this puddle of water that has separated us for so long. This trip won't be quite as luxurious as when I came across on the Queen Elizabeth—but better because it brings me closer to you. I miss you so much. I wish I had even a wee snapshot of you. I never carried my wallet on missions, so when I went down, I didn't have a picture of you with me (except in my heart).*

> *I've been assigned as PX ration officer for the 400 enlisted men on board. I don't mind—it helps to pass the time. There's nothing much to do except eat, sleep, read, and stand on deck. This ship definitely isn't the master of the Atlantic. It rocks, rolls, leaps, and lunges!! Lots of the boys have been and still are victims of seasickness. I haven't got it yet. Of course, there's still plenty of time left on the ocean— so we'll see.*

> *We're getting two very good meals a day and a light snack for lunch—along with all the P-nuts, candy, and cookies we can eat. We also see shows at night and listen to some of the latest hit songs. "Don't Fence Me In" is still my current favorite.*

The Merchant Marines didn't build the Liberty ships to be comfortable. Their basic design caused them to pitch in rough seas, tossing and turning, and sliding from side to side. During her conversion to a troop transport ship, the tween (middle deck), was modified to accommodate tiered hammock-like bunks, which filled up nearly the entire deck. Although this configuration made things tight for the passengers, it allowed room on the other decks for extra toilet and shower facilities.[436]

The next night, Don wrote:

> *How's my honey tonight? Gee, but I wish I knew. I've been lying in bed all day long just dreaming. And you've been in every one of them. I seem to get more lonesome and homesick every day.*

Here I am speeding on my way home and complaining 'cause it isn't fast enough, when I should consider myself very lucky to be ahead of millions of other guys. I am truly grateful. Perhaps if there were something to do on the ship to keep my mind occupied—but there isn't.

The ship is very crowded. I'm second from the bottom in a tier of five "hammock style" bunks. It's too dark to read, so when we're in our bunks we just try and sleep. I've spent way more time doing <u>nothing</u> since I went overseas than I have doing <u>something</u>.

Time to hit the sack. So, until the next time I take pencil in hand, "I'll Be Loving You Always."

Halfway to the U.S. mainland, the returning soldiers' excitement began to wane and feelings of boredom returned:

Things are pretty dull around here. We've seen all the movies they have on board, and the PX has run out of P-nuts and cookies. I'm still on a six-hour shift of OD duty in the officer's mess. After I finish, I'll get my orders in for PX rations tomorrow.

They say it's a beautiful day today, but I won't get off duty in time to see it. But I'm not complaining. The Army teaches us not to complain. The Army has taught me three other things as well. First, salute everything that moves. Second, if it doesn't move then pick it up. And third, if you can't pick it up, then paint it!!! Well, that just about covers it.

The next day, the seas turned rough. Don wrote:

Greetings from the Mid-Atlantic Ocean. I'm in a restless mood tonight, probably influenced by the ocean, which seems to be in the same mood. It's very awkward trying to write in one of these sacks while the ship rocks and rolls from side to side. The ocean has been a bit choppy the past couple of days. Whitecaps decorate the water as far as the eye can see in every direction. I still haven't been seasick yet (knock on wood). I get woozy occasionally, but my flying experience got me used to motion.

If our luck holds out, we should be seeing the Statue of Liberty about Tuesday morning. What a beautiful sight that will be! We're supposed to be off the boat within three hours of docking and go to a staging area for 24–48 hours to be processed. Then I'll be put on a train for Ft. Douglas, where, supposedly, they'll have our leave papers ready within 24–48 hours after our arrival. That sounds too efficient for the Army, but I hope it's true.

The men's spirits lifted as their Liberty ship sailed closer to America. The day before the New York coastline came into view, Don wrote his final letter of the war to Laura Jeanne:

Gee, I wish you were here with me now, darling. It's a beautiful day with a few scattered clouds and a slight summer breeze. The ocean is so very, very calm today. It's really perfect—that is, it would be, if you were here.

I'm sitting aft of the smoke stack sunning myself, and of course, writing to my "li'l pigeon." The morale is running high today, and everyone (including myself) is getting excited. Tomorrow at this time we'll all be straining our eyes for land. It still seems like a dream to me.

If at all possible, I'm going to make a "collect" call from the first telephone I see, even if it's in the middle of the night. I can't wait to finally hear your voice again.

On June 12, 1945, Don's boatload of Kriegies came to the end of their twelve-day voyage, sailing past Liberty Island on their way to disembark at New York Harbor. The freed POWs jumped up and down and cheered as they approached Lady Liberty. That night, Don wrote the following in his YMCA notebook:

My heart swelled with pride and gratitude when we came into view of the Statue of Liberty. I feel so grateful for the freedoms that I fought for. I can't describe how wonderful it felt to finally step back on American soil. For me—the war is finally over!

After landing, we were processed, and I got temporarily located prior to my train ride home. I called Laura Jeanne as

*soon as I could get to a telephone. How great it was to hear
her voice!*

Don and Laura Jeanne hadn't spoken to each other since the day
before he left New York—nearly a year ago. She wrote the following
about that long awaited telephone call:

*As soon as he arrived in the USA, Don called me from New
York City, telling me he'd soon be on his way back home,
but had no idea when he'd arrive. I don't have the words to
explain how wonderful it was to hear his voice again, and
hear him repeat the words "I love you, I love you, I love
you!" We both did more crying than talking.*

*After I hung up the phone, I silently thanked God for bringing
Don safely home to me. The anticipation of his homecoming
turned my world upside down. I could hardly eat, or sleep, or
think of anything else.*

Don concluded the account of his long journey home, writing:

*It was a long three-day train ride from New York. I remember
how good it felt to see and be in the Rocky Mountains
again. To my surprise, the Army had my leave papers ready
to go when I arrived at Fort Douglas, and I boarded the
southbound train a few hours later. Although it was late at
night, I recognized the Mill Pond and the sugar factory just
outside town.*

*I was able to talk the train conductor into stopping at the Lehi
station, hoping that L.B. [Laura Jeanne's father] would be
working the graveyard shift. He was, and wondered who was
important enough on the train to get the engineer to make an
unscheduled stop in the little town of Lehi, especially in the
middle of the night.*

*Once he recognized that I was the soldier getting off the
train, L.B. rushed out of his office into the street and hugged
me. He wanted to immediately call and alert Laura Jeanne
that I was home. I just wanted to surprise her! It was a dark,
exciting night, as I carried my bag through the sleepy town
of Lehi.*

The porch light was on, making the Brown residence easy to find. It didn't matter. Don had dreamed about doing this for so long, he could have found Laura Jeanne's home with his eyes closed. After quickly walking up the steps and crossing the porch to the front door, he paused for a moment to gather himself—then rang the doorbell.

New Beginning

EPILOGUE

In her life history, Laura Jeanne completed the story of her reunion with Don, writing:

> *It was ironic after all my planning and waiting that my dad would be the first one to see Don. He arrived home a couple of days earlier than I'd expected and in the middle of the night—catching me completely by surprise.*
>
> *I'd gone to bed that night wearing an old nightgown, with curlers in my hair. I was sleeping soundly, until I heard my mother answer the front door. I jumped out of bed, opened my bedroom door, and there he was! I rushed into his arms and burst into tears as we hugged each other tightly. My heart nearly stopped with our first embrace. Between hugs and kisses, I tried to apologize for how I looked, but it didn't seem to matter. As he wiped away my tears of joy, Don looked into my eyes and said, "You look so beautiful!"*

After the excitement had subsided, Don's mother-in-law looked him over carefully, concerned at what she saw:

> *My mother finally asked Don how he felt and what we could do for him. It was then that I noticed the strain in his face and the puffiness of his skin. Much of the lost weight he'd regained was in his face and belly area, leaving the rest of his body still quite thin. He told us that he was completely exhausted, and his first request was to have a hot bath, followed by one of my "professional" backrubs.*
>
> *After seeing the terrible condition of Don's feet, we soaked them in Epson salts to ease the pain and swelling. After eating some hot soup, he lay down on my bed and quickly fell into a deep sleep. The ravages of war had taken their toll on my*

husband. Then and there, I determined that I'd do everything possible to help him recover from the nightmare he'd been living.

Tomorrow would bring a new day—and with it, the start of a new beginning for Mr. and Mrs. Donald N Evans.

That new beginning included Don's decision to get out of the Air Force Reserve Unit at Fort Douglas as soon as possible. Although he loved to fly, he was eager to distance himself from anything that reminded him of the war. Laura Jeanne quit her job and the two of them became inseparable, spending his leave time visiting friends and family and getting to know each other again.

Near the end of August, two months after he returned home, they finally went on their long overdue honeymoon—courtesy of Uncle Sam. The Army flew most of the POWs from the European Theater of Operations to hotels on the beaches at Santa Monica, California. Laura Jeanne wrote the following about their two-week, all-expense-paid trip:

We stayed at a gorgeous hotel on the beach and were treated royally with every luxury at our command. Thousands of POWs (most of them not married) were there, including Grant Ash and many of the men Don knew from prison camp. He was thrilled to see Bob, Kenny, and Pat again, who were now stationed at nearby Santa Anna.

The government spared no expense in showing us a great time. There were all kinds of sightseeing tours available, marvelous food at famous restaurants, parties, and dances with renowned big name bands. We hated for the two weeks to come to an end.

We arrived home on September 7 and were met by Don's parents at the airport. His dad looked really tired. The next morning, Don's sixteen-year-old little brother brought us news that his father had suffered a heart attack while working on his farm. We rushed to the hospital, but we were too late. Don's father was only 47 years old.

On September 26, 1945, Don received an honorable discharge from the Army Air Corps. During his military service, he received the Air Force Air Medal with three additional oak leaf clusters, the European Theater Ribbon with four clusters, and the Purple Heart. Later, the Army awarded him the Prisoner of War Medal.

––––––––––

The day after the war ended, Bob, Kenny and Pat took off from their air base at Frankfurt to make a final search for Jerry's plane. Bob had to borrow the CO's P-47 because his plane had been shot up and damaged in a forced belly landing on its final flight of the war. They flew repeated search patterns over the dense Schnee-Eifel woods where Jerry's plane had last been seen. When this proved fruitless, they finagled a Jeep from the Army motor pool and spent the next day searching the area from the ground. Unable to find any evidence of Jerry's plane, they finally gave up their search.

The 368th Fighter Group remained in Germany for one more month before the Air Force began to ship the pilots home. In his memoirs, Bob wrote:

> We ended the war up in Nuremburg and were the only ones of the Five who came home normally. Kelly was still MIA (now presumed killed) and Evans came home through the POW program. The three of us milled around in a French port with what seemed like a million other guys, finally loading on a Liberty ship named the SS Thomas Marshall that was headed for the United States.
>
> We were all sick the entire 12 days on the water. The boat trip was an experience I wouldn't want to repeat. We landed in New York Harbor, then transported to Camp Kilmer in New Jersey, where we were treated like kings. It was there that I was fed the largest steak I've ever seen. After being processed, we were sent to our homes by train for a short furlough.
>
> Not one to write or call, I just appeared on the doorstep at home, surprising my Mom. That wasn't fair and she was just about floored—not a very good son.

Kenny later wrote the following about their discharge from the Army and the last time the remaining members of the Five were all together:

After a brief visit to our homes, the three of us were sent to Santa Anna, California, for discharge from the Air Force. This is where I met Don and his wife again. All of us enjoyed being together for about two weeks. Don and I had become good friends while serving together in the 397th Fighter Squadron.

Since I had friends in Utah, I spent an extra two or three days there on my way home after being discharged. I stayed with Bob and enjoyed seeing Don and Laura again. As we were all together at the train station in Salt Lake City on my way home to Kansas City, Missouri, Don's wife whispered in my ear that they were going to name their first son after me. That was the last time I ever saw them.

Kenny and Pat returned to their home in Missouri after the war and continued their close friendship. They enrolled in college together, both earning engineering degrees from the University of Missouri. Pat later moved to Texas, working as an engineer in Houston until his death at age fifty-six. Kenny started his career working as an engineer with Panhandle Eastern Pipe Line, eventually becoming president of the large multistate company. In 1983, he was the recipient of the Missouri Distinguished Service in Engineering Award, complementing the Distinguished Flying Cross and Air Medals he earned while serving in World War II. He remained in the Kansas City area after his retirement, keeping in touch with Bob until his death in 2015 at age ninety-one.

———————

Nearly four years after the war, a local Catholic priest discovered Jerry Kelly's grave in Frauenkron, six miles west of Stadtkyll, and notified the Army. The War Department changed his status from MIA to KIA—Killed in Action—and sent a letter to the Kelly family, informing them of the discovery. The Army gave the family the option of having their son's remains returned to Salt Lake City or buried in one of the European cemeteries with tens of thousands of other soldiers killed in the ETO during World War II. They also leaked the story to someone in the press. Mrs. Kelly learned about the fate of her son a few days before the War Department notification arrived while reading the *Salt Lake Tribune*—on Mother's Day 1949. Jerry's younger sister Ruth remembered her mother saying: "If they think they have him, then I want him home."[437]

The following month, on the fifth anniversary of the D-Day invasion, the Kelly family held a memorial service for Second Lieutenant Gerald B. Kelly in Salt Lake City. Members of his family, Mormon Church leaders, and close friends attended the funeral. The Air Medal Jerry had hoped to earn during the war and a Purple Heart were both displayed on the outside of his closed casket. Although the talks at the service were inspirational, providing hope and comfort to most in attendance, Mrs. Kelly was inconsolable over the loss of her son.[438]

Whoever buried Jerry in the woods outside the small German town of Frauenkron had hung his dog tags on the cross that was used to mark the grave. Six of the serial numbers debossed into the tags matched Jerry's, but one was illegible. Clinging to the remote chance this uncertainty offered, Mrs. Kelly refused to believe the remains were those of her son—hoping beyond hope that someday he might still return home.[439]

Following the twenty-year-old hero's funeral service, family and a few close friends gathered on a grassy knoll at the cemetery to dedicate the gravesite. Don and Bob stood solemnly at the rear of the small gathering as the casket was lowered into the ground. Tears filled their eyes as memories of their fallen friend came flooding into their minds.

After the war ended, Bob met Jackie Devereaux on a blind date. The young man Don once described as "not too forward when it comes to women" surprised everyone when he quickly proposed. They were married a year later. She and Laura Jeanne became lifelong friends, further cementing the close bond shared between their husbands. Bob returned to the University of Utah to finish school, but couldn't get flying out of his system. While still attending college, he joined up with a newly organized National Guard unit, which was looking for experienced fighter pilots to build a P-51 Mustang Fighter Squadron.

After graduating with a degree in education, Bob taught elementary school until the Air Force activated his fighter group during the Korean War, where he served honorably for another two years. After his second war stint, Bob decided to make a career change and returned to the U in pursuit of an aeronautical degree. The following year, he landed a job with Lockheed Aircraft Corporation in Burbank, California, working as a Flight Test Analyst. Later he became editor of the Lockheed *L-1011 Service Digest Magazine.*

Still in love with flying, Bob became a flight leader with the Van Nuys Air National Guard and was soon in the cockpit of an F-86 Sabre jet, flying 670 mph. He retired from the military as a lieutenant colonel and a decorated combat veteran, having been awarded the Distinguished Flying Cross and the Air Medal with ten Oak Leaf Clusters. At age ninety-four, Bob remains active, enjoys life, and is in good health. No longer able to fly airplanes or drive fast cars, he settles for going on long walks nearly every day.

After Don's discharge from the Army, he and Laura Jeanne registered for the fall quarter at BYU. Laura Jeanne loved everything about college. She made the honor roll and performed with the Women's Glee Chorus as they toured several Western States.

Coach Dixon welcomed Don back to the BYU tennis team with open arms. He never fully recovered from the foot injuries he suffered during his hard parachute landing and forced march, which cost him some speed on the court. He compensated for it by increasing the kick of his topspin serve and adding a deceptive drop shot to his repertoire. Don quickly moved up the team ladder, finishing out the season playing in the number two singles slot.

Don and Laura Jeanne enjoyed the simple college life. Although they lived frugally in a small basement apartment near campus, by the end of the spring quarter, they'd run out of money. Don's $75 monthly G.I. education allowance and $25 per quarter scholarship wasn't enough for both of them to attend college. They were each forced to give up something they loved—Laura Jeanne quit school and started working full-time, and Don resigned from the tennis team his senior year and picked up a part-time job.

Following Don's graduation, the couple moved to Orem, Utah, where they raised their four children. He started his career as a bookkeeper and salesman at a used car dealership. Within five years, he had become a successful entrepreneur in the grocery industry and an astute investor, which allowed him to retire early, at age fifty-five. Don was actively engaged in civic and church responsibilities throughout his life, but he always had time for his children and grandchildren, especially when it involved sports or spending time in the mountains at the family cabin. He found his greatest solace being near his beloved Laura Jeanne, seldom leaving her side after he returned from the war.

In many of his letters to her during the war, Don had written, "I'll tell you more about that when I return home." He probably would have if the war had gone differently for him, but it hadn't and he returned a different man than he was when he wrote those words. In her life history, Laura Jeanne wrote:

> I was surprised that Don refused to talk about the war after he returned home. Whenever I'd ask him about his experiences overseas, he'd often get pale and break out in a cold sweat, unable to answer my questions. I soon learned not to bring it up anymore and just wait until he was ready and willing to share feelings and events. It was over the course of many years before I learned about some of his Missing in Action and Prisoner of War experiences.

Laura Jeanne continued, sharing the following story:

> In late December 1965, twenty-one years after Don was shot down, we went together to see the movie "The Battle of the Bulge." It was a popular movie and we were both excited to see it. Partway through the show, Don experienced a panic attack—breaking out in a cold sweat, as flashbacks of old memories flooded his mind. He was relieved when I suggested that we leave the theater, not saying a word as we drove back home.

SECRETARY OF THE AIR FORCE
WASHINGTON

.15 AUG 1990

MEMORANDUM FOR RECIPIENTS OF THE PRISONER OF WAR MEDAL

In accordance with your request, it is a pleasure to forward the enclosed Prisoner of War Medal.

This medal was authorized by Congress for any person who served honorably as a prisoner of war after April 5, 1917. It is estimated that 142,000 United States Service members were held as prisoners in World War II, the Korean Conflict, and the Vietnam Conflict. The medal recognizes the special service prisoners of war gave to their country and the suffering and anguish they endured while incarcerated.

The United States Army's Institute of Heraldry was tasked to design the medal. Designs were solicited from the military Services, veterans associations, and private citizens. Over 300 proposals were submitted. A Joint Service Panel reviewed all of the proposals and selected the design submitted by Mr. Jay C. Morris, a civilian employee of the Department of the Army.

On the front of the medal is an eagle, symbol of the United States and the American spirit. Although surrounded by barbed wire and bayonet points, it stands with pride and dignity, continually on the alert for the opportunity to obtain freedom, symbolizing the hope that upholds the spirit of the prisoner of war. On the reverse, below the words "Awarded to," is space where the recipient or next of kin may engrave the prisoner of war's name. Below it is an inscription naming the purpose of the award, "For honorable service while a prisoner of war." The shield is from the coat of arms of the United States of America.

The public law authorizing the Prisoner of War Medal specified that the medal shall be accorded a position of precedence in relation to other awards and decorations, immediately following decorations awarded for individual heroism, meritorious achievement or service, and before any other service medal, campaign medal or service ribbon authorized to be displayed.

Please accept this medal with my best wishes.

Donald B Rice

Donald B. Rice

1 Atch
Prisoner of War Medal

Don's traumatic combat and prisoner of war experiences taught him that he could endure nearly anything. Sadly, he also learned that dealing with the memories of those experiences was almost as difficult as living through them. His horrific war memories, combined with his father's death so soon after he returned, triggered a complex set of pent-up emotions—some of which remained locked in his mind for the rest of his life.

Before the POW Act of 1981, post-traumatic stress disorder (PTSD) wasn't even on the radar for clinical psychologists. The focus of the Veteran Administration for POWs was on physical issues, such as injuries and restoring lost weight. The prevailing medical view was that adult trauma, the kind combat veterans and POWs had suffered, "did not lead to long-term effects, except among those who were emotionally disturbed before they went off to war."[440]

Most of the 93,000 prisoners captured in the ETO during World War II manifested symptoms of trauma after the war. The government responded by treating them to an all-expense-paid, two-week vacation in Santa Monica. During a meeting held in California, Army brass and medical officers told the former POWs "that they should return home and get on with their lives, and that they would get over any emotional problems they were experiencing. Any problems they experienced after the war would be due to their own inability to cope with the aftermath of their wartime experiences." As a result, many POWs chose to remain silent, hesitant to talk about their war experiences even to those closest to them.[441] The country waited until 1981, thirty-six years after the war ended, before honoring them with the Prisoner of War Medal.

Don was able to suppress the worst of his war memories, pushing them somewhere in the back of his mind, but they never disappeared. As the years passed, he learned to cope better with his past, even taking Laura Jeanne to see Paris and Europe, as he'd once promised her in a letter during the war. However, he was unwilling to visit any of the places where his POW experiences took place.

Although Don eventually shared some of his war experiences during the last few years of his life, most of them were of the uplifting and inspirational variety told to youth and church groups. He rarely opened up about the ugly experiences of the war that he wrote about in his YMCA notebooks, instead choosing to take them with him to his grave.

Unlike Bob, Kenny, and many other members of his old Jabo Angel Squadron, Don never attended any of the 368th Fighter Group Association annual reunions. However, he did donate to his old fighter group and looked forward to reading each edition of the association newsletters, writing notes, comments, and memories beside many of the articles and photographs. And he enjoyed hearing Bob's reports about the events.

Don was a patriot and proud of his service during the war. He loved his country and always reverenced her flag, proudly standing at attention, with his hat removed and his hand over his heart, during the playing of the "Star Spangled Banner." As he did, memories of that Christmas Eve spent long ago under a tall, stately pine tree in the Ardennes Forest flooded his mind. It seemed fitting that he passed away on the fifty-fifth anniversary of that experience.

Following his death in 1999 at age seventy-six, Don's family discovered a dog-eared copy of the 368th Fighter Group membership roster in his desk drawer. He'd written notes of recent telephone conversations and attempts to make contact with several of the Jabo Angel pilots he'd flown with during the war. He made no mention of the calls to any family members, not even to Laura Jeanne. Although his flashbacks and nightmares had long since vanished, his recollections of the war and the men he'd flown with had endured— memories filled with life lessons and defining moments that most never experience. Winning his own war, he emerged a kind and gentle man.

Don gained appreciation for the best qualities of human behavior by experiencing their opposites during the war. He always held the door for others and went out of his way to be accommodating, even to strangers. When others, particularly women, entered a room, he stood to show respect. Having known the pangs of hunger and starvation, he anonymously provided food to families in need throughout his lifetime. He valued the kindness of others as well, never forgetting his experience with the little old German woman in Koblenz. And from his many brushes with death, he developed a calm demeanor and learned to maintain control of his emotions, qualities that served him well as a parent and leader.

The last check he wrote before he died was made out to the 368th Fighter Group Association. Along with his donation, he included a short note. The editor included it in the September 30, 2000 edition of the 368th newsletter:

> A week before he died (December 24, 1999), Don Evans was reading our "From Invasion to Victory" newsletter insert and wrote the editor as follows from his home in Orem, Utah:

> On December 24, 1944, the 397th had a support mission to troops in Bastogne. I was shot down strafing Tiger tanks under 3,000 ft. cloud cover—captured December 25 by SS Troops—interesting experience.

> Don

> We had many comments on the newsletter of November 1999, but none quite so poignant.

Four months after Don's death, Laura Jeanne decided to write her life history. An avid scrapbooker, she'd completed picture albums covering both of their lives, filled with handwritten memories, photographs, and memorabilia. She wrote her own compelling story based on her personal journal, letters written between her and Don, and her meticulous scrapbook diaries.

Laura Jeanne lived for twelve more years. She claimed that her most meaningful accomplishments in life were being a devoted wife and loving mother. "I'll Be Loving You Always" remained her favorite song until the day she died.

Stalag Luft 1 Memorial

AFTERWORD

In a conversation with my wife a few days before Thanksgiving 2013, I lamented not knowing more about Jerry Kelly, the member of the Three Musketeers lost during the war. After all my research and interviews, he remained an enigma to me, leaving a gaping hole in my book. Bob and my father loved him like a brother and considered him the finest young man they'd ever known. Bob had named a son after him and still had Jerry's picture hanging on his den wall. In some of my father's church sermons to young people, he held Jerry up as an example of how to live high moral standards, stick to your principles, and still be a well-liked, fun-loving person, regardless of your circumstances.

During one of my conversations with Bob, he told me he'd lost contact with Jerry's family after moving to California. The only Kelly family member he thought might still be alive was a younger sister named Ruth, but he didn't have a clue how to find her. My attempts to discover more about Jerry failed. Not knowing where else to turn, I finally gave up. The lost musketeer's story seemed destined not to be told. Then fate stepped in.

While growing up in Salt Lake City, Ryan Kelly heard a few stories about his great-uncle Jerry, a pilot who died fighting in World War II, but no one in his family knew much about him. After losing two close friends in a tragic accident during the summer of 2013, Ryan pondered why death comes so early for some. While watching an interview with Pulitzer Prize-wining historian David McCullough, Ryan was profoundly moved by one of his statements: "We are all shaped by people we have never met." Ryan's thoughts turned to his great-uncle. He wondered why his family knew so little about him. There wasn't even a picture of Jerry in their family albums. Eager to test the validity of McCullough's statement, Ryan began a journey to rediscover his great-uncle—a quest that would take him from the dusty basement vault at Granite High School in Salt Lake City, where old yearbooks were stored, to California, where the two people who knew Jerry best still lived.[442]

Setting aside his other personal interests, Ryan spent nearly all his free time focused on his new pursuit. He discovered an old copy of Jerry's senior class yearbook, old newspaper stories, military records, and even a few of Jerry's old friends. They shared memories that painted the picture of a special young man everyone seemed to like and respect. Each of them recalled how deeply saddened they were when he didn't return home from the war, still missing his smile and sense of humor. While visiting the home of Jerry's best high school friend, Ryan learned that he and Jerry had joined the military together and had corresponded during the war. He introduced Ryan to a son he'd named after Jerry.[443]

Ryan felt prompted to write a sketch of his great-uncle's life and share what he'd discovered with family members and friends. At his father's suggestion, he mailed a copy to Jerry's younger sister, Ruth Kelly Worthen. She enjoyed reading the biographical sketch and shared additional memories of her brother with him over the phone. Once he learned that his widowed great-aunt had saved all of the letters Jerry had written to his family during the war, Ryan hopped on a plane and headed to Santa Cruz, California, to meet her in person.

While reading the box of letters Ruth had saved for more than seventy years, Ryan discovered that Jerry had two close friends in the Air Force—so close in fact, that members of their squadron called them the Three Musketeers. Ruth told him that she'd met Bob before Jerry went overseas, and that Don and his wife visited her family a few times after the war ended. She remembered reading that Don had passed away years earlier, but she didn't know about Bob, having lost track of him after he moved to the Los Angeles area.

Re-energized by his visit, Ryan continued his search. Finding Bob wasn't easy. However, his persistence finally paid off when the right Robert Sharp picked up the phone. Ryan's call startled Bob, who never expected to hear from anyone in Jerry's family again. After becoming acquainted on the phone, Bob excitedly told him, "Ken

Evans is writing a book about his father's military experiences, and Jerry is an important figure in the book. You need to get in contact with him!"

On the evening of November 29, 2013, I received the following e-mail:

My name is Ryan Kelly, and I live in Salt Lake. Over the past few months, I've been trying to learn more about my grandpa's younger brother, Jerry Kelly, who was killed in World War II. Our family has known very little about Jerry, and so I've made the effort to learn more about him.

I recently spoke with Bob Sharp, and he said that my great-uncle was good friends with your father, Don Evans. I have all the letters Jerry wrote to his mom during the war. Jerry mentions your dad often and wrote what a great guy he was.

Bob Sharp said you've done a lot of research about your dad's service in the war. I'd love to talk with you, if that would be okay. I have attached an essay I wrote about Jerry. I thought you'd be interested in reading it.

Surprised and excited, I immediately replied to Ryan's email. After corresponding several times, we agreed to meet for lunch. We hit it off as we talked about Bob, Jerry and my father. I brought him several pages from my manuscript that included information and stories about his great-uncle. He shared information from a few of the letters Jerry had written home to his mother during the war. Time that afternoon passed quickly, and we agreed to meet again soon.

Since that first luncheon, Ryan and I have met many times and become good friends. His great-aunt Ruth agreed to give me copies of all Jerry's letters. When I finally met her in person, she shared several memories of her brother with me. Thanks to Ryan's research, Ruth's stories, and the box of letters she saved, I was able to fill the void that surrounded the youngest member of the Three Musketeers and ringleader of the Five.

There was one more thing that I needed to do before completing my writing. In May of 2017, I traveled to Europe with my wife and sister and walked where my father had walked.

We visited the English countryside where he flew his final training missions. We crossed the English Channel and strolled along the beaches of Normandy where his first air base was located. We visited Paris, Reims, Versailles, and other places my father had written about during the war. We hiked through the rolling hills and dense forests of the Ardennes where he was shot down during the Battle of the Bulge.

As I sat under a tall pine tree near my father's crash site, I tried to imagine what it must have been like for him that Christmas Eve so many years ago, huddled under a similar tree, wondering if he'd ever see my mother again. Walking back to our car, I pictured his capture by SS Troops the following day and was unable to hold back the tears.

Next, we drove east through the beautiful Belgium countryside along his forced march route toward Frankfurt, Germany, where he experienced the best and the worst of human behavior.

Our final stop was Stalag Luft I just outside Barth, Germany. Nearly all traces of the POW camp and the nearby women's concentration camp are now gone. We had difficulty even finding the site. No one seemed to know anything about it. Finally, we had a chance encounter with a kind German woman who had discovered the camp on a bike ride the previous summer. After hearing our story, she graciously agreed to guide us to the isolated location. We were the only visitors there that day.

A simple stone monument with plaques in English and German stands in the middle of a secluded grassy area. There are also concrete markers identifying the location of each compound. As I wandered through the trees, grass, and wildflowers growing on the North 3 Compound site where my father was imprisoned, I was struck by how peaceful and serene it now appears. It was hard to imagine this had ever been a POW camp.

Suddenly, everything I knew my father had experienced flooded my mind—bitter cold barracks, near starvation, boredom, depression, poor sanitation, lice, infection, abusive treatment by guards. I envisioned the machine guns in the guard towers and the fenced compounds surrounded by coils of barbed wire.

That both my father and the POW campsite emerged as they had from their horrific war histories is truly inspiring.

I've known Bob and Jackie Sharp my entire life and have fond memories of visits with their family when I was growing up. Bob is the only veteran of World War II my father remained friends with after the war. In many ways, the two of them were very much alike—kind and friendly, fun loving, and blessed with the same witty, sarcastic sense of humor. I don't ever remember hearing them talk about the war when they were together. Bob knew it was a sensitive topic for my father and respected his desire to keep it in his past. During the years between the deaths of my parents, I lost track of him. When I discovered the regulation-bending letter he had written to my mother after my father was shot down, I called him on the phone. Since then, we have become close friends.

Through his war memoirs, mission reports, interviews, phone calls, and e-mails, Bob provided me with an inside look into the life of a fighter pilot during World War II. In doing so, he also helped me learn and understand more about my father. Bob knew him in a way no one else did. They loved, trusted, understood each other, and shared an uncommon bond. Even though the Three Musketeers were together for less than a year, they both developed that same relationship with Jerry and never fully recovered from his death.

As Bob and I collaborated on my writing project during the past few years, certain events have transpired in ways, according to him, "that are beyond coincidence." His explanation is that "Don and Jerry are having fun on the other side, using us as marionettes to ensure that we tell their story right." I want to believe that's true.

ACKNOWLEDGMENTS

I owe a debt of gratitude to many people for their help in writing my book, but none more so than to my mother. Her dedicated efforts to preserve detailed accounts of her and my father's early lives through writing, scrapbooking, and saving letters and memorabilia is truly remarkable. Later in her life, she finally gave me her blessing to write their story, but made me promise to wait until after she passed away to do so.

I'm deeply grateful to Bob Sharp as well. Reading his mission reports and listening to him recount his World War II memories was captivating. The details he shared and the images he painted while telling his stories made me feel like I was there with him and that the experiences had taken place recently, not seven decades before. I can't thank him enough for his unending support and friendship.

While searching out the missing story of his great-uncle, Ryan Kelly fortuitously found me as well. I'm indebted to Ryan for helping me fill in the missing pieces of Jerry's story and for his constant encouragement to "stick with it" to the end.

My deep appreciation goes to Doug Robinson, whose contributions far exceed those of an editor. He loved the story from the start and helped me believe that I was the right one to tell it. Thanks also to my talented graphic art designer, Dan Ruesch, and to my publishing consultant, Bruce Bracken, for their help in getting my manuscript published.

Prior to my father's death, he agreed to meet with Don Norton, a noted oral historian and retired English professor, who recorded memories of some of my father's World War II experiences. When Don learned that I was writing my book, he volunteered to help, hoping that others could hear the stories as well. Andrea Christensen, author and former English professor and author, Rebecca R. Merrill also took a special interest in my writing project. I'm grateful to each of them for their invaluable assistance editing and proofreading my early manuscripts.

Two authoritative works provide the foundation for nearly all credible World War II historical writings: *The United States Army in World War II* and *The Army Air Forces in World War II*. I relied heavily on these authoritative sources, finding them invaluable in my research and writing. I also gratefully acknowledge Timothy M. Grace, author of *Second to None: The History of the 368th Fighter Group*, along with the many other dedicated World War II organizations whose mission is to preserve the history of their fighting units and the stories of the brave men who were part of them.

My dear wife, Sandy, and my sister, Sue, have been my most devoted supporters. They patiently proofread countless manuscript drafts, providing support and encouragement. I can't thank them enough. It was fitting that the three of us were finally able to walk together where my father walked over 70 years ago.

NOTES

CHAPTER ONE

1   Yearbook Staff, *Lehision 1941: Volume 25*, Lehi High School Yearbook.
2   "Portrait of Educational Attainment in the United States: 2007," U.S. Census Bureau, Current Population Survey and Decennial Censuses, Figure 1.
3   Edith M. Stern, "Denver Students Learn Movie Making in the Classroom," Popular Science Monthly, April 1941, Issue 228.
4   Yearbook Staff, *Lehision 1941*.

CHAPTER TWO

5   Utah History to Go, "Utah's Interurbans: Predecessors to Light Rail," https://historytogo.utah.gov/utah_chapters/mining_and_railroads/ utahsinterurbans.html (accessed 15 Feb. 2013).
6   Susan King, "Before Lois Lane, Torchy Blane got the Scoop," http:// herocomplex.latimes.com/uncategorized/lois-lane-torchy-blane/ (accessed 15 February 2013).
7   Susan Evans, Donald N Evans, and LaRae Shelley, "Life History of Noble Evans."

CHAPTER THREE

8   University of Utah, "A Brief History of Fort Douglas," http://web.utah. edu/facilities/fd/history/history.html (accessed 13 Feb. 2013).

CHAPTER FOUR

9   Dr. Bruce Ashcroft, *We Wanted Wings: A History of the Aviation Cadet Program*, (Staff Historian: HQ AETC Office of History and Research 2005), 33, https://media.defense.gov/2015/Sep/11/2001329827/-1/-1/0/ AFD-150911-028.pdf. (accessed 15 Feb. 2013).
10   Ibid., 34
11   Ibid., 33

CHAPTER FIVE

12 Ashcroft, *We Wanted Wings*, 3.
13 National Museum of the U.S. Air Force, "Military Ballooning: The Spanish American War," http://www.nationalmuseum.af.mil/Visit/ MuseumExhibits/Factsheets/Display/tabid/509/Article/196758/lighter- than=air-flight.aspx (accessed 9 Mar. 2013).
14 W. Kevin Durden, "World War I from the Viewpoint of American Airmen," Airpower Journal: Summer 1988.
15 Ashcroft, *We Wanted Wings*, 9.
16 Durden, "World War I from the Viewpoint of American Airmen."
17 Ibid.
18 U.S. Air Force, "Missions Part One: From the Signal Corps to the Air Corps," http://www.airforce.com/learn-about/history/part1/ (accessed 9 Mar. 2013).
19 Ibid.
20 Wesley F. Craven and James L. Cate, eds., *The Army Air Forces in World War II*, Volume 6, *Men and Planes* (Chicago: The University of Chicago Press, 1955), 558–59.
21 Ibid., 560
22 Ashcroft, *We Wanted Wings*, 42.

CHAPTER SIX

23 Craven and Cate, *The Army Air Forces in World War II: Men and Planes*, 568.
24 Ibid, 569
25 Ibid.
26 National Museum of the U.S. Air Force, "Fairchild PT-19 Cornell," http://www.nationalmuseum.af.mil/Visit/MuseumExhibits/FactSheets/ Disply/tabid/509/Article/198088/fairchild-pt-19a-cornell.aspx (accessed 15 Mar. 2007).
27 Brady School of Aviation, *Curtis Field Flight Book: Class 44-B*, (Brady, Texas), 1943.

CHAPTER SEVEN

28 Goodfellow Air Force Base, "A History of Goodfellow," http://www. goodfellow.af.mil/AboutUs/FactSheets/Disply/tabid/365/Article/372978/ goodfellow-ari-force-base-history.aspx (accessed 15 Mar. 2013).
29 Texas State Historical Association, "Goodfellow Air Force Base,"http:// www.tshaonline.org/handbook/online/articles/qbg01 (accessed 15 Mar. 2013).
30 Craven and Cate, *The Army Air Forces in World War II: Men and Planes*, 569–71.

31   National Museum of the U.S. Air Force, "Vultee BT-13B Valiant," http://
      www.nationalmuseum.af.mil/Visit/MuseumExhibits/FactSheets/Display/
      tabid/509/Article/196294/vultee-bt-13b-valiant.aspx (accessed 20 Apr.
      2013).

32   Robert D. Sharp, "War Memoirs."

                            CHAPTER EIGHT

33   Moore Field, *Class 44-B: Volume Three, Number Two* (Moore Field,
      Mission, Texas, 1943).

34   Craven and Cate, *The Army Air Forces in World War II: Men and
      Planes*, 572–73.

35   History Flight, "North American AT-6 / Texan," http://www.
      historyflight.com/nw/aircraft_at6texan.php (accessed 8 Apr. 2013).

36   Matagorda Island, "Matagorda Island: A True History," http://www.
      matagordaisland.com/history.htm (accessed 29 Mar. 2013)

37   Ibid.

38   "Matagorda Island," Calhoun County Museum, http://www.
      calhouncountymuseum.org/?page_id=94 (accessed 30 Mar. 2013).

39   Matagorda Island, "Matagorda Island: A True History."

40   Wayne H. McAlister and Martha K. McAlister, *Matagorda Island, A
      Naturalist's Guide* (Austin: University of Texas, 1993), 78.

41   Abandoned & Little Known Airfields, "Matagorda Island AFB," http://
      www.airfields-freeman.com/TX/Airfields_TX_Corpus_NE.htm (accessed
      20 Mar. 2013).

                            CHAPTER NINE

42   "Republic P-47D," National Museum of the US Air Force: Factsheet,"
      http://www.nationalmuseum.af.mil/Visit/MuseumExhibits/FactSheets/
      Display/tabid/509/Article/196276/republic-p-47d-bubble-canopy-version.
      aspx (accessed 4 Apr. 2013).

43   Defense Media Network, "Classic Wings: P-47 Thunderbolt," http://
      www.defensemedianetwork.com/stories/classic-wings-p-47-thunderbolt/
      (accessed 4 Apr. 2013).

44   "Republic P-47 Thunderbolt," The Aviation History Online Museum,
      http://www.aviation-history.com/republic/p47.html (accessed 4 Apr.
      2013).

45   Ryan Kelly, "Loving Those Who Have Gone Before Us."

46   Ibid.

47   SportsLifer, "Great NCAA Basketball Tournament Upsets," http://
      sportslifer.wordpress.com/tag/college-basketball (accessed 24 April
      2013).

48   William B. Colgan, *Allied Strafing in World War II*, (Jefferson, North
      Carolina: McFarland & Company, Inc., 2010), 42–43.

49   Ibid., 41, 43

50   Ibid., 44

51   National Museum of the USAF, "AAF Fighter Escort," http://www. nationalmuseum.af.mil/Visit/MuseumExhibits/FactSheets/Display/ tabid/509/Article/196181/aaf-fighter-escort.aspx (accessed 1May 2013).

CHAPTER TEN

52   Sloan E. Dawson, "World War II Nebraska Army Airfields Bruning Army Airfield," http://www.oldcottonmill.com/Research/research_n/NE%20 Air%20Bases.pdf (accessed 16 Apr. 2013).

53   "Bruning Army Airfield," Nebraska State Historical Society http://www. nebraskahistory.org/publish/markers/texts/bruning_army_air_field.htm (accessed 16 Apr. 2013).

54   Army Air Forces Statistical Digest: World War II, "U.S. World War II Aircraft Loss Statistics During Flight Training," http://www.taphilo.com/ history/WWII/Loss-Figures-Aircraft-USA-Training.shtml (accessed 3 Apr. 2013).

55   "Yanks Launch New Attack on Peninsula," *The Stars and Stripes: Continental Edition*, July 4, 1944, http://www.army.mil/d-day/ (accessed 14 Jul. 2014).

CHAPTER ELEVEN

56   Rueben Goossens, "R.M.S. Queen Elizabeth," http://www.ssmaritime. com/RMS-Queen-Elizabeth.htm (accessed 22 Apr. 2013).

57   Ibid.

58   Ibid.

59   Ibid.

60   "Atcham," American Air Museum in Britain, http://www. americanairmuseum.com/place/19 (accessed 23 Apr. 2013).

61   Robert D. Sharp, "War Memoirs."

62   The National WWII Museum, "Take a Closer Look at Ration Books," http://www.nationalww2museum.org/learn/education/for-students/ww2- history/take-a-closer-look/ration-books.html (accessed 24 Apr. 2013).

63   Ames Historical Society, "World War II Rationing on the U.S. Homefront," http://www.ameshistory.org/ (accessed 28 Apr. 2013).

64   Maury Klein, *A Call to Arms America for World War II* (Bloomsburg Press, 2015), p. 432.

65   Ames Historical Society, "World War II Rationing on the U.S. Homefront."

66   Roger Mola, "The Army Back Home," Air and Space/Smithsonian, May 2015, p. 38.

CHAPTER TWELVE

67 9th Air Force Association, "Ninth Air Force History," http://www.home. earthlink.net/~iversonom/9afhistory.html (accessed 29 Apr. 2013).
68 Ibid.
69 Timothy M. Grace, *Second to None, The History of the 368th Fighter Group s* (The 368th Fighter Group Association, 2006), 20.
70 "Cardonville A-3," Abandoned, Forgotten & Little Known Airfields in Europe, http://www.forgottenairfields.com/france/lower-normandy/ calvados/cardonville-a-3-s1104.html (accessed 29 Apr. 2013).
71 National Museum of the U.S. Air Force, "V-1 Buzz Bomb," http:// www.nationalmuseum.af.mil/Visit/MuseumExhibits/FactSheets/Display/ tabid/509/Article/196158/v-1-buzz-bomb.aspx (accessed 1 May 2015).
72 National Museum of the U.S. Air Force, "Republic/Ford JB-2 (V-1 Buzz Bomb)," http://www.nationalmuseum.af.mil/Visit/MuseumExhibits/ FactSheets/Display/tabid/509/Article/196227/republicford-jb-2-loon-v-1-buzz-bomb.aspx (accessed 23 Apr. 2015).
73 National Museum of the U.S. Air Force, "V-1 Buzz Bomb."
74 456th Fighter Interceptor Squadron, "V-1 Flying Bomb: Defense of the Realm," http://www.456fis.org/V-1_FLYING_BOMB.htm (accessed 2 Oct. 2014).
75 Ibid.
76 National Museum of the U.S. Air Force, "V-2," Rocket," http://www. nationalmuseum.af.mil/Visit/MuseumExhibits/FactSheets/Display/ tabid/509/Article/196226/v-2-meillerwagen.aspx (accessed 23 Apr. 2015).
77 National Museum of the U.S. Air Force, "German V-Weapons: Desperate Measures," http://www.nationalmuseum.af.mil/Visit/MuseumExhibits/ FactSheets/Display/tabid/509/Article/196145/german-v-weapons-desperate-measures.aspx (accessed 1 May 2015).
78 National Museum of the U.S. Air Force, "German V-Weapons Fact Sheet," http://www.nationalmuseum.af.mil/Visit/Museum-Exhibits/Fact-Sheets/Display/Article/196722/slave-labor-built-v-weapons/ (accessed 30 Apr. 2013).
79 Father Don Cleary, *Chaplains Diary,* Newsletter published for friends at Cornell University, Printed in the 368th Fighter Group Association Newsletter, September 1988.

CHAPTER THIRTEEN

80 "Chartres Cathedral," The City of Chartres, http://chartrescathedral.net/ the-city-of-chartres/ (accessed 14 Sept. 2013).
81 Grace, *Second to None, The History of the 368th Fighter Group*, 81–82.
82 Ibid., 83–84

83   Office of Air Force History United States Air Force, *Condensed Analysis of the Ninth Air Force in the European Theater of Operations* (Washington, D.C.: 1984), 8–9, http://www.afhso.af.mil/shared/media/document/AFD-100924-018.pdf (accessed 14 Sept. 2013).

84   Ibid., 27

85   Ibid., 81–83

86   Cleary, *Chaplains Diary*, September 1988.

87   France.fr Official Website of France, "Liberation of Paris," http://ww2db.com/battle_spec.php?battle_id=153 (accessed 15 Sept. 2013).

88   C N Trueman "The Liberation of Paris," http://www.historylearningsite.co.uk/liberation_of_paris.htm (accessed 15 Sept. 2013).

89   Ibid.

90   Ibid.

91   France Interactive, "Relive the Liberation of Paris in WWII," http://www.france24.com/en/20140820-paris-wwii-liberation-nazi-occupation-battle-france-world-war-two-webdoc/ (accessed 20 Aug. 2014).

92   Kelly Bell, "Is Paris Burning? Liberating the City of Light," http://www.warfarehistorynetwork.com/daily/wwii/is-paris-burning-liberating-the-city-of-light/ (accessed 18 Oct. 2016).

93   Ibid.

94   France, "Liberation of Paris."

95   Jay Nordlinger, "A Colonel at Chartres," *National Review,* http://www.nationalreview.com/corner/266849/colonel-chartres-jay-nordlinger (accessed 14 Sept. 2013).

CHAPTER FOURTEEN

96   Laon Tourist Guide, "Laon: Town Guide," http://www.informationfrance.com/laon.php (accessed 14 Sept. 2013).

97   Ronald V., "Abandoned and Little Known Airfields: France, Laon-Athies," http://www.ronaldv.nl/abandoned/airfields/FR/picardy/aisne.html (accessed 14 Sept. 2013).

98   Grace, *Second to None, The History of the 368th Fighter Group*, 90.

99   Richard P. Hallion, "The Day After D-Day," Air and Space/Smithsonian, May 2015, 47.

100 Grace, *Second to None, The History of the 368th Fighter Group*, 91.

101 Ibid.

102 National Museum of the U.S. Air Force, "Fighters and Flak," http://www.nationalmuseum.af.mil/Visit/MuseumExhibits//FactSheets/Display/tabid/509/Article/196165/fighters-and-flak.aspx (accessed 1 May 2015).

103 Lloyd Clark, "Operation Market Garden Reconsidered," *World War II Magazine*, http://www.historynet.com/operation-market-garden-reconsidered.htm (accessed 23 Nov. 2013).

104 Ibid.

105 Ibid.

106 Ibid.

107 Ibid.

108 Grace, *Second to None, The History of the 368th Fighter Group*, 91.

109 French Moments, "The Coronation of the Kings of France in Reims" https://frenchmoments.eu/the-coronation-of-the-kings-of-france-in-reims/ (accessed 21 Aug. 2014).

110 Grace, *Second to None, The History of the 368th Fighter Group*, 92.

111 Ibid.

112 Ibid.

113 Ibid., 93

114 Ibid., 95

CHAPTER FIFTEEN

115 Jennifer Rosenberg, "Hitler Facts," http://history1900s.about.com/od/hitleradolf/a/Hitler-Facts.htm (accessed 9 Mar. 2014).

116 Ibid.

117 Ibid.

118 Stephanie L. McKinney, "Stalin Joins the Allies," About.com, http://history1900s.about.com/od/people/ss/Stalin_11.htm (accessed 25 Aug. 2014).

119 This Day in History, "Assassination plot against Hitler fails: July 20," http://www.history.com/this-day-in-history/assassination-plot-against-hitler-fails (accessed 12 Nov. 2013).

120 Ibid.

121 Ibid.

122 Hugh M. Cole, *The Ardennes: Battle of the Bulge* (United States Army in World War II, European Theater of Operations), (Washington D.C.: 1965), 1–6, http://www.history.army.mil/books/wwii/7-8/7-8_CONT.HTM (accessed 21 Oct. 2013).

123 Ibid., 2, 9

124 Ibid., 12

125 National Museum of the U.S. Air Force, "Messerschmitt Me 262A Schwalbe," http://www.nationalmuseum.af.mil/Visit/MuseumExhibits/FactSheets/Display/tabid/509/Article/196266/messerschmitt-me-262a-schwalbe.aspx (accessed 20 Apr. 2015).

126 C. Peter Chen, "Peenemünde Army Research Center," https://m.ww2db.com/facility/Peenem%C3%BCnde_Army_Research_Center/ (accessed 20 Apr. 2015).

127 Charles B. MacDonald, *The Siegfried Line Campaign* (Center of Military History, United States Army, Washington D.C., 1993), 30–36, http://www.history.army.mil/html/books/007/7-7-1/CMH_Pub_7-7-1.pdf (accessed 14 Jan. 2014).

CHAPTER SIXTEEN

128 "Our Lady of Chièvres," Devotion to Our Lady, http://
devotiontoourlady.com/november.html (accessed 14 Sept. 2013).

129 "Chièvres Air Base," *NSOS*, https://www.nshq.nato.int/nsos/about/
chievres-air-base/ (accessed 14 Sept. 2013).

130 Ibid.

131 Grace, *Second to None, The History of the 368th Fighter Group*, 96.

132 Ibid.

133 Vernon V. (Pat) Murphy, "Mission #51," Printed in the 368th Fighter
Group Association Newsletter, rewritten with additional comments by
Donald N Evans.

134 Grace, *Second to None, The History of the 368th Fighter Group*, 97.

135 Ibid., 98

136 Ibid., 99

137 Amy Berish, "FDR and Polio," Franklin D. Roosevelt: Presidential
Library and Museum, http://www.fdrlibrary.marist.edu/aboutfdr/polio.
html (accessed 7 Mar. 2014).

138 Ibid.

139 Ibid.

140 Grace, *Second to None, The History of the 368th*, 99.

CHAPTER SEVENTEEN

141 "Aachen (Germany)," *Encyclopedia Britannica*, http://www.britannica.
com/EBchecked/topic/200/Aachen (accessed 2 Nov. 2013).

142 Mac Donald, *The Siegfried Line Campaign*, 281, 307.

143 Ibid., 307

144 Stephen E. Ambrose, *Citizen Soldiers: The U.S. Army from the
Normandy Beaches to the Bulge to the Surrender of Germany* (New
York City: Simon & Schuster, 1998), 147.

145 Ted Ballard, "Rhineland: The U.S. Army Campaign of World War II,"
U.S. Army Center of Military History, http://www.history.army.mil/
brochures/rhineland/rhineland.htm (11 Apr. 2013).

146 Mac Donald, *The Siegfried Line Campaign*, 307.

147 Grace, *Second to None, The History of the 368th Fighter Group*, 99.

148 Lt. Colonel Dave Grossman, "Trained to Kill," 10 Aug. 1998, http://
www.waldorflibrary.org/images/stories/Journal_Articles/RB6201.pdf
(accessed 11 Apr. 2013).

149 Kendra Cherry, "Pavlov's Dogs," http://psychology.about.com/od/
classicalconditioning/a/pavlovs-dogs.htm (accessed 11 Apr. 2013).

150 Grace, *Second to None, The History of the 368th*, 101.

151 MacDonald, *The Siegfried Line Campaign*, 317.

152 Ibid., 320

153 Ibid.

CHAPTER EIGHTEEN

154 Grace, *Second to None, The History of the 368th Fighter Group*, 356–60.
155 Ibid., 104
156 Ibid., 106
157 Andreas Parsch, "5-Inch Rockets," Directory of U.S. Military Rockets and Missiles, http://www.designation-systems.net/dusrm/app4/5in-rockets.html (accessed 28 Aug. 2014).

CHAPTER NINETEEN

158 Grace, *Second to None, The History of the 368th Fighter Group*, 107.
159 Ibid., 239–40
160 Ibid., 108
161 Ibid., 109
162 Ken Barrett, "The Battle of Hürtgen Forest: World War II," http://www.hurtgen1944.homestead.com (accessed 25 Oct. 2015).
163 Ibid.
164 Grace, *Second to None, The History of the 368th Fighter Group*, 109.
165 Ibid., 109
166 Ibid.
167 Ibid.
168 "World War II on the Radio," ORTAC.com: Old Time Radio Catalog, http://www.otrcat.com/wwii-on-the-radio.html (accessed 26 May 2015).
169 Ibid., 110
170 Ibid.
171 Cleary, *Chaplains Diary*, March 1990.
172 Kelly, "Loving Those Who Have Gone Before Us."

CHAPTER TWENTY

173 Grace, *Second to None, The History of the 368th Fighter Group*, 114.
174 "Fighter-Bomber is easiest to fly: Bad weather over target balks at publisher's start on mission," Hearst Newspaper Series #3, reprinted in Second to None, The History of the 368th Fighter *Group*, 365.
175 Grace, *Second to None, The History of the 368th Fighter Group*, 115.
176 C.J. Schexnayder, "Army vs. Navy, 1944: The original game of the century," SBNation.com, http://www.sbnation.com/ncaa-football/2011/12/9/2623172/army-navy-game-2011-history (accessed 17 Sept. 2016).
177 Ibid., 118
178 Ibid., 119

179 "The Bombing of Civilians in World War II," World Future Fund, http://
     www.worldfuturefund.org/wffmaster/Reading/war.crimes/World.war.2/
     Bombing.htm (accessed 4 Nov. 2013).
180 Ibid.
181 Ibid.
182 Grace, *Second to None, The History of the 368th Fighter Group*, 120.

CHAPTER TWENTY-ONE

183 Office of Air Force History United States Air Force, *Condensed Analysis*,
     40.
184 Cole, *The Ardennes*, 21.
185 Carlo D'Este, "December 16, 1944: Ardennes Offensive Begins," The
     History Reader, http://www.thehistoryreader.com/modern-history/
     december-16-1944-ardennes-offensive-begins-abysmal-failure-allied-
     intelligence/ (accessed 2 Oct. 2013).
186 Ibid.
187 Roger Cirillo, "Ardennes-Alsace," Office of the Chief of Military History
     (2003), 5–6, http://www.history.army.mil/brochures/ardennes/aral.htm
     (accessed 2 Oct. 2013).
188 Ibid., 5, 7
189 Cole, *The Ardennes*, 50.
190 Ibid., 17, 22
191 Ibid., 22, 28
192 Ibid., 12
193 Ibid.
194 "*Schutzstaffel,* The Waffen-SS," Jewish Virtual Library, https://www.
     jewishvirtuallibrary.org/jsource/Holocaust/waffenss.html (accessed 9
     Sept. 2014).
195 Glen B. Infield, *Skorzeny: Hitler's Commando* (New York: St. Martin's
     Press, 1981), 78.
196 Ibid., 12, 16
197 Ibid., 22, 26
198 Ibid., 37, 41–45
199 Ibid., 80, 82
200 Ibid., 83–84
201 Samuel W. Mitcham, Jr., *Panzers in Winter* (Mechanicsburg, PA, 2006:
     Stackpole Books), 32.
202 Ibid., 33
203 Cole, *The Ardennes*, 650.
204 Ibid.

CHAPTER TWENTY-TWO

205 Cole, *The Ardennes*, 260.

206 Ibid., 259–60
207 Elizabeth M. Collins, "The Battle of Lanzerath," *Soldiers Magazine"* http:// soldiers.dodlive.mil/2014/12/the-battle-of-lanzerath/ (accessed 16 Dec. 2014).
208 Cole, *The Ardennes*, 260.
209 G. Infield, *Skorzeny: Hitler's Commando*, 84.
210 Cole, *The Ardennes*, 261.
211 Wesley F. Craven and James L. Cate, eds., *The Army Air Forces in World War II*, Volume 3, *Europe: Argument to V-E Day* (Chicago: The University of Chicago Press, 1955), 683.
212 Ibid.
213 Ibid.
214 D'Este, "December 16, 1944: Ardennes Offensive Begins."
215 Cole, *The Ardennes*, 90.
216 Ibid., 261
217 Ibid.
218 Ibid.
219 Ibid.
220 "The Malmedy Massacre," Jewish Virtual Library, http://www. jewishvirtuallibrary.org/jsource/ww2/malmedy2.html (accessed 9 Oct. 2013).
221 Ibid.
222 Cole, *The Ardennes*, 263.
223 Ibid., 265–66
224 Ibid., 170
225 "Remembering the Invisible Soldiers of the Battle of the Bulge," U.S. Memorial Wereth, http://www.wereth.org/en/history (accessed 24 Nov. 2013).
226 Torsten Ove, "Wereth 11 of WWII," *Pittsburgh Post-Gazette*, 7 Nov. 2010, http://www.post-gazette.com/pg/10311/1101015-109.stm (accessed 24 Nov. 2013).
227 Ibid.
228 Cole, *The Ardennes*, 272.
229 Ibid., 277–80
230 Craven and Cate, *Europe: Argument to V-E Day*, 685.
231 Colonel S. L. A. Marshall, *Bastogne: The First Eight Days* (Washington, D.C.: Infantry Journal Press, 1946), 8–10, http://www.history.army.mil/ books/wwii/Bastogne/bast-fm.htm (accessed 26 Oct. 2013).
232 Craven and Cate, *Europe: Argument to V-E Day*, 687.
233 Grace, *Second to None, The History of the 368th Fighter Group*, 123–24.
234 Ibid., 123
235 Confidential Combat Statement filed by 2nd Lt. Donald N Evans on December 17, 1944, with additional personal mission comments later added by Donald N Evans.
236 Grace, *Second to None, The History of the 368th Fighter Group*, 124.
237 G. Infield, *Skorzeny: Hitler's Commando*, 78.

CHAPTER TWENTY-THREE

238 Rick Atkinson, *The Guns at Last Light: The War in Western Europe, 1944–1945* (New York: Henry Holt and Company, 2013) 440–42, 449.

239 Cole, *The Ardennes*, 265–66.

240 Ibid., 266–67

241 Ibid., 267

242 Ibid., 267–68

243 Ibid., 267

244 Ibid., 268

245 Ibid.

246 Ibid., 268–69

247 Ibid., 268

248 Ibid., 268

249 "Bastogne," Bastogne Municipal Website, http://www.bastogne.be/ (accessed 21 Nov. 2013).

250 Marshall, *Bastogne*, 1.

251 Ibid., 15

252 Cole, *The Ardennes*, 309.

253 Colonel Edward Shames, "The Siege of Bastogne," American Veterans Center, http://www.americanveteranscenter.org/wwiichronicals/issue-xxxiii-winter-200506/the-siege-of-bastogne-e-company-506th-parachute-infantry-101st-airborne-the-band-of-brothers/ (accessed 21 Nov. 2013).

254 Marshall, *Bastogne*, 16.

255 Cole, *The Ardennes*, 284.

256 Ibid., 670

257 Grace, *Second to None, The History of the 368th Fighter Group*, 125.

258 Cole, *The Ardennes*, 338.

259 Samuel W. Mitcham, Jr., *Panzers in Winter*, 85.

260 Cole, *The Ardennes*, 339–42

261 Ibid., 268, 337–39

262 Marshall, *Bastogne*, 110.

263 Cole, *The Ardennes*, 670.

CHAPTER TWENTY-FOUR

264 G. Infield, *Skorzeny: Hitler's Commando*, 78, 88.

265 Ibid., 91, 165

266 Stanley Weintraub, "General George S. Patton and the Battle of the Bulge," MHQ: The Quarterly Journal of Military History (Winter 2007 Issue).

267 Ibid.

268 Cole, *The Ardennes*, 509–10.

269 Weintraub, "General George S. Patton.

270 D'Este, "December 16, 1944: Ardennes Offensive Begins."

271 Weintraub, "General George S. Patton."
272 "Biography," The Official Website of General George Patton, http://www.generalpatton.com/ (accessed 28 Oct. 2013).
273 Ibid.
274 Ibid.
275 Alan Axelrod, *Patton: a Biography*, (London, United Kingdom: Palgrave Macmillan, 2006), 105–07.
276 Weintraub, "General George S. Patton."
277 Charles M. Province, "The Slapping Incidents,"*93rd Evacuation Hospital,* http://www.members.tripod.com/msg_fisher/93evac-9.html (accessed 22 Nov. 2013).
278 Ibid.
279 From the excerpts of President Roosevelt's Press Conference, December 17, 1943.
280 Charles M. Province, "The Third Army in World War II," The Patton Society Research Library, http://www.pattonhq.com/textfiles/thirdhst.html (accessed 22 Nov. 2013).
281 John Elliot, "Guns of George S. Patton," *Guns.com,* http://www.guns.com/2011/06/17/the-known-and-lesser-known-carry-guns-of-george-s-patton/ (accessed 22 Nov. 2013).
282 Weintraub, "General George S. Patton."
283 Ibid.
284 "Biography," The Official Website of General George Patton

CHAPTER TWENTY-FIVE

285 Cole, *The Ardennes*, 393–96.
286 Ibid., 345, 369
287 Marshall, *Bastogne*, 99–106.
288 Cole, *The Ardennes*, 357.
289 G. Infield, *Skorzeny: Hitler's Commando*, 88.
290 Craven and Cate, *Europe: Augment to V-E Day*, 688.
291 Cole, *The Ardennes*, 364, 369–70.
292 Ibid., 407
293 Ibid., 407–09
294 Ibid, 411, 422
295 Marshall, *Bastogne*, 107–10.
296 Weintraub, "General George S. Patton."
297 Cole, *The Ardennes*, 390.
298 Grace, *Second to None, The History of the 368th Fighter Group,* 126.
299 Cole, *The Ardennes*, 371, 376.
300 Mitcham, *Panzers in Winter*, 91.
301 Cole., 373
302 Marshall, *Bastogne,* 115–16.
303 Ibid., 116
304 Ibid., 117–18

305 Cole, *The Ardennes*, 390.
306 Grace, *Second to None, The History of the 368th Fighter Group*, 126–27.
307 Craven and Cate, *Europe: Argument to V-E Day*, 688.

CHAPTER TWENTY-SIX

308 Weintraub, "General George S. Patton."
309 Office of Air Force History United States Air Force, *Condensed Analysis*, 42.
310 Craven and Cate, *Europe: Argument to V-E Day*, 689.
311 Cole, *The Ardennes: Battle of the Bulge*, 470.
312 Craven and Cate, *Europe: Argument to V-E Day*, 689–93.
313 Mitcham, *Panzers in Winter*, 150.
314 Cole, *The Ardennes*, 374–76.
315 Atkinson, *The Guns at Last Light*, 444.
316 G. Infield, *Skorzeny: Hitler's Commando*, 87, 88.
317 Grace, *Second to None, The History of the 368th Fighter Group*, 127.
318 Ibid.
319 Cole, *The Ardennes*, 376.
320 Atkinson, *The Guns at Last Light*, 462.

CHAPTER TWENTY-SEVEN

321 Marshall, *Bastogne*, 531.
322 "What Is Angle of Attack?" http://www.boeing.com/commercial/aeromagazine/aero_12/whatisaoa.pdf (accessed 18 Nov. 2016).
323 Junaid Ali, "Can Airplanes Fly Upside Down?" http://www.decodedscience.org/can-airplanes-fly-upside-down/25167 (accessed 12 Nov. 2016).
324 "Very Low-Level Military Static Line Parachute Systems," http://www.combatreform.org/llparachute.htm (accessed 15 Jan. 2014).
325 Marshall, *Bastogne*, 134–35.

CHAPTER TWENTY-EIGHT

326 Craven and Cate, *Europe: Argument to V-E Day*, 697.
327 Ibid.
328 Ibid., 701
329 Ibid., 698
330 Gifford B. Doxee, "The Experiences of a POW: Transfer to Muhlberg," http://www.go2war2.nl/artikel/1730/Gifford-E-Doxee-the-experiences-of-a-POW.htm?page=11 (accessed 2 Nov. 2014).
331 Craven and Cate, *Europe: Argument to V-E Day*, 699, 701.
332 Atkinson, *The Guns at Last Light: The War in Western Europe*, 469–70.

333 Grace, *Second to None, The History of the 368th Fighter Group*, 130.
334 Ibid.
335 Craven and Cate, *Europe: Argument to V-E Day*, 701.
336 Ibid., 702
337 Grace, *Second to None, The History of the 368th Fighter Group*, 131–32.
338 "Koblenz—Germany's most beautiful corner," Koblenz Verbindet, http://www.koblenz.de/stadtleben_kultur/koblenz_allgemeine_infos_e.html (accessed 7 Mar. 2016).
339 Grace, *Second to None, The History of the 368th Fighter Group*, 132.
340 C. Peter Chen, "World War II Database: Battle of the Bulge," http://ww2db.com/battle_spec.php?battle_id=42 (accessed 7 Nov. 2014).
341 The U.S. Army, "Battle of the Bulge: December 1944–January 1945." http://www.army.mil/botb/ (accessed 8 Mar. 2016).

CHAPTER TWENTY-NINE

342 Grace, *Second to None, The History of the 368th Fighter Group*, 133.
343 Kenneth W. Simmons, *Kriegie*, (New York: Thomas Nelson & Sons, 1960), 54–56.
344 Dale Andrade, "Luzon 1944–1945," U.S. Army Center of Military History, http://www.history.army.mil/brochures/luzon/72-28.htm (accessed 7 Mar. 2016).

CHAPTER THIRTY

345 "World War II Encyclopedia--Forty and Eight Boxcar," Skylighters, http://www.skylighters.org/encyclopedia/fortyandeight.html (accessed 11 Nov. 2014).
346 Grace, *Second to None, The History of the 368th Fighter Group*, 135.
347 Ibid.

CHAPTER THIRTY-TWO

348 Vinetastadt Barth, "History of the City" http://www.stadt-barth.de/englisch/history.htm (accessed 23 Nov. 2014).
349 Ibid.
350 Military Intelligence, "American Prisoners of War in Germany: Stalag Luft I," Prepared by the Military Intelligence Service, War Department, 1 November 1945.
351 Ibid.
352 Ibid.
353 Hubert Zemke as told to Roger A. Freeman, *Zemke's Stalag: The Final Days of World War II* (Washington and London: Smithsonian Institution Press, 1991), 19–20.

354 Ibid.

355 Ibid., 20, 35

356 Ibid., 35–36

357 Ibid., 37

358 Military Intelligence, "American Prisoners of War in Germany: Stalag Luft I."

359 David Rolf, *Prisoners of the Reich: Germany's Captives 1939–1945* (London: Leo Cooper, 1988), 98.

360 Donald L. Miller, *Masters of the Air: America's Bomber Boys Who Fought the Air War Against Germany* (New York: 2006), 405.

361 Ibid., 408–09

362 Robert R. Swartz, "The Kriegies," Stalag Luft I Online, http://www.merkki.com/swartzrobert.htm (accessed 11 Nov. 2014).

363 Zemke and Freeman, *Zemke's Stalag,* 24–27.

364 Ibid., 27–28

365 Ibid., 28

366 Ibid., 17

367 Military Intelligence, "American Prisoners of War in Germany: Stalag Luft I."

368 Ibid.

369 "Hitler Descends into his bunker," History.com This Day in History, https://www.history.com/this-day-in-history/hitler-descends-into-his-bunker (accessed 22 Nov. 2014).

370 "POW-WOW," Stalag Luft I Online, http://www.merkki.com/powwow.htm (accessed 18 Jan. 2015).

371 Rolf, *Prisoners of the Reich,* 87.

372 Zemke and Freeman, *Zemke's Stalag,* 33, 34.

373 Ibid., 31–32

374 Ibid., 32

375 Ibid., 33

376 "POW-WOW," Stalag Luft I Online.

377 History Learning Site, "The Red Cross: and World War Two," http://www.historylearningsite.co.uk/red_cross_and_world_war_two.htm (accessed 17 Nov. 2014).

CHAPTER THIRTY-THREE

378 Military Intelligence, "American Prisoners of War in Germany: Stalag Luft I."

379 Mayo Clinic, "Diseases and Conditions: Lice," http://www.mayoclinic.org/diseases-conditions/lice/basics/definition/con-20021627 (accessed 19 Dec. 2014).

380 "Listing by Rooms of the POWs at Stalag Luft I," Stalag Luft I Online, http://www.merkki.com/north3.htm (accessed 19 Nov. 2014).

381 Military Intelligence, "American Prisoners of War in Germany: Stalag Luft I."

382 Allen D. Young, "Allen Dahl Young: The Diary of a Prisoner of War," *Utah Historical Quarterly*, Summer 1998.

CHAPTER THIRTY-FIVE

383 Zemke and Freeman, *Zemke's Stalag,* 57.

384 Military Intelligence, "American Prisoners of War in Germany: Stalag Luft I."

385 Andy Rooney, "Nazi Camp Held Galaxy of U.S. Aces," *Stars and Stripes: May–June* 1945.

386 Zemke and Freeman, *Zemke's Stalag,* 60–61.

387 Ibid., 61–62

388 Ibid.

389 John Vietor, "Time Out," Stalag Luft I Online, http://www.merkki.com/the_guards.htm (accessed 12 Jan. 2015).

390 "Patton's Third Army Crosses the Rhine," World War II Day by Day: The Daily Chronicles of World War II, https://ww2days.com/pattons-third-army-crosses-rhine-2.html (accessed 28 Dec. 2014).

391 Ibid.

392 Zemke and Freeman, *Zemke's Stalag,* 65.

393 Atkinson, *The Guns at Last Light: The War in Western Europe,* 522–23.

394 Forrest C. Pogue, *The Supreme Command* (Washington, 1954), United States Army in World War II, 479–91.

395 "President Franklin D. Roosevelt Dies," The History Channel, http://www.history.com/this-day-in-history/president-franklin-d-roosevelt-dies (accessed 13 Jan. 2015).

396 Zemke and Freeman, *Zemke's Stalag,* 66.

397 Ibid., 69

398 Ibid., 73–74

399 Ibid., 71

400 Ibid., 75–77

401 "Hitler Descends Into His Bunker."

402 Zemke and Freeman, *Zemke's Stalag,* 79

403 Ibid., 81–82

CHAPTER THIRTY-SIX

404 Ibid., 85

405 Ibid.

406 Military Intelligence, "American Prisoners of War in Germany: Stalag Luft I."

407 Zemke and Freeman, *Zemke's Stalag,* 87.

408 Ibid., 91

409 Miller, *Masters of the Air*, 513.
410 Tilman Remme, "The Battle for Berlin in World War Two," http://www.bbc.co.uk/history/worldwars/wwtwo/berlin_01.shtml (accessed 14 Jan. 2015).
411 Ibid.
412 Ibid.
413 Ibid.
414 Ladislas Farago, *The Last Days of Patton* (New York: McGraw-Hill Book Company, 1981), 207.
415 Miller, *Masters of the Air*, 514.
416 Zemke and Freeman, *Zemke's Stalag*, 102–03.
417 Miller, *Masters of the Air*, 513.
418 Zemke and Freeman, *Zemke's Stalag*, 97, 110.
419 "Germany surrenders unconditionally to the Allies at Reims," This Day in History, http://www.history.com/this-day-in-history/germany-surrenders-unconditionally-to-the-allies-at-reims (accessed 15 Jan. 2015).
420 Barbara Maranzani "Remembering V-E Day," The History Channel, http://www.history.com/news/remembering-v-e-day (accessed 17 Jan. 2015).
421 Miller, *Masters of the Air*, 510.
422 Zemke and Freeman, *Zemke's Stalag*, 111.
423 Ibid., 113–14
424 John W. Howland, "Operation Revival: Rescuing the POWs from Stalag Luft I," http://www.91stbombgroup.com/91st_tales/07_operation_revival.pdf (accessed 20 Jan. 2015).

CHAPTER THIRTY-SEVEN

425 Zemke and Freeman, *Zemke's Stalag*, 113.
426 The Cigarette Camps: U.S. Army Camps in the Le Havre Area – Camp Lucky Strike, http://www.skylighters.org/special/cigcamps/cigbib.html (accessed 21 Jan. 2015).
427 Oscar G. Richard III, *Kriegie: an American POW in Germany*, (Baton Rouge, Louisiana State University Press 2000), 104–05.
428 Ibid., 105
429 Stalag Luft III, "The Long March," http://www.stalagluft3.com/long-march/ (accessed 12 Mar. 2015).
430 Grace, *Second to None, The History of the 368th Fighter Group*, 186.

CHAPTER THIRTY-EIGHT

431 "Liberty Ships," The National Park Service, http://www.nps.gov/nr/twhp/wwwlps/lessons/116liberty_victory_ships/116facts1.htm (accessed 28 Jan. 2015).
432 Ibid.

433 Ibid.

434 Ibid.

435 William H. Geoghegan, "Liberty Ship Walk-Around: S.S. John W. Brown," http://www.geoghegan.us/brown/JWB-walkaround.htm (accessed 30 Jan. 2015).

436 Ibid.

EPILOGUE

437 From an interview with Ruth Kelly Worthen (Jerry's sister) at the 90th memorial birthday celebration held in Jerry Kelly's honor on July 13, 2014.

438 Ibid.

439 Ibid.

440 Brian Engdahl, PhD, and Charles Stenger, PhD, "Serving America's Former Prisoners of War," http://brain.umn.edu/pdfs/Engdahl_Praeger.pdf.

441 Ibid.

AFTERWORD

442 Kelly, "Loving Those Who Have Gone Before Us."

443 Ibid.

INDEX

Antwerp

Allied front
line, Dec. 25

NETH.

Maastricht

Leuven

Brussels

Aachen

Duren

Roer R.

BELGIUM

Liege

Hürtgen
Forest

Mons

Meuse R.

West Wall

Charleroi

Sambre R.

Malmedy

Shot down—
captured
Christmas Day

Stavelot

Stadtkyll

Time Bomb
incident

St.-Vith

Freyneux

Prüm

La Roche

A R D E N N E S

Houffalize

LUXEMBOURG

Wrapped
like a
mummy in
cloth strips

Bastogne

Our R.

Allied front
line, Dec. 25

Luxembourg

Meuse R.

FRANCE

Moselle R.

N
W   E
S

Verdun

Metz

0   10   20 Miles

0   20 Kilometers